# ICT
## Practitioners
### 2nd Edition

K. Mary Reid • Alan Jarvis • Jenny Lawson
Allen Kaye • Matthew Strawbridge

**www.heinemann.co.uk**
✓ Free online support
✓ Useful weblinks
✓ 24 hour online ordering

**01865 888058**

**Heinemann**
*Inspiring generations*

Heinemann Educational Publishers
Halley Court, Jordan Hill, Oxford OX2 8EJ
Part of Harcourt Education

Heinemann is the registered trademark of Harcourt Education Limited

First published 2006

10 09 08 07
10 9 8 7 6 5 4 3

British Library Cataloguing in Publication Data is available
from the British Library on request.

10-digit ISBN: 0 435 40204 8
13-digit ISBN: 978 0 435402 04 4

Edited by Ken Brown
Typeset by TechType, Abingdon, Oxon

Original illustrations © Harcourt Education Limited, 2006

Cover design by Wooden Ark

Printed in China through Phoenix Offset

Cover photo © Powerstock

Picture research by Natalie Gray

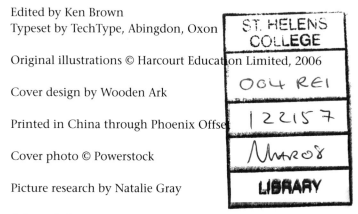

Acknowledgements
Every effort has been made to contact copyright holders of material reproduced in this
book. Any omissions will be rectified in subsequent printings if notice is given to the
publishers.

**Websites**
There are links to relevant websites in this book. In order to ensure that the links are up to
date, that the links work, and that the sites are not inadvertently linked to sites that could
be considered offensive, we have made the links available on the Heinemann website at
www.heinemann.co.uk/hotlinks. When you access the site the express code is 2048P.

**Tel: 01865 888058   www.heinemann.co.uk**

# Contents

The units listed below are available for download from the Heinemann website. Go to www.heinemann.co.uk/vocational, click on **IT & Office Technology** then click on **Free Resources**. The password for these units is **BTEC1stICTprac**

# Acknowledgements

The publisher and authors would like to thank the individuals and organisations who granted permission to reproduce materials in this book.

Page 1: Dennis MacDonald / Alamy
Page 51: The Image Bank / Getty Images
Page 64: Harcourt Education / Trevor Clifford
Page 68: Epsom (*left*); courtesy of HP (*right*)
Page 69: Photodisc / Siede Preis (*left*); courtesy of HP (*right*)
Page 115: Imagebroker / Alamy
Page 169: Creasource / Corbis
Page 207: Harcourt Education / Gareth Boden
Page 208: Harcourt Education / Gareth Boden
Page 209: Harcourt Education / Gareth Boden
Page 210: Harcourt Education / Gareth Boden
Page 215: Getty Images / Photodisc
Page 265: Jonny Le Fortune / Zefa / Corbis
Page 301: Rachel Royse / Corbis
Page 343: Image Source / Rex Features
Page 383: Randy Lincks / Corbis
Page 389: Alan Jarvis
Page 407: Alan Jarvis

*Unit 5*
Page 1: C. Devan / Zefa / Corbis

*Unit 15*
Page 1: Eyewire

*Unit 17*
Page 1: Jim Craigmyle / Corbis
Page 14: courtesy of HP
Page 14: Harcourt Education / Gareth Boden
Page 14: Photodisc / Siede Preis
Page 14: courtesy of HP
Page 23: Harcourt Education / Gareth Boden
Page 27: Harcourt Education / Gareth Boden
Page 31: LightOnLand.com / Alamy

# Introduction

The BTEC First Diploma and First Certificate for ICT Practitioners are Level 2 qualifications which provide you with a broad foundation in the subject. There is a sufficiently large choice of units to allow you to follow specialist interests if you wish.

## Achieving a qualification

This book includes sufficient material, selected from the units on offer, to enable you to achieve either of these qualifications.

To achieve the First Diploma you must pass:
- Unit 1: Using ICT to present information
- Unit 2: Introduction to computer systems
- Any four further units (or equivalent)

To achieve the First Certificate you must pass:
- Unit 1: Using ICT to present information
- Any two further units (or equivalent)

Some units have a value of 0.5, but any two of these are equivalent to one full unit.

## Units in this book

This book covers all the units shown in this table:

|  | Unit value |
|---|---|
| Unit 1: Using ICT to present information | 1.0 |
| Unit 2: Introduction to computer systems | 1.0 |
| Unit 4: Website development | 1.0 |
| Unit 6: Networking essentials | 1.0 |
| Unit 7: Software design and development | 1.0 |
| Unit 8: Customising applications software | 1.0 |
| Unit 9: Database software | 0.5 |
| Unit 10: Spreadsheet software | 0.5 |
| Unit 16: Mobile communications technology | 0.5 |

In addition, three extra units are available for downloading from the website:

|  | Unit value |
|---|---|
| Unit 5: ICT supporting organisations | 1.0 |
| Unit 15: Providing technical advice and guidance | 1.0 |
| Unit 17: Security of ICT systems | 0.5 |

These units can be downloaded from the Heinemann website. Go to www.heinemann.co.uk/vocational, click on **IT & Office Technology**, then click on **Free Resources**. The password for these units is **BTEC1stICTprac**

You may decide you would like to study Unit 3: ICT project. Although there is not a chapter devoted to this unit in the book, guidance is available for tutors.

## Assessment

You will find assessment guidance at the end of each unit in this book.

All the units included in this book are internally assessed. You will be required to put together a portfolio of evidence to show what you have achieved against the grading criteria.

## Assessment and Delivery Resource

The Assessment and Delivery Resource consists of a folder of photocopiable materials and a CD-ROM. It provides additional guidance and resources for tutors, and covers all the units in the book, the three downloadable units, and Unit 3: ICT project.

## Software versions

Throughout this book and in the CD-ROM you will find examples taken from commonly used software. What you see on your screen may differ from the examples if you have different versions or updates of the software.

Very best wishes for your studies.

K Mary Reid
August 2006

# 1 Using ICT to Present Information

## About this unit

This unit will give you the skills and confidence to produce a variety of documents for a range of audiences. You will probably already be familiar with a number of software packages and will be comfortable using them.

Standard software packages offer a very wide range of facilities, and we will be looking at some of them in this unit. It is said that most users use no more than 10% of the facilities in their software. So it is a good idea to explore the applications that you use and see what you are missing.

▶ Continued from previous page

# Learning outcomes

When you have completed this unit you will:

1 understand the purpose of different document types

2 understand the basis for selecting appropriate software to present and communicate information

3 be able to use commonly available tools and techniques in application packages

4 be able to review and adjust finished documents.

# How is the unit assessed?

This unit is internally assessed. You will provide a portfolio of evidence to show that you have achieved the learning outcomes. The grading grid in the specification for this unit lists what you must do to obtain Pass, Merit and Distinction grades. The section on Assessment Tasks at the end of this chapter will guide you through activities that will help you to be successful in this unit.

# The purpose of different document types

## Types of document

In this unit the term 'document' is used to describe information produced in either printed or electronic (on-screen) format. All documents can be produced using standard applications packages. You will be looking at six different types of document designed for presenting information: short formal documents, extended formal documents, graphical documents, promotional documents, presentations and informal documents.

### Short formal documents

#### Memo

A memo is a short note to someone else in the same organisation. It can be sent by email, hand-written, or printed out and delivered by hand. Memos are usually informal in style, but most organisations have a set format to ensure that essential information is not missed out, such as subject, date, originator's name and contact details.

#### Business email message

Emails are often used for informal personal notes, but are now widely used for more formal business purposes as well. Although a chatty style may be suitable for personal emails, in business it is still important to write clearly, and you should avoid the abbreviations used in text messaging. As anything said in an email is as legally binding as in a letter, many organisations insist that business emails follow the conventions of business letters. In any case, the email should always end with a 'signature', which is a few lines of stored text giving the name, job title and contact details of the sender.

#### Letter

A formal letter is a form of correspondence from an organisation to an external client or other contact. Business letters normally have a standard structure and should include:

- Business heading – this could be pre-printed on the stationery or included in a letter template. It will include the name, address, phone and fax numbers, email address etc. of the organisation. It will probably also have a company logo.
- Address of the recipient – this is often placed on the left side of the page below the heading.
- Date the letter was written – this can be placed on either side, depending on the design of the business heading.
- The salutation – normally in the style 'Dear Mr Jones'; if the name is not known, then 'Dear Sir or Madam' may be used.

- The text of the letter, written in clear English. Do not be tempted to use a very formal, old-fashioned style of language, as today it is considered pompous.
- The ending – normally 'Yours sincerely', although 'Yours faithfully' is used with 'Dear Sir or Madam'.
- Signature of the sender.
- The printed name of the sender.
- A copy list – this is a list of anyone else who is being sent a copy of the letter, and is written 'Cc: Jane Davies, Gerry Smith' at the bottom of the letter.

## Further research – business letters

Find some examples of business letters and check them against the standard structure listed above.

### Order form

When a customer decides to order goods, they may fill in an order form. This will have been designed so that it captures all the information that the business needs:

- name of customer
- address of customer
- delivery address – if different from customer's address
- phone number
- items ordered – description or stock code of each type of item, plus the quantity required
- method of payment.

When orders are taken over the phone, the information may still be written down on an order form. Similar information will be captured when goods are ordered online.

### Invoice

An invoice is a bill sent to a customer after the goods have been delivered. When you buy something in a shop you will normally pay for it on the spot, and when you order something from a mail order company you are usually expected to pay for the goods before you receive them. If a business orders items, such as stationery, the supplier will deliver the goods, then send an invoice, which should be paid within a month. An invoice should have a business heading.

### Agenda

An agenda is a list of items to be discussed at a formal meeting. A typical agenda might have these items:

- Apologies for absence
- Minutes of the last meeting
- Matters arising from the minutes
- Item 1 .....
- Item 2 .....
- Item 3 .....
- Date of next meeting
- Any other business.

### Minutes

The minutes of a meeting are a report on what was discussed and the decisions taken. The minutes should follow the same structure as the agenda. Someone at the meeting is given the task of taking the minutes, i.e. making notes and writing them up. At each meeting, the minutes of the previous meeting are checked and any corrections are agreed.

## Extended formal documents

Some documents are from a few pages long up to hundreds of pages. They need to be structured in some way, usually with headings and subheadings.

### Article

An article may be written for the staff newsletter, or for a national or local newspaper. In style, an article falls between a report and an essay. It will have a heading and one level of subheadings.

### Newsletter

Many organisations produce newsletters for their staff or customers, keeping them up to date with new products and news about the company. Newsletters can incorporate photos and graphical headings. They will often be laid out in columns or text boxes.

### Report

A report is any document that is written to explain a project, provide facts or generally convey information. Internal reports will be used by managers to help them make decisions. Companies may also have to produce reports, such as an Annual Report. Reports are usually written in a formal structured style, with heavy use of headings, subheadings and numbered points.

### User guide

A user guide is designed for a person who is not completely familiar with a product, especially a software application. User guides can be presented as printed books or on-screen as multimedia presentations.

## Graphical documents

The terms **image** and **graphics** are often used interchangeably in normal language. In ICT we tend to use graphics to refer very broadly to any pictorial information or decoration, including photos, backgrounds, lines, diagrams, charts, graphs and drawings. An image is a type of graphic that shows an actual picture of something. But in practice the two terms are used quite loosely.

### Illustration

An image can be used to illustrate text, in a logo or as decoration. Be very careful about the use of images in business documents, especially as decoration, as they can look amateurish. Always ask yourself whether the image is necessary and whether it adds to the meaning.

### Chart

A chart or graph can be printed out as a single document or it can be embedded into a word-processed document. In either case it must have a heading and be properly labelled.

### Flowchart

A flowchart is a kind of diagram that uses standard boxes to show how events follow one another. Flowcharts often have decision boxes, with different paths followed depending on the choices made.

### Diagram

Diagrams use basic shapes to represent objects, and to show how they relate to each other.

## Promotional documents

A promotional document advertises goods, events or organisations to the public.

### Advertisement

A printed advertisement can be a page in a magazine or newspaper, a single-sheet flyer or a poster. They are carefully designed to catch the eye, and to use the logos that represent the product or organisation. Advertisements are always designed with a particular audience in mind.

 Further research – target audiences

Collect the bulk mail adverts that are delivered to your home, together with any that fall out of newspapers and magazines. Can you identify the target audience for each? Do you think the designs are effective?

### Leaflet

A leaflet is usually a single sheet of paper, printed on both sides and folded so that the pages can be turned. There are several ways of folding leaflets, with one, two or more folds. Leaflets can contain more information than simple advertisements but they should still be worded concisely.

### Web page

A web page can hold a great deal of information, because the page can be scrolled down for as long as necessary. However, it is much better if the main information is held at the top of a page where it can be seen when the page is loaded. Web pages are highly versatile and can be used for any type of public information or for information restricted to a chosen audience, e.g. within a company or club.

Information can be printed from web pages, by either copying the text or printing out a complete page. Printing can sometimes cause problems as the page may have a fixed width that cannot fit on to A4 paper. Use *Print Preview* (in the *File* menu) to check what the page will look like and, if necessary, change the paper orientation to *Landscape*.

## Presentation

A presentation is a combination of live talk and ready-prepared graphical materials (a slide show). The alternative could be a video on its own, or a simple talk without illustrations. Combining visuals and speech into one presentation has many advantages:

- The slides add impact to a talk – the audience is much more likely to listen and understand if the message is reinforced by text and pictures.
- You can feel confident that the main points of your talk are included in the slide show.
- You can take the presentation at your own speed.
- You can respond to the audience as the presentation proceeds, going back to earlier slides if necessary.

There are two main ways of creating the display for a presentation:

- **Projecting from a computer.** A multimedia projector is connected to a PC or laptop. This projects on to a screen whatever is shown on the computer monitor. You are able to face the audience while controlling the presentation.
- **Viewing a computer display.** The presentation can be viewed directly on a computer screen. A large display screen can be added as a second monitor, so you can still control the presentation from a PC or laptop. For a presentation to a couple of people it is possible to simply view the display on a PC's normal monitor.

Both methods display the output from a computer in real time. This means that the presentation can include animation and video. It can also include sound, provided that suitable speakers have been installed.

## Informal documents

### Personal email

A personal email can be as informal as you like. There are no rules to follow!

### SMS – texting

You will be familiar with SMS (Short Message Service) messages, commonly known as text messages, that can be sent from one mobile phone to another. These are limited to 160 characters per message. You will know some of the many clever abbreviations that are used to save space, such as l8r (later) and u r (you are). You should avoid using these in any other kind of communication where space is not so limited.

Creative writing

There are many other ways of communicating with people through writing. Some of these require a great deal of creativity, such as novels and poetry. There are some standard formats, such as the crime novel or the sonnet, but writers are free to write and present their thoughts in any way they please.

## Further research – document types

Gather together examples of documents of different types, all produced using ICT. Make sure that you have two or three contrasting examples of each of these types:

- short formal
- extended formal
- graphical
- promotional
- presentation
- informal.

## Audience types

Documents that convey information are always prepared with a particular type of reader in mind. We call this the target audience. When deciding who the audience is for a document you should ask:

- Is the document intended for one individual, for a specific group or for the public in general?
- Is it written for other members of the same organisation, e.g. internal staff, or for people external to the organisation, e.g. customers?
- Is it meant for people in a particular age group, e.g. children, young persons, the elderly?
- Is it designed for people with particular interests or needs?
- Is it for people who live in a specific area?

## Appropriate communication

A document can communicate information only if it is written and presented in a way that makes sense to the reader. You should ask 'Does my reader understand what I am trying to tell them?' not 'Have I written this in a way that shows off my skills?'

At the same time, if the document is from an organisation then it should follow the styles and standards that the organisation expects.

## Meeting user need

The first thing to consider is whether the language and writing style are suitable both for the kind of document it is and for the audience.

### Language and writing style

We all use variations on our language in differing circumstances. Spoken language uses different vocabulary and simpler sentences than written language. Formal language uses more complex phrases and a richer vocabulary than informal language. You should notice the differences and try to match them in your communications. It is not a matter of using 'correct' language but of using 'appropriate' language.

Many organisations encourage employees to use Plain English. This can be understood by most people and is helpful for those for whom English is not their first language.

### Further research – Plain English

Check out the website of the Plain English Campaign. You can download guidelines on how to make your written English easier to understand.

Many organisations use a logo on all their printed materials. Their documents will also often have a very specific style. This will be achieved by always using the same fonts, font sizes, text and page colours and page layout. This is known as the corporate style of the organisation.

The managers in an organisation will probably produce some templates that match the rules of the corporate style. All employees will be expected to produce documents using the templates, or that conform to the same style.

Electronic 'documents' such as web pages and presentation slides should also be produced in the corporate style.

### Further research – corporate style

Collect examples of several printed documents that are produced by the same organisation. Can you work out what the corporate style is?

Collect and analyse documents for two other organisations. Compare the documents of the three organisations. Are the corporate styles applied consistently?

### Summaries

It is often helpful to provide a summary of a document. A summary can be placed at the end of a report or alternatively at the beginning, where it is sometimes known as an Executive Summary. This will extract the key points from a long letter or a complex report.

## Specialist tools

There are a number of specialist tools that you can use to check your communications:

- **Readability tests** check whether the vocabulary and style of writing are suitable for people of specific ages or with particular reading levels.
- **Accessibility tests** check whether a website can be understood easily by someone with impaired vision who is using a voice output system, or with some other disability.

## Netiquette

The term 'netiquette' refers to some basic rules that you should use when communicating with someone over the Internet. It includes such principles as:

- Adhere to the same standards of behaviour online as you would in real life.
- Share expert knowledge.
- Respect other people's privacy.
- Be forgiving of other people's mistakes.

## Templates

Most people who use standard applications at work find that they produce similar documents over and over again. For example, someone may write a monthly newsletter with the same layout each month, just varying the content. Also most organisations have a corporate style: a set of rules about what fonts and colours to use and how the logo is to be displayed.

A template is a document that has all these features built in, so that it can be used every time a new document of that type is created.

### What does it mean?

*A **template** is a document, written in a software package, that can be used over and over again for a variety of purposes. Typical examples are headed letter stationery or memo formats.*

## Test your knowledge

1. Do you know the difference between a report, a memo and an invoice?
2. What are agendas and minutes?
3. Describe two occasions when someone might use presentation software.
4. What is the target audience for this book?
5. What is the corporate style used by your centre of learning or place of work?
6. What is the purpose of a summary?
7. What are the main principles of netiquette? Do you think people generally stick to them?

# Selecting appropriate software

## Applications for presenting and communicating information

This unit concentrates on the common applications that are used to present and communicate information. They include:

- **text editors** – used to produce very simple text files for technical use
- **word processing** – used to produce letters, reports, simple publications and labels
- **desktop publishing** – used to produce publications that require complex layouts and combinations of text and graphics
- **graphics** – used to create and manipulate images
- **spreadsheets** – used to produce tables, graphs and charts
- **presentation** – used to create slide presentations
- **communications** – used to create, send, receive, store and organise emails and text messages.

Some of these applications are designed to produce printed material, others present the information electronically. We describe the outputs as 'documents' in both cases.

### Text-based applications

#### Text editors

The simplest text editors, such as Microsoft Notepad, allow you to write and save text files. These have no formatting at all and use the characters from the basic ASCII (American Standard Code for Information Interchange) character set. Text files take up the minimum amount of storage space.

Text files have a number of important uses:

- for texting on mobile phones
- for non-formatted emails
- to store important information about an application, for example in a Read Me file
- to create web pages using HTML.

You will probably be most familiar with text files from your use of a mobile phone. SMS text messages are small text files. Your phone has a very simple text editor that allows you to create and edit text messages.

#### Word processors

Word processors are the most widely used software packages. They have developed from simple text editors to become the highly sophisticated and rich applications that we are all familiar with. Although Microsoft

Word is well known, there are other products available, such as Corel Word Perfect.

### Desktop publishing

Desktop publishing software combines text and graphics. The layouts can be as flexible as you like, but you do need a higher level of skill to use them effectively. Commonly used packages include Adobe Pagemaker and Microsoft Publisher.

## Graphics software

Graphics are stored in two basic formats – bitmap or vector. You need to understand the difference between these in order to know which applications package to use.

A **bitmap** image is made up of thousands of tiny cells of colour known as pixels. If you zoom in on a bitmap image you can see clearly that it is made up of lots of individual square dots (Figure 1.1).

Each pixel has a colour value stored as a binary code. If the value for each pixel is stored in one byte (8 bits) then 256 different colours will be available – this is just about adequate for line drawings such as cartoons, but is not good enough for photographs. Two bytes (16 bits) per pixel, gives over 64,000 different colours which is known as High Colour. True Colour can be achieved with three bytes (24 bits) per pixel, which gives a choice of millions of colours; in fact, this is more than can be distinguished by the human eye.

Software packages for creating bitmaps are often known as painting applications. They offer many different pens and brush shapes that can be used for drawing images.

**Figure 1.1** *Enlarged bitmap image showing the individual pixels*

Photographs are stored as bitmaps and they can be edited in painting packages, but specialist photo editing packages are usually used for this purpose.

A **vector** image consists of one or more separate objects, such as lines, circles and other shapes. Each object can be manipulated individually without disturbing the others. For example, a rectangle can be drawn, and then it can be moved around the page, enlarged or reduced in size, filled with a colour, or deleted. When a vector image is saved, what is actually stored is information about the properties of each of the objects. These will specify the shape, position, colour etc. So a more complex image with lots of objects will require more information than a simpler image. It will therefore need more storage space. Generally speaking, a vector image takes up less memory than a bitmap. Software packages for creating vector images are often known as drawing packages.

It is possible to convert a vector image to a bitmap by a process known as rasterising.

### Standalone graphics applications

Bitmap graphical packages, such as Microsoft Paint and Corel Painter, can be used to create 'paintings' and other images.

Other bitmap graphical packages, such as Microsoft Picture Manager, Adobe Photoshop and Corel Paint Shop, cannot easily be used to create new images, but are used to edit photographs.

Vector graphical packages, such as Adobe Illustrator, CorelDraw and Macromedia Freehand, can be used to create technical drawings, such as maps and product designs, and to create diagrams, cartoons and other line drawings.

When you create a graphic in a standalone package, the image is saved as a separate file. It is a document in its own right. Bitmap images often have the file extension *.bmp*, so, for example, a picture you create in Paint may be saved as *mypicture.bmp*.

### Embedded graphics applications

Many applications, such as Microsoft Word, include mini-applications within them. These are known as embedded applications. For example, within Microsoft Word, PowerPoint and Excel you can find these embedded graphics applications: Drawing, WordArt and Diagram. Note that all these embedded applications produce vector graphics.

Each will create a box on the page. When you click inside the box, you will be using the functions of the embedded application to create a graphic of some kind. Normally a toolbar appears that offers you the options associated with the application.

When you have finished creating the graphic, you can click outside the box and the graphic becomes integrated into the word processing document or spreadsheet. However, you can always go back into the graphic and edit it with the embedded application.

The Drawing application also offers you some autoshapes, which help you to draw a number of standard diagrams very quickly. See Figure 1.2.

Microsoft Publisher has the WordArt embedded application, but when you use desktop publishing software you should normally create and edit graphics in another package then import them.

There are embedded applications for drawing charts and graphs in Word, PowerPoint and Excel. The Chart tool in Excel is considerably more sophisticated and allows

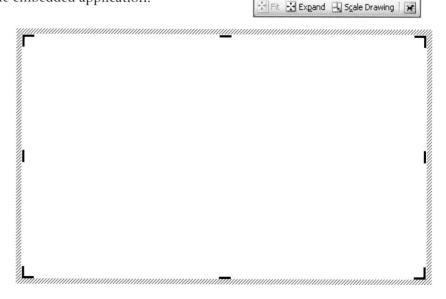

**Figure 1.2** *Using the Drawing embedded application in Word*

you to use data stored anywhere in the spreadsheet. Charts are also vector images.

In addition, many applications, such as Word, have an embedded application for editing bitmap graphics. This cannot be used to create images but can be very useful if you have inserted a bitmap image developed in a standalone application. To use this tool, click on an image and the *Picture* toolbar will appear. See Figure 1.3.

**Figure 1.3** *Editing an image in Word using the Picture tool*

## Presentation software

Microsoft PowerPoint is the most widely used presentation software package. You can use it to create a digital slideshow for a multimedia projector. Although it is possible to look at the slides on a desktop PC, you would be wise to learn how to make a presentation with a talk supported by slides.

The PowerPoint package includes an online tutorial. If you have not used the software before, you are advised to work through the tutorial before you try anything else.

You can create a presentation in three ways:

■ Use the AutoContent Wizard to create a slideshow, which you can then customise for your needs.
■ Use a design template.
■ Start with a blank presentation.

You will probably want to start with the AutoContent Wizard, but you will not want your slides to look just like everyone else's so you should move on to the other two methods as soon as you feel confident.

## Other technologies

Information can be presented through a number of other widely used technologies.

### Texting

You can use texting (SMS) facilities on a mobile phone when that is the most appropriate way of making contact with another person. Texts should not be used to convey important information, and cannot provide a permanent record.

Most phones offer predictive texting, which allows you to hit each key once rather than having to tap through to the correct letter. The software then displays the word in its dictionary that best matches the sequence of key presses.

### Email

In order to compose, send, receive and organise emails you can use:

- email client software, such as Outlook or Outlook Express, which communicates with your Internet Service Provider (ISP) that handles all the emails for you
- webmail software, such as Hotmail, Gmail or Yahoo! Mail, which is provided by an online provider and which you can only access online.

Email client software normally lets you compose a message using:

- plain text – using the basic ASCII characters
- HTML – this allows you to use fonts, colours, images etc.

Note that some webmail systems are not able to display HTML text.

### Multimedia

A multimedia presentation combines text and graphics with video and sound. You can create one yourself using multimedia authoring software. Although multimedia lies outside the scope of this unit, the skills you learn now will be invaluable when you start to work with such applications.

## Features of applications software

### Interface

Whenever you use a computer, you interact with it through a user interface. All the software applications that you use – from games to finance packages – are interactive. They give information to the user and they require input from the user.

For more information on user interfaces, see Unit 2.

### What does it mean?

*A **user interface** is the point of contact between a user and the software. It consists of a visual display on the screen, which may be controlled using both the keyboard and a mouse or other device. Some user interfaces incorporate sound as well.*

Graphical user interface (GUI)

Graphical user interfaces are used for both applications software and systems software.

Figure 1.4 shows an example of a GUI for desktop publishing software.

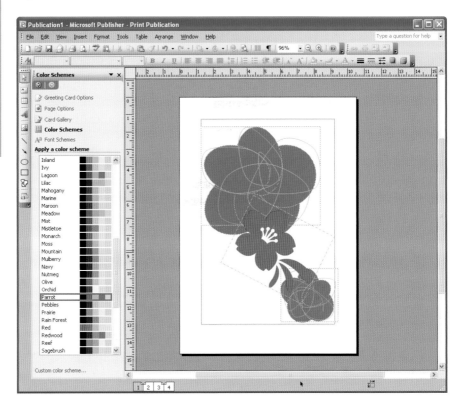

**Figure 1.4** *A graphical user interface*

Many software applications have user interfaces that are similar to this one. It allows the user to carry out a large number of actions, such as printing the document, zooming into the document, selecting drawing tools, viewing help pages etc. The graphical components help the user to make sense of the options in what would otherwise be a very crowded display.

There are very many software packages on the market, produced by many different companies. Although software developers can create their own distinctive GUIs, they know that they will be able to sell more if the software is easy to learn. So most business applications software tends to conform to a fairly standard presentation, largely based on the style of Microsoft Windows.

Today, end users expect all software to be user-friendly. They want to spend their time using the computer to do the tasks they have planned; they do not want to waste any more time than necessary in learning how to use it.

WIMP

Graphical user interfaces usually make use of four elements, which together are known as WIMP:

- **Window** – windows hold the activities within one application and can be layered on top of each other so that you can switch between applications
- **Icon** – a small image that can act as a button
- **Menu** – drop-down and pop-up menus hide the choices from view until you actually need them
- **Pointer** – a moving image that is controlled by the mouse.

Voice recognition and voice output options

Most interfaces take input from the user via a keyboard or mouse. Specialist input devices can analyse sound and accept speech instead. Voice recognition input devices are particularly helpful for visually impaired users and also for those who have difficulties with movement and are unable to control mouse or keyboard.

Interfaces can also provide output in a format to meet a user's needs. Sound output, especially the spoken word, allows visually impaired users to understand what is on their screen.

## Software suites and integrated packages

Manufacturers of software often develop suites of applications. These consist of several applications that work well together. Examples of these would be Microsoft Office Suite, Adobe Creative Suite, Lotus SmartSuite and CorelDraw Graphics Suite. Within each suite the applications will be designed to:

- provide a similar user interface
- handle the same file formats
- use the same embedded applications.

At one time, integrated packages, e.g. single programs, such as Apple Works, were popular because they presented all the common office tools within one application. Over time, business users demanded more from their applications and manufacturers moved towards providing several inter-related applications within a suite instead of one large one. However, integrated packages are still seen as very useful for young people and for home users, who just need basic functions and may be confused by over-complicated software.

## Variety of outputs

We have already seen that applications can produce output in printed or electronic format. In addition to normal printed documents and on-screen presentations, these outputs can include:

- **Audience notes.** These are printouts containing pictures of the slides and may include space for notes. They can be given out at the beginning of the presentation, so that the audience can make notes as they go along. Alternatively, you may just want to give them out at the end as a reminder of the content.

■ **Speaker's notes.** These are notes on the slides in presentation software. They can be printed out for the speaker to refer to when making a presentation.

■ **Mail merge.** You will probably at some time have received a letter that is addressed to you, but you will know that very similar letters will also have been sent to many other people. These letters are generated by a process known as mail merge. The name and address data is held in a simple database, which is then merged with a standard letter document to produce personally addressed letters.

## File formats

Files can be created in applications in a number of standard formats. You can tell which format is being used by looking at the last part of the full file name, known as the file name extension. For example, an image with the filename *dogs.bmp* has the filename extension *.bmp*, which tells us that it has been stored in bitmap format.

■ **Text files** *(.txt)* are also known as ASCII files. These are created by text editors and simply contain basic characters in the ASCII character set. You can also save a word-processed document in text format but you will lose all the character formatting and any special characters that you have used.

■ **Rich text files** *(.rtf)* are produced by word processors and preserve a certain amount of character formatting, such as colours and fonts. They can usually be exchanged between applications from other software houses.

■ **Word-processed files** use different formats depending on which application has been used. Microsoft Word files use the filename extension *.doc*, and are not necessarily compatible with other word processing applications.

■ **HTML files** are text files that contain the programming code for web pages. They are saved with the filename extension *.htm* or *.html*, which tells a browser that they can be interpreted as web pages.

■ **Bitmap images** can be stored in full with the *.bmp* extension. They can also be compressed, which reduces the amount of information stored about the image and, hence, requires less storage space. There are various compression techniques, but you are most likely to come across the *.jpg* or *.gif* formats.

■ Plain text **emails and text messages** use their own file formats, but they are based on simple text files.

## Automated procedures – wizards

You will be familiar with wizards – those clever features that take you step-by-step through a process. Most wizards ask you to make some choices, then they create a ready-made document or presentation for you. These are often a very useful way to get started with a new application, but you will soon want to create your own work from scratch.

How to –

## Use a wizard in Microsoft PowerPoint

### 1. Use the wizard

- Launch PowerPoint. In the *Task Pane* click on *Create a New Presentation*.
- Select *From AutoContent Wizard*.
- Click on *Presentation Type*, and then click on *All*. You will see a list of standard presentation topics, such as *Business Plan* and *Company meeting*. You can check them all out, but start with *Generic* (Figure 1.5).

**Figure 1.5** *The AutoContent Wizard in PowerPoint*

- On the next screen select *On-screen presentation*.
- Next, choose a title for your presentation (e.g. Travel to work) and make sure that your name is inserted in the footer.
- When the wizard has finished, a complete

presentation will be displayed. The *Slide Pane* on the right shows the first slide. The *Outline Pane* on the left shows the structure of the complete slideshow, with all the text that each slide contains (Figure 1.6).

- To view another slide, click on one of the numbered slide icons in the *Outline Pane*.

### 2. Customise the presentation

You will want to put in your own words and add new slides:

- You can change the text on any slide by typing over the text in the *Outline Pane*. Alternatively you can type directly on to the slide itself, replacing the existing text.
- You can move text by dragging and dropping it either in the *Outline Pane* or directly on the slide.
- You can delete a slide by clicking on the slide icon in the *Outline Pane* and then selecting *Delete Slide* from the *Edit* menu.
- You can add a new slide by clicking on the slide icon immediately before the point where you want the new slide. Select *New Slide* from the *Insert* menu, then select the style of slide that you want from the options in the *Task Pane* (Figure 1.7). The boxes on each slide are known as placeholders.

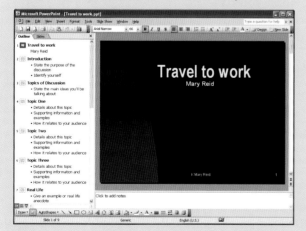

**Figure 1.6** *The Generic presentation created by the wizard*

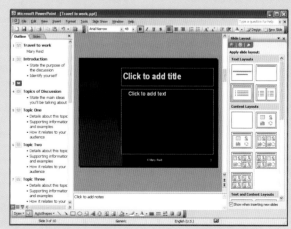

**Figure 1.7** *Selecting a slide layout*

3. **View the slides**

   In the *View* menu, you can switch between four different 'views' of the slides:

   - **Normal View** displays three panes: the *Outline* pane on the left, the *Slide* pane on the right and the *Notes* pane under the *Slide* pane. The *Outline* pane lists the slides and the text on them. To view a slide, click on the slide icon in the *Outline* pane. The text in the *Notes* pane will be printed in the speaker's notes.
   - **Slide Sorter** shows thumbnails (small pictures) of all the slides. If you want to change their order

   you can drag and drop a slide to a new position.

   - **Notes Page** displays a document with the slide at the top and the notes from the *Notes* pane underneath. These can be printed as the speaker's notes.
   - **Slide Show** (or F5) displays the slides full-screen, as they will be seen in the presentation. Click anywhere on the screen to move to the next slide. You will also find a button at the bottom of each slide that presents a pop-up menu, which allows you to go back to previous slides or to end the slideshow.

## Further research – working with wizards

Find out what wizards are built into all the applications that you have access to. Can you manage without them?

For assessment purposes, you may use any wizards that are available, but you should always customise the output to meet the specified needs. You also need to prove that you are capable of working with the application on your own. Do not forget that the assessor will also have used the wizards and will recognise work that is purely automatically generated.

### What does it mean?

**Shortcut keys** *(also known as **hot keys**) are combinations of key presses that achieve the same effect as making certain selections from a menu.*

## Shortcuts

You can use an application much faster if you learn a few keyboard shortcuts. It is often quicker to press a couple of keys than to click on a menu and make a selection. For example, Ctrl+C means that you should press down the Ctrl and C keys at the same time to copy text you have highlighted. Other shortcuts are shown in Figure 1.8. You should get used to using at least the shortcut keys for copying (Ctrl+C), cutting (Ctrl+X) and pasting (Ctrl+V), because there are times when the menus may be hidden.

If you click on a menu, you will normally be able to see the shortcut keys for each option.

## Use of templates

You should certainly set up templates for any documents that are likely to be used more than once. For example, headed stationery should be set up in a template.

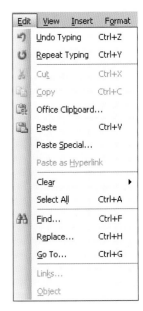

**Figure 1.8** *Shortcut key combinations*

Many packages have built-in design templates that you can make use of. See Figure 1.9. Try some of them out by selecting *New* from the *File* menu.

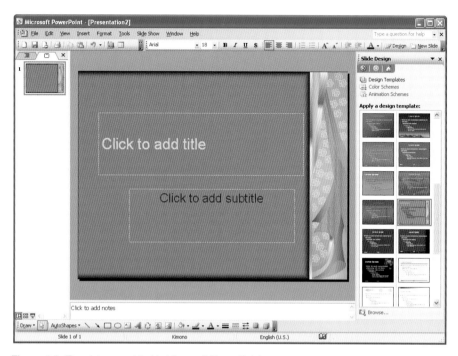

**Figure 1.9** *Templates provided in Microsoft PowerPoint*

You can create your own templates in many software packages. First, open a new document. You can use an existing template as the basis for your own template or you can start with a blank document.

Add all the features that you want in your template. Depending on the purpose of the document, you might want to add a heading, logo, headers and footers, address and date, columns etc. You can set the size of the page and margins in *Page Setup*. You can also add styles to the style list.

Make sure that you save it all as a template, then it will appear with the other templates when you create a new document. Usually you do this by selecting *Save As*, then choosing *Template* in the *Save as Type* box.

# Information to be communicated

## Types of information

We are so used to receiving information in text, either written or spoken, that we sometimes forget that information can be conveyed effectively in other ways as well. Information can be presented through text, numbers, images and graphics, charts or tables.

## Structured and unstructured information

Some information is presented in a structured way. Here are some examples.

### Lists

Lists can be presented with each item numbered, lettered or with bullets. There are several numbering and lettering styles to choose from:

> 1, 2, 3, 4, …
> i, ii, iii, iv, …
> a, b, c, d, …

Sometimes you find lists within lists:

> 1.  First topic
>     1.1 first point
>     1.2 second point
>     1.3 third point
>
> 2.  Second topic
>     2.1 first point
>     2.2 etc.

Sorted lists present the information sorted alphabetically, numerically, by date or by importance. Some software applications only allow you to sort data into alphabetical, numerical or date order.

### Formal reports

Formal reports often structure the information into topics, with headings and subheadings for sections. List numbering is also used within sections.

### Tables

Tables arrange information in two dimensions.

## Finding information

### ICT sources

There are many sources of information in an electronic format, including websites, CDs, DVDs, and information displays such as train times at a railway station.

Large amounts of data are stored on the Internet. But the right information has to be extracted by sifting and sorting it from the data. It must then be presented in a way that makes it meaningful to the user.

- **Searching for information on the Web.** You retrieve data from the Internet when you successfully download the information that you need. There are a number of tools that can help you to find the right information, the most common being search engines.
- **Searching for information on a specific website.** Many websites have site search engines. Alternatively they may offer a site map that lists all the pages, and this may help you to find what you want.

**What does it mean?**

*A **search engine** is a software tool that can be used to find pages on the Internet. Search engines track millions of web pages and create an index based on the text appearing on the pages, or on the keywords provided by the web designer. The user enters search terms (one or more words) and the search engine then finds and lists relevant websites. Well-known search engines include Google and Yahoo.*

- **Searching for information in a document.** Sometimes you need to search for information within a specific document. For example, to find where a phrase appears within a Word document, select *Edit*, then *Find*, then key in the words.

### Non-ICT sources

You can find information from many other sources, such as books, newspapers, magazines, radio and television broadcasts, talks and lectures, or conversations with experts.

## Further research – collect information for future use

Keep a note in a document or database of any information that you find, from both ICT and non-ICT sources, over a period of time. This could be information that is relevant to your studies, or information that you need in your daily life.

For each item of information, record what the information was, the date you found it, where the information was or who said it. Store any source material, such as printed documents, recordings, or links to relevant websites.

## Checking the validity of information

Not all the information that you gather is true. Sometimes people make mistakes, sometimes they misunderstand the facts and sometimes they deliberately mislead you. You need to check whether the information you have is correct.

Anyone can place anything they like on the Internet. There are two main ways of checking the validity of information you discover:

- **Check the source itself.** Is the information provided by a well-known organisation or expert? If not, are there any indications that the author is a trustworthy source?
- **Check the information against other sources** that you can trust, e.g. your teacher, a reliable website such as the BBC's, or a book written by an expert.

## Further research – Wikipedia online encyclopedia

Wikipedia is an online encyclopedia. It differs from others because anyone can write an entry or add to one that is already there. How reliable do you think the information is? Go to the website and check out the information on a topic that you do know something about.

## Test your knowledge

8    What are the main differences between text editing, word processing and desktop publishing software?

9    Name one software application that can be used to create bitmap images and another that can be use to create vector images. Briefly explain the differences between the way they handle images.

10   What is an embedded application?  Give one example.

11   How does a graphical user interface make it easier for the user to work with the software?

12   What is a template?

13   Outline two ways of checking the validity of information.

# Tools and techniques

This section should introduce you to some new skills, and get you to think in a new way about the software packages that you use.

Many packages offer very similar facilities, so if you can do something in one package it is worthwhile seeing whether you can do the same in another. This similarity is most noticeable if you use software applications that are produced by the same company.

The examples in this unit all come from commonly used Microsoft products – Word, Excel, Publisher, PowerPoint, Paint, Outlook and Outlook Express. You should be able to find similar functions in other packages.

## Formatting and editing tools

### Formatting text

#### Formatting characters

Applications packages allow you to change the appearance of text in many ways – this is known as formatting. Most Microsoft packages allow you to format the text using a *Formatting* toolbar. Packages produced by other companies offer very similar facilities.

You highlight the text you want to format then select from a wide range of formatting options. The formatting options can be selected using any one of these methods:

- clicking on icons in the *Formatting* toolbar (Figure 1.10)

**Figure 1.10** *The Formatting toolbar*

- selecting from the *Format* menu (this offers you the biggest choice of options)
- using hotkeys, e.g. Ctrl+B for bold
- right-clicking on the text and selecting from the options.

You should use the basic formatting options with care:

- **Bold** should be used to emphasise words or phrases. It is normally used for headings.
- *Italic* is also used for emphasis, and is sometimes used for quotes or for additional comments.
- <u>Underline</u> should be used very rarely in printed documents. It is mainly used in handwritten scripts as a substitute for bold. Today, underlined text normally indicates a hyperlink, and can be used for that purpose in a document that is going to be viewed electronically, such as a web page, presentation or help file.

## Further research – formatting characters in Outlook or Outlook Express

You can format the characters in an email created in Outlook or Outlook Express, although you must realise that some recipients will not be able to view the formats in their email software.

Create a new email in the usual way. Select *Rich Text* from the *Format* menu. This brings up a *Formatting* toolbar, which you can use just as you would in any other package. You can even insert pictures using the *Insert* menu.

### Formatting paragraphs

Paragraphs of text can be positioned on the page using a number of different tools.

Text **alignment** arranges text in relation to the margins of the document or the textbox. Normally the text is highlighted then aligned. In some packages, all the text in a textbox is automatically given the same alignment. In many packages, the alignment buttons can be found in the *Formatting* toolbar. Alignment is sometimes referred to as justification. See Figure 1.11.

Text can also be indented (Figure 1.12). Tabs can be used to indent individual words.

### Formatting pages

Paper is produced in International paper sizes from A0 (largest) down to A10 (smallest). The normal paper used in most printers is A4, which is 210 mm by 297 mm.

One special feature of the International sizes is that, if you cut any standard sheet of paper in half, you get two sheets of paper in the next size down. This means that you can print out two A5 pages side by side on one A4 sheet of paper.

In the USA, an alternative set of paper sizes is used. You need to know about these as some software may be set up for American papers. The US

---

This text is aligned to the left, which means that it is lined up against the left margin of the page. Left alignment is commonly used for all kinds of documents, although it does mean that the text looks 'ragged' along the right margin.

This text is aligned to the right. Right alignment is normally only used for positioning addresses on letters. It is sometimes used to create special effects. But generally it looks rather odd and is difficult to read.

This text is aligned to the centre.
Headings are often centre aligned, but otherwise use it with care, as eyes finds it difficult to dart from one starting point on a line to another.

This text is fully justified. The characters have been spaced out so that they line up on both the left and the right margins. This looks neat in formal printed documents, although you may find that some words are stretched a little too much.

**Figure 1.11** *Text alignment*

---

This is the start of a normal paragraph.

This paragraph has been indented. The section of text is highlighted then moved to the right or left using the Text Indent buttons. Indented text can also be aligned in any of the available ways.

If you press the tab key on the keyboard (above the Caps Lock key), as I did at the beginning of this sentence, the cursor moves a short distance to the right.

If you press the tab key more than once, the cursor makes a number of jumps.

| You can | use tabs | in the same line | to space out words |
| And then | use them | on the next line | to keep them in columns |

**Figure 1.12** *Indenting and using tabs*

sizes are A (smallest) to K (largest). Size A is also known as Letter size and, at 8.5 inches by 11 inches (216 mm by 254 mm), it is the nearest to A4.

Other specialist paper sizes are used, and special sizes are used for envelopes.

You can choose the paper size in most software applications by going to the *File* menu and selecting *Page Setup*. Select the *Paper Size* tab, and then make your choice from the list. The default is usually set as A4, but it is worth checking that it has not been set at Letter (USA) size instead. If it has, you can click on the *Default* button to change the default page size.

Some further features of page formatting:

- **Page orientation.** You can arrange a document so that the text runs across the length of the paper (landscape) or across its width (portrait). This is the orientation of the paper, and it can be set in the *Page Setup* dialogue, in the *Paper Size* tab.

- **Starting a new page.** In most applications you can usually insert a page break or create a new page from the *Insert* menu, or by using shortcut keys.

- **Setting the size of margins.** Margins can be set at the left, right, top and bottom of the page in most applications. This is usually done through the *Page Setup* dialogue. The left and right margins should normally be the same size. But if you are producing a document in which pages are to be printed back-to-back and then bound as a book, you will probably want a larger margin on the inside edge – this will be on the left edge of odd-numbered pages and on the right edge of even-numbered pages. The top and bottom margins contain the header and footer, so you need to make them large enough to hold whatever text you want there.

- **Page numbering.** Most software applications will automatically number pages for you, although they vary in how this is achieved. In Word, select *Page numbers* from the *Insert* menu. You can choose to have the number at the top or bottom of the page, and positioned to the left, right or centre. The usual position is at the bottom of the page in the centre.

## Editing text

Once text has been placed in a document, you can edit it in a number of ways.

### Inserting text

You can insert text using one of these methods:

- Click in the correct place and type in extra text. In most applications you can switch between *Insert* mode (where new text is simply added between existing text) and *Overtype* mode (where new text replaces existing text). This can usually be done by pressing the *Insert* key on your keyboard. In Word, you can switch *Overtype* on or off by

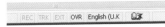

REC TRK EXT OVR English (U.K

**Figure 1.13** *The Overtype mode button (OVR) in Word*

double-clicking on *OVR* in the status bar at the bottom of the window (Figure 1.13).

■ Paste in text that has been cut or copied from another document. You will find it helpful to highlight the text and use the shortcut keys: Ctrl+C to copy, Ctrl+X to cut and Ctrl+V to paste.

■ Drag text from one part of a document to a new position. In many applications you can highlight the text to be moved, click anywhere inside the highlighted text and hold the mouse button down as you drag the text to where you want it to appear then release the mouse button.

### Inserting special characters

You are probably aware that different fonts offer you a large choice of special characters, some of which can be selected using shortcut keys. If you can find a suitable character then it is often easier to insert it into a document instead of inserting an image. But you must remember that someone who receives your document electronically will be able to see the characters on screen as intended only if the same font is installed on their system.

You can insert a special character using one of these methods:

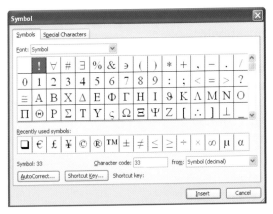

**Figure 1.14** *Selecting a special character*

■ If you know which font and character to choose then select it from the drop-down list of fonts and key in the character.

■ Select *Symbol* from the *Insert* menu. This usually displays the characters in the *Symbol* font. You can change to any other font in the *Font* box. You may find useful characters in *Wingdings* and similar fonts. See Figure 1.14.

■ Select *Symbol* from the *Insert* menu and click on the *Special Characters* tab. This displays the shortcut keys that can be used. For example, the symbol for 'trademark' in the UK is ™. This can be written by using the shortcut keys Alt+Ctrl+T. See Figure 1.15.

### Amending text

You can change text using one of these methods:

■ Overtype the existing text with new text.

■ Highlight the text, then start typing. The new text will replace the highlighted text.

### Deleting text

You can delete text in a number of ways, including:

■ Highlight the text and press the *Delete* or *Backspace* keys.

■ Highlight the text, then use Ctrl+X to cut it. This method stores a copy of the cut text in the clipboard, so if you decide you need the text after all you can paste it back.

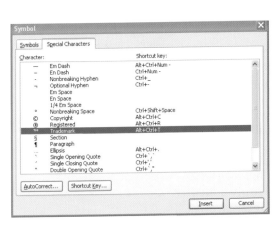

**Figure 1.15** *Using shortcut keys for special characters*

## Formatting graphics

### Formatting bitmap images

You can create simple bitmap images in Paint, or in a number of other more sophisticated painting packages. Paint offers you a number of tools – brushes, pens, and spray cans – as well as lines and freeform shapes. A new colour can be applied to an area with the *Fill* tool. Once lines and colours have been placed on the image, they are fixed and can be removed only by painting over them with another colour.

When a bitmap image has been created in a standalone application, you may want to insert the image into a word-processed document or a presentation. Although you can often copy and paste the image, you will get much more satisfactory results if you insert the image from the *Insert* menu. In Word you should select *Insert*, then *Picture*, then *From File*, then browse to find the image file you want.

### Formatting vector images and basic shapes

Vector images can be created in specialist graphics applications, but you will probably find it easiest to use one of the embedded applications.

You can create vector images by using the Drawing application that is embedded in Word. In the *Insert* menu, select *Picture*, then *New Drawing*. A drawing area appears on the page and the *Drawing* toolbar appears (Figure 1.16).

**Figure 1.16** *The Drawing toolbar in Word*

A vector image is made up of one or more individual objects, such as lines, rectangles and text boxes. Try using the rectangle, oval, line, arrow and autoshape buttons. You can change the line and fill colours, and the style of lines and borders, by clicking on an object and then using the *line style*, *line colour* and *fill colour* buttons.

When you click outside the drawing area, the toolbar disappears and the drawing becomes part of the document. But you only have to double-click on the drawing for the drawing tools to appear again. This means that you can edit the drawing at any time.

### Formatting charts and graphs

Charts and graphs are vector graphics that can be created easily in a spreadsheet. They can then be copied and pasted into another document.

The purpose of any chart or graph is to bring the data to life by turning it into a diagram. You need to choose the type that is most appropriate for the data you have.

You can create a wide variety of charts and graphs in Excel. Do not be tempted to produce more than one chart for a set of data, or to draw a fancy chart when a simple one would do.

|  | Jan 2006 |
|---|---|
| Times | 685,081 |
| Telegraph | 917,043 |
| Guardian | 394,913 |
| Sun | 3,319,337 |
| Mirror | 1,727,672 |
| Mail | 2,389,011 |

**Table 1.1** *Daily sales for six newspapers (Source: Audit Bureau of Circulations)*

How to –

## Create charts and graphs in Excel

- Enter the data in Table 1.1 (see previous page) into a new spreadsheet and save it.

- Highlight all the cells shown in the table, including the heading Jan 2006. Then click on the *Chart Wizard* button in the main toolbar.

- In the *Chart type* box (see Figure 1.17) select *Column* for a vertical bar chart. In the *Chart sub-type* box select the first option in the top left-hand corner. Then click on *Next*.

- The next page will show you what the chart will look like. Click on *Next*.

- In the *Chart Title* box key in 'Newspaper Sales in January 2006'. You can put in a title for the category (X) axis – it could be 'Name of newspaper'. You could also add the title 'Daily sales' for the value (Y) axis. Click on *Next*.

- In the next page you can choose whether the chart will be placed on the same sheet or on a new sheet. Click on *Finish*.

- The chart will appear on the sheet and you can move it to the correct position.

- At Step 1 of the *Chart Wizard* you could choose *bar* for a horizontal bar chart, or *pie* for a pie chart. In each case, select the first option in the *Chart sub-type* box.

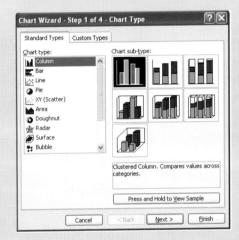

**Figure 1.17** *The Chart Wizard in Excel*

| | A | B | C |
|---|---|---|---|
| 1 | Task | Deadline | Completed |
| 2 | Write to Smith Ltd about the contract | Feb 28th | Feb 28th |
| 3 | Talk to Linda about the new printers | Mar 3rd | |
| 4 | Fix meeting with Mark | | Feb 27th |
| 5 | Write report | Mar 5th | |
| 6 | | | |
| 7 | | | |

**Figure 1.18** *A simple table created in a spreadsheet*

| Task | Deadline | Completed |
|---|---|---|
| Write to Smith Ltd about the contract | Feb 28th | Feb 28th |
| Talk to Linda about the new printers | Mar 3rd | |
| Fix meeting with Mark | | Feb 27th |
| Write report | Mar 5th | |

**Figure 1.19** *The same table printed out with formatted cells*

**Figure 1.20** *Creating a table in Word*

## Formatting tables

Spreadsheets are naturally arranged as tables. Although they are designed for numerical calculations, they can be used to arrange information neatly even where no numbers are included. See Figure 1.18.

Individual cells, or groups of cells, can be shaded or given borders. In Excel, highlight the cells, use the *Format* menu, select *Cells*, then use the *Border* and *Patterns* tabs. The text in each cell can be formatted in the usual way. See Figure 1.19.

Tables can also be created in Word, PowerPoint and Publisher, although they work in slightly different ways. In Word or PowerPoint, click on the *Insert Table* button in the main toolbar, then highlight the number of cells that you need. See Figure 1.20.

In Publisher, click on the *Tables* button in the toolbox, drag an outline of the table on to the document, then follow the instructions in the dialogue box.

You can then add data to the cells. Cells can be formatted by highlighting one cell or a set of cells and using the options in the *Format* menu. Drag the edges of the cells to make them bigger or smaller.

## Editing graphics

All bitmap and vector graphics packages allow you to edit an image. Each package offers its own choice of functions that can be applied to an image. You might like to explore several different packages to see what they offer.

Photographs are bitmap images and these can be edited like any other. Specialist photo-editing applications have additional features that allow you to touch up and manipulate photos. You can use Microsoft Picture Manager for this (Figure 1.21).

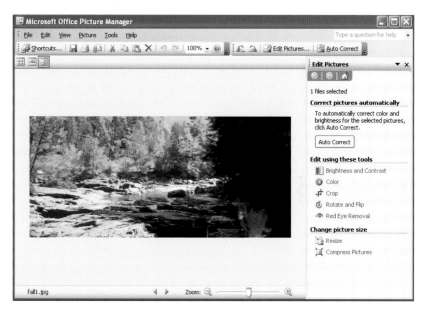

**Figure 1.21** *Microsoft Picture Manager*

## Further research – exploring Microsoft Picture Manager

To do this you should have saved a photo in the *My Pictures* folder.

- Open the folder and find the picture.
- Right-click on the image file, select *Open With*, then *Microsoft Office Picture Manager*.
- Click on *Edit Pictures* in the toolbar. You can now try out all the editing facilities.

## Resizing

A bitmap image can be resized without removing any parts of it. This is also known as stretching, although you can 'stretch' an image by making it smaller as well as larger. In Paint you should select *Image*, then *Stretch/Skew*. See Figure 1.22. Change the percentages in the *Stretch* boxes – the figures should normally be the same. For example, if you enter 50% for both horizontal and vertical, the image will be halved in size along each edge. You can stretch or squash the image in one direction by entering different horizontal and vertical percentages.

When you click on an object in a vector image, handles appear at each corner and along each edge (Figure 1.23). The object can be stretched by dragging on the handles. To keep the shape in proportion, hold down the *Shift* key while dragging on a corner handle.

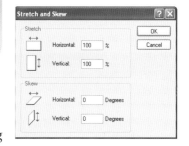

**Figure 1.22** *The Resizing dialogue box in Microsoft Paint*

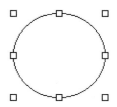

**Figure 1.23** *The corner and edge handles on a vector object*

A whole vector image can also be resized in Word by clicking once on the image and then dragging on one of its handles.

### Rotating and flipping

Sometimes you want to rotate a bitmap image, or part of an image. In Paint you are limited to rotations of 90º, 180º or 270º, and angles are measured anticlockwise. You can rotate the whole image or you can outline an area with one of the selection tools. Use *Image*, then *Flip/Rotate*. In Picture Manager you can rotate the image by any angle you choose.

The objects in a vector image created in the *Drawing* tool can also be rotated by any angle. You will find the *Rotate or Flip* option in the *Draw* menu at the left end of the *Drawing* toolbar.

Flipping an image creates its mirror image. The mirror can be horizontal or vertical.

### Copying and pasting

When you create a bitmap image in Paint, you can copy or cut areas of the picture. First select an area using one of the selection tools, then copy or cut it in the usual way. The selected area can then be pasted on to the same document, and can be moved around to a new position.

With all bitmap graphics packages, once a selection has been placed it merges into the rest of the image and cannot be picked up again.

Vector graphics store each line or other element on the page as a separate item, so each can be copied and pasted individually within the drawing area.

## Advanced tools

### Cropping

When you crop a bitmap image, you cut off the parts that you do not need, often using a selection tool. This is sometimes known as trimming.

In some applications, such as Microsoft Picture Manager, you can drag on special cropping handles on the edge of the image to remove the sections that you do not need. See Figure 1.24.

Paint does not have a specific cropping tool but you can achieve the effect very simply. Outline the area that you want to keep with the selection tool and copy it. Create a new blank image and paste the copied image to it.

If you have inserted a bitmap image into a Word document, you can still crop it by using the *Picture* tools. Click on the *Crop* button. You cannot crop a vector graphic.

**Figure 1.24** *Cropping an image in Picture Manager*

## Paste Special

Sometimes, when you copy and paste items from other applications, you want to be able to continue to edit them as if they were in the original package. Or perhaps you want to store them in a different format. This is where *Paste Special* comes in. If you select this from the *Edit* menu, you are given a number of format options. The exact options you see will depend on what you have copied. For example, if you copy some text in a Word document then use *Paste Special* to paste it into another Word document, you will be given the choice of pasting it as a picture, as a text box, as HTML or as unformatted text.

## Arranging

If you create a vector drawing use the Drawing embedded application, you can arrange the various lines and shapes in a number of ways. You can understand how this works if you draw three different shapes and fill each one with a different colour. You can move the drawing objects on top of each other, but which one will be in the front? Right-click on one of the objects, select *Order*, then try out the options.

## Paragraph styles

When you create a document, you normally select from the wide range of fonts, font sizes, font styles (bold, italic, underline) and effects (shadow, outline etc.), font colours and alignment options (centre, left, right, justified). Each combination of these options is known as a style.

If you use more than one style in a document then it is irritating to have to recreate a style each time you need it. There are several ways of speeding up this process. You can then add styles to a template for future use.

## How to –

### Use and create styles in Microsoft Word

**To use the *Style* list**

- Key in some text and then highlight some or all of it.

- Click on the down arrow on the *Style* list box, which is at the left end of the *Formatting* toolbar (next to the list of fonts). This will show the list of default styles (Figure 1.25).

- Select the style you want to apply to the text.

**Figure 1.25** *The default style list*

- Click on the *Styles and Formatting* button to the left of the styles list.

- In the *Task Pane*, right-click on *Heading 1*, then select *Modify*.

- In the dialogue box, make your choice of font properties for the heading. Do not change the name of the *Heading 1* style. Then click *OK*.

- Repeat for the other heading styles and for the *Normal* style. You will notice that the *Header* and *Footer* styles are based on the *Normal* style.

**To change an existing style**

You can change the *Heading* styles and the *Normal* style to ones that you want.

**To add a style to the *Style* list**

■ Click on the *Styles and Formatting* button to the left of the styles list.

■ In the *Task Pane*, click on *New Style*.

■ In the dialogue box, key in a name for the new style.

■ Make your choice of font properties, then click *OK*.

■ Your new style has been added to the *Style* list, and can be used anywhere in the document. See Figure 1.26.

**Figure 1.26** *Style list with modified heading and new style*

## Animation

You can add animation to the slides that you create in PowerPoint. But you should do this with some care. It is very easy to be entranced by the effects that you can produce and not realise that they can be deeply irritating to the audience. Ask yourself whether the animation actually adds extra value to the presentation. For example, if you have a number of items of information on a slide, you may like to introduce them one by one rather than all at the same time.

How to –

## *Add animation to a presentation*

### Slide animations

You can animate the text by letting it fly on to the screen one line at a time.

■ On a slide, click on the placeholder that you want to animate, then select *Animation Schemes* in the *Slide Show* menu.

■ Click on an animation (e.g. *Faded Wipe*) from the *Task Pane*, then watch the effect.

■ You can apply an *Animation Scheme* to several slides at the same time. Hold down Shift then click on each of the slides in the *Outline Pane*.

■ When you are happy with the effect you have chosen, click on *Apply to all Slides*. (This will apply the animation to all the slides you selected.)

### Slide transitions

The switch from one slide to another can be made more interesting by applying a transition effect. For example, the next slide could appear to move in from one side, or the previous slide could dissolve away.

■ Click on the next slide, then select *Slide Transition* from the *Slide Show* menu. You can apply the transition to the chosen slide, or to all the slides.

## Tracking

Some documents are written by more than one person. You might want to create a group report on a project you have all been working on. One person is given the task of writing the first version of the report, which is then passed on to another person. The second person may want to suggest some changes, which are then discussed with the original writer.

The report will be changed and may be changed back again several times before both are happy with it.

There is a useful tool in most word-processing software to keep track of the changes. The original text is written with a black font. In Word, once the tracking tool has been switched on, the changes suggested by the second person are shown in another colour and by underlining. The amended text will also be sidelined in the margin. The first writer can then decide whether to accept each of the changes or not.

## How to –

### *Track changes in Word*

Two people should carry out this task together.

**First person**
■ Create a new document and write some text in the usual way. Save the document.

**Second person**
■ Open the document. Select *Tools*, then *Track Changes*. The *Reviewing* toolbar will appear (Figure 1.27).

**Figure 1.27** *The Reviewing toolbar*

■ Insert some extra text in the document. It will appear in red and underlined. A vertical black line is shown in the left margin to draw attention to the change.

■ Now delete some words from the original text. They will be shown in red with a line through the words.

**First person**
■ You can now decide whether to accept each change. Click on one of the changes and then click on the *Accept Change* button in the *Reviewing* toolbar.

■ To reject a change, click on the *Reject* button.

■ When you are satisfied with all the changes, select *Tools* and *Track Changes* to switch off tracking.

If the changes appear differently on your page it is because it is possible to change the styles. Look under *Tools*, then *Options*, then the *Track Changes* tab.

## Combining information from different sources

### Inserting or importing a file
If you are working in a word processing or desktop publishing application, you can often bring in a different type of file and make it part of your current document. This is sometimes known as importing a file.

Desktop publishing packages usually allow you to combine files from many different sources into one document. In Publisher, draw a text box then select *Insert* from the main menu, then *Text file*. You will then be able to search for a file created in a word processing package and drop the contents into the box.

You can also insert picture files. In Publisher, select *Insert*, then *Picture File*. You can then find an image file – which can be a bitmap or vector image – and place the image on the page. When you click on the image, handles will appear that will allow you to resize the image.

A similar facility is found in most other packages. In Word, Excel and PowerPoint, select *Insert* then *Picture*, then *From file*.

### Editing inserted graphics

You may intend to create an image in a standalone package and then insert it into a word processing document or presentation. You can edit the image in two ways:

- You can use all the tools in the standalone application and save the image exactly how you want it to be seen in its final form. You then open the document or presentation and insert the image.
- You can save and then insert the image into your document, then use the *Picture* tools to edit it within the document. The changes will be saved in the document, but the original image will not be altered.

### Mail merging

Mail merge allows you to create a simple database of records that can be used in conjunction with a main word processed document. Mail merging can be used for direct marketing mailings, club membership mailings, billing etc.

You need a **main document** and a **data source** attached to it. In Word, a data source is a simple database, saved with the file name extension *.mdb*. The steps are:

- create a main document
- create or identify a data source
- merge the data with the main document to produce a set of printed documents.

## How to –

### Set up a mail merge

In this activity you will be setting up a mail merge letter to the customers of a small business telling them about a new product.

- Create a new document in Word in the usual way. If you have already saved a template for a business letter then use that. If not, create a simple letter heading, with the name and address of the business and its logo. Add today's date to one side below the heading. This is your main document for the mail merge. Save it as 'Letter'.

- In the *Tools* menu, select *Letters and Mailings*, then *Mail merge*.

- You will be asked a series of questions in the Task Pane. Answer as follows:

- **Step 1** Select document type *Letters*.

- **Step 2** Select *Starting document* then *Use the current document*.

- **Step 3** Select *Select recipients* then *Type a new list*. Then click on *Create…*

- The *New Address List* box will appear (Figure 1.28). Key in the name and address of one customer. You do not have to fill in every box, but make sure that you include the postcode. Zip code is the American term for a postcode.

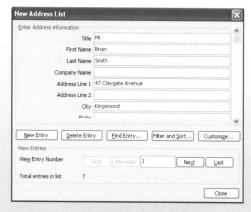

**Figure 1.28** *Creating an address list in Word*

- Click on *New Entry* to add another customer. Add five or six customers. Click *Close*.

- You will be prompted to save the address list in the *My Data Sources* folder. Call it 'Customers'.

- The next box displays all the addresses in a table and allows you to sort them if you wish. Click *OK*.

- Go to **Step 4**. You will be placing the name and address of each customer on the left of the page and below the letter heading. Click in the correct position then, in the *Task Pane*, select *Address Block*. Click *OK* in the dialogue box. A placeholder for the address will appear on the letter like this: <<AddressBlock>>.

- Click a little below the address block and then select *Greeting Line*. You can then choose what type of greeting to use. The default is Dear followed by the person's title and name.

- Now write the rest of the letter to customers.

- **Step 5** displays the merged letter using the first name and address. The arrows on the *Task Pane* allow you to browse through the remaining letters.

- **Step 6** lets you print the letters, one for each customer. You will not be popular if you print copies of all the letters, so, if you are just trying out this feature, when the *Merge to Printer* dialogue appears, choose *Current Record*.

# Presentation techniques

You can improve the appearance of any document by adding bullets, lines, borders and shading. But do not overdo them; the careful use of one or two features can make a document look professional, whereas a jumble of unrelated additions can look messy and amateurish.

Depending on the software used, bullets, lines, borders and shading can be added to a highlighted selection of text, to a text box, or to a cell (or set of cells) in a table or spreadsheet. You first select or highlight the item, then choose the feature you want.

## Choice of font and size

A font is a style of character that can be used on screen and for printing. Different fonts have been around since the invention of printing. Many more have been designed for use on computers, and there are now thousands to choose from.

There are three main kinds of **typeface** used for fonts – serif, sans serif and cursive. These are shown in Figure 1.29.

| Serif fonts | Sans serif fonts | Cursive fonts |
|---|---|---|
| Sample of Times Roman | Sample of Arial | Sample of Bradley Hand |
| Sample of Palatino | Sample of Verdana | Sample of Calligraphic |
| Sample of Bookman | Sample of Comic | Sample of Script |
| Sample of Goudy | Sample of Papyrus | Sample of Freestyle |

**Figure 1.29** *Types of font*

### Size of fonts

The **size** of each font is measured in points – another old printing term. There are 72 points to an inch, or approximately 29 points to a centimetre. A font size of, say, 12 points, measures the length from the top of the highest character to the bottom of the lowest character. But some fonts are long and thin and others are short and fat, so fonts with the same font size may look very different on the page.

Generally speaking, you should not use less than 12 points for normal text, although smaller sizes can be used for footnotes and captions.

### Serif fonts

**Serif** fonts have extra marks (serifs) at the ends of the strokes. These imitate the chisel marks left when letters are carved into stone. The most widely used serif font is Times Roman – so called because it was used by the Times newspaper and imitated the lettering used in ancient Rome.

Serif fonts create a definite impression for the reader. They suggest tradition, stability, honesty and good old-fashioned values, so they are sometimes used in logos when an organisation wants to appear to be substantial, long-established and trustworthy. However, they can sometimes be a bit difficult to read.

### Sans serif fonts

**Sans serif** fonts lack the extra marks and appear much plainer. But you will find a greater variety of shapes amongst sans serif fonts.

Sans serif fonts look modern and friendly. They are often used to give an impression that an organisation is up-to-date, customer-centred and forward-looking.

### Cursive fonts

**Cursive** fonts imitate handwriting, although some of them are based on handwriting styles from over a century ago.

Cursive fonts look warm and informal, but should be used with great care. They are not as legible as the other fonts, so should not be used for large areas of text. One obvious use would be for mock signatures, but they can also be used for headings.

### Selecting a font

How are you going to choose which fonts to use? It is a good idea to analyse printed materials and work out what looks professional and what looks amateurish. Here are a few suggestions:

- Think carefully about the impression you want to give. Choose fonts to convey a hidden message to your reader.
- Use a maximum of two fonts in a simple document like a letter or a report – one font for the main text and another one for headings.
- If you use a serif font for the main text, then you can use either a serif or sans serif font for headings.
- If you use a sans serif font for the main text then a serif font will often look odd when used for headings.

- Only use a third font for special emphasis, or for text in a separate section such as a footer.
- For the main text use at least 12 point, and larger sizes for headings.

## Use of colour

You can use colours for text, headings, borders and backgrounds. You should use colour with care, and restrict colours to no more than two or three toning colours in a document. Some applications offer you colour themes, which link colours that work well together. Subtle colours are usually more effective, especially for printed materials, although the occasional use of a bright colour can draw attention to promotional documents.

Some people are unable to distinguish between a range of colours, so you should make sure that all your documents are equally readable in grey scale.

## Layouts

Most applications offer you a choice of layouts through the use of templates. You should explore these as they will give you ideas.

### Text boxes

In many packages, text is created within a text box, which can then be positioned anywhere on the document. Here are some examples:

In Word, PowerPoint or Publisher, click on the *Text box* button or select *Text box* from the *Insert* menu. A text box appears in Word, which you can then resize (Figure 1.30). In the other applications, you draw out the text box on the page. Start typing your text in the box. You can apply all the usual font options from the *Formatting* toolbar. You can change the appearance of the text box, for example giving it a border, by right-clicking on it and selecting *Format Text box*.

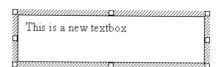

This is a new textbox

**Figure 1.30** *A text box in Word*

The advantage of using a text box is that it can be moved around the document. You can normally do this by moving the mouse to the edge of the text box until the Move pointer appears, then dragging it to its new position.

A text box can also be resized by dragging on any of the handles around the edge of the box. You may need to enlarge it to contain all your text.

### Columns

Many documents arrange the text in columns. This can easily be seen in newspapers and magazines, but many businesses also use a column layout for publicity leaflets, newsletters and staff information.

In Word, select *Columns* from the *Format* menu, then select the number of columns that you want. You can add a line between the columns if you like.

As you enter your text it will flow from the bottom of one column to the top of the next. See Figure 1.31.

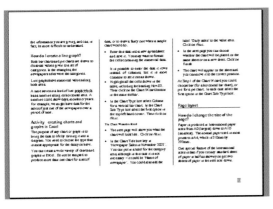

**Figure 1.31** *Three-column layout in landscape orientation*

In a desktop publishing package, you have a lot of freedom to place text boxes anywhere on the page, and these could be laid out as columns. You can make the text flow from one text box to another.

### Tables

A table can be used to display statistical data, but it can also be used to organise your text and images on a page. You can choose whether to have visible borders on a table or its cells. For example, the fonts in Figure 1.29 were displayed in a three-column table with five rows, and no borders. Web pages are very commonly laid out using tables without visible borders.

## Headers and footers

A header is an area at the top of each page, and a footer is at the bottom. The content of the header or the footer is usually the same on each page. Text in a header or footer is normally smaller than the main body of the text, to distinguish it from the rest of the document.

If you have set up page numbering in a wizard, the numbers will appear in the header or footer. You can add extra information to the header or footer. For example, you might want the name of the document, the date it was written or your own name to appear on each page.

In most applications, select *Header and Footer* from the *View* menu. Packages have different dialogue boxes, so you would be wise to check them out.

Word opens directly in the *Header* section with a floating *Header and Footer* toolbar (Figure 1.32). Check what the buttons do by passing the mouse over each. You can insert the date or page numbering, or you can choose from the *Insert AutoText* list. Text can be formatted using the usual *Formatting* toolbar. You can also apply any of the paragraph styles that you have created. You can switch to the footer by clicking on the *Switch* button.

**Figure 1.32** *The header section and the Header and Footer toolbar in Word*

## Titles and headings

Headings should be consistent throughout a document. You can either use a template, or you can set up heading and other styles in the style list before you start work on a document.

If you are writing a formal report then a title page may be required, although some reports simply have a heading on the first page instead.

## Use of bullets

- **Bullet points.** The symbol at the beginning of this paragraph is a bullet point. It is used to separate out the paragraphs and to draw attention to them. Bullet points are found in many documents and are widely used in PowerPoint presentations.

In most applications, highlight the text then click on the *Bullets* icon. You will notice that a new bullet point is created every time you use the *Enter* key.

In many applications you can choose a different image for the actual bullet by selecting *Format*, then *Bullets and Numbering*.

## Graphical images

You can add a number of graphical images to most documents:

- **Lines.** Straight and freeform lines can be drawn on most text documents and images. In Word and PowerPoint you can use the line tool from the *Drawing* toolbar. Paint and Publisher also have line tools in their toolboxes.
- **Borders.** A border can be placed around a selected section of text, a cell or a text box. You can usually do this by right-clicking the object and then formatting it. Most packages allow you to choose the style, colour and thickness of the border.
- **Backgrounds.** A complete document can be given a suitable coloured or patterned background in Word, Publisher and PowerPoint. Just select *Format*, then *Background*.

## Advanced techniques

### Tables of contents

A contents page is often given at the beginning of a long document. This lists the main sections and their page numbers. Although you can create this yourself, you will find that you will have to change it if you add extra text. The best approach in Word is to use the Table of Contents feature.

 How to –

### *Create a table of contents*

You can create a table of contents for a long document provided you have used the *Heading* styles from the style list for all the headings and subheadings:

- Place the cursor where you want the table of contents to be inserted.

- In the *Insert* menu select *Reference*, then *Index and Tables*.

- In the dialogue box click on the *Table of Contents* tab.

- You can make some changes to the default layout of the table of contents, but to start with just click on *OK*. The contents will be created using your headings.

### Indexes

At the end of this book you will find an index. You can use a tool in most word processing applications to create an index automatically.

## How to –

### *Create an index*

**Mark the entries**

- Highlight one of the words that you want to appear in the index.

- In the *Insert* menu, select *Reference*, then *Index and Tables*, then click on the *Index* tab.

- Click on *Mark Entry*, then *Mark*. The text will reveal the hidden text, including {XE …} following the word you have highlighted.

- You can hide or reveal the hidden text by clicking on the *Show/Hide* button in the *Standard* toolbar.

- Carry on marking the words to appear in the index.

**Create the index**

- Hide the hidden text.

- Click where you want the index to appear at the end of the document.

- In the *Insert* menu, select *Reference*, then *Index and Tables*, then click on the *Index* tab.

- Choose a format from the *Formats* box, then click on *OK*.

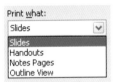

### Speaker notes

You can print out speaker's notes, audience notes or images of all the slides in a presentation. See Figure 1.33.

**Figure 1.33** *Printouts from PowerPoint*

## How to –

### *Print out notes or slides in PowerPoint*

- Select *File*, then *Print*. In the *Print* dialogue box you will see a *Print What:* list. You can choose to print thumbnails of all the slides, *Handouts* for the audience, *Notes Pages* (speakers notes), or an outline of the whole presentation.

## Information storage

### Files

When you use a software package, you can usually generate a file which you then save on backing storage. You are invited to give the file a name. The software will then add a filename extension, which identifies the type of file.

Files produced by a word processor or desktop publishing software are usually called documents. But other files can be referred to as data files, image files, sound files etc.

## File details

When you open *My Documents* you can choose to display the files in a number of *Views*. Click on the *Views* button, and select *Details*. See Figure 1.34. For each file you will be able to see its name, its size in KB or MB, the type of document it is and the date it was last modified.

**Figure 1.34** *Views options*

## File management

You should develop good practices when handling your files:

- You should give your document files sensible and clear names. It should be obvious to another person what the file contains.
- If you expect to work on a document over a period of time, you should create new versions as you go along. The first draft could be called 'ICT system project, V1'. The next time you open the document, save it immediately as 'ICT system project, V2'. You will gradually build up a series of versions. If anything goes wrong with one version, you can go back to the previous one. Sometimes you may decide to revisit something that you had written in a previous version but deleted in a later one. Keeping old versions leaves your options open.
- Create sensible folders, and folders within folders, for storing your work. It will then be easy for you to find a specific file.
- Delete old files if you are sure you will not need them again. Usually you have plenty of storage space so it is wiser not to delete files unless you really have to.

## Test your knowledge

**14** What is the difference between resizing and cropping an image? Explain how you resize bitmap and vector images.

**15** What are bullet points used for?

**16** Select a number of fonts and describe what each might be used for.

**17** Given that an A4 sheet is 210 mm by 297 mm, what are the dimensions of an A2 sheet?

### What does it mean?

A **file** is a collection of data that is stored as one item and is given a specific name. There are many kinds of file including program files (which hold the actual code that makes up the program), document, database, image and sound files.

### What does it mean?

A **filename extension** is the last part of a full filename. For example, the full filename for a word-processssed document could be mydocument.doc. In this case, doc is the filename extension and identifies the type of file that it is.

### What does it mean?

A **folder** is a way of organising files on a storage medium, such as a hard disk. Folders are also known as directories. A folder may have further folders within it.

# Review and adjust documents

## Review

When you have finished creating a document, you should review and check it very thoroughly before making it public or submitting it for assessment. This section gives you some techniques for doing this.

### Use of media

You will present your documents either in a printed form or electronically.

#### Printed documents

The quality and type of paper that you use can have quite an impact on readers.

Printer papers are identified as being suitable for use in either a laser or an inkjet printer, or both. Do not use other papers, as they may contain fibres that can come loose and damage the printer.

The weight of paper affects its look and feel. Paper is weighed in grams per square metre (gsm or $g/m^2$). Here is a selection of printer papers:

- **Business-quality** paper is everyday paper for internal use and is usually 80 $g/m^2$. It can be obtained in a number of tints.
- **Letter-quality** papers are often 100 $g/m^2$ and can be tinted, or given a more interesting surface to imitate woven papers or parchment.
- **Photo-quality** papers can be heavy and glossy and produce prints that look just like normal photos. Other photo-quality papers give good images on high-quality matt papers.
- **Card** can be used in most printers, and is available in many colours and up to 250 $g/m^2$.
- **Label stationery** is used to print out sticky labels for mailings.

Some papers, such as glossy photo paper, can be printed on only one side. Make sure that you load the paper the correct way up in the printer tray.

Each printer offers a number of options, using its own dialogue box. You can find this by clicking on the *Properties* button alongside the name of the printer in the *Print* dialogue.

- **Print quality.** You can choose usually between *Best*, *Normal* and *Fast* (sometimes known as Draft) mode. Draft mode uses a lower resolution, with fewer dpi (dots per inch), but produces a fast printout, so is useful for doing a quick check. Best mode uses a high resolution, but takes much longer to print, and uses more ink. You will be able to see a difference in quality between photos printed in Best and Normal mode, but the differences for text will be barely noticeable.

- **Paper type.** You can also identify the type of paper you are using, and the printer software will automatically select the right settings.
- **Colour printing.** Colour printers use mixtures of the three standard colours cyan, magenta and yellow to reproduce any colour at all. They also use black ink for pure black printing. Documents that include colours can be printed in full colour or in shades of grey. Grey is, in fact, produced by mixing colours, so true grey scale can only be achieved on a colour printer. Note that the American spelling of grey ('gray') is often used in applications.

## Quality control

The first version of a long document is known as a draft. This should be printed out and checked, and corrections should be made. An important document may go through several drafts before it is ready for the final printing.

### Proofreading

When a book is being prepared for publication, each trial printout is known as a proof. This is then read carefully by a proofreader, who checks that the text matches what the author intended and that any errors of spelling, grammar and layout have been corrected. The proofreader marks up any errors, which are then sent back to the publisher. Your work is going to be published in some form or another, either as a document to be used by an organisation, or as an assessment task, so it should be proofread just as carefully.

It is good practice to ask someone else to proofread an important document. They will often spot errors that you have missed. They should be looking for:

- spelling errors
- grammar errors
- wrong punctuation
- sentences in the wrong order.

You should understand the difference between proofreading and rewriting. It is perfectly acceptable to ask someone else to proofread and mark up the errors in your work. You should include their marked-up copy as evidence. You should then go through the marked-up copy yourself and decide whether you agree with the changes suggested. In other words, you have to take final responsibility for any changes.

### Accuracy

The information you give should be as accurate as possible. You should check any crucial facts against at least two sources. It is a good idea to ask an expert to look over your work for factual errors.

### Functionality

Your documents should be easy to read and use, given the nature of your audience. A long document can be enhanced with a table of contents or an index. A document in electronic format will benefit from links to different sections of the text. Do not write a long document when a short one would be more appropriate.

### Aesthetics

Aesthetics refers to the attractiveness of the document.

## Further research – aesthetics and graphical styles

Make a note of any documents that you find visually pleasing. Try to analyse what makes them attractive. Is it the choice of colour, font, layout, backgrounds, or some combination of these. You can create your own graphical style based on a successful design used elsewhere. Do not copy it exactly, but use it to give you ideas.

### Spell checking

You should have the spell checker switched on as a matter of course when you are using a text-based application. Even if you are good at spelling you will still make typing errors.

Make sure that the spell checker is set for UK English spellings.

You will still have to use your intelligence to decide between the alternatives offered for a word that is spelt incorrectly. You also need access to a dictionary, either printed or online, to check the meaning of the word you have substituted.

## Further research – using the spell checker

A student wrote this sentence, making some typing errors on the way:

**I herad about the holliday from my fiend.**

After using the spell checker, the sentence became:

**I herald about the Holliday from my fiend.**

What has happened here?

### Grammar checking

The grammar checker in word processing applications is quite sophisticated and it is a good idea to look at the options available. In Microsoft Word select *Options* from the *Tools* menu, then click the *Spelling & Grammar* tab.

### Thesaurus

A thesaurus groups words and phrases together that have similar or related meanings. If you would like to improve your vocabulary, you can use the thesaurus in two ways:

- Right-click on a word and select *Synonyms* for a quick list of words that mean much the same.
- Right-click on a word, select *Synonyms*, then *Thesaurus*. This will open a *Task Pane,* which will give you a greater choice of alternatives.

Once again, you need to use your intelligence to make sure that what you write still makes sense. Remember that the mark of good writing is that it is clear, not that it uses exotic words.

## Feedback from other people

It is acceptable to ask someone else to read your document and feed back any comments. You should include their comments as evidence, and then decide whether the comments are helpful or not.

You should not allow anyone else to amend your documents directly or to rewrite sections.

## User requirements check

You should check your document against the original requirements. Your document was originally designed to present information for a specific purpose and for a particular audience. Ask yourself whether you have been successful in meeting those intentions:

## Explaining decisions and actions taken

When you review a document for assessment purposes you should be ready to explain some of the choices you made:

- **Choice of packages.** You probably had a choice of applications (including embedded applications) that you could have used to create the document. You will have chosen one of them because it had features that were useful for your task.
- **Choice of techniques and tools.** You have read about a great many techniques and tools that you can choose from. You will have selected tools and techniques because they work well with the type of document and the audience. Do not simply select the tools that you already know; use the task as an opportunity to increase your skills.
- **Layout.** The choice of layout may be restricted by the house style of an organisation. Alternatively, you may be able to point to other publications aimed at the same audience, which are similar in layout and design to yours.

## Test your knowledge

**18**  Suggest a suitable type of paper for each of these business documents:

- letter to a job applicant inviting him or her to an interview
- invoice to a customer
- three-fold publicity leaflet, with photos
- internal memo
- printout of an email
- notice for the staff notice board.

**19**  What should someone be checking when they proofread a document?

**20**  Why is it important to spellcheck every document?

**21**  What is a thesaurus?  How can you use the thesaurus feature to improve your writing style?

# Assessment tasks

The assessment tasks in this unit are based on the following scenario:

*Carlton Studios are a graphic design company. They use a combination of manual methods and ICT to design and present all sorts of documents for their clients. The managing director, Susan Cooper, has hired you to work in ICT support. She would like you to review the types of documents that they produce, and the tools that they use, and to recommend how they can make better use of their ICT resources. She will also need you to support the graphic designers, so you will need a thorough understanding of the ICT tools they use to produce documents.*

> To work towards a Distinction in this unit you will need to achieve **all** the Pass, Merit and Distinction criteria in the unit and have evidence to show that you have achieved each one.

## How do I provide assessment evidence?

Your evidence can be presented in any suitable form, such as written reports, presentations or verbal explanations, together with the documents that you create for Task 3. These can be supported by other documentation, such as printouts, screen shots, witness statements, observation records and transcripts of conversations. If you make a presentation, include speaker's notes, and print off both slides and notes.

All your evidence should be presented in one folder, which should have a front cover and a contents page. You should divide the evidence into four sections corresponding to the four tasks.

## Task 1 (P1)

Collect examples of a number of documents, at least one from each of these types:

- short formal
- extended formal
- graphical
- promotional
- presentation
- informal.

Describe the structure and the purpose of the documents in each category. You can present this as a report, in a talk or electronically.

## Task 2 (P2)

Describe the different types of information and sources. Illustrate this with examples that you have collected.

Describe how you can check the validity of information and show that you have done so for some of the items of information that you have used.

# Assessment tasks continued

## Task 3 (P3, P4, P5, M1, M2, M3, D1)

This is a practical activity and will form the bulk of your assessment. You should spend time to ensure that the work you submit is of the highest quality and covers all the requirements.

For this task you should create at least six documents yourself, one at least from each of the document types listed in Task 1. You may use documents that you have prepared for other units in your course, or for other aspects of your life.

Each document should be designed to present information to a specific audience and you should identify the audience for each.

You should aim to demonstrate that you can use tools and techniques that are appropriate for the subject matter, for the style of document and for the audience. Over the whole set of documents you should show that you can use a wide range of tools.

For at least two of the documents you should select and use different document templates.

Two or more of the documents should present the same information to different audiences and using different types of document. For example, you could create a presentation for children in a local primary school explaining a religious or cultural festival. You could also write an article for a local newspaper covering the same information, but for an adult audience and in a journalistic style.

At least one of your documents should be more complex and should combine text, numerical and graphical information. For example, you could write a report for a manager describing a project that you have been involved in. This could include photos and statistical tables.

Take one of the documents that you have prepared and then show how advanced tools and techniques can improve it. Provide the earlier and later versions as evidence.

You should provide evidence that you have saved documents with appropriate filenames, and have stored them in suitable folders.

> To work towards a Distinction you should create document templates using two different applications. Your templates should be used to create some of the documents that you submit.

## Task 4 (P6, D2)

Review and check all the documents that you have created for Task 3. Read through the last section of this unit for an outline of the types of checks that you should be doing. There are several ways in which you can provide evidence that you have reviewed and checked the documents, such as 'before' and 'after' documents, feedback comments, or logs.

> To work towards a Distinction you should review the complex document that you created in Task 3. You should justify the tools and techniques that you used and explain why they were appropriate for your audience.

# 2 Introduction to Computer Systems

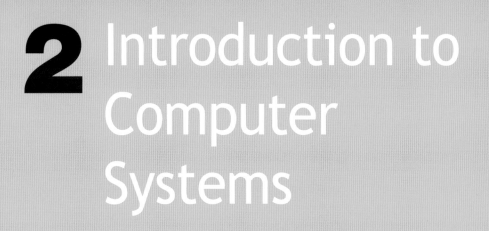

## About this unit

This unit introduces you to the basic concepts of computing. Most of the topics are dealt with in more depth in other units.

If you have taken courses in ICT before, you may find that you already know some of the theory. You are still advised to study this unit carefully, as it does require you to apply your knowledge in practical contexts.

As you work your way through, you should be asking some questions about the computer systems in use at your centre, and a discussion with the technical staff would be very beneficial. If you own a computer yourself then you will probably want to experiment with some of its facilities.

▶ Continued from previous page

# Learning outcomes

When you have completed this unit you will:

1 know different uses of computers in homes and businesses

2 be able to explain the use of common types of hardware in a personal computer system

3 know how to select software for a specified user

4 be able to connect hardware devices safely and configure software for a specified user.

# How is the unit assessed?

This unit is internally assessed. You will provide a portfolio of evidence to show that you have achieved the learning outcomes. The grading grid in the specification for this unit lists what you must do to obtain Pass, Merit and Distinction grades. The section on Assessment Tasks at the end of this chapter will guide you through activities that will help you to be successful in this unit.

# Uses of computers in homes and businesses

## Types of computers

### Personal computers

A personal computer is one that is designed for a single user. A personal computer may be standalone, or may be linked to a network.

Personal computers fall into two types:

- desktop computers, which are usually known as personal computers (PCs)
- laptop computers, which are portable.

All personal computers, must have, as a minimum, a monitor, some form of keyboard and some kind of pointing device. The processor and other essential parts need to be stored in a base unit, which in laptop computers in usually under the keyboard.

The familiar desktop PC houses the base unit in a tower or desktop unit. A mouse is the most common pointing device, although touch pads are common on laptops.

**What does it mean?**

*A **standalone** computer is one that is not linked permanently to others in a network.*

### Servers

A PC can be connected into a network. For a small network, say between two or three computers in an office or home, no additional computers are needed. But the task of managing a large network requires a powerful computer known as a server.

A server has several storage devices (hard disk drives) and a means of connection to all the computers in the network.

### Embedded devices

Computer systems are also hidden away inside many other kinds of machine. They all need a processor, plus some form of input and output but these need not take the familiar form of keyboard, mouse and monitor. These computer systems are known as embedded systems, and they can be found in music systems, cars, games consoles, phones and domestic appliances, such as DVD players and washing machines.

### Mainframe computers

Although networks of personal computers are widely used in businesses today, there are still some circumstances where a more powerful system is needed. Mainframe computers are the large and expensive systems that are used for very active systems which handle a lot of data. For example, a mainframe could be used by a major bank or to support a heavily used online shopping or travel website. Sometimes a single mainframe computer is used to replace a number of servers. It is usually possible to connect a large number of users to a mainframe through terminals.

### Personal digital assistants

A personal digital assistant (PDA) is a hand-held computer, which can carry out many of the functions of a full-size system. The small screen size does limit its capabilities. Some PDAs are now combined with a mobile phone, and can be used to handle emails and browse the Web. Although PDAs can be used independently, most users link them to a personal computer on a daily basis, so that they can synchronise some of the data, such as the entries in a calendar.

## Users

Computer users fall into two broad categories:

- **home or commercial end users** who use applications software
- **ICT practitioners** such as administrators who work with operating systems, or developers who create software.

Most people who use ICT at work are end users, which means that they use computers and data communications as tools within their normal work.

End users can use ICT successfully only because of the many ICT practitioners who have developed the hardware and software, who manage the data and networks, and who help them to use it.

Both end users and ICT practitioners are users of the computer systems, although they interact with computers in different ways. In a work environment, users will not usually stray from one category to another. Most of the users in an organisation will be end users, and they will not be expected to do any programming or to carry out technical tasks.

But today many people own computers for their own personal use, and they have to act both as end users and as ICT practitioners.

 Further research – jobs in ICT

Look through advertisements for jobs in the ICT industry. You may find these in local newspapers and in local employment agencies. National newspapers often cover ICT jobs on a particular day of the week. There are also some specialist papers and magazines, such as Computer Weekly, which carry a large number of job advertisements. You can also find employment agencies on the Internet that specialise in ICT work. Note down the kinds of jobs you have found and what the post-holders will be expected to do.

## Home/commercial end users

Whenever a person uses applications software, they are working as an end user. Today we do not expect end users to have any technical skills in managing their computer systems. Instead they should be able to concentrate on their business tasks, using a computer as a tool.

### Types of tasks that end users might perform on a computer

End users work with applications software in order to carry out the business of the organisation or for their personal use. Tasks may include:

- communicating with others through the Internet
- creating documents, spreadsheets and presentations
- creating and editing images
- interacting with a database
- working with specialist software related to their work.

### Levels of technical expertise that end users might need

All end users have to have basic ICT skills, even if they do little more than read and reply to emails. But most end users have some training in specific software applications, and can become very proficient at using them.

An end user may have to do some simple maintenance with the 'engine' of their computer – the operating system. They may:

- launch applications software
- set up new directories
- move or delete files
- configure the display.

## ICT practitioners – developers

Developers create new software applications for end users to use.

If the software project is a large one, several people will be involved in the task. The software may have been designed by a systems analyst, who looks at the ways in which information is handled in an organisation and then designs a better system. The software developers will then create and test the software to match the design.

In a small project the software developer will carry out all the tasks, from analysing the problem, to designing, creating and testing the software.

### Types of tasks that developers might perform on a computer

There are three main types of software developers:

- A **programmer** takes the design for a new piece of software and then writes the computer program. Programmers can use a number of programming languages such as Visual Basic, Java or C++.
- An **applications developer** will use an applications generator to create a new application. Applications generators, such as Microsoft Access, allow the developer to create an application very quickly, using a number of tools such as a form or report designer. These tools

generate the program code directly. The developer can then add further features to the basic application by adapting and extending the program code.

■ Web pages are programmed by **website developers**. They use Hypertext Mark-up Language (HTML) together with other specialist languages. Many sites are also linked directly to a database.

You will learn more about programming if you study Unit 7, about applications development in Unit 8 and about website development in Unit 4.

### Levels of technical expertise that developers might need

All developers need to have advanced skills in the languages and other tools that they use. They also have to understand how end users will work with their products, and how they will fit into the wider work of the organisation.

All programs have to interact with the operating system, so the people who write the programs also have to understand how this works.

## ICT Practitioners – technical users

The technical users look after all the computer systems in an organisation. Most companies run a network, so the technical staff will be responsible for managing both the network and the individual desktop computers linked to it.

### Tasks that technical users might perform on a computer

In order to support the computer system, technical users carry out a number of tasks:

■ **Maintain the computer system**. This includes configuring the operating system, setting up user accounts, ensuring that data is backed up, preventing unauthorised access and viruses, maintaining supplies for peripherals (e.g. printer paper), and dealing with day-to-day problems with hardware and software.

■ **Plan and carry out changes**, by installing new hardware and software, and planning major upgrades.

■ **Support end users**, often by providing a helpdesk for end users.

A number of job titles are used when referring to the technical staff who maintain computer systems:

■ An **administrator** (or systems administrator, or network administrator) is a computer professional who works directly with the network operating system to ensure that the network functions as intended. A **network manager** (or systems manager) is the senior administrator; the network manager is in charge of the network and its administration, and will plan and manage any large upgrade projects. You can read more about this role in Unit 6.

■ A **helpdesk worker** (also known as user support) helps end users if they have any problems with their software and hardware. You can read more about what they do in Unit 15.

- A **technician** carries out the day-to-day maintenance tasks relating to hardware and software. They may check and configure individual desktop computers, install new hardware and software, check the connections, and provide help to users.

In a small organisation, one person may carry out all three roles.

Technical users work directly with operating systems. This will normally mean configuring the network operating system as well as the operating systems running on each of the computers that make up the network.

## Further research – ICT practitioners

Try to meet as many ICT practitioners as you can, and ask them about their work. Select two kinds of jobs that exist in ICT and find out as much as you can about them. If at all possible, talk to people who hold the jobs. Try to decide which of the jobs appeal to you as a possible future career.

### Levels of technical expertise that technical users might need

Technical users are highly knowledgeable people who have high levels of understanding of the systems that they work with. They are able to look into and change many aspects of the system. Administrators become very skilled at managing and troubleshooting network operating systems.

# User interface

Some of the software that is loaded on your computer works invisibly in the background and you rarely need to communicate with it; this is true of some of the core components of the operating system. But you still need to interact with many components of the system, so all operating systems have some kind of user interface.

The user can interact with the operating system in two distinct ways:

- Through a command line interface, such as MS-DOS. The user gives instructions to the operating system by keying in coded commands.
- Through a graphical user interface (GUI), such as Microsoft Windows. The user gives instructions by clicking on buttons, selecting from menus or moving icons around the screen.

### Command line interfaces

Before GUIs were introduced, all interaction was through a command line interface.

Many network operating systems use GUIs, but technical users often like to use the command line interface instead. Many find that it is quicker to enter a command than to search through a menu for an option.

Years ago, all computer systems were managed by ICT practitioners. They would configure and control the operating system on a large and expensive mainframe computer.

For a number of years, MS-DOS was the main operating system used on PCs. Microsoft Windows was originally built as an interface to make it easier for the user to use MS-DOS without having to learn the commands. You can still use the MS-DOS commands on a PC that has Windows.

There are some other operating systems that use a command line interface, the most used of which is Linux.

## Further research – MS-DOS command line interface

If you are using a version of Microsoft Windows, you can switch into a command line interface and find out what computing was like for everyone years ago. You may not be able to do all this on a network computer at your centre.

If you select *All Programs* in the *Start* menu, then *Accessories*, you should find *Command Prompt*. Click on this and a blank window will open. See Figure 2.1.

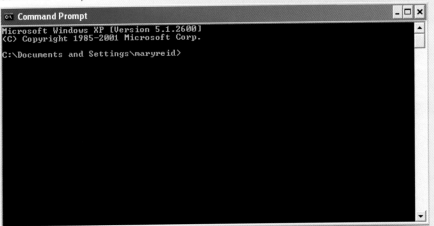

**Figure 2.1** *The MS-DOS window*

There are a few icons, such as the *Minimize* button, at the top of the window, but you have to imagine that they do not exist. Once you move into the main black screen you will find yourself in a world in which the mouse does not work, and there are no icons or drop-down menus. To make anything happen at all you will have to enter some commands from the keyboard.

Before you start, you need to know that folders are referred to as directories. A directory inside another one is called a subdirectory. You will probably find you are in the *Documents and Settings* directory that holds your personal files.

Try keying in these commands:

- **DIR** This is short for 'directory', and is the command to list all the files in the current directory. At the end of the list, the system will state how many files and subdirectories there are. See Figure 2.2.

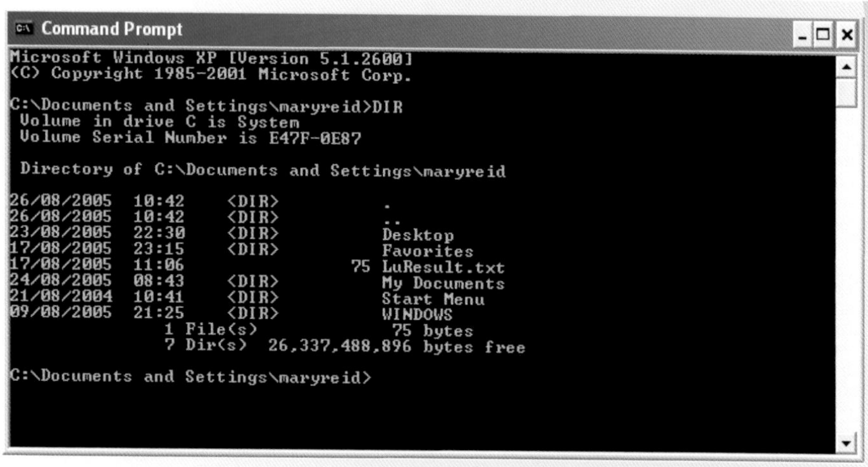

**Figure 2.2** *The result of the DIR command*

- **CD FAVORITES**  CD stands for 'change directory'. You may have noticed a subdirectory called Favorites. This command opens that directory. Use DIR to see its contents.

- **DIR /P**  You may have found that the screen scrolled rapidly as the details of all the files and subdirectories were displayed. This will slow down the display and allow you to read the information one screen at a time.

- **CD..**  This changes the directory to the one above it. You can use it more than once to get back to the root directory, which is the directory for the C drive itself.

- Most of the files are data files rather than programs. The filenames for programs end with *.exe*. To run (execute) a program you have to find it in a directory then key in the first part of the filename.

- **EXIT**  This is the command to leave MS-DOS.

## Graphical user interface (GUI)

The first desktop computers were introduced in the 1970s and became common in offices and homes in the 1980s. New computer owners found that they were in charge of a complete computer system. Each user had to act as both an ICT practitioner and an end user of applications software. So ordinary users had to learn to use the operating system for their computer, which meant that they had to use a command line interface.

But the command line interface made many people think that it was difficult to use a computer. It made sense for the computer industry to develop an interface to the operating system that would be easy for a non-professional to use.

End users almost always use GUIs to carry out their tasks. GUIs are used for both operating systems and software applications, and you will probably be familiar with Microsoft Windows (Figure 2.3). The operating system for Apple Macintosh computers has had a GUI right from the start.

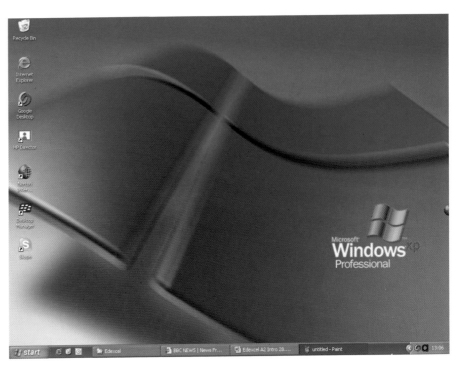

**Figure 2.3** *The graphical user interface for Microsoft Windows*

**Multi-tasking** *is the ability to hold several programs and files in memory simultaneously, so that the user can switch between one task and another.*

Modern GUIs usually support multi-tasking. That means that the user can launch more than one application at a time and can switch between them. For example, you may start writing a document in a word processor, then open a spreadsheet and switch between the two.

The GUI for an operating system makes it easy to identify which software applications are launched and to switch between them. In Windows, the Taskbar and the facility to minimise windows both support multi-tasking. See Figure 2.4.

**Figure 2.4** *Taskbar displaying four tasks that are currently open*

 Further research – multi-tasking

In Windows, the Taskbar displays shortcuts to all the documents that are currently open. Each of these represents a different task. All of these documents, and the applications software they are using, are being held in memory at the same time. Windows supports multi-tasking, so the user can switch between one task and another. Do you use multi-tasking effectively yourself? Or do you tend to close down a program before opening another one? Have you experienced any difficulties with multi-tasking? For example, has your computer crashed because you have opened too many applications and documents?

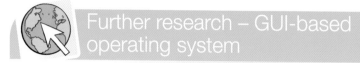

## Further research – GUI-based operating system

Use the GUI-based operating system that you are familiar with and show how the GUI helps you to carry out maintenance tasks. Think how this might compare with a command line interface.

## Specialised user interfaces

Although GUIs are widely used, they do not suit all users in all circumstances. Here are a couple of examples of specialised user interfaces:

- **Voice output** – users with visual impairments can use voice systems that read back to them the text on a screen.
- **Voice control** – users who cannot manipulate a mouse can use voice commands to control the system. This is useful for users with visual impairment as well as those with other disabilities. Voice controlled systems may become used more widely in the future for embedded systems, so that you could, for example, talk to your washing machine!

## Advantages and disadvantages of different types

A GUI has many advantages:

- A good GUI is said to be intuitive, i.e. the user can usually see straightaway what they need to do to carry out an action.
- A non-technical user can interact easily with the operating system and will not need technical support to carry out basic tasks.
- Users do not need expensive training to learn to use a GUI.
- Paper manuals (which can easily get lost or damaged) are also not needed.
- Once a user is familiar with one GUI they can usually adapt easily to another one.

The disadvantages of a GUI are quite specific:

- Users with disabilities may not be able to use a GUI.
- Experienced users may find that they can work more quickly using shortcuts, such as hotkeys.
- Technical users may prefer to work in a command line interface, as they have direct control over the actions.

## Test your knowledge

1  What are the differences between a personal computer and a server?

2  What is an embedded system? Give examples.

3  What technical skills might you expect an average end user to have?

4  List four jobs that an ICT practitioner might apply for.

5  What does a network administrator do?

6  Describe one situation where a command line interface might be preferable to a GUI.

# Hardware in a personal computer system

You will probably be familiar with the main components that make up a personal computer system:

- The **processor** or **CPU** (central processing unit) carries out the instructions in a program, and controls all the other components. The processor is normally stored on one chip.
- The **main memory** holds all the data that is being used by a computer system while it is active. Main memory requires power to work, so it is emptied when the computer is switched off. Main memory is normally provided on one or more RAM (random access memory) semiconductor chips.
- **Storage devices** are used to store data, but, unlike the main memory, do not lose the data when they are switched off. Backing store devices include various types of disk and tape drive. All storage devices store data on storage media, such as disks and tapes. Most storage devices allow the system to write new data to the storage media as well as to read it back; the exception to this would be the CD-ROM drive, which can only read disks.
- **Input devices** transfer data to the CPU. Input devices include keyboard, mouse and microphone as well as a variety of specialised devices like barcode readers and scanners.
- **Output devices** receive data that is transferred to them from the CPU. Output devices include screen, speakers and printer. Some devices, such as a modem, can act as both input and output devices.
- A **modem** links the computer system with the Internet and converts the signals from the computer into the format used by the connection. It acts as both an input and an output device.
- A **network interface card** is a combination of software and hardware that enables a computer to be linked to a network.

Of these, the input, output and storage devices are often known as **peripheral devices**, or just peripherals.

The processor controls the whole computer system. None of the other components can do anything unless they are in communication with the processor. All the input and output ports on a computer receive control signals from the processor. Any device that has to pass data to or from the processor can only do so under the control of the processor.

These devices all work at different speeds, and the processor has to ensure that they all receive signals at the right time and in the right order.

**What does it mean?**

**Storage media** *are the actual disks or tapes that are used to store digital data. Storage media are placed in a disk or tape drive, which then reads or writes data. Storage media include hard disks, floppy disks, CDs, DVDs and digital tapes.*

*Note that 'media' is the plural for 'medium'.*

# Hardware

## Processors

The majority of desktop and laptop computers have very similar processors installed. They currently fall into three groups:

- Intel Pentium series and Intel Celeron series
- equivalent processors, such as the AMD Athlon series
- Apple G series.

In the past if you bought an Apple system then it would have an Apple processor (Apple have recently announced that they are changing to use Intel processors). On the other hand, the Intel Pentium and equivalent processors are virtually interchangeable with each other, and are used by many different manufacturers, although they do differ in their performance.

The speed of a processor is measured in hertz (Hz), where 1 hertz = 1 cycle per second. This refers to the fetch-execute cycle, which is the process of copying one program instruction from main memory to the processor, then carrying out the instruction. Today's processors can carry out many millions of cycles per second, so the processor speed is measured in MHz or GHz.

The speed of the processor is not the only measure of a processor's performance. Some processors with slower cycle times are constructed to handle instructions more efficiently, so may actually work through programs faster than processors with higher speeds.

## Memory

### RAM

Main memory is made up of RAM semiconductor chips. See Figure 2.5. RAM means 'random access memory', which indicates that all data stored in memory can be accessed equally quickly.

RAM chips require power to hold on to their data. When a computer is switched off, the data in RAM is erased.

**Figure 2.5** *A RAM chip*

The main property of RAM is its capacity, which is measured in megabytes (MB) or gigabytes (GB). This is the number of bytes that can be stored in memory while the computer system is switched on.

For a program to run, it must first of all be copied from storage to main memory. As it runs, it creates additional data files; for example, when you load word processing software into memory you create a document that contains further data. Documents and other data also have to be stored in main memory.

**What does it mean?**

**Capacity** *is the amount of data that can be stored. Capacity is measured in bytes, kilobytes (KB), megabytes (MB) or gigabytes (GB). 1 KB is approximately one thousand bytes, 1 MB is approximately one million bytes, and 1 GB is approximately one thousand million bytes.*

Several programs and their data files can be held in different parts of main memory at the same time. So the capacity of main memory determines how many programs can be loaded, and how many documents you can create.

If you try to load too many programs, or work on too many documents at the same time, you will get a system message telling you that the system is running out of resources. If this happens frequently, then you can add extra RAM to a system, or replace existing RAM chips with larger ones.

### Further research – capacity of main memory

You can find out the capacity of the main memory in your system in Windows. Go to the *Start* menu, select the *Control Panel*, then select *System*. The amount of RAM will be displayed in the *General* tab.

### Cache

Cache is a small and very fast memory that is part of the processor. It holds recently used data, so that if the processor needs to use that data again it can read it from the cache instead of having to read it from main memory.

## Storage devices

Data is stored on storage media, such as disks and tapes. Main memory only holds the programs and other files that the computer is actually using, and only for as long as it needs them. Thus all programs and data files have to be stored on a medium so that they can be loaded into memory when needed.

Storage media may be:

- **Read-only memory (ROM)** – the data is stored permanently and cannot be erased, and no new data can be added. The most common type are CD-ROMs.
- **Recordable (R)** – data is stored permanently and cannot be erased. But new data can be added until the media is full up. This is also known as WORM (Write Once, Read Many) technology.
- **Read and write (RW)** – the data can be erased and new data can be added.

Three technologies are used for storing the data:

- **Magnetic** – tiny spots on the surface are set up as individual magnets. The magnetic field of each spot is aligned in one of two directions, which represent the binary values 0 or 1. The importance of these numbers to ICT is explained on page 70. Magnetic storage is used on tapes and floppy disks.

- **Optical** – tiny pits on the surface represent a binary value 1, while flat areas represent 0. The light from a laser reflects cleanly from a flat area but is scattered by a pit.
- **Flash** – this uses a memory chip, rather like RAM, but it does not need power to hold on to the data.

The main types of storage media are as follows:

- **Hard disks** are magnetic read and write media. They can have a high capacity and are used as the main backing store for virtually all computer systems.
- **Floppy disks** are small, magnetic read and write media. They can hold only 1.44 MB of data each. Because of their limited capacity they are not used very frequently today.
- **CD-ROMs** are read-only optical disks. They can hold up to 700 MB.
- **CD-R** are CD disks that are recordable. Recording on a CD-R is often referred to as 'burning'.
- **CD-RW** are CD disks that can also be erased and written to again.
- **DVDs** (Digital Versatile Discs) are high-capacity CDs that can be used for a wide range of digital data, including video. They come in plain DVD (i.e. ROM), DVD±R, DVD±RW and DVD-RAM formats. DVD drives have largely superseded CD drives on the most recent systems.
- **Flash memory** is used in memory cards and USB flash drives. They are rewritable.
- **Tapes** are magnetic media mainly used for security purposes. The complete contents of a hard disk may be copied to tape daily, and the tapes stored carefully in case the hard disk is damaged or corrupted. Digital Audio Tapes (DAT) are commonly used, although other formats are available.

Backing store devices are used to read data from and write data on to storage media (disks and tapes). They are normally known as **drives**. Some drives are designed so that the storage media cannot be removed, while others are removable.

- Most drives work with **removable media**. Removable media can be used to transfer data from one computer system to another. New software is often presented on a removable medium, so that users can install it on their own system. Removable media include floppy disks, CDs and DVDs of all types, flash memory cards and tapes.
- The disks used in hard disk drives (HDDs) are **fixed media** and cannot usually be removed, though removable ones are available that can be locked away for security. Hard disks are able to work fast because the individual disks are held in a sealed, dust-free casing. This means that the head that reads and writes the data can be positioned very close to the surface of the disk, without actually touching it. Sometimes hard drives are referred to as internal drives, simply to emphasise the fact that they are placed inside the main tower or desktop unit.

It is useful to compare the speeds of the drives, but this is not as easy as it sounds because of the different technologies used. The speeds of CD and DVD drives can be directly compared with each other. The first CD drives that were produced read the data at 150 KB per second. Today the speed is given as a multiple of the original speed. So, for example, a CD with a speed of 52x reads data fifty-two times faster than 150 KB per second, i.e. at 7.8 MB per second.

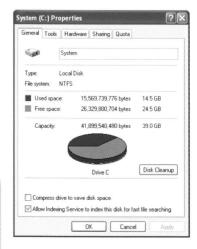

Figure 2.6 *Capacity of a hard disk*

### Further research – finding out the capacity of storage media

You can find out the capacity of the storage media on a computer system that you are using by opening *My Computer* from the *Start* menu. You will see a list of all the drives. Right-click on each in turn and select *Properties*. In Figure 2.6 the hard disk in drive C has a capacity of 39 GB, of which 14.5 GB has been used.

## Input devices

There are many input devices that can be used with a PC:

- **Mouse.** A mouse is a pointing device that controls a pointer on the screen. The standard mouse has two buttons, which you can click or double-click to send instructions to the operating system. A further button or fingertip wheel is sometimes added to carry out extra actions.

- **Keyboard.** The standard keyboard uses the QWERTY key layout, named after the top row of letters. The standard keyboard includes a numeric keypad, some control keys (such as Insert, Page Up and the arrow keys), and programmable function keys (F1, F2 etc.). An ergonomically designed keyboard uses a similar layout to the standard one, but is shaped to make it more comfortable to use.

- **Graphics tablet.** This is a flat surface that you can 'draw' on with a stylus. It can be used to interact with the GUI, or in applications to draw images.

- **Microphone.** A microphone linked to a PC can capture sounds for Internet voice conversations or for recording purposes.

- **Scanner.** A scanner 'reads' paper documents and turns them into computer files, usually saved as images. But it can also scan in text; then special optical character recognition (OCR) software can recognise the letters and turn the text into a word processor document.

## Output devices

### Printers

The most common types of printer used today are shown in Figure 2.7:

- **Inkjet printers** squeeze tiny bubbles of ink on to the paper to form the characters and images. The quality of the output is measured in dots per inch – more dots per inch give better pictures, but take longer to print. Inkjet printers can print to a variety of papers, including glossy photo paper. The ink is stored in ink cartridges. Four colours are used – black, cyan, magenta and yellow.

■ **Laser printers** use the same technology as photocopiers. The laser places an electrostatic charge on a drum to match the image. Toner powder is attracted to the charged areas on the drum, and the image is printed when the paper is pressed against the drum and briefly heated. Colour laser printers use the same colours as inkjet printers, but the paper has to be charged and printed four times, once for each colour.

Laser printers produce high-quality output but cost more than inkjet printers. Colour laser printers are considerably more expensive than black laser printers. Laser printers are generally faster than inkjet printers.

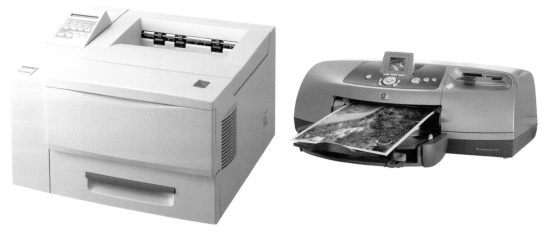

**Figure 2.7** *Inkjet and laser printers*

### Monitors

The main output device for a computer system is the monitor, or screen. Monitors are measured in two ways:

■ **size** – the length along a diagonal of the display area
■ **resolution** – the number of pixels (colour dots) that it can display horizontally and vertically.

Generally speaking, the larger screens give higher resolution and cost more.

There are two main types of screen, shown in Figure 2.8:

■ **CRT monitor.** A Cathode Ray Tube monitor is the traditional type of monitor that is still widely used.
■ **LCD screen.** A Liquid Crystal Display gives a completely flat screen and is commonly used for laptops and hand-held systems. LCD monitors can also be used with desktop systems.

LCD screens use far less power than CRT ones, but they do need back lighting. The display cannot be easily seen from an angle. LCD screens are more expensive than CRT screens.

**Figure 2.8** *LCD and CRT monitors*

The quality of the pictures on a screen depends to a certain extent on its resolution. But of far greater importance is the graphics card that has been installed. A graphics card is, in fact, a second processor that carries out all the calculations needed to display high-quality graphics. Provided the card carries enough memory, it enables the user to change the resolution of the screen (up to the maximum allowed by the screen itself), and the number of colours that can be displayed. The graphics card also handles video and 3D animations fast enough for them to appear realistic.

### Modems

The connection between a computer and the Internet falls into two main types:

- A connection can be made through a **dialup modem**. The modem has a serial connection to the CPU, which then sends the signal along an ordinary telephone line. Modems usually transfer data at a speed of 56 kilobits per second. The meaning of bits is explained on page 72.
- A **broadband connection** is one that can carry more data than the traditional dialup method. Broadband connections can carry data at speeds from 512 kilobits per second right up to hundreds of megabits per second.

The most common broadband methods are as follows:

- **ISDN** (Integrated Services Digital Network), which uses a dedicated digital network
- **ADSL** (Asynchronous Digital Subscriber Line), which works over ordinary BT telephone lines
- cable connections provided by the cable TV companies.

### Network interface cards (NICs)

A NIC must be fitted to a PC before it can be connected to a network. There are a number of different types of NIC, depending on the kind of network that is needed, but the most common type is an Ethernet card.

You will learn more about network cards if you study Unit 6.

## Costs

The costs of complete PCs and of individual peripherals tend to come down over time, but these devices are then replaced by new ones with higher specifications. You would be wise to keep in touch with the current prices by reading magazines, visiting computer shops or searching on the Internet.

Do remember to consider the price of media, both for storage (disks etc.) and for printing (paper). When comparing the price of printers it is important to remember the cost of the ink cartridges or toners, and to calculate how often these will have to be replaced.

### Further research – current prices

Use computer magazines and the Internet to find out the current costs of a range of devices that you might want to add to the PC that you use.

## Data representation

Computers store incredibly large amounts of data. This data can represent:

- numbers
- characters – e.g. the letters and symbols on a keyboard
- instructions – from which whole programs are made
- many other kinds of data, such as colours and sounds.

Although the data can be very complex, it is all stored in a very simple fashion.

### Binary representation

Our alphabet has 26 characters and our number system uses 10 digits, but the computer has only two 'characters' to play with. These are known as bits. We refer to these two bits with the symbols 0 and 1.

So how can the computer store so much information with only two characters? Think about our number system for a moment – we have only 10 digits and yet we can combine them in different ways to represent billions of numbers. To state something obvious, the position of each digit is important, so that the number 372 is a different number from 723, even though they both use the same digits. In the same way, even though the computer only has two bits, they can be combined to give billions of arrangements. These patterns of bits are known as binary patterns.

Each of these binary patterns can be used to represent a different piece of data. Whenever binary patterns are used to store data, we describe it as digital data.

Binary patterns are also transferred from one part of a computer to another. Whenever a computer is running, many millions of pieces of

### What does it mean?

A **character** is any letter or symbol that can be stored in a computer system. The standard characters include all the letters of the alphabet (both upper and lower case), the digits from 0 to 9, and all the punctuation marks and symbols shown on a normal keyboard (including the space). Additional characters can be stored as well, such as letters and symbols used in other languages, like é, ß, and ¥.

### What does it mean?

A **binary (or bit) pattern** is any combination of bits in a sequence.

### What does it mean?

**Digital** data is any data which is stored or transmitted using binary patterns.

data are being moved around inside the processor every second. And every time data is transferred to or from one of the devices that make up the computer system (such as a keyboard, disk drive or printer) then binary patterns are sent as signals.

Binary patterns are combinations of bits.

How many binary patterns can be made with exactly two bits? Here they are:

00            01            10            11

So we can create four different binary patterns with exactly two bits. Note that $4 = 2 \times 2$.

Next, how many binary patterns can be made with exactly three bits? Here they are:

000    001    010    011    100    101    110    111

The answer this time is 8. Note that $8 = 2 \times 2 \times 2$.

Can you predict how many binary patterns you can make with four bits? Write down all the patterns systematically, and you should find 16. Note that $16 = 2 \times 2 \times 2 \times 2$.

Can you now predict how many binary patterns you can make with 5, 6, 7 or 8 bits?

Look at Table 2.1:

| Number of bits | Number of binary patterns | |
|---|---|---|
| 2 | 4 | $4 = 2^2 = 2 \times 2$ |
| 3 | 8 | $8 = 2^3 = 2 \times 2 \times 2$ |
| 4 | 16 | $16 = 2^4 = 2 \times 2 \times 2 \times 2$ |
| 5 | 32 | $32 = 2^5 = 2 \times 2 \times 2 \times 2 \times 2$ |
| 6 | 64 | $64 = 2^6 = 2 \times 2 \times 2 \times 2 \times 2 \times 2$ |
| 7 | 128 | $128 = 2^7 = 2 \times 2 \times 2 \times 2 \times 2 \times 2 \times 2$ |
| 8 | 256 | $256 = 2^8 = 2 \times 2 \times 2 \times 2 \times 2 \times 2 \times 2 \times 2$ |
| 9 | 512 | $512 = 2^9 = 2 \times 2 \times 2 \times 2 \times 2 \times 2 \times 2 \times 2 \times 2$ |
| 10 | 1,024 | $1024 = 2^{10} = 2 \times 2 \times 2 \times 2 \times 2 \times 2 \times 2 \times 2 \times 2 \times 2$ |
| ... | | |
| 16 | 65,536 | $65,536 = 2^{16}$ |
| ... | | |
| 24 | 16,777,216 | $16,777,216 = 2^{24}$ |
| ... | | |
| 32 | 4,294,967,296 | $4,294,967,296 = 2^{32}$ |

**Table 2.1** *Number of bit patterns that can be created with a fixed number of bits*

You will see that the number of binary patterns doubles each time. In general, if there are $n$ bits then these can be combined to give $2^n$ different binary patterns.

32 bits can be combined to give over 4 thousand million binary patterns – far more than we could ever need.

## Bits and bytes

Binary patterns are usually stored and transmitted in groups of 8 bits. An 8-bit pattern is known as a byte. For example, the binary pattern 10010111 is one byte in length. From the table above you can see that there are 256 ways of combining the 8 bits in one byte.

We measure the amount of data stored in a computer by counting how many bytes are used.

You will remember the standard ways of measuring metric units, as shown in Table 2.2:

| Metric units | Name | Abbreviation |
|---:|:---:|---:|
| 1,000 | kilo | k |
| 1,000,000 | mega | M |
| 1,000,000,000 | giga | G |

**Table 2.2** *Metric units*

Sometimes the abbreviations are used, and sometimes the full word is given. For example, when measuring distance, 1,000 m = 1 km, and when measuring power 1,000 watts = 1 kilowatt, and 1,000 kilowatts = 1 megawatt.

But when it comes to digital data, bytes are never counted in thousands. They are always counted in groups of 1,024 bytes. This is because of the way they are physically stored and accessed. You will have realised that powers of 2 feature very heavily in computer storage and $1,024 = 2^{10}$.

1,024 is close to 1,000, so the accepted convention is that 1,024 bits = 1 kilobyte (abbreviated to 1 KB, or 1 KByte). See Table 2.3.

| Metric units | Name | Abbreviation | Computer units |
|---:|:---:|:---:|---:|
| 1,000 | kilo | K | 1,024 |
| 1,000,000 | mega | M | 1,048,576 = 1,024×1,024 |
| 1,000,000,000 | giga | G | 1,073,741,824 = 1,024×1,024×1,024 |

**Table 2.3** *Computing units*

The right hand column of the table shows that in a computer system the terms mega and giga mean approximately 1 million and 1 thousand million respectively. But for all everyday purposes you can think of 1 MB as 1 million bytes, and 1 GB as 1 thousand million bytes.

Note that the abbreviation for a bit is 'b' and for a byte is 'B'.

### How can binary patterns be used to represent data?

Binary patterns can be used to represent any data that is stored or transmitted digitally. In a computer the data could be numbers, characters or program instructions. The numbers themselves can stand for ordinary numbers as we use them, or for the elements that make up pictures and sound.

So one byte, such as 01100011, could represent a number, or a character, or part of a program instruction, or something in an image, or a fraction of a sound. How then does the computer know which one it means? Whenever a computer system is doing anything at all it is running a program, and that program will be expecting to receive data of a particular type, so will interpret the data in the way it is expecting.

### Further research – wrong interpretation of data

Have you ever opened a document in a word processor and seen something like this?

DHHþ BÎ

]Y:ôLßiúÔc×®½w=º{µ=çöTĺ÷êªêx\
¡oMÓ«Ï~u™^Mÿüåešÿ1ÿ÷ñôzþÿÓå2}cþüöÓo¿úã—•¿¾óô¬¿ûéĺ»7—
WÓ›ùóûÿüáï¿wûþ¶÷›s  æÏwOÓt"õüüütÛÿÉü [ëÿ} Óî½Ü÷þè…Œ§ËÓýÛx— ï
}öáO¦/æ ÿkþfþˉþöƒß}üïÿþáËŸßÛÞößtýpJmx¯ T _¹•Î\»ÎÚ¢–³ÙL  èŽ†qÐdM
"£…#*ëòç ÿœ'y_<X•Ù?[½£ñ

This may look like nonsense, but what has happened is that perfectly valid data has been interpreted wrongly by the software. The data represented by the binary patterns was, in fact, instructions in Word for laying out the document, but the software has interpreted the patterns as characters. This happens when documents have been stored in the format used by one software package and then loaded into another package which works with a different format. Most of the time the software does interpret the bit patterns correctly.

Have you come across other examples of the wrong interpretation of data?

### How are characters represented in a computer system?

Many years ago the computing community agreed on a standard method for representing characters in binary patterns. This is known as the American Standard Code for Information Interchange (ASCII). Each character is allocated 8 bits (one byte), and these bit patterns are used whenever text is being stored or transmitted. Here is a selection of ASCII binary patterns:

| Binary pattern | Character |
|---|---|
| 01000001 | A |
| 01000010 | B |
| 01000011 | C |
| 01000100 | D |
| 01000101 | E |
| | ... |
| 01100001 | a |
| 01100010 | b |
| 01100011 | c |
| 01100100 | d |
| 01100101 | e |
| | ... |

| Binary pattern | Character |
|---|---|
| 01110010 | r |
| 01110011 | s |
| 01110100 | t |
| | ... |
| 00110000 | 0 |
| 00110001 | 1 |
| 00110010 | 2 |
| | ... |
| 00100000 | space |
| 00100001 | ! |
| 00100010 | " |
| | ... |

**Table 2.4** *Some ASCII binary patterns*

Notice that the upper case (capital) and lower case letters are treated as different characters. But can you see the relationship between the bit patterns for each?

## Check your understanding

Work out what this message means. Each byte of data represents one character in ASCII.

01000010 01100101 00100000 01100001 00100000 01110011
01110100 01100001 01110010 00100001

## Further research – calculating the size of text files

A text file consists entirely of characters, using the ASCII coding system. For example, a simple email or a text message will be sent as a text file.

If the words in this book were all stored in a text file, how many kilobytes would it take up?

To answer the question, estimate how many characters there are in the book. Don't forget to include the spaces. Since each character needs one byte to store the character code, you can see immediately how many bytes are needed.

In practice, this book contains a great many illustrations and these use up far more storage space than the text on its own. But you could do a similar exercise for a novel without any illustrations.

# Performance

Tables 2.5 and 2.6 show typical specifications for computer systems at the time of writing (early 2006). Buy a computer magazine and check these against systems currently on sale.

| Device | Capacity | Speed |
|---|---|---|
| Processor | | 3 GHz to 4 GHz |
| RAM | 512 MB to 2 GB | |
| Cache | 1 MB to 2 MB | |
| Hard disk drive | 40 GB to 500 GB | |
| Floppy disk drive | 1.44 MB | |
| CD-ROM drive | 700 MB | Data transfer speed = 32× to 48× * |
| CD-RW drive | 700 MB | Data transfer speed = 32× to 48× * |
| DVD drive | 4.7 GB to 17 GB | Data transfer speed = 16× * |
| Flash drive | 64 MB to 1 GB | |
| Tape drive | 8 GB to 40 GB | Data transfer speed = 3 to 12 MB per second, equivalent to 20× to 80× |

\* The speeds shown are for reading data; writing data is a slower process.

**Table 2.5** *Technical specifications for computers and memory*

| Screen | Size (diagonal) | Resolution |
|---|---|---|
| CRT monitor | 15" to 21" | 1024 × 768   to  2108 × 1536 |
| LCD monitor | 12" to 21" | 1024 × 768  to  1600 × 1024 |

**Table 2.6** *Technical specifications for monitors*

**Performance** *is a way of describing how well a device in a computer system does its job. This often relates to the speed at which it works.*

*The* **technical specification** *of a device in a computer system is a list of its properties. It usually refers to the capacity and performance of the device.*

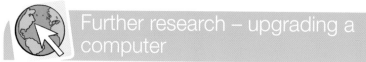

## Further research – upgrading a computer

If you want a bit of a challenge, have a look at the computer owned by a friend. Find out what they want to use the computer for, and whether the current system meets their needs. Produce a short report for them in which you recommend some upgrades that would improve the performance of the system, at the lowest cost.

## Logical representation of a PC system

A computer system can be illustrated by a simple diagram as shown in Figure 2.9.

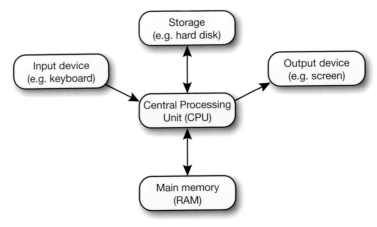

**Figure 2.9** *A PC system*

## Case study

### *Systems to suit a user's requirements*

1 Problem: George is the Secretary of a Residents' Association. He wants to buy a standalone computer so that he can write letters and agendas for meetings.

   Solution: George needs, as a minimum, an entry-level system with the simplest processor on the market, with basic RAM and hard drive capacity. He would need a CD or DVD drive in order to install the word processing software that he chooses. Once he starts using the computer he will probably become a little more ambitious and want to produce newsletters and other printed material. He might want to spend a little more on a good quality colour inkjet printer.

2 Problem: Margaret is elderly and wants to use the Internet to search the Web and send emails to her family.

   Solution: Margaret's computer system could be similar to George's with the addition of a modem or broadband connection. She would also benefit from a good quality graphics card, and a higher resolution screen. Although she may not think of using the computer for other purposes, in the future she may find that she wants to switch to the Internet while using other software. More RAM would be a good idea.

3 Problem: Asad maintains a database for a small company that tracks down and sells old comic books. The database has grown quite large as it holds details

of many comic books over a long period and where they can be found.

   Solution: Database software tends to use quite a lot of memory, so Asad needs a moderately fast processor with sufficient RAM and hard disk capacity. He will probably want to print out lists, so will need a fast printer. He may not need colour printing, so a basic laser printer will probably be suitable.

4 Problem: Elisha is a garden designer. She uses specialist software to create 3D drawings of her designs so that she can see what they look like from all angles. She also prints these off to give to her customers.

   Solution: Elisha needs a high-quality graphics card with a high-resolution screen. To support the heavy use of graphics she also requires the fastest processor she can afford, a substantial amount of RAM and extensive hard disk space. If the graphics are to be printed then she will have to find a printer that produces a suitable quality of output, probably in colour.

   Can you draw up a shopping list of hardware for each of these users? You will have to look through computer magazines and websites to find the best solutions.

## Test your knowledge

7   What are storage devices and storage media?

8   What are RAM chips used for?

9   Explain the differences between ROM, R and RW media.

10  Why are some storage disks fixed and others removable?

11  What is the difference between the size and resolution when referring to monitors?

12  List three ways of providing a broadband connection.

13  Why might you need to install a network interface card?

14  How many bit patterns can you make with 8 bits? What can these bit patterns represent?

15  List three changes that could be made to a computer system to improve its performance.

# Select software for a specified user

Software is a general term used for programs. Hardware refers to the physical components of a computer system, but on its own it can do nothing. Software is needed to control the hardware and to turn it into a useful machine.

Software falls into two categories:

- **systems software**, which controls a computer system
- **applications software**, which carries out specific tasks for an organisation or for an individual user.

Systems software must be in place on a computer system before applications software can be used.

You need to know how to select a combination of systems and applications software to meets the particular needs of an individual user. So before you begin you should ask these questions about your user:

- What tasks will the user be doing on the computer system?
- Are these tasks being carried out at home or at work?
- What level of ICT skills does the user already have?
- Which software is the user already familiar with?
- Does the user have any particular needs or requirements, e.g. disabilities?
- What is the maximum cost?

These should allow you to identify the **minimum** specification for a computer system.

In practice it is always a good idea to go beyond the minimum specification. This is because:

- New software and hardware come on to the market all the time, and users do not want to find that they cannot use them.
- Once users have started using a system, they normally discover its capabilities and want to do new tasks with it.

## Systems software

Systems software includes the operating system, together with add-on programs known as system tools. An end user is not usually aware of the systems software. In comparison, the technical users in an organisation, such as systems administrators, spend most of their time working directly with the systems software.

The processor controls the use that the computer system makes of resources, such as memory, input devices, output devices and storage devices. These can be controlled only through the instructions in the systems software.

Systems software often works in the background while a user is doing something useful with applications software. For example, when you are word processing a document and you send it to the printer, you are not aware of all the processes that the systems software has to go through to make it happen. The applications software works directly with the systems software, so that the user does not have to worry about it.

## Operating systems

The core of the systems software is the operating system. You will probably be familiar with a version of Microsoft Windows, which is an operating system that is widely used on desktop computers.

Windows was originally the name of the graphical user interface that Microsoft built on top of its original operating system MS-DOS. But today it is difficult to separate the core operating system components from the user interface that communicates with it; and current versions of Windows do not need MS-DOS at all.

But there are several other operating systems that you may also have heard of, such as the Apple Mac OS. More complex operating systems are used for network systems, such as Windows Server, OS/2, Unix and Linux.

The operating system is never a single program but a collection of programs, each of which carries out a specific task. Extra programs can often be added to the main operating system. For example, when a new printer is added to a system, the relevant printer driver has to be installed to enable the operating system to communicate with the device.

The operating system carries out these tasks as needed:

- allows the user to select and launch programs, as well as launching some programs automatically
- allocates space in memory to programs
- loads programs, by transferring them from storage into main memory
- runs programs, by transferring instructions one at a time from memory to the processor, then executing them
- manages the backing store, by creating, opening, moving, deleting and renaming files
- manages input and output devices, by controlling the data that flows between them and the processor
- allows the user to configure the system, i.e. make changes to the way in which the operating system works.

The operating system is designed to make the computer system as efficient as possible.

The user is able to make certain changes to the way the operating system functions – these may or may not improve the performance of the system.

## Further research – check out your operating system

If you are running Windows on your own desktop computer at home you can look at the *Windows* directory on the C: drive. In it you will find a very large number of programs, which together control the computer system.

If you want to make any changes to the system you should go to the *Control Panel* (see Figure 2.10) by selecting *Settings* from the *Start Menu*. You will not be able to change the core functions of the operating system. But you could, if you like, modify aspects of the display, add or remove fonts, install new software, install new hardware drivers, change how the mouse responds, defragment a drive etc.

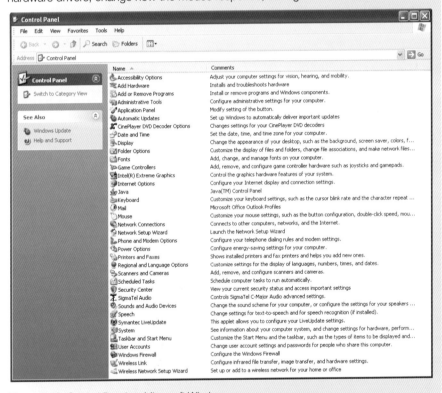

**Figure 2.10** *Control Panel on Microsoft Windows*

## Systems software tools

A number of programs support the operating system and are known as system tools, or utilities. Some of these can be found in Windows by going to the *Start* menu, selecting *All Programs*, then *Accessories*, then *System Tools*.

## Diagnostic tools

One very useful system tool for technical users is *System Information*, which can give you detailed data about almost any aspect of your computer system. Figure 2.11 shows the data about *Running Tasks*, i.e. the programs that are currently running.

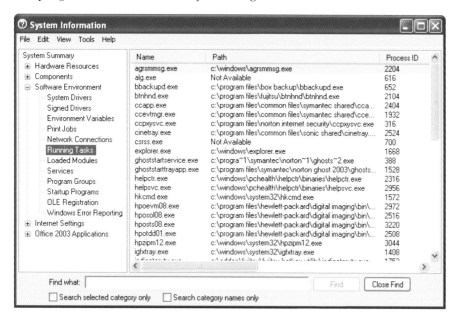

**Figure 2.11** *The System Information tool*

## File managers

The operating system allows you to organise files into folders (or directories). End users as well as technical users can easily delete files and folders, or move them to new locations. Windows XP offers you a number of file management tools to support this. When you open *My Documents* do you see something like Figures 2.12 or 2.13 – or neither?

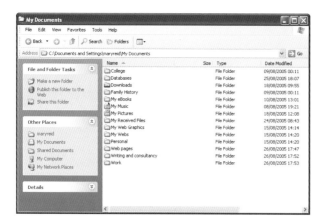

**Figure 2.12** *Details view*

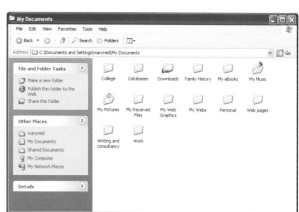

**Figure 2.13** *Icons view*

To switch between different views of the folder, click on the *Views* icon in the toolbar. For serious use of the file manager you would be advised to use the *Details View*.

In all views, the window is divided into two panes. The right pane displays the files and folders. The left pane is called the *Explorer Bar* and displays tasks that can be carried out on them.

You can change the contents of the *Explorer Bar* in a number of ways from the *View* menu.

## Further research – using Windows Explorer

Windows Explorer is a particular view of folders and files which is the most useful for technical use.

First select the *Details* view. Then click on the *Folders* icon in the main toolbar. See Figure 2.14. You can now easily move files from one folder to another by dragging the file from the right pane to the folder on the left. You can also go straight to Windows Explorer from the *Start* menu by selecting *Accessories* in *All Programs*.

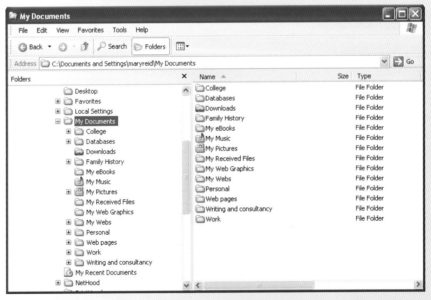

**Figure 2.14** *Windows Explorer*

## Disk utilities

You may notice that your operating system has become quite slow, especially when it is saving or loading files. One option is to defragment the disk using a system tool called the *Disk Defragmenter* (Figure 2.15). This rearranges all the files so that they make the best use of the space. It only really improves performance if the disk is more than 75% full.

You can find the defragmenter in the *System Tools*. Click on *Analyze* first to see whether your disks do need to be defragmented. If you then go ahead, be warned that it can take a long time to defragment a disk.

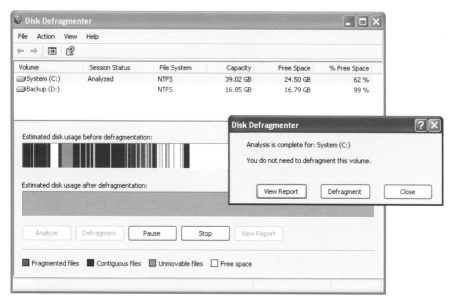

**Figure 2.15** *The Disk Defragmenter*

# Applications software

A computer system can do nothing at all without systems software. But for a computer system to be useful it must also have applications software. Examples of applications software include a hospital patient records system, a desktop publishing package, an arcade game or an Internet browser.

Software may be bought ready-made, or may be designed specifically for one organisation. Applications software is used by an end user, who may be very experienced at using it, but will probably not have any specific technical knowledge about the operating system.

Applications software can be used for many purposes. Here are a few general categories that might be used in an organisation:

- Carry out business transactions, such as dealing with customer orders for a mail order company, sending out mobile phone bills, booking facilities in a health club or managing bank accounts.

- Create business documents, such as letters and reports.
- Handle communications, such as access to the Internet and internal email.
- Manage finances.
- Present information to an audience, whether in printed or electronic form.

What does it mean?

*A **transaction** is a single action such as placing an order, making a phone call, making a booking or withdrawing cash.*

- Create and manipulate images.
- Manage projects.
- Design products.

Applications software is also used outside the business environment for many purposes, such as for playing games, recording music, genealogy, and a host of other leisure pursuits.

Sometimes an organisation will have applications software developed specifically to meet their own needs. This is known as **bespoke software**. For example, the system for air traffic controllers is a special, one-off bespoke system.

In many cases an organisation will find that standard office applications software meets their needs perfectly well. For example, virtually everyone uses one of the standard word processing packages, and it would be very surprising if an organisation developed its own word processing software.

## Office applications software

Office applications software is software that can be used for many different tasks, in business and at home. Anyone can buy this software, so it is designed to meet the needs of a wide range of users.

Office applications software is ready-made, and can be installed and used immediately. It is normally sold as a complete package and can be bought through a high street store, from an Internet retailer or through a mail order software supplier. It is often supplied on an optical medium, such as a CD or DVD, or it can be downloaded from the Internet.

An application or software **package** is, as the name implies, an extensive collection of programs which form one application. This description applies to most applications software these days.

A software package will be marketed like any other product under its own trade name. You will be familiar with a number of software packages such as Microsoft Word, Adobe Photoshop and Macromedia Dreamweaver.

The term package implies that the end user will be able to choose which components of the package to install. Users would also expect to receive full documentation, so that they could use the package straightaway. The documentation may be in the form of a printed manual, but is more likely to be provided in electronic form.

Office software packages are available for word processing, spreadsheets, database management, graphics (drawing and painting) and presentation graphics.

**Further research – office applications packages**

Make a list of all the office applications packages that you have access to at your centre. Are there others that you would like to use?

## Word processing

Word processing software is the most commonly used type of package in business. Before word processing facilities became widely available, documents were first handwritten and then typed up on a typewriter. It was very difficult to correct errors once they had been typed, so sometimes a document had to be typed several times before it was correct. Sometimes a document would be dictated by a manager to a secretary, who would jot it down in shorthand before returning to a typewriter to type it up. Typing and shorthand-writing were skilled tasks and specialist staff were employed to do them.

Today, many employees use word processors to prepare their own documents. They can create standard documents, such as letters, which they can use more than once with only minor changes.

Word processors have reduced the time taken to produce standard documents and have reduced staff costs. Many employees find that they enjoy outlining and then developing a document directly on the computer.

Word processing packages, such as Word Perfect, Lotus Word-Pro or Microsoft Word, can be used to produce letters, reports, memos, articles, orders and invoices, notices, leaflets, newsletters and books.

Word processing packages also offer additional features, which can be used to create email messages, web pages, mailing labels or mail merge letters.

## Spreadsheets

Spreadsheet applications were the first business software packages to appear, after word processors, for desktop computers. A worksheet is laid out as a very large table consisting of many cells. Each cell can hold a value or a formula. A formula can carry out calculations based on values held in other cells. Each cell can also be formatted to hold data of a specific type, such as a number, date or simple text.

Spreadsheets also include graphing and charting functions, which will generate all kinds of charts using data held in the cells.

A spreadsheet can be interactive, allowing the user to enter 'what if' queries.

Many users have discovered that spreadsheets can also be used to print forms and other documents that need cells or tables.

A spreadsheet package, such as Lotus 1-2-3 or Microsoft Excel, can be used in business for accounts, budgets, scientific calculations, statistical analysis, simple databases, interactive 'what if' calculations and form designs.

### Database management systems
Database management systems structure and organise the data used in a database. You can read more about databases in Unit 9.

A database management system, such as Lotus Approach or Microsoft Access, can be used in business to store data about stock in a shop or factory, orders from customers, orders sent to suppliers, case notes (for doctors, social workers etc.), personnel (employees), mailing lists or log sheets.

### Graphics software
The term 'graphics' covers all kinds of images stored in digital form. They include photos that have been scanned in or downloaded from a digital camera, or images 'painted' or 'drawn' using graphical software. Clip art is used to describe pre-drawn images that you can use freely in your documents. There is more information about the difference between bitmap and vector images in Unit 1.

You can choose from a wide range of graphics software, including photo editors and general image design packages. Windows XP includes a number of useful wizards that can be used to view, change and print images. For many purposes the simple bitmap Paint program, which can be found in the *Accessories* folder in *All Programs*, is very useful.

Graphics software can be used in business to create or edit images for use in standard stationery (as logos), publicity materials (leaflets, brochures, posters) or web pages.

### Presentation packages
Presentation packages, sometimes known as presentation graphics, are used to provide the illustrations for talks and lectures. They offer many useful templates, which can be customised by the addition of your own text and images.

Presentation packages, such as Microsoft PowerPoint and Lotus Freelance, can be used to create a slideshow that can be projected directly from the computer on to a screen, and to print notes for the speaker and the audience.

### Desktop publishing packages
Desktop publishing software was originally designed for newspapers and magazines. Before the software was available, editors would assemble stories provided by journalists, and literally cut and paste the stories on to a board. They would then add photographs, illustrations, headings and lines.

Desktop publishing offers the same facilities, but in electronic format. Individual contributors can send their word processed stories to the editor's system, who can then import them into the page layout. Stories, headings and images can be easily edited and moved around to fit the space.

Once a page is ready, it can either be printed directly or sent, still in electronic form, to produce a plate for large-scale printing.

Desktop publishing software packages can usually combine material created in a number of other formats and using many different packages.

On a smaller scale, a desktop publishing package makes it easy to arrange text and images on a page for a notice, for a leaflet, or for some other kind of publicity.

Desktop publishing software, such as Adobe Pagemaker or Microsoft Publisher, can be used in business to create newsletters, notices, leaflets, publicity materials or invitations.

## Games software

Games are widely enjoyed in the home. They can also be very useful in an educational context, where children can learn and explore ideas through the medium of games. The competitive nature of games can make them addictive, and the high quality of the graphics and animation add to the enjoyment.

### Further research – animation

Look closely at the animated objects, such as people and cars, in computer games. They will have been drawn using a specialised vector drawing package, rather like a CAD package. Each object will be composed of many smaller objects, each of which will have a lot of data associated with it. These objects will have been drawn as **wireframes**, with surface textures added.

You will have seen the same techniques at work in film animation. Again, very specialised software is used for animation, but it is widely used for live action films as well as cartoons.

Share your observations with fellow students.

### What does it mean?

A **wideframe** is a basic visual guide used to establish the layout and placement of fundamental design elements.

## Communications

People working in industry and commerce need to communicate with each other. They communicate with other people in the same organisation, people in other organisations and the general public.

The main means of communication are face to face conversation, printed documents, telephone and electronic media. ICT can be used to support most means of communication, but is particularly important for the last type.

Electronic communications include internal email through the organisation's local area networks, external email via the Internet, intranet (web-style pages that can only be viewed within the organisation) and web pages on the Internet.

The main software applications for these uses are browsers and email clients.

### Browsers
A browser is a piece of software which is used to view pages on the Web. The most commonly used browsers at present are Internet Explorer and Mozilla Firefox. When a user visits a web page, the HTML code is downloaded to their computer and the browser interprets the code to create the web page itself. A browser also supports hyperlinks, so that when a user clicks on a link the browser will find the correct page and download it.

### Email clients
You have to use a specialist software package, known as an email client, to send or receive an email. The most commonly used email clients are Outlook and Outlook Express, but there are many others. Some Internet Service Providers, such as AOL, supply their own email client software.

## Other specialist software
A software application can be designed for a wide range of uses, or it can be designed for specialist use.

Word processing packages are used by all kinds of people for all sorts of reasons. In comparison, a specialist software application concentrates on one particular task and offers extra facilities that cannot be found in more general packages.

You will not see specialist packages advertised widely. Instead, they will be marketed directly to the businesses that are likely to want to use them. But if you search on the Internet you should be able to find examples of packages for these types of application: computer-aided design (CAD), programming languages, web development tools, route planning, voice recognition, voice synthesis and project planning.

### Computer-aided design (CAD)
General vector-drawing packages can be used for many tasks, but they do not usually have all the facilities that an engineer or product designer might need. CAD software includes thousands of pre-drawn standard objects.

CAD packages usually allow the user to zoom in and out, and to pan round an object. Or the object itself can be rotated. Objects can be shown as plans (seen from above), as elevations (seen from the sides) or as 3D images. Sometimes an object is developed as a wireframe and then a surface is added to make it appear realistic.

Each element of a vector drawing is a separate object, and many CAD packages exploit this by allowing the user to add extra data about each object. So, for example, information about the cost of the materials used for each component can be entered and then the package can automatically calculate the total cost of the whole product.

CAD packages, such as AutoCAD by Autodesk, are used to design products to be manufactured (such as furniture and cars), large structures (such as bridges and motorways), integrated circuits (the electronic circuits built on to silicon chips) and maps.

## Case study

### *English Heritage*

English Heritage looks after the world's first cast iron bridge, which was built in 1779 in Coalbrookdale. In order to keep it in good repair they needed to understand how it was constructed. The only information they had about how it was built was a painting of it under construction. So English Heritage used AutoCAD to create engineering drawings of the bridge. See Figure 2.16.

Use the Internet to find other examples of drawings created in AutoCad or other CAD packages. If you know someone who uses a CAD package at work then you could ask if you could view some finished drawings.

**Figure 2.16** *Part of the structure of the bridge drawn in AutoCAD*

*(Source:* www.autodesk.co.uk)

## Programming languages

Programs are written in a programming language. You may have heard of a number of these including Visual Basic, C++ and Java.

Here are some program instructions written in the programming language Visual Basic. You do not have to understand them, but just notice that they are made up of words and abbreviations that look a bit like ordinary English.

```
Function IsLoaded(ByVal strFormName As String) As Integer
   Const conObjStateClosed = 0
   Const conDesignView = 0
   If SysCmd(acSysCmdGetObjectState, acForm, strFormName) <>
       conObjStateClosed Then
     If Forms(strFormName).CurrentView <> conDesignView Then
       IsLoaded = True
     End If
   End If
End Function
```

In **machine code**, *binary patterns represent each of the instructions in a program. When a computer runs a program, it is carrying out the machine code instructions.*

Programs in Visual Basic (or any other programming language) have to be converted into the code that the CPU uses, known as machine code. This conversion is done by a piece of software known as a compiler.

Machine code instructions are the actual instructions that control the computer. Machine code instructions are, like all other data, stored in binary patterns.

Programmers often use a programming environment designed for the language they have chosen. A programming environment is complex software that has two main components – an editor and a compiler. The editor is a bit like a word processor, in which the programmer can write a program in the programming language. The compiler then converts the program into machine code instructions.

If you take the Software Design and Development unit (Unit 7) then you will learn how to design software applications and write programs.

### Web development tools

Website developers use specialist software to create their sites. Web pages are stored in a simple computer language called Hypertext Markup Language (HTML). Professional developers will be skilled at creating the code in an HTML editor, or even in a simple text editor like NotePad.

There are also a number of web authoring packages, such as Macromedia Dreamweaver and Microsoft FrontPage. These are more like programming environments designed specifically for developing web pages. They include an HTML editor, but the users are more likely to prepare web pages using a page layout mode, which is rather like working with desktop publishing software.

### Route planning

Route planning software works out a route to take you from one place to another. The most common use of this is for car drivers. They can ask for the route to be the shortest or quickest (taking into account areas that get congested) or they can opt for a scenic route. The selected route is then presented as a map or detailed directions.

Software that is sold for use in a vehicle uses satellite navigation systems so that the exact current position of the vehicle can be plotted. The directions can be given by voice output so that the driver does not have to watch the map closely.

### Voice recognition

Voice controlled user interfaces are highly complex. They have to carry out two separate tasks before they can carry out spoken instructions:

- **voice recognition** – recognise the words that are being spoken and convert them into text
- **natural language processing** – analyse the text and convert the words into the commands of the system.

Voice recognition is itself a complicated process. The sounds of a human voice are picked up by a microphone. The patterns of sound are then matched against standard patterns that are stored in the computer. People speak with different accents; some have high voices and some low. Because of the huge variation in speech, a voice recognition system is often set up for one specific speaker.

Voice recognition is a very useful method for communicating with a computer for someone who is unable to use a keyboard through disability.

## Further research – voice recognition

You can sometimes see examples of voice recognition on television. To do this you have to set up subtitles. If you have a digital receiver (e.g. Freeview, satellite or cable) then use the interactive options to switch on subtitles. If you use only analogue reception then find page 888 on teletext. Some subtitles are prepared in advance of the broadcast, so in order to see voice recognition at work you need to check this during a live broadcast, such as a sports event. Sometimes the software makes mistakes, so make a note of them.

### Voice synthesis

You will have heard announcements at railway stations or on trains. In some cases the sentences are put together from individual words or phrases that have been recorded by a human. In other cases, true voice synthesis is used, where the sound is generated from within the software itself.

A voice synthesis system starts with text and converts it into sounds. Once again, this is a complex process, especially if the sound is to appear lifelike. Each of us can say the same word in a number of different ways, depending on the context. For example, the last word of a sentence is usually spoken at a lower pitch than the rest of the sentence, unless it is a question. The system has to analyse the text and decide how the word should sound.

Voice synthesis is sometimes used by people who are unable to speak. If they are able to use a pointing device to choose letters and words on a screen, the system can then convert it into speech.

### Project planning

In business, a project is a task that may take days or months to complete. For example, a building project would start with the specification and design of a new building and carry on until the building is complete. Such projects are very complex and involve a lot of people and materials, all of which have to be scheduled so that the project runs smoothly.

Software projects are very similar, especially the large ones where many people work together to create a new software application.

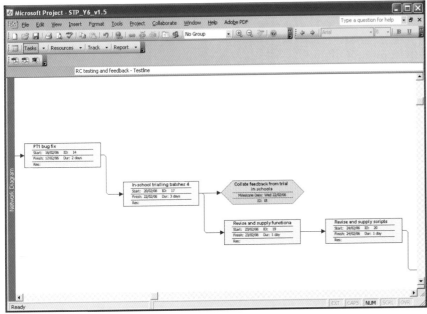

**Figure 2.17** *Planning a project with* *Microsoft Project*

Project planning software helps the project manager to plan the whole project from beginning to end. The manager will want to make best use of the employees so that they are kept busy all the time and are not idly waiting for another part of the project to be completed. The manager also needs to ensure that any materials needed are ready in time. The software usually allows the user to draw diagrams, which show how the project should progress. See Figure 2.17.

Project planning packages, such Microsoft Project, let the user list and schedule all the tasks, make changes to the schedule if necessary, produce reports and keep account of how long individual employees have worked on the project.

## Bespoke software

Bespoke software is custom-made to meet the needs of a single organisation, or very occasionally for a single user. It is one-off, so no-one else will have the same software.

A large business, such as a bank, may employ its own software developers, who will devote thousands of person-hours to produce a substantial piece of bespoke software, such as a system for handling all the transactions at its Automatic Teller Machines (ATMs, or cash machines).

A smaller organisation may use an outside consultant to develop bespoke software for them, if they cannot find anything ready-made that is suitable.

There are quite a few advantages in using bespoke applications software:

- Bespoke software should meet the precise needs of the organisation. This is important if the needs are unique.
- Bespoke software will carry out exactly the tasks that the organisation wants. It will cover everything that they ask for, but will not include unnecessary functions.
- The user interface for bespoke software will be designed in collaboration with the organisation, to meet their preferences.
- The developer of bespoke software will normally be available to provide support when it is new, and also as problems arise later.

There are also some disadvantages in using bespoke applications software:

- Bespoke applications software is bound to be expensive, as one organisation has to pay all the costs.
- Bespoke software will not have been tested thoroughly by other users in other organisations.
- The organisation will have to wait for the software to be developed.
- The organisation may find that the final software is not up to expectations.

## Further research – bespoke applications packages

Find out whether your centre uses any bespoke packages. If there are any, they will probably be used by office staff rather than by students.

## Compatibility

Systems are compatible if they can work together. There are two questions that you need to ask about any software that you may be selecting for a user:

- Is the software compatible with the user's hardware?
- Is the software compatible with other software on the system?

The term PC was introduced by IBM when they created their first desktop personal computer. The only real competition at the time was the range of computers manufactured by Apple. Since then, the majority of desktop and laptop computer systems have been made to be compatible with the PC standards, and have used Intel or equivalent processors. But over the years the Apple Mac series has remained as a distinctive alternative.

Whichever system you have in place, you also have a choice of operating system. In fact, you can run several different operating systems on a given processor. But in general, you can run Apple operating systems only on an Apple processor.

Having selected an operating system that is compatible with the processor, you can then select applications software that will run on it. Operating systems have gone through many versions over the years, and you do need to know what version you are using, as applications packages are designed for particular versions of operating systems. Information about compatibility will be supplied in the technical documentation, but it should also be stated in any marketing material.

Finally, if a user wants to be able to send data from one software package to another, you should check that the two are compatible with each other. Some software packages are part of a family of applications produced by the same software manufacturer. Examples of these would be the Microsoft Office suite, or the packages produced by Adobe or Corel.

## Test your knowledge

16 What does the term 'systems software' cover?

17 What are the main functions of an operating system?

18 What are the advantages to the user of having folders?

19 List the main types of applications that might be used in an office.

20 Give three uses for a spreadsheet package.

21 What is an email client?

22 Why do web developers need specialist software?

23 Name two things that can be designed with CAD software.

24 What are 'voice recognition' and 'voice synthesis'? Give one example of each in use.

25 Why is compatibility important?

# Connect and use hardware devices and configure software for a specified user

## Health and safety

If you are going to set up a computer system for a user, you do need to be able to do this safely. There are many laws and regulations that apply to people who are employed. Many of these are designed to reduce the risk of injury. Although they do not apply to students, nevertheless you should always adopt good health and safety practices when carrying out practical activities as part of your studies.

In this section we will be looking at the risks and the regulations that especially apply to computer users.

### Electrical hazards

Computer equipment is electrically powered, so all computer users are at some risk:

- Electric shock can stop the heart beating properly or prevent a person from breathing. A shock can also cause burns inside the body, or can make the muscles go into spasm.
- Thermal burns can occur if faulty electrical equipment overheats.
- Electrical faults may cause fires.

### Manual handling

If you are involved in setting up computer systems then you may have to lift heavy boxes and equipment. You may be at risk of injury:

- You may damage your back through incorrectly lifting objects.
- You may injure other parts of your body through dropping objects.

### Impact on users

Using computers for a long time can cause a number of problems:

- Repetitive strain injury (RSI) gives pain in the shoulder, neck, arm, wrist or hand. It can result from repeatedly doing small actions, such as keying in at a keyboard or manipulating a mouse.
- Eyestrain can be caused by spending long periods looking at a computer screen, and can give the user headaches and sore eyes. It does not actually damage the eyes but it can make it difficult to concentrate on the work.
- General aches and pains can be the result of uncomfortable seating and badly positioned equipment.

# Working practices

## Working procedures

If users cannot reach the computer equipment easily, or are uncomfortable, then they will not be as productive as they could be:

- **Work surfaces** should be large enough for the tasks to be done, should be clear of obstructions and should have a matt surface. Ideally, it should be possible to raise or lower the work surface to suit the user. There should be sufficient space for a mouse mat.
- **Chairs** should be fully adjustable. The best office chairs can be raised and lowered, the tilt of the seat can be altered and the angle that the back makes with the seat can be changed.
- **Screens** should have brightness controls and be capable of tilt and swivel. They should be positioned at 90 degrees to a window to avoid glare and reflections. A document holder can be attached to a screen to hold documents at eye level.
- **Keyboards** should be movable, and the angle of the slope should be adjustable. A wrist support should be built into the keyboard or provided separately. The pressure required to depress the keys should be checked – if too much pressure is required then the user's hands will ache, but if too little then the fingers will tend to slip off the keys.
- **Storage** for books, files, manuals, disks, stationery, pens and office equipment should be designed so that items are easy to reach but do not interfere with work.
- **Cabling** should be ducted or fixed in place so that it cannot cause an accident.

## Assess and minimise risks

All organisations should identify someone with responsibility for health and safety. It is the duty of all employers to assess the risks to their employees, and to minimise those risks.

A risk assessment includes these steps:

- Identify the hazards.
- Decide who might be harmed and how.
- Evaluate the risks arising from the hazards, and decide whether the existing precautions are sufficient or whether more needs to be done.
- Record the findings.
- Review your assessment from time to time.

After the risks have been assessed then the employer should take steps to minimise risks, i.e. make the chance of an accident occurring as low as possible. It is usually impossible to remove risks entirely.

Risk assessments should cover all kinds of hazards, but, where employees are using computers, the **Health and Safety (Display Screen**

**Equipment) Regulations** apply. Under the regulations employers have to do the following:

- **Analyse workstations, and assess and reduce risks.** This means that they must look at the complete workstation, including all the furniture. They have to take into account any special needs of individual staff.
- **Ensure workstations meet minimum standards.** The regulations list the standards that have to be met by keyboards, desks, chairs and lighting, as well as the screens themselves.
- **Plan work so there are breaks or changes in activities.** It is up to the employer to negotiate these breaks with employees, but short, frequent breaks are better than longer, less frequent ones.
- **On request, arrange eye tests, and provide spectacles if special ones are needed.**
- **Provide health and safety training and information.**

## Obtaining resources

In the UK, the Health and Safety Executive deals with all the regulations that apply in the workplace and in public places. Their website provides a large amount of information and advice for employers and for employees. Go to www.heinemann.co.uk/hotlinks, insert the express code 2048P and click on this unit.

## Communicating progress and outcomes

All employers must provide employees with instruction, training and information that they need to keep them safe, and they should also provide supervision where necessary.

Any organisation that has five or more employees must do the following:

- Record publicly the findings of the risk assessment.
- Draw up a Health and Safety Policy.

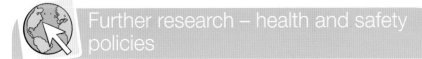

Further research – health and safety policies

Find out if there are any health and safety policies at your place of study that apply to you as a student. If you have a job, find out who the Health and Safety Officer is.

# Hardware connections

## Connection of peripheral devices to a PC

The various devices that make up a computer system have to be connected to each other. Computers themselves are then connected into networks.

These connections use various types of data transfer. Whatever the method, each consists of:

■ A **method** of transferring the binary data. This could be through a cable made of copper or optical fibres. Alternatively the method could use radio, infrared or microwave signals.

■ An **interface**. This consists of a **port**, which is a socket where cables can be plugged in or signals picked up, plus built-in software that controls it.

There are a number of types of connection, including these:

■ **Serial connections** use cables that transfer binary patterns in a steady stream from one component to another.

■ **Parallel connections** transfer many bits at the same time along a set of parallel wires. If one byte (8 bits) is transferred along a parallel cable, each bit will travel along a different wire, so will be about eight times faster than using a serial cable. Parallel connections are only used over short distances.

Some parallel cables are easily recognised by their flat ridged structure. Not all parallel cables look like this, and most bundle the wires together inside an outer casing so that they look much the same as serial cables.

In the past, each device in a computer system had its own direct connection to the CPU.

■ Many devices, such as the keyboard and monitor, use serial connections. The standard serial interface to connect the CPU to its peripherals is RS232.

■ A parallel connection was often used to connect a printer to the CPU.

Today it is more common for several devices to be linked together in a 'daisy chain', sharing a single port. Examples include:

■ **USB** (Universal Serial Bus) is a widely used interface that can be used with most peripherals, especially the slower ones. You will find two or more USB ports on the base units of most computers. Up to 127 devices can be linked to each port. USB cables also carry a power supply, which means that small peripherals, such as speakers, do not need a separate power cable.

■ **Firewire** (also known as IEEE 1394) was originally developed for Apple computers but can now be used on others as well.

Inside the base unit other types of connections are used, such as EIDE (Enhanced Integrated Drive Electronics), which is often used to connect the hard disk drives to the processor.

There is a growing use of wireless connections to connect devices, such as a mouse and keyboard, to a PC. These use radio instead of cables to carry the data communications.

A list of devices with common connections is shown in Table 2.7.

| Device | Type of connection |
|---|---|
| Printer | USB or Firewire mostly, but parallel connections still available |
| Speakers | Standard audio ports |
| Digital camera | USB or Firewire for direct connection; alternatively portable USB memory devices are used |
| Scanner | USB or Firewire |
| Web cam | USB or Firewire |
| Bar code reader | USB, Firewire or serial RS232 |
| Graphics tablet | USB, Firewire or serial RS232 |

**Table 2.7** *Typical computer connections*

## Testing functionality

When a device has been connected to the PC, you normally have to run some software to initiate it. For example, this will install a printer driver on the system and check that the communications are working satisfactorily.

At this stage the peripheral should be thoroughly tested to make sure that it is functioning correctly.

# Configuration of software

Software can often be configured to suit an individual user. Configuration changes can be made both to the appearance of the user interface and to the way in which it operates. Configuration allows users to personalise the software so that it matches their own way of working. The configuration choices the user makes are often known as preferences.

Both systems software and applications software can be configured. In Windows, the information about the user's preferences is stored in the registry.

## Personalising applications software

Many business applications software packages are built to the Windows standard. They include Microsoft software as well as software produced by other companies. That means that many of the configuration options that you select in Windows will also affect these applications. For example, the choice of colours that you make in *Display* will also be active in these applications.

Some applications (such as most games, as well as some specialist software) are not built to the Windows standards. These may or may not allow you to change how they appear.

All the examples in this book will relate to widely used Microsoft software, but you might like to check how much applies to other applications.

## Toolbars

A toolbar contains a set of icons which represent options that the user can choose from. One or more toolbars often appear at the top of the window. Toolbars that 'float' anywhere on the screen are known as toolboxes. See Figure 2.18.

**Figure 2.18** *Typical toolbars in Microsoft Word*

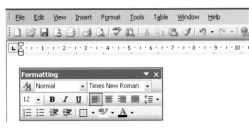

**Figure 2.19** *The formatting toolbar is now a floating toolbox*

Here are some changes that you can make to toolbars or toolboxes:

■ You can move a toolbar, or detach it from the top of the window and change it into a toolbox. Click on the small bar at the left edge of the toolbar and drag it to wherever you want it to go. See Figure 2.19. Move it back to the top of the window to turn it back to a toolbar.

■ You can add extra toolbars from the selection that are offered. Right-click anywhere on one of the toolbars to select the toolbars you are likely to need. Do not overload the screen or there will be little space left for the document (Figure 2.20). Just choose the toolbars that will help you with your work.

**Figure 2.20** *Displaying many toolbars in Microsoft Word clutters the screen*

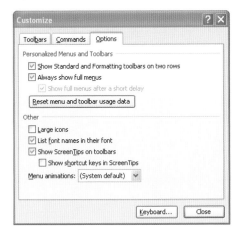

■ You can change the appearance of the icons on the toolbars. At the right-hand end of each toolbar you can find a small down arrow. Click on this and select *Add or Remove buttons*. You can now remove buttons from the toolbar or add some extra ones. If you select *Customize* you will be presented with more advanced options. See Figure 2.21.

**Figure 2.21** *Customising the appearance of toolbars*

Other configuration options

## Further research – customising toolbars

Use a standard software package and try out some of the methods for customising the toolbars that have been suggested in this section.

Most software packages offer you a number of other configuration options, usually by selecting *Preferences* or *Options*.

For example, the *Internet Options* in Internet Explorer (found in the *Tools* menu) lets you select your home page. See Figure 2.22. This is the page that is opened when the browser is launched. Most users do not realise that they can change this. The home page can be any page on the Internet, or a web page that you have created and stored on the hard disk.

Figure 2.23 shows the *Options* dialogue (from the *Tools* menu) from Microsoft Excel. The *General* tab allows you to identify the default file location. This is the folder where it will initially look for files and save files. You can change this to another folder. You can also specify the standard font to be used on spreadsheets, and how many sheets will be provided in a new workbook.

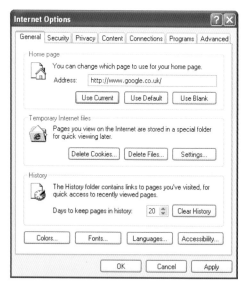

**Figure 2.22** *The Options box in Internet Explorer*

## Personalising the operating system GUI

Users can make many changes to the configuration of their own standalone computer system. But when a desktop computer is linked into a network, the network administrator may limit the changes that can be made. In this section we will assume that you have full access to all the configuration options on a computer.

All the examples refer to Windows, but you should find similar options available to you if you use another operating system. Different versions of Windows vary in the way they present options to users, so the illustrations may not exactly match what you can see on your computer system.

**Figure 2.23** *Options in Microsoft Excel*

The safest way to configure the operating system is to use the *Control Panel*, which can be found in the *Start* menu. The *Control Panel* contains a number of programs that allow you to configure different aspects of the system. You are warned not to make any changes unless you are sure you want to do them.

## How to –

## *Use the* **Control Panel** *in Windows*

Try these out in the *Control Panel* in Windows:

Select *Display* (see Figure 2.24). This allows you to do the following:

- Select a background for the desktop – known as a wallpaper – or create a pattern of your own.

- Select and configure a screen saver from the ones available.

- Choose colours, fonts and icons to be used in each window.

- Place a web page on the desktop instead of wallpaper (only advisable if you have broadband access to the Internet).

- Select the screen resolution – this is the number of pixels (dots of colour) that make up each screen. Larger screens can comfortably display more than smaller ones. But users may also prefer to have more or less information displayed at one time, or may find the text in one setting easier to read. Most people use the settings 1024 by 768, or 1280 by 1024. Smaller screens may be set at 800 by 600.

Select *Date/Time* from the *Control Panel* (see Figure 2.25) to do the following:

- Adjust the date and time that is displayed on screen.

- Change the time directly to another time zone.

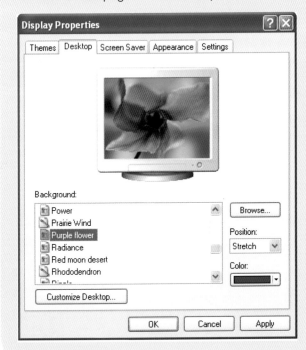

**Figure 2.24** *Display properties in Windows*

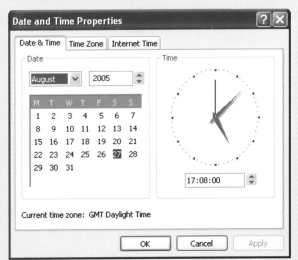

**Figure 2.25** *Setting the date, time and time zone in Windows*

You can make a limited number of configuration changes directly from the desktop. Here are some ideas:

- You can move the icons around on the desktop.
- You can go directly from the desktop to many of the *Control Panel* options. For example, if you double-click on the time (in the bottom right corner) the *Date/Time* properties box will open.

- You can drag the Taskbar (at the bottom of the screen) and any of the toolbars to the top or sides of the desktop. (If it will not move, then right-click on the Taskbar and make sure it is not locked.)

## Shortcuts

A shortcut is an icon that allows you to go directly to a file without having to search through all the folders in *My Computer* to find it. You can create a shortcut to a program, to a document or to a folder. If you click on a shortcut, it will carry out the most appropriate action – a program shortcut will launch the software, a document shortcut will open the document, and a folder shortcut will display the contents of the folder.

You will find a number of shortcuts on the desktop. A large icon for a shortcut, like the one in Figure 2.26, displays a small bent arrow to indicate that it is a shortcut.

When you select *All Programs* in the *Start* menu, what you actually see are shortcuts to the programs, like the *Calculator* icon, for example. You can:

**Figure 2.26** *A shortcut icon*

- **Delete a shortcut.** Right-click on it and select *Delete*. This will not delete the actual software or document, but only remove the shortcut.

- **Create a new shortcut** to an important document. Open the *My Documents* folder and locate the document. Right-click on the document icon and select *Create Shortcut*. The shortcut icon will appear in the folder. You can now drag this to wherever you would like it to be, including the desktop.

- **Copy a shortcut.** Right-click on it and select *Copy*. Go to wherever you want to place the shortcut, right-click and select *Paste*. For example, if you want to have a program shortcut on the desktop, go to the *Start* menu and find the program. Right-click and select *Copy*. You can then right-click on the desktop and paste the shortcut in place.

Using either dragging, or copying and pasting, you can place a shortcut:

- in any folder
- on the desktop (e.g. you can copy a program shortcut from the *All Programs* menu to the desktop).

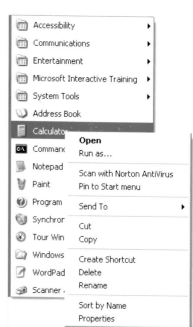

**Figure 2.27** *Right-click on a program in the All Programs menu, then select Copy*

Finally, you can easily add a shortcut in the *Start* menu to any program that you use frequently. Find the program in the *All Programs* menu, right-click on it and select *Pin to Start menu*.

## Taskbar

The Taskbar is the area at the bottom of the screen. It displays a shortcut to each of the documents or software that you have opened – these are the tasks - so you can switch between them. You can make a number of changes to the Taskbar.

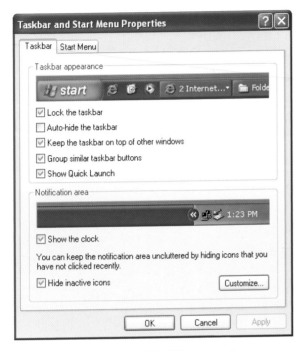

Figure 2.28 *The Taskbar and Start Menu properties*

- In the *Control Panel*, select *Taskbar and Start Menu* (Figure 2.28). You can instead right-click on the Taskbar and select *Properties*.

- You can add extra features to the Taskbar. Right-click on a blank area of the Taskbar, and then select *Toolbars*. Select *Quick Launch* (if it is not already ticked). This useful toolbar holds shortcuts to programs that are frequently used. You can delete some of the shortcuts and add others of your own if you like. See Figure 2.29.

Figure 2.29 *The Quick Launch toolbar in the Taskbar (to the right of the Start button)*

### Mouse

The *Control Panel* has a *Mouse* option. This can be used to set various properties, depending on the model that you have installed, such as:

- switching the functions assigned to the left and right buttons – useful for left-handed users
- changing the on-screen pointer image
- changing the speed at which the pointer moves across the screen
- changing the speed of double-clicking – useful for anyone with slow movements.

## Further research – improving the desktop display

Can you suggest some improvements that could be made to the desktop display on the computer systems you use at your centre? Do you know how to make the changes?

### Folder structures

Files are stored in computer systems in directories, also known as folders. Any user can set up their own folders, and this is a sensible way of organising a lot of personal documents and other files.

The appearance of the folders and files can be configured to suit the user. For more details see the section on File managers on page 81.

### User feedback

If you configure software for a particular user, it is very important that you let them try it out and give you feedback. In fact, if you can show them what the possibilities are and how to configure it for themselves they will be able to continue to experiment until they find a layout that suits them perfectly.

# System security

The hardware used in organisations can be worth many hundreds of thousands of pounds. If any of it is damaged or stolen then it may take a while to replace it. The cost of replacement will usually be covered by insurance, so the main problem will be the delay in installing replacement hardware. The delay can mean that business is lost and the company will lose money.

Although the computer hardware in an organisation may be very valuable, damage to software and data is of far greater significance to most businesses. The software can be replaced (as copies will always be available), but the real risk lies in loss of business data. Imagine what could happen if an airline lost all its data about the tickets it had sold for flights in the future. It would not be able to issue the tickets to passengers who had already booked but not yet received their tickets; it would not know whether flights were full, so would not be able to sell more tickets; it would not be able to provide airports with security information about passengers. Data is far more valuable to a business than either the hardware or the programs.

Because business data is so important, it is confidential. Other companies might be very interested to know what it contains, so security is also needed to ensure that information is only available to those with a right to know it.

Any work that you do on a computer as part of your studies, especially your assessment work, will have taken you many hours. It is very important to you and you need to protect it.

## Threats to data stored on a computer

ICT systems have to be protected from a number of threats. Someone may access a system illegally in order to read sensitive information and, even though they may not cause any damage to the system, they may create all kinds of problems to the organisation. Worse still, they may actually change data or even delete it.

The main aims of security are:

- to maintain the system as intended
- to protect the system from unauthorised changes being made to the software or data
- to protect the system from both accidental and deliberate illegal access
- to detect successful and unsuccessful attempts at illegal access
- to provide a means of recovery if things go wrong.

ICT systems can be kept secure only if the people who look after them remember to do tasks laid down to achieve this on a regular basis.

It is very important for people who use computers to consider all the ways in which their computer systems could be threatened.

### Viruses

Computer viruses can cause a lot of damage to software, by deleting and altering programs and data. They can be spread from one computer to another through a network system, or on disks.

Most viruses are carried on email attachments. These can then infect the computer system by deleting or altering files. Many viruses that come via email can also automatically send out new emails, with the virus attached, to any addresses in the email address book. Since the process is automatic, viruses can spread from organisation to organisation around the world very rapidly.

### Spyware

Spyware is another kind of program that is installed on a computer without the user being aware of it. This can happen when free software is downloaded from a website. As its name suggests, spyware monitors the way in which the computer is being used and scans files for passwords and other confidential data. This is then transmitted back to its originator.

As well as the security dangers, spyware can take up memory, and can slow down a computer. There are a number of programs available that can remove any spyware that has been installed and prevent further installations.

Spyware should not be confused with cookies, which are very small data files. Cookies are usually harmless, and indeed they speed up access to websites as they can remember passwords and preferences.

### Data theft and hacking

Data or software should only be altered or deleted by someone who is allowed to do so. But just reading data can also cause damage to an organisation, even if it is not deleted or altered in any way.

The main threats from unauthorised access are that:

- software or data is deleted
- software or data is altered
- confidential data is read or copied
- information is passed on to another person who is not allowed to read it – this is known as data theft
- software is used by someone who is not allowed to use it.

Most cases of unauthorised access are carried out by people deliberately.

### Media failure

If a disk becomes damaged then the data stored on it may be lost. This can be true of fixed hard disks as well as all the removable media. It is sometimes possible to recover data from a disk, even if some of it has

**What does it mean?**

A **virus** *is a small computer program that can cause damage to a computer system. Viruses are usually spread by being attached to programs or documents, which are then distributed on disk or by email.*

**What does it mean?**

**Hacking** *refers to the actions of people who gain access to computer systems when they have no right to do so. The technical term for hacking is* **'unauthorised access'**, *and the Computer Misuse Act is the law in the UK that deals with this offence.*

been corrupted. But to protect against the loss of data, all disks should be backed up regularly.

## Further research – security threats

If you would like a challenge then think about all the threats to security of data, and answer these questions:

- Which threats can cause the most damage to data?
- Which threats can cause the most damage to the business? How?
- Which threats are the easiest to protect against?

## Relevant and current legislation

### Data Protection Act 1998

Most organisations collect and store personal data. For example, they hold details about their employees.

Many businesses will also have information about their customers, and some of this information can be quite detailed. For example, supermarket chains issue loyalty cards to their customers, and the customers can gain loyalty points or other incentives like AirMiles when they do their shopping. But whenever the customer buys anything, the system will also be gathering information about the type of goods that the person prefers, what time of day they go shopping etc.

The Data Protection Act applies whenever information about living persons is stored, but only if it is possible to identify the individual from the data. So if a survey is done but the names of the people who respond are not collected then this usually does not count as personal data.

In the Act a **data controller** is someone who is responsible for storing personal data. **A data subject** is a person that the data refers to. The data controller is obliged to protect the data in a number of ways, but all the data subjects have rights to view the data about themselves.

The Information Commissioner is a Government officer who regulates data controllers. Every organisation or individual who processes personal data must complete a form, explaining how they intend to collect, store and use personal data. This is then sent to the Commissioner for approval.

There are eight data protection principles:

1   **Personal data must be processed fairly and lawfully.** The data controller in an organisation must complete a notification form for the Information Commissioner. They must tell the Information Commissioner what data they intend to collect, how they intend to collect it, what they want to use the data for and who they may pass the information on to. They also have to explain how they intend to

keep the data secure. The data subject must give permission for any data to be used.

2 **Personal data must be obtained and processed for limited purposes.** The organisation must only use the data in the way they described on their notification form and they must not use it for any other purpose.

3 **Personal data must be adequate, relevant and not excessive.** The data must be just what is needed and nothing more.

4 **Personal data must be accurate.** The organisation has to try to ensure that the data is correct, although it cannot be held responsible if the data subject made a mistake when they gave the information in the first place.

5 **Personal data must not be kept longer than necessary.**

6 **Personal data must be processed in accordance with the data subject's rights.** Any data subject (i.e. the person that the data refers to) is entitled to read the information that is held about them. The data controller in the organisation must provide the information so that it is easy to understand. The data subject has the right to ask for their name to be removed from any marketing lists.

7 **Personal data must be secure.** The data must only be available to people within the organisation who need to know it. Anything else will count as unauthorised access.

8 **Personal data must not be transferred to countries outside Europe without adequate protection.** This is because all the countries in the European Union (EU) have similar data protection laws, but countries outside the EU vary a great deal.

An earlier Data Protection Act only related to data stored on a computer system. But the 1998 Act covers all personal data, including documents stored in a filing cabinet or lists written on paper.

There are some exceptions. The Data Protection Act does not apply to data held for 'personal, family or household purposes', so you do not have to worry about declaring your personal address book or mobile phone. In addition, data collected for national security, for the investigation of crime and for taxation purposes does not have to be declared to the Commissioner.

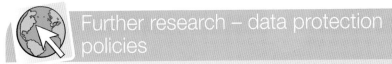

## Further research – data protection policies

At your centre of learning or place of work, find out what data protection policies the organisation has in place. Do they seem to cover the requirements of the Data Protection Act?

Computer Misuse Act 1990

The Computer Misuse Act 1990 was designed to deal with unauthorised access to computer systems. Sometimes hackers gain unauthorised access simply out of bravado. In many cases they have criminal intentions, as they wish to either shut down systems or to steal or alter information.

Three kinds of offence were made illegal by the Act, and they are, in ascending order of seriousness:

1   **Unauthorised access to computer material.** An employee who uses a computer at work will be given permission (be authorised) to use certain software and to work with particular data in a database. Normally the systems administrators will set up access privileges on the network. These will ensure that when each employee logs on with their own user ID and password they will only be able to use and see those parts of the system that they are allowed to use.

    If an employee logs on with someone else's user ID (without permission) then they would be gaining unlawful access. Also, if they find loopholes in a system and use them to access parts of the system that they are not allowed to visit, then that too counts as an illegal activity.

    If someone accidentally gains access to a system, they are not guilty of an offence, although they would be if they continued to explore the system once they realised what had happened. Notice that gaining access as an experiment or 'for a laugh' is still a criminal act.

    The law does not just apply to employees and their organisation's computer systems, but to anyone who uses a computer and to any computer system.

    Examples of offences under this section include logging on to a system with someone else's user name and password or simply reading programs or data when not authorised to do so.

2   **Unauthorised access with intent to commit or facilitate commission of further offences.** If someone gains unauthorised access to a computer system and does so in order to commit a crime then they are guilty of a more serious offence. For example, a person might try to transfer money illegally from one bank account to another, or might want to find out incriminating information that they could use to blackmail someone.

3   **Unauthorised modification of computer material.** If a person deliberately alters or deletes information held on a computer system, when they do not have the authority to do so, then they are acting illegally. This part of the Computer Misuse Act is also designed to catch people who introduce viruses to systems.

## Further research – how does the Computer Misuse Act affect me?

The Computer Misuse Act will only affect you if you deliberately try to gain access to a computer system, or to change computer data, when you do not have permission to do so. If you do any of these things by accident, then you should not be in trouble, but you should take steps to tell the right people and prevent damage occurring.

- What should you do if you do delete some data by accident?

- What should you do if you find that you have been given access to parts of the system that you should not visit?

- What should you do if you discover that you have passed on a virus?

- Have you received any information or warnings about the Computer Misuse Act at your centre? If not, you could offer to create a summary of the Act and its implications for students, and this could then be used as part of your assessment evidence.

## Virus checking

The best way to prevent virus damage is to install virus protection software on networks or on standalone computer systems. Virus protection software works with a virus data file, which contains information about all known viruses. The software uses the data file to check whether programs or data have been infected. It can be configured to check every new file that is placed on the system, including all emails, and it will also spot any unexpected changes to the system. A full virus check can be run periodically to check that nothing has slipped through. Since new viruses are being released all the time, it is very important to update regularly the virus data files that enable the software to detect and identify the viruses.

## Backup procedures

The main aim of security is to maintain the system – hardware and software – as intended. So if things do go wrong it is important to be able to re-create the system that existed before the damage was done.

Hardware can often be replaced by suppliers, with the cost covered by insurance. It is far more difficult to replace the software and data. But if proper backup procedures have been followed then the software and data can be copied from the backups and the system can revert to how it was before.

Every single file on an ICT system should be copied and the copy kept on a disk or tape of some sort. This copy is known as a backup, and it can be used if the original is damaged.

When you use a word processor you will probably find that you can set it up so that it always saves a backup copy of each document. This can

### What does it mean?

*A **backup** is a copy of software and data that is kept in case the original becomes damaged.*

be very useful if you save something then realise that you have made a mistake and want to go back to a previous version. But as the backup is usually saved on the same disk as the original file, it is not much help if the disk itself is damaged.

An end user on a standalone computer is much wiser to save a backup copy of a file on to another storage medium as a security measure.

### Backups for large amounts of data

On a network, all the files will be backed up regularly. This is an automatic process during which all the files on the system will be copied on to a removable disk or digital tape. In most organisations this will happen in the middle of the night when no-one is at work on the system. The disk or tape will then be removed by a network administrator in the morning and locked in a fire-proof safe. You can read more about backups on networks in Unit 6.

It is now possible for someone to backup their standalone PC on to a remote server through the Internet.

The two main types of backup are:

- **Full backup.** The operating system can be set up so that it automatically makes a backup on a regular basis. This is best done at night, when users will not be trying to access it.
- **Incremental backup.** Several of these may be done between one full backup and the next. An incremental backup copies only the files that have been changed since the last backup. Although incremental backups will be done during the working day, they will be much quicker than full backups so should not noticeably interrupt normal work. If the files need to be restored then the last full backup will be used together with any incremental backups made since.

### Storing backups

Backup files should be stored on a medium that:

- makes fast copies
- can be stored in a secure place away from the original.

So if a full backup is taken of all the files on a network server (i.e. on the network's hard disk) then it should be stored on a medium that can be removed and locked away in a safe. Digital tape is commonly used for this purpose, as data can be copied to tape very rapidly.

All backup tapes and disks need to be labelled very carefully with the date and time.

## Firewalls

A firewall is a piece of systems software that protects the system from unauthorised access. Firewalls are commonly used to check all the communications between a system and the Internet. If it detects any unexpected attempts to access the system via the Internet then it will block them and report them immediately to the user.

## Physical security and damage to equipment

All ICT systems have to be protected from loss and damage. This applies to the hardware – the components of the computer system and the network cabling – as well as to the software and data held on the system.

An ICT system can be damaged by:

- catastrophic events, such as fire, flood or major damage to the building
- environmental problems, such as high temperatures or damp
- electrical and magnetic interference
- minor faults, such as damaged cables or broken components
- lost disks, keys or components.

Most of these problems are caused by accidents. But someone who wants to harm an organisation could cause such damage deliberately. Any damage to the hardware puts the software and data at risk as well.

In addition, unauthorised access to ICT systems can happen as a result of:

- people gaining entry to buildings and rooms
- theft of hardware, disks and documents
- tapping into networks.

Unauthorised access is normally deliberate. But if the security in a building is not good enough then someone may innocently wander into a forbidden area.

ICT systems can be protected by:

- locks and burglar alarm systems
- keeping all disks in locked boxes and drawers
- placing computer systems in a part of the building that cannot be reached easily from outside
- keeping the room at an even temperature.

### Further research – security measures by retailers

If you would like a challenge, then investigate the security measures used by an online retailer. How do they protect their data and the data given to them by customers? How do they stay within the law? You will be able to find out some of this by making a purchase yourself (you can drop out at the last minute if you do not want to buy). The company will not let you into most of their security secrets, but you could make a good guess about the procedures that they follow and the software that they use.

## Test your knowledge

26  Describe three hazards that could cause injury to someone working with computers.

27  How can the risks posed by those hazards be minimised?

28  What is USB and what is it used for?

29  Why is it a good idea to personalise the user interface?

30  List five things that can be changed through the Control Panel in Windows.

31  How could you configure the mouse to meet a person's individual needs?

32  What problems can be caused to a business if it suffers from data theft?

33  According to the Data Protection Act, what is personal data?

34  What are viruses and how can you protect a computer from them?

35  Why should you back up data?

## Assessment tasks

The assessment tasks in this unit are based on the following scenario:

*Suppose you have started work as a trainee ICT support technician for TLA Technical Support. You and a colleague will be visiting local businesses and organisations to advise them about ICT and to fix any problems they have. Your supervisor has asked you to compile a report about the things you have learnt and the work you have done.*

> To work towards a Distinction in this unit you will need to achieve **all** the Pass, Merit and Distinction criteria in the unit and have evidence to show that you have achieved each one.

### How do I provide assessment evidence?

Your evidence can be presented in any suitable form, such as written reports, presentations, posters or verbal explanations. These can be supported by other documentation such as photos, charts, diagrams, printouts, screen shots, witness statements, observation records and transcripts of conversations. If you make a presentation, include speaker's notes, and print off both slides and notes.

All your evidence should all be presented in one folder, which should have a front cover and a contents page. You should divide the evidence into six sections corresponding to the six tasks.

### Task 1 (P1, P2, P3, M1)

For this task you need to do some research and then present your findings in any suitable format.

- List a number of different types of computer and for each one describe its purpose.

- Compare a command line and graphical user interface for an operating system, and show how each could be used to perform the same task.

- Sometimes a command line interface is more efficient than a graphical interface; describe circumstances when this could be true, and explain how it is more efficient.

- Use a diagram to show how data flows around a standalone personal computer. Make sure you have described what is going on in the diagram.

## Assessment tasks continued

### Task 2 (P4, M2, D1)

You will be given a scenario by your tutor that describes a particular user.

- Give a list of suitable hardware and software that would meet the user's needs. You should show that they are compatible with each other.
- Justify your choice of hardware and software for the user.

> To work towards a Distinction you should outline two possible computer systems that would meet the user's needs. You should include both hardware and software. Then evaluate both systems in terms of their performance and also in terms of value for money.

### Task 3 (P5)

This task is a practical activity.

- Connect at least two peripherals to a personal computer.
- You should show that you have done this safely and you should test the peripherals to make sure that they work properly once connected.

### Task 4 (P6, M3)

This is another practical activity. You will be given a scenario that describes a particular user. This could be the same one that you used for Task 2. You will also be told which software to work on.

- Configure the software to meet the needs of the user.
- Explain how the way you have configured the software will help the user carry out their tasks on the computer.

### Task 5 (P7, D3)

You should identify a particular situation where a computer is being used. You may be given this by your tutor or you may be able to agree on one together.

- Outline the data security issues when using the computer in this situation.
- Outline the legal issues that are relevant in this situation.

> To work towards a Distinction you should make sure that you have considered a commercial system. You should do the following:
> - Recommend actions that could be taken to protect the system.
> - Recommend what should be done to ensure that the system complies with the law.

### Task 6 (M4, D2)

Describe, in general, how a computer system can be protected from potential threats. You should consider threats to the hardware, software and data.

> To work towards a Distinction you should evaluate the current threats to the security of data held on computer systems. Make sure that you consider both commercial and personal systems. You should think about the kinds of threat that are prevalent at the present time.

# **4** Website Design

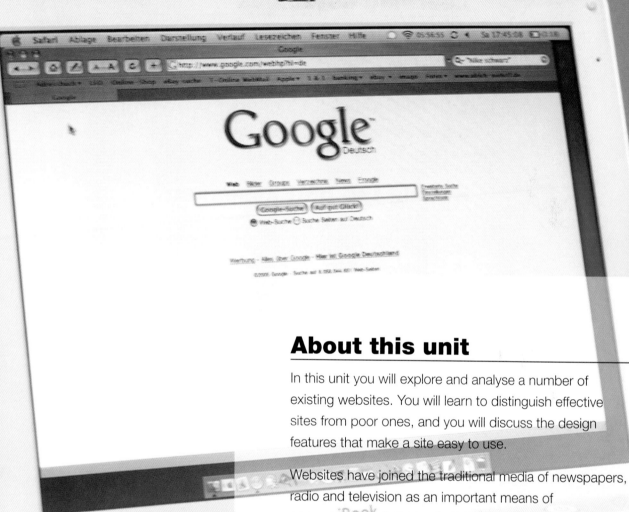

## About this unit

In this unit you will explore and analyse a number of existing websites. You will learn to distinguish effective sites from poor ones, and you will discuss the design features that make a site easy to use.

Websites have joined the traditional media of newspapers, radio and television as an important means of communication between individuals and organisations. In the past, the media offered one-way communication only, although digital interactive television is now changing that. But websites can be used very easily for two-way communication, so had a clear advantage over the other media when they first appeared in the 1990s.

You will have the opportunity to design and build a website for a client, and will learn a number of useful skills.

In order to succeed in this unit you will need to have easy access to the Internet and a good search engine. You should also have the use of one or more web authoring packages.

▶ Continued from previous page

# Learning outcomes

When you have completed this unit you will:

**1** understand the purpose of websites and the laws and guidelines that concern their development

**2** understand the principles of multipage website design

**3** be able to create a multiple page website.

# How is the unit assessed?

This unit is internally assessed. You will provide a portfolio of evidence to show that you have achieved the learning outcomes. The grading grid in the specification for this unit lists what you must do to obtain Pass, Merit and Distinction grades. The section on Assessment Tasks at the end of this chapter will guide you through activities that will help you to be successful in this unit.

# Purposes of websites and the laws that affect them

In 1991, Tim Berners-Lee developed the World Wide Web while he was working at CERN (the European Organisation for Nuclear Research). He was a computer scientist whose job was to ensure that physicists got the very best use out of the Internet.

The World Wide Web (also known as the Web, or WWW) very rapidly became the universal standard way of displaying and linking documents on the Internet.

The Web is a hypermedia system, which embeds hyperlinks to other web pages. All the pages on the Web are ultimately linked together.

Berners-Lee developed three important elements that together make the Web work for users:

- **Hypertext MarkUp Language (HTML)** – the code used to create all web pages
- **HyperText Transfer Protocol (HTTP)** – the rules for transferring HTML files from one computer to another
- **browsers** – software applications that enable the user to view web pages.

Since 1991, HTML has been extended quite considerably, so that it can now include snippets of programming languages, known as scripts. At the same time, a number of different browsers have been launched, and they are frequently updated to reflect the new developments in HTML.

The most commonly used browser is Microsoft Internet Explorer, but other browsers, such as Mozilla Firefox, are also used.

A browser does a number of tasks:

- It sends a request for a page to the web server where the website is stored. The request identifies the page by its Uniform Resource Locator (URL) – often referred to as its web address. The HTML code for that page is then transmitted over the Internet.
- It interprets the HTML code and displays the web page.
- It sends requests to the web server for additional files that are referred to in the HTML code for the page – these could be for graphics or sounds. Each image or sound is transmitted as a separate file.
- When the user clicks on a hyperlink, the browser sends a new page request to the webserver.

Browsers have been updated to match the developments in HTML, but it is important to realise that not all users use the latest versions. Web pages can appear differently in different browsers and in different versions of the same browser.

## What does it mean?

**Media.** *The traditional ways of providing news to the general public, such as newspapers, radio and television, became known as communication media (or simply, 'the media'). The word 'media' is the plural for 'medium', i.e. the means whereby information is transmitted. Websites, email, interactive television and mobile phones are referred to as the new media.*

**Multimedia** *systems handle data in a variety of formats, such as sound, graphics and animation.*

**Hypermedia** *is a multimedia system that includes hyperlinks to other pages.*

## Purposes of websites

Websites can do the following:

- **Inform.** All websites provide some information, which is one reason why the Internet became known as the Information Superhighway.
- **Sell.** Websites can be used to promote products and services to visitors.
- **Interact.** Websites can easily offer interactivity, allowing the visitor to send information and ideas back to the organisation and to engage in dialogue.

It is interesting that we use the terms 'reader', 'listener' and 'viewer' for people who use newspapers, radio and television, whereas a person who goes to a website is referred to as a 'visitor'. Visitors, of course, do not just passively accept what is given to them; instead they make choices about what they want to see and where they want to go. It is the interactive nature of websites that distinguishes them from the traditional media.

Websites created by organisations fall into a number of categories:

- commercial
- non-commercial
- educational
- governmental
- internal communications.

### Commercial websites

#### Marketing

As the Internet has grown, so more and more businesses have emerged that exist only on the Web. There are many examples of online banks, shops, travel agencies and insurance companies. These companies sell goods and services directly to the customer.

Customers normally pay for products online with a credit card, and they need to be reassured that their payments will be safe. Online payments are usually routed through a secure server, which encrypts all the data.

Goods have to be sent to the customer either by post or using a distribution company, and successful online businesses usually guarantee delivery within 24 hours or a few days.

Some Internet businesses offer services that avoid the need to deliver goods. For example, online banking has grown very rapidly, and customers can view their balances, make payments and generally manage their accounts at any time of the day. Similarly, travel companies can send documents, such as ticket confirmations, by email and may not need to use the post at all.

Many high street chains now have online e-commerce operations as well. Large supermarkets offer a home shopping service, which can be

**What does it mean?**

**e-commerce** *is the use of the Internet for selling goods and services to customers.*

## Further research – e-commerce websites

Amazon, the online bookstore (Figure 4.1) describe themselves in this way:

*"What we do*

*Amazon.co.uk is famous for selling books, but did you know that we now sell millions of other products too? From cameras to coffee machines, exercise videos to Elvis CDs, there's something for everyone. We also enable independent sellers to sell new and used items on our website via Amazon.co.uk Marketplace. In addition, we give you a variety of resources to help you make your choice, including customer reviews and personal recommendations."*
(Source: www.amazon.co.uk)

Use your usual search engine to find other e-commerce websites. Can you work out which kinds of business have gone in for e-commerce? And what kinds of business are rarely to be found on the web?

**Figure 4.1** *Amazon's e-commerce site*

very helpful for people who are housebound, have young children or lead busy lives.

## Information repositories

Many commercial websites promote a service or product without actually offering online sales. For example, most rock bands have websites that promote the band and their music, although visitors may not be able to buy albums directly from the site. These can be described as repositories of information.

Many tourist attractions use the Internet to give people information about location and opening times and to encourage people to attend. Similarly, hotels often provide basic information even though you may have to phone to book a room.

## Further research – leisure attraction websites

Disneyland Paris uses its website to show what it offers and to encourage people to visit. Can you find other leisure attractions that market their services on the Web?

## Non-commercial websites

Here are some non-commercial organisations that have websites:

- schools, colleges and universities
- charities
- political parties
- churches and other religious organisations.

All these organisations are trying to persuade the visitor to do something in response and are not simply providing interesting information.

Some of these sites also offer some online sales, and start to develop an e-commerce angle.

### Personal

Many sites are developed to support online communities. We refer to communities of place (based on people living in a particular area) and communities of interest (based on people who share a common interest wherever they live). Communities of interest thrive on the Internet as they can bring together people from around the world who would otherwise never meet. But communities of place are also important and a website can act as a focal point for local concerns.

At the smallest level, individuals can develop their own personal websites where they can write about the things that matter to them. Many of these are created in the form of a weblog, often referred to as a blog. This is a website that can be easily updated by the owner, often on a daily basis, and provides a kind of online journal of thoughts and personal descriptions of events.

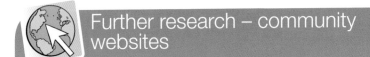

## Further research – community websites

Hampton Online is a community website serving an area in SW London. It includes news, local information, letters (with the ability to reply), notice-boards and links to local websites. To see the site go to www.heinemann.co.uk/hotlinks, insert the express code 2048P and click on this unit.

Can you find other examples of online communities on the Web?

### Advice and guidance

Many public services have sites, such as the well-used NHS-Direct, that specialise in communicating information to members of the public. Go to www.heinemann.co.uk/hotlinks, insert the express code 2048P and click on this unit.

There are also a few online organisations that have built huge databases of articles and external links, which they then provide as a service to visitors. One example is About (*www.about.com*).

You may wonder how an organisation can finance a free information service. You will usually find that sites are sponsored by other businesses and their advertisements appear in banners and pop-up screens. Some information sites, such as the Government's site DirectGov, are paid for out of public taxation. Go to www.heinemann.co.uk/hotlinks, insert the express code 2048P and click on this unit.

### Clubs

Many clubs and local organisations have websites that provide information to members and the general public about their activities.

## Educational

There are many websites to support students, teachers and parents. A good place to start is the National Grid for Learning, which is a huge collection of links to all kinds of educational websites.

The Young People section in DirectGov takes you to many useful sources of advice on money, health, work, travel and, of course, learning.

You will probably already know about the BBC Bytesize website, where you can revise any of the more popular GCSE subjects.

The Qualifications and Curriculum Authority is in charge of all the standard qualifications in the UK. You can find out about courses that you could take after this one.

TeacherNet brings together all the information that teachers need, including online resources and lesson plans. You may have benefited from some of the teaching materials yourself.

There are also websites to help parents support their child's learning. The Department for Education and Skills runs the ParentsCentre site, which gives advice about all aspects of education.

## Further research – educational websites

Make up a list of educational sites that would help you in studying this course, or in deciding what to do next. Share this list with fellow students.

## Government

### National government departments

You can now carry out many interactions with government departments online. For example, you can:

- book your driving test
- apply for a passport
- claim Child Benefit
- fill in your Income Tax return and pay any tax you owe
- get health advice
- find out about your rights as an employee

and many, many more things.

For some tasks, such as applying for an Educational Maintenance Grant, you do have to fill in a paper form and post it with supporting documents. In all these cases you can download the forms and read the information about them online.

Each government service has its own website, but you can find your way to the right one from the Directgov site.

### Local authority

From Directgov you will also be able to locate your local authority's (Council) website, where you should be able to:

- report graffiti
- book adult education classes
- raise a petition
- respond to a consultation
- express your views about local issues
- pay council tax.

You should be able to find out easily online who your elected representatives (Members of Parliament and councillors) are. Many have their own websites, and all can be contacted by email.

## Communication within organisations

The Internet is essentially a public-access network, so that anyone can visit any site they choose. An organisation may want to maintain a site for internal communications that can be accessed only by employees or members. To do this they can set up an intranet (note the spelling).

An intranet is created on the organisation's own network system and can be used only by users who log on to stations on the network. It will normally include email services and an internal 'website'. Strictly speaking we should not really refer to the pages as a 'website' as it does not appear on the World Wide Web.

**What does it mean?**

*An **intranet** is a closed system that has many of the features of the Internet but which is accessible only within an organisation.*

An intranet can hold confidential information that should not normally appear outside the organisation, as well as day-to-day administrative arrangements.

By definition, members of the public do not normally have access to intranets, but you may find that you have an intranet at your place of study.

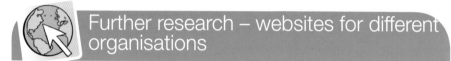

## Further research – websites for different organisations

Use a search engine or portal sites to find a wide range of websites developed for organisations. Keep notes on all the sites that you visit. You may be able to use them later for the assessment tasks. For each site you visit, jot down:

- web address and name of the organisation
- purpose of the site
- type of site – commercial, non-commercial, educational, governmental
- brief description of the content.

Eventually you will have to select at least four of these sites and write about them in more depth. But it is useful to build up a list at this stage from which you can choose.

# Client need

Before a web designer starts work designing a website for a client, the designer has to ask a number of questions, in particular:

- **What is the purpose of the site?** The effectiveness of a website can be judged by referring to its purpose. It would not be sensible or fair if all websites were assessed against the same standards. A website that is designed for a fan club will be very different from one for a company selling computer supplies.
- **What is the target audience?** These are the groups of people that the organisation wants to communicate with through the website.

You can ask the same questions about any site you visit. You can judge whether the designer has made sensible decisions about the content and layout of a site, and you will then be in a position to form a judgement about the quality of the site and how it could be improved.

## Target audience

A web designer needs to know whether the site is aimed at the world in general or at a specific section of the population, e.g. young people, car owners, parents, football supporters, women, members of a particular religion, or residents in a particular town. Most sites are built with a typical visitor in mind.

Here are some questions that you can ask about a website to help you judge whether it is right for its target audience:

■ Does the home page give a good idea of what the site contains?

■ Is the home page informative and interesting?

■ Does the site provide the expected information?

■ Is there too much information or too little? The right amount will depend on the purpose of the site.

■ Is there basic information about the organisation, who it includes and what it does?

■ Does the site say how to contact the organisation? This information should always be provided somewhere on the site.

■ Does the site allow a visitor to contact the organisation directly? This may be offered through an online form, or an email address may be given.

■ Is there a Privacy Policy? This is a statement about how the organisation will handle any information given to them by a visitor. It is necessary to comply with the Data Protection Act and to give the visitor the confidence to do business with the organisation.

■ Is the site kept up to date? Sites should be maintained as frequently as appropriate; for example, a news site will be updated every day, while a site that gives advice on buying a kitchen freezer needs to be updated only when new freezers come on to the market.

## What does it mean?

*A **link** is a text or graphic on a page. When it is clicked, another page in the same file or directory is loaded. For example, a page in the Help file for an applications package will contain links to other pages in the same file.*

*A **hyperlink** is the common term for a link on the Internet. Hyperlinks can link to pages that are in different files or directories, and that can be anywhere on the Web.*

## User need

Visitors to a site will stay on the site only if they find it easy to use. A web designer needs to think carefully about how the pages are designed, how quickly they download and how the pages are linked together.

### Navigation

Navigation refers to the way visitors find their way around a site, using links provided on the pages. Text or images can act as navigation links, and image links are often called buttons. Some of the most important links may be positioned together in a navigation bar. Here are some questions to consider:

■ Is it easy for a visitor to find their way around the site? The main navigation bar is often along the top of the screen, or it may be down the left-hand side; other links may be provided anywhere on the page.

■ Are the methods of navigation consistent? The navigation bar should be in the same position on each page, and the colours and images that identify them should be consistent throughout the site.

■ Can visitors find most of the information they want with no more than three mouse clicks? The 'three click rule' should apply to almost all information, as visitors leave a site if they cannot find information quickly.

- Does the site offer a search box? A visitor can enter a key word in a search box and a list of possible pages will be displayed.
- Does the site offer a site map? A site map is a diagram that shows how the pages link together; a complete site map cannot be provided for large and complex sites.

What does it mean?

**Navigation** *refers to the way visitors finds their way around a website, using links provided on the pages. Text or images can act as navigation links, and image links are often called buttons. Some of the most important links may be positioned together in a navigation bar.*

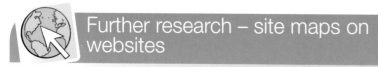
Further research – site maps on websites

NHSDirect provides a site map for visitors. This is a separate page laid out as shown in Figure 4.2. Have you seen site maps on other sites? Do they help the visitor?

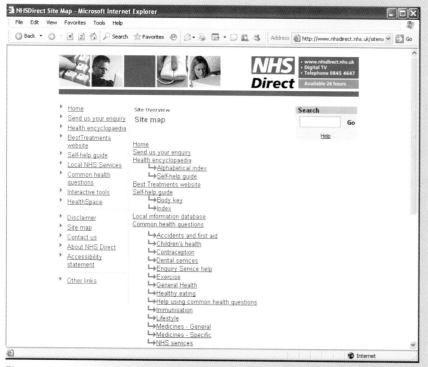

**Figure 4.2** *A site map for NHSDirect (Source: www.nhsdirect.nhs.uk)*

## Download speeds

Visitors will leave a site if they have to wait too long for a page to download. Although many people now use fast broadband connections, the web designer always has to remember the people using the oldest equipment and dialup modems. These questions should be asked with the slowest connection in mind:

- Do pages download quickly? A page should normally download in less than a minute on the slowest communication channel at the busiest time of day.
- Are visitors warned in advance if a page is likely to take some time to download? Visitors may want to view pages with high-quality photos,

or to download a file in a graphical format like pdf; in these cases they should be warned about the size of the download before requesting it.

## Client's requirements

### Suitability of language

The language used on a website should be clear, simple and straightforward. It is more difficult to read text on screen than when it is printed out, so, generally speaking, sentences should be short and uncomplicated.

Sometimes a page will provide a link to a formal document, and this may contain technical information, legal detail, and much longer passages of text.

You should ask:

- Does the site use language in a style that is appropriate to the subject matter and for the target audience? Business sites tend to use more formal language than sites devoted to leisure interests; the age of expected visitors is also relevant.
- Does the site use technical or specialist terms? If so, are they ones that would be understood by the target audience?

### Choice of images

Images give life to a website. But using them effectively is quite an art. In particular, too many images can simply confuse the user. Images give information and the designer needs to be clear about their use, as well as their appearance.

- Do images convey additional information? Images, such as photos or drawings, often impart information.
- Do images enhance the impact of the site? Some images are used as decoration, and to create a mood or style.
- Are the images appropriate for the site? The purpose and audience must not be forgotten.
- Do images have alternative text? When you pass the mouse over an image, a short text description may pop up; this is the alternative text for the image and should ideally be provided to support users of non-standard browsers and for visitors with visual impairment.
- If Flash, video or other animations are used, do they add to the quality of the site? Lengthy introductions can be very irritating.

### Appropriate formats

The visual appearance of a site should match the purpose and target audience:

- What impression is the site trying to give to visitors? It could be businesslike, friendly, busy, formal or casual.
- What impression does a visitor form of the organisation from the site?

- Is the text easy to read on screen? Short paragraphs are easier to read than long ones; text that spreads itself across a wide screen can be difficult to read.
- Can the text be downloaded or printed so that a visitor can read it offline?
- Is the text presented in a consistent style? Sites will probably use a number of different text styles, but they should be used consistently.

### Layout

The layout of the pages of the site should make the site easy to use:

- Are the most important items on the home page visible without scrolling down? Some visitors never use the scroll bar, so all the most important items should be towards the top of the page.
- Is the page laid out in columns? If not, is it easy to read text?
- Is the page still visible when the window is made smaller? Does the page expand when the window is enlarged?
- Is the layout consistent from page to page?

### Colour

Colour should be used carefully – too many contrasting colours can be distracting, too few can be dull.

- Does the site use an appropriate colour scheme? Sometimes an organisation will have corporate colours; in other cases a set of colours should be chosen to convey the desired impression.
- Do the colours of the text and background make it easy to read? Dark text on a light background is best.
- Is the colour scheme used consistently?

### Font

In Unit 1 you will have learnt about how fonts can be used to create an impression. A wide range of fonts can be used in website graphics. Fonts that can be used for website text are more limited. Ask yourself:

- Are the fonts used on the site suitable for the target audience?
- Are the fonts suitable for the subject matter?

## Laws and guidelines

A number of UK laws apply to websites. As a web designer you need to be aware of these and abide by them, even when developing a small personal website.

### Data Protection Act 1998

You learnt about the Data Protection Act in Unit 2, which applies to all data about living persons. Websites have to comply with it, so you should not disclose personal information, such as the address of someone, without their express permission.

## Copyright Designs and Patents Act 1988

Writing, music, films and works of art are described as intellectual property, and the creators (or their employers) normally own the copyright to their work. This means that no-one else may copy, print, perform or film work without the copyright owner's permission. In the UK, copyright normally extends for 50 years after the creator's death, and the rights extend to their heirs.

For many years it was not clear whether copyright applied to software products. The **Copyright Designs and Patents Act 1988** states that software (including websites) should be treated in the same way as all other intellectual property.

The copyright for a website belongs to the organisation that commissions it, not to the web designer.

All content on a website should fall into one of these three categories:

- material created within the organisation
- material used with the permission of the copyright owner
- copyright-free material.

Permission must be sought before using text, photographs, images, videos, music and other sounds that have originated elsewhere. This applies whether they are found on a website or in books or recordings. Software used on websites, such as scripts in Java, Visual Basic and other languages, as well as Flash animations, are also covered by copyright. Copyright holders will usually charge for permission to use their materials.

In general, it is wisest to assume that any material published in any format, including on the Web, is covered by copyright, unless it explicitly states that it is copyright-free. **Copyright-free** material is not necessarily cost free, but on the Web there are many sources of copyright-free materials that can be downloaded and used at no charge.

There are several other terms used for software and other materials in relation to their copyright status:

- **Shareware** is software that has been copyrighted by the originator, but is sold (or given) to users with permission to copy it and to share it with others. Sometimes the conditions of use prevent the shareware from being used for commercial purposes. Shareware may be offered for free on an evaluation basis, but with payment required for continuing use. Many scripts are offered as shareware.
- **Open source** software is software that can be distributed without restrictions, so that all users can view and modify the code. Open source software is not necessarily free of charge. Originally it was known as free software – in the sense of 'free to share' rather than 'at no cost'.
- **Public domain** materials are items that are completely free of copyright and can be used by anyone.

## Further research – copyright free material

Find sources of copyright-free no-cost materials on the Web that can be used legally on a website. You could look for images, photos, animations, literature, articles and music.

In the USA the **Digital Millennium Copyright Act** covers similar ground to the UK's Copyright Designs and Patents Act 1988.

## Other legislation

We have seen that the Data Protection Act and the Copyright legislation have implications for the publication of websites. There are a number of other UK laws, regulations and guidelines that apply to any published materials that can be accessed from the UK, and some of these relate to offensive material.

The content of a website could be judged to be offensive if it is libellous, pornographic, racist, blasphemous, sexist, homophobic, over violent or inciting hatred, although there is not one single definition in law.

- The **Computer Misuse Act**, which you studied in Unit 2, protects the private information held on databases that support websites, and protects the communication of private information that a visitor may send to a website.
- The **Child Protection Act** makes it a criminal offence to possess child pornography, such as indecent pictures of children or pictures of a person under the age of 16 in a sexual act. The publication of such materials, on the Web or elsewhere, is an even more serious offence. The **Obscene Publications Act** covers the publication of other pornographic and violent material.
- The **Race Relations Act**, **Sex Discrimination Act**, **Disability Discrimination Act** and **Equal Opportunities Act** all identify areas of discrimination that could lead to actions in the criminal or civil courts. In general, material should not be published that encourages discrimination on the grounds of race, ethnic origin, colour, nationality, sex, sexual orientation, disability or religious beliefs.
- **Libel** is a civil offence, not a criminal offence, which means that someone can take a private action in the civil courts if their reputation has been damaged.

## Internet guidelines

### Employer defined

Most organisations issue **internal guidelines** to staff, identifying unacceptable behaviour that would lead to disciplinary action. Some of these may relate to material that might be published on the website, but which could be offensive to visitors. Such guidelines would be in addition to the legal constraints.

### National regulation

Many industries have their own codes of practice. These are agreed by all the members. If a business violates the code of practice, it often means that they lose membership of the industry body or that they can be publicly reprimanded.

One example of this, that is relevant to websites, is the **Code of Practice for Advertisers**, which is produced by the Advertising Standards Authority. This requires all advertisements to be legal, decent, truthful and honest. This is self-regulation by the advertising industry, but is very effective. The Office of Fair Trading can take out an injunction in the courts against persistent offenders.

On the Web, banners and pop-up advertisements are covered by the Code of Practice, as are any online sales promotions.

### International agreements

A number of global organisations have produced guidelines that they hope members will abide by. These cannot replace laws in individual countries, but they can be quite powerful. One example of this is the 'Guidelines on Advertising and Marketing on the Internet' produced by the International Chambers of Commerce.

## Test your knowledge

1   What is meant by a target audience?

2   What is e-commerce? What features will you always find on e-commerce websites?

3   Name three commercial and three non-commercial websites.

4   What is navigation? Why is it so important in a website?

5   What is the difference between the Internet and an intranet?

6   What should you use images for on a website?

7   How does the Copyright Designs and Patents Act affect you as a web designer?

# Principles of multipage website design

Before you can learn to design and create a web page, you should analyse a selection of sites to see if you can work out what makes them good or bad. To do this you need to understand how sites are constructed.

## Construction features

When you download a web page into a browser, the HTML code is transferred to your computer. This is referred to as the source code. HTML code is always stored and transmitted in a simple text file (ASCII file). It usually has a file name with *.htm* or *.html* as its file extension; for example, *homepage.htm*.

In Internet Explorer you can view the HTML by selecting *View* then *Source*. This usually opens up Notepad and displays the code. Notepad is a text editor, and is the simplest means of viewing and creating text files. If you use a different browser you should still be able to view the source code from the *View* menu.

If you scan through an HTML file, you will see references to other files that must be downloaded to complete the page. For example, you may see something like this:

```
<IMG src="http://www.example.com/cats.jpg" width=100
height=80 border=0 alt="Picture of cats">
```

This tells the browser that it needs to download the picture stored as *cats.jpg* from the site *www.example.com*.

**What does it mean?**

**Source code** *is the HTML program that makes up a web page file. A browser interprets the source code and presents it on screen as a web page.*

You may also spot some links to other files that may be used, such as video or sound, or files that contain program code.

### Frames

When you have visited websites you may have noticed that sometimes only a section of the page moves when you use the scroll bar. This happens when the page has been divided into two or more frames.

One of the frames may act as a header, and this will remain the same as other pages are downloaded. Alternatively a side frame may hold the main navigation links, and this too will remain static as pages are selected. See Figure 4.3.

**Figure 4.3** *Three possible frame layouts*

The HTML code that specifies the size and position of all the frames is held in a separate frame page. This page is not visible to the visitor. Instead it defines which pages are to be first downloaded into each frame.

Frames are less popular than they once were. One reason for using frames was to reduce the time taken to download each page, but this has been largely overcome by faster connections.

## Action buttons

A button is an image that represents an action. When you click on it with a mouse some action happens. On websites, the action is often to link you through to another page.

Buttons can be used for other purposes as well. You may have completed an online form, and at the bottom of the form you clicked a button labelled 'Submit' or something similar. This action button triggered off a small program, which made sure that the information you entered was sent to the right place.

## Hyperlinks

### Text links

Any section of text or any image can be used as a hyperlink to another web page. But how does the visitor recognise that text or an image is a link? Originally text links were all identified by underlining. Blue was the traditional colour for a link, with a link that had already been visited changing to magenta.

Text can, in fact, be used as a link without underlining, and in any colour, but this should only be done if the visitor is left in no doubt that this is, in fact, a link. Usually a different colour from the main text is used for the link, or all the links are placed together in a navigation bar.

### Image links

Images can also be used as links. Buttons are image-based links that look like the kind of buttons that you might press in the real world. But any image can be used as a link.

If an image is used as a link, the image has to be downloaded into the browser before the link will work. If a page has many image links then it may take some time for them to appear on a slow Internet connection, and the visitor may become impatient.

As a general rule, images used as links should be as small as possible, in terms of memory. Images in gif format usually take less memory than photos stored in jpg format.

Text links do not suffer from this problem, and they can be customised to appear quite interesting. Sometimes buttons created as image links can be replaced by text links with no loss of visual style.

# Further research – text and image links

The About site has a great many text links on one page (Figure 4.4). In comparison, *lastminute.com* prefers to use images as links (Figure 4.5). Almost all the graphical elements – photos and boxes – on this page are links. Colour is used to identify the text links in the navigation bar on the left.

Which do you prefer, and why? Find and compare other sites that make heavy use of either text or image links.

**Figure 4.4** *Using text for links (Source: www.about.com)*

**Figure 4.5** *Using graphics for links (Source: www.lastminute.com)*

## Internal links

Internal links allow the visitor to find their way around the site. No-one is going to find a page unless it is linked from another page.

Unless the site is very small there will not be links from any one page to all the other pages. Designers have to think about how the pages are related to each other and work out what pages a visitor might want to see next.

Visitors can be divided into two types: those who are looking for specific information, and those who just want to look round. The site must provide links to suit both.

A site can use either, or both, of these linking styles:

- **Linking by structure.** The website may naturally fall into a number of main sections, and links to the first page in each section should be given in the main navigation bar. This bar should be visible on every page on the site. Each section may then have its own secondary navigation bar. Each page should always carry a link back to the home page, and this is usually included in the main navigation bar.

- **Linking by theme.** Not all sites can be as tightly structured as others. The Web allows visitors to browse to any page they like and in any order they like, so it is sometimes helpful to provide links to other pages that cover similar topics. Linking by theme helps the visitor who just wants to surf.

### External links

One of the great advantages of the Web is that it allows websites to provide links to other related sites. External links like these help to join all the sites on the Web into one vast network.

Some very useful websites are specifically designed to provide lists of external links arranged by subject matter – these are known as portal sites.

However, some sites, especially commercial ones, would prefer visitors to stay on their site, so they give few, if any, external links.

## Hotspots

A large image can be placed on a web page, which has within it a number of spots that act as links. An image like this is known as an image map and the spots as hotspots. Hotspots can be used for geographical maps, but they can also be used as graphical navigation bars.

## Further research – hotspots on a map

On the website shown in Figure 4.6 each spot on the map is a separate link to the relevant page about that location. Notice that when the mouse points to a spot it also shows a text label. Can you find similar hotspots on other websites?

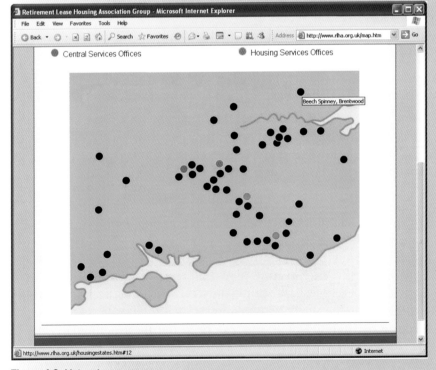

**Figure 4.6** *Hotspots on a map*

## Download speeds

When we use a computer graphic we can refer to its size in two senses:

- **The memory needed to store the image.** Most computer graphics use a very large amount of memory. For example, a photograph taken with a digital camera will be 2MB or more. On a slow connection, a picture this size could take half an hour or more to download from the Internet!

- **The dimensions of the image measured in pixels.** Images are composed of many tiny spots of colour known as pixels. The width and height of an image are measured in pixels. It is very important that, when you create an image for a web page, you make it exactly the right size for the space it is going to occupy. This ensures that it has no more pixels than it really needs.

Because of the size problems, all images used on websites are stored in a compressed format:

- **jpg** – used mainly for photos and to give photorealistic quality
- **gif** – used for most other images, but limited to 256 different colours
- **png** – a new format, which is gradually replacing gif.

The gif format usually takes up far less memory than the jpg format.

Compression reduces significantly the amount of memory needed to store an image of given dimensions.

You can check the size of an image on a web page by right-clicking on it and selecting *Properties*. See Figure 4.7. In this example, the image has been saved in compressed jpg format. The memory required is 28,406 bytes (around 26 KB) and the dimensions are 617 pixels wide by 500 pixels high.

**Figure 4.7** *The properties of an image on a web page*

## Interactive features

### Email links

An email link enables the visitor to send an email directly to the organisation. When the visitor clicks on it, a *New Message* window is opened in the visitor's email client software, such as Outlook or Outlook Express.

### Registration login

A number of sites ask the visitor to sign in before they can access some pages on the site. On an e-commerce site, the organisation will need the name and address of the visitor if they choose to make a purchase. On other sites, the pages can be personalised to suit the visitor's interests. If a site encourages contributions from visitors in a discussion forum or chat room then they do need to identify the visitor, who can be barred if they make unsuitable contributions. In all cases, personal data should be transmitted securely, which usually means that the data has been encrypted (i.e. turned into a secret code).

# Design

Websites should always be designed before they are created. It may be tempting to get started on the creation of a site straightaway, but changes to the fundamental design can result in many hours of extra work, which could have been avoided if the design had been sorted out first.

If you are creating a website for a client then you need to discuss their requirements with them. For assessment purposes you will be asked to develop a website to meet a particular purpose. This could be based on an idea suggested by your tutor, or you could suggest one yourself. The important thing is to ensure that the requirements of the client (real or imaginary) are set out before you begin. At the end of your project you should review your website by comparing it with the initial requirements.

## Tools

A number of techniques, including storyboards and prototypes, are used at the design stage.

### Storyboards

A **storyboard** is a series of pictures of what the site will look like. It is usually sketched by hand on paper. It can then be checked with the client to make sure that it matches what they need.

The storyboard should indicate:

- layout of the home page and other pages
- links on the main navigation bar
- use of colour for background and text
- use of images for information and decoration.

The storyboard should be reviewed with the client. This discussion will often highlight things that were forgotten in earlier discussions or that were not clearly described. At this stage, the client will often be inspired with new ideas for the site and these can also be included.

### Sample pages

A **prototype** is a set of sample pages from the site which can be used to check whether the design works and pleases the client. The prototype will normally consist of the home page plus a small number of indicative pages.

Once the client has agreed on the prototype, the remaining pages can then be created in full.

## House style

Most organisations have rules about how their communications should look. They may specify:

- a logo to be used on all letters, leaflets and adverts
- where the logo should be positioned and what size it should be

- what colours can be used for background, text and as highlights
- what font styles and font sizes should be used
- where elements of the text should be placed, e.g. in a letter, where the date should appear
- level of language
- designs of signs placed on buildings
- styles used within a shop, e.g. designs of carrier bags, direction signs and display cards.

All this, taken together, is known as the house style for that organisation.

House styles are used because they help to create an impression of the organisation. An organisation may want to appear professional, technical, environmentally friendly, family orientated, international, local, approachable, efficient etc. The impression they create is known as the **corporate image**.

## Further research – house styles

Visit the websites of some well known shops. Have they successfully used a house style on the website that matches the one used in the shops?

# Interactivity

One of the advantages of websites over many other forms of communication lies in their interactivity. Visitors do not simply look and read, but also respond in some way to the content.

## User input

The visitor can interact with a website using the keyboard or the mouse.

Here are some interactive actions that visitors can do:

- select the pages they want to view, either via the navigation links or using a search tool
- log in to access extra features
- enter information in a form
- select and purchase goods
- send an email
- post a comment to an online forum or chatroom
- answer a quiz or survey
- play a game.

## Underpinning database

Databases can be used to support a website in a number of ways. This is most obvious when you visit the website for a large supermarket chain.

You might imagine that a web designer has individually created every one of the pages that you see displayed, but in fact most of the pages will be generated on demand.

A database will hold all the information about each of the items for sale. The web designer will have designed the overall look of the page and then created the code that calls up the right data from the database.

A visitor to the site will be able to search the database by typing in keywords, and the results will be displayed on a web page that is automatically created.

The people who maintain the database do not have to be web designers. The database may also be the one used by the shops, displaying data on the point-of-sale terminals.

## Form design

Many websites encourage visitors to leave information on an online form. Several different types of response boxes can be used on a form:

- **text field** – this can hold a single line of text
- **text area** – this can hold longer pieces of text
- **radio buttons** – the visitor can select one from a number of choices
- **check boxes** – the visitor can select as many as they like from a number of choices
- **select fields** – the visitor can select from a drop-down list of options.

See Figures 4.8 and 4.9.

At the end of the form there will be an action button, often labelled 'Submit'. The coding for this button carries out the next action, which may store the data in a database or convert it into an email.

**Figure 4.8** *Text fields and a text area in a form*

**Figure 4.9** *Fields, radio buttons and check boxes on a survey form*

## Test your knowledge

8   List all the factors that affect how long it takes for an image on a website to download.

9   Why might you want to use a text link instead of an image link (button)?

10   What is a storyboard? Why should you create and use one?

11   What is a prototype?

12   Why do commercial companies want to keep a consistent house style for all their communications, including the website?

13   Give four situations where interactive features on a website can be of benefit to an organisation.

# Create a multiple page website

## Web development software

This section introduces you to the general principles of constructing a website. These principles should be useful whichever software you are using. The case studies in this section provide a short tutorial in the use of Microsoft FrontPage. If you are using a different package then you should check the Help file on your software or visit its associated website. There are also many tutorials available on the Web.

Web pages are created in the computing language HTML. But you do not need to learn HTML in order to create a website.

Many websites are created using specialist web authoring software packages. These let you create a web page in much the same way as you would create a document in a word processing or desktop publishing package. The web authoring software then generates the HTML for you. You are free to look at the HTML code at any time, and to change it or add to it directly. But it is perfectly possible to create a straightforward website, which meets its purpose, without knowing any HTML.

### Specialist software

There are a number of useful web authoring packages available, such as Microsoft FrontPage and Macromedia Dreamweaver.

You can use a web authoring package in three different ways:

- **Using templates and wizards.** A number of templates and wizards can be used to create web pages. Although some of the results can be quite pleasing, you will find them rather limiting. Websites produced in this way are difficult to modify and update, and they do look very similar to each other.

  You may enjoy looking at some of these templates for ideas for websites of your own, but you are advised **not** to use them for completing your assessment tasks.

  Although templates and wizards produce immediate results, you will not learn a great deal about web development by using them, and you will not be able to adapt them easily to your needs.

- **Writing HTML code directly.** Professional web developers often work directly in HTML. Some of the advanced features of websites can only be created in this way. This is recommended only if you already have considerable experience in web design. However, you will be learning how to read the HTML code and making some minor changes to it.

- **Using the page design mode.** This is by far the best tool for a beginner to use. At first you will use it to create page layouts in much the same way as you would use presentation or desktop publishing software. As you develop your skills you will be able to read and edit the HTML that the software generates, and will be able to view the effects immediately.

In this unit all the case studies will be based on Microsoft FrontPage 2002, also known as FrontPage XP. Similar features will be found in later versions of FrontPage, and also in other web authoring packages.

## How to –

### Start a web in FrontPage

You are going to create a website for a small specialist shop, called Keiss Designs, who sell traditional handmade knitwear from a remote island in Scotland. You could, of course, decide on your own subject.

In FrontPage each website that you create is stored on your system in a separate web folder. FrontPage refers to these as webs.

■ Launch FrontPage. To the right of the window you will see the task pane (Figure 4.10) with a heading New Page or Web. If you cannot see this, then go to *File / New / Page or Web*.

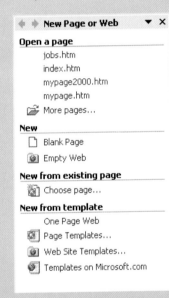

Figure 4.10 *The task pane*

■ In the task pane, select *Web Site Templates*.

■ In the Website Templates dialogue box, click on *One Page Web*.

■ To the right you will see a text box in which you can specify the location of the new web (see Figure 4.11). Click inside the text box and you will see the path. The default location for all FrontPage webs is in a folder called *My Webs*. The default name for a web folder is '*mywebnn*' but you should change this to a meaningful name, such as 'keiss'. FrontPage will create the folder for you when you click on OK.

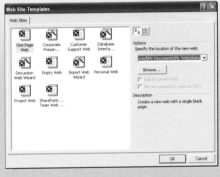

**Figure 4.11**
*Creating a new web in FrontPage*

■ You should see the *Views* bar on the left side of the window. If you cannot see this, then click on *Views bar* in the *Views* menu.

■ In the *Views* bar you will be using the *Page view* and the *Folders view*. Click on *Folders*.

■ You will now see what FrontPage has created (Figure 4.12). It contains:

  a. a folder called *_private* that is used by FrontPage

  b. a folder called *images*, where all the graphics will be stored

  c. a page called *index.htm*.

You can close a web folder by selecting *Close Web* from the *File* menu or by simply exiting from FrontPage. To open a web folder, select *Open Web* from the *File* menu,

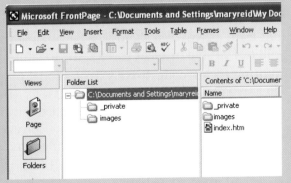

**Figure 4.12** *Folders view of the new web*

All web pages are saved with either *.htm* or *.html* as the filename extension. Web authoring packages will usually allow you to display the page in three modes:

- *Normal* – this is the page editor
- *HTML* – this is the HTML editor
- *Preview* – this lets you check what the page will look like in a browser.

You can also check the final appearance of a page in a normal browser, such as Internet Explorer or Netscape. There are some differences in the way different browsers (and different versions of the same browser) interpret HTML code, so it is important to check web pages in a range of standard browsers before they are published. We will cover this under 'Format and edit web pages' later.

The first page that your visitor will see is the page called *index.htm* or *index.html*. This is often known as the home page for the site. Sometimes it is best to create other pages before creating the index page.

## How to –

### Create a page

The web will have four pages:

- *index.htm* – the index (or home) page, which will be a graphical welcome page
- *about.htm* – a page describing the company
- *products* – a page listing the products that the company sells
- *contact.htm* – a page with information about how to contact the company.

You will create the index page last.

- Make sure you still are in *Folders* view.
- Select *File / New / Page or Web*, then select *Blank Page* from the task pane.
- A new page appears in the folders list. Click on its name and rename it *about.htm*.
- Double click on *about.htm* and it will open in *Page View*.
- Type in some text, as you would in a word processor.

FrontPage, like most web authoring packages, will allow you to display the page in three modes, which you switch between at the bottom of the window:

- *Normal* (page editor)

- *HTML*
- *Preview*.

You create the page in Normal mode, then you can check what it will look like when displayed by a browser in the Preview mode (Figure 4.13). At this stage they will look very similar, but differences will emerge as you use more advanced features. Notice that the text wraps at the end of lines, just as it does in a word processor.

Save the page by clicking on the *Save* button.

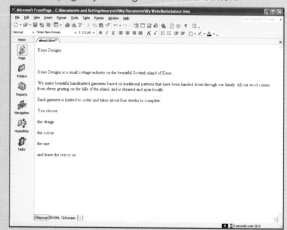

**Figure 4.13** *Entering text in Normal (page editor) mode in FrontPage*

## Embedded facility in other packages

You can find web templates and wizards in a number of Microsoft products, such as Word or Publisher. You can also convert documents created in Adobe PageMaker into web pages.

This can be useful for creating quick pages, especially for creating sample pages to illustrate your initial ideas. However, you are advised not to use any of these methods for serious web development, or for assessment on this course.

## Other software used in web design

Some websites make very good use of animation. Animations are short movies that use images and diagrams rather than photographs. Animation can be used:

- as an introductory sequence
- as a short film to educate or demonstrate
- as a decorative feature.

Most website animations will have been developed in Macromedia Flash or similar software. These software packages allow you to select images, then move them around the screen and apply effects such as fading.

If an animation sequence is used as an introduction to the site then returning visitors may not want to watch it again. They should always be offered the option of skipping the sequence.

## Further research – use of animation

Find a website that uses animation. Does it enhance the website, or does it irritate the visitor? Look for good and bad examples of animation.

## Use of HTML

Web authoring software always includes an HTML editor. You can switch between the page editor and the HTML editor at any time. It is possible to write HTML code in any text editor, such as Notepad. Before web authoring software was introduced, web designers created web pages by writing the code directly. They would then have to save the file and open it in a browser to see what it looked like.

The HTML code for the page shown in Figure 4.13 looks like this:

```
<html>
<head>
<meta http-equiv="Content-Language"
content="en-gb">
<meta http-equiv="Content-Type" content="text/
html; charset=windows-1252">
```

```
<meta name="GENERATOR" content="Microsoft
FrontPage 5.0">
<meta name="ProgId" content="FrontPage.Editor.
Document">
</head>
<body>
<p>Keiss Designs</p>
<p> </p>
<p>Keiss Designs is a small cottage industry on
the beautiful Scottish island of Keiss.</p>
<p>We make beautiful handknitted garments based
on traditional patterns that have been handed
down through our family. All our wool comes
from sheep grazing on the hills of the island,
and is sheared and spun locally.</p>
<p>Each garment is knitted to order and takes
about four weeks to complete.</p>
<p>You choose</p>
<p>the design</p>
<p>the colour</p>
<p>the size</p>
<p>and leave the rest to us.</p>
</body>
</html>
```

The markup codes placed between triangular brackets are called tags. Tags are not case sensitive. Most tags come in pairs – the start tag (e.g. <p>) and the end tag (e.g. </p>).

This is the overall structure of the HTML code:

```
<html>
<head>
</head>
<body>
</body>
</html>
```

The HTML code is divided into two sections. The head section holds information about the web page; lines placed between the head tags are hidden from the visitor, but contain information used by browsers and search engines. The body section holds the actual contents of the web page.

- <html> and </html> mark the beginning and end of the page
- <head> and </head> mark the beginning and end of the head section
- <body> and </body> mark the beginning and end of the body section
- <p> and </p> mark the beginning and end of a paragraph
-   is a non-breaking space and is the code for a normal space.

# Format and edit web pages

## Fonts and text formatting features

You will want to add variety to your page by using different font styles.

But a word of warning: a visitor's browser will only be able to display a font that is already resident on their computer. So although you may want to use an attractive but obscure font for a heading, the visitor will be able to see the characters displayed in the font only if they already have the font installed. If they do not have the required font then the browser will display the text in the default font for that browser; on a Microsoft Windows system the default font is normally Times New Roman, but the user can change the default font to whatever they wish.

To begin with you would be wise to stick to Times New Roman, Arial or other widely used fonts.

You can format text styles in much the same way as you would in a word processor. Your package probably offers a *Format Font* function which shows you all the options you can use.

How to –

### *Use text formatting options*

- If the web is closed, open it using *Open Web* in the *File* menu. Click on *Folders View* and double-click on the *about.htm page* to open it in *Page View*.

- Highlight the heading. On the *Formatting* toolbar, use the *Font*, *Font Size*, and *Font Color* buttons to format the text.

- Highlight other sections of text and format those.

- Use the *Bullets* button in the toolbar to create bulleted text.

- Use the alignment buttons as you would in a word processor.

- Do not forget to save your page. See Figure 4.14 for the result.

**Figure 4.14** *A formatted page*

This is the HTML code for the body of the page shown in Figure 4.14:

```
<body>
<p align="center"><font color="#009900" size="7"
face="Verdana"><b>Keiss Designs</b></font></p>
<p> </p>
<p><font color="#009900" size="5"
face="Verdana"><b>Keiss Designs</b></font>
<font color="#800000" face="Arial" size="4">is a
small cottage industry on the beautiful Scottish
island of Keiss.</font></p>
<p><font color="#800000" face="Arial" size="4">We
make beautiful handknitted garments based on
traditional patterns that have been handed down
through our family. All our wool comes from sheep
grazing on the hills of the island, and is
sheared and spun locally.</font></p>
<p><font color="#800000" face="Arial"
size="4">Each garment is knitted to order and
takes about four weeks to complete.</font></p>
<p><font color="#800000" face="Arial"
size="4">You choose</font></p>
<ul>
  <li><font color="#800000" face="Arial"
size="4"><b>the design</b></font></li>
  <li><font color="#800000" face="Arial"
size="4"><b>the colour</b></font></li>
  <li><font color="#800000" face="Arial"
size="4"><b>the size</b></font></li>
</ul>
<p><font color="#800000" face="Arial"
size="4">and leave the rest to us.</font></p>
</body>
```

- <font> includes all the font properties that apply up to the next </font> tag
- <b> and </b> mark the beginning and end of bold text
- <ul> and </ul> mark the beginning and end of an unnumbered list
- <li> and </li> mark the beginning and end of a line in a list.

Note the American spellings of the words 'center' and 'color'.

The *Preview* mode in FrontPage lets you check how the page will appear eventually. But it is always useful to view it in a browser, to see it as a visitor would see it.

## How to –

### View a page in a browser

- Open your page in FrontPage. If you make any changes to it, you should save the page again before viewing it in a browser.

- In the *File* menu select *Preview in Browser*. The *Preview in Browser* dialogue box (Figure 4.15) lists any browsers on your system that have already been identified to FrontPage.

- If no browsers are shown, or you want to use a different one from those listed, click on *Add* then browse to the program file for the browser you want to use.

- Select the browser from those listed in the *Preview in Browser* dialogue box. Select the window size that you want to use, then click *Preview*.

- The browser window opens with your page displayed.

**Figure 4.15** *Preview in Browser dialogue*

## Lines and backgrounds

A **horizontal line** can be added to the page, usually using the *Insert* menu on the web authoring package. The tag for this is simply <hr>, for horizontal rule, and there is no end tag in this case.

The **colour of the background** can be changed, usually through a *Page Properties* dialogue. Most web authoring packages offer a palette of colours. The HTML adds the 'bgcolor' attribute to the <body> tag.

```
<body bgcolor="#FFFF00">
```

- **bgcolor** gives the background colour, with the value expressed as a six digit hexadecimal code, e.g. #FFFF00, as an RGB code, e.g. rgb(255, 255, 0) or as a standard colour word, e.g. yellow.

- **background** gives the location and name of the image that is used for the background.

## How to –

### Add lines and a background

- In *Normal* mode, use *Insert / Horizontal Line* to add a standard grey line that extends across the page.

- A horizontal line is an object on a web page. You can change the properties of most objects by right-clicking. In this case, right-click on the line and select *Horizontal Line Properties*. In the dialogue you can change the colour and height (thickness) of the line.

- To change the colour of the background, select *Format / Background*. Under *Colors*, select a new background colour.

- See Figure 4.16 for both these effects.

**Figure 4.16** *Background colour and horizontal line inserted*

## Using graphics

Images viewed on web pages are stored as independent files. This means that when a page is downloaded into a browser, the browser then has to download each of the image files from the server as well. So all the image files that are used on a web page are stored on the server alongside the page files.

It is common practice to store all the images on a website in a folder called *images*. A web authoring package always provides a means of inserting images on a page, usually from an *Insert* menu.

Images on a web page should be in jpg or gif format, which are both compressed formats. If you want to use an image that is in uncompressed bitmap (*.bmp*) format, then you have two options: you can use graphics software to save an image in one of these formats; alternatively, web authoring software like FrontPage will convert it for you when you save the page.

In FrontPage you can resize an image directly on the page, but you must resample it to save it again at its new dimensions. This ensures that the image file is no larger than it needs to be.

## How to –

### Add a photograph

To do this activity you need a photo that is in jpg format, and that has already been reduced to the right size for the page.

- Open the page you were working on before in *Normal* mode.

- Place the cursor at the point where you want an image to appear, then select *Insert*, then *Picture*, then *From File*. You will have to click on the folder icon in the dialogue box in order to navigate to the location where the image is stored on your system. The image should appear on the page, as in Figure 4.17.

- Save the page. FrontPage prompts you to save the image as well, with the dialogue shown in Figure 4.18. FrontPage has already created an images folder for you. The image should be saved in the images folder, so if *images/* does not appear in the *Folder* field, click on *Change Folder* and open the images folder.

A word of warning: when you are working in FrontPage, do not use Windows Explorer to copy images directly into the *images* folder. You have to find them elsewhere, insert them on your page, then allow FrontPage to place them in the *images* folder.

**Figure 4.17** *An image inserted on to a web page*

**Figure 4.18** *Saving an image for a web page*

You can make images smaller using the image manipulation features of FrontPage. Although you can also make images larger, they will not look good, as they will lose their definition.

You can also move a picture to its exact position on the page.

## How to –

### Make an image smaller in FrontPage

For this activity you can use a photo that is too large to fit in the page.

- Insert a photo on the web page as before.

- Resize the image by dragging on the corner handles. If you drag on one of the side handles, the image will be squashed in one direction only. If you drag on one of the corner handles, the image will get smaller but still keep the same proportions.

- Click on the image, and the *Pictures* toolbar will appear (Figure 4.19).

- Click on the *Resample* button (Figure 4.20) in the *Pictures* toolbar. Not only does this reduce the size of the image file but it also improves the appearance of the image.

- Save the page. The *Save Embedded Files* dialogue window will appear. The name of the images folder should appear under *Folder*. As before, if the word *images/* does not appear under *Folder*, then click on *Change Folder*, and select the *images* folder.

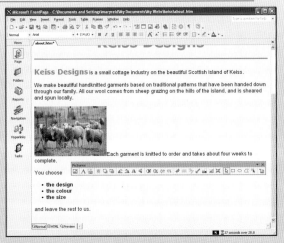

**Figure 4.19** *Resizing an image in FrontPage*

You can check which image files have been saved by clicking on the *images* folder in the *Folders* list.

**Figure 4.20** *The Resample button*

## How to –

### Move an image to its exact position

- Click on the photo.

- In the *Pictures* toolbar click on the *Position Absolutely* button (Figure 4.21).

**Figure 4.21** *The Position Absolutely button*

- Now click on the picture and move it to wherever you want it to be.

- Save the page again and look at it in *Preview* mode. It should now look like Figure 4.22.

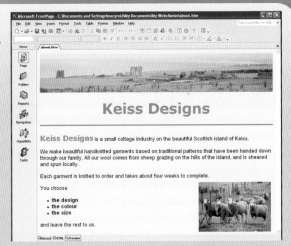

**Figure 4.22** *Resizing and positioning an image*

## Background images

A background image can be applied to a page instead of a background colour, although backgrounds should be chosen carefully, as too much detail can distract the visitor from the text. Backgrounds are automatically tiled (i.e. repeated to fill the space) so quite a small image can be used.

Web authoring packages sometimes provide a selection of background images, which are defined in the HTML like this:

```
<body background="images/ripple.gif">
```

You can also find many sources of copyright-free background images on the Internet. Background images are usually only successful if they are very subtle.

## How to –

### *Add a background image*

You are going to start a new page in the web and give it a background image. You may like to apply the same background to the page you have already created.

- Look at your web in *Folders View*.

- Select *File / New / Page or Web*, then select *Blank Page* from the task pane.

- Rename the page *contact.htm*.

- Double click on the page to open it in *Page View*.

- Select *Insert / Background*.

- In the *Background* dialogue box, under *Formatting* click on *Background Picture*.

- Now click on *Browse* to find the image that you want to use as a background. In the example, we have used a small part of the pattern on one of the garments (Figure 4.23). This is tiled to give the background (Figure 4.24).

**Figure 4.23** *A part of a photo used for a background*

- Most photos used as backgrounds need to be washed out (i.e. made much paler) so they do not dominate the page. FrontPage has a *Wash Out* tool on the *Pictures* toolbar (Figure 4.25).

- In this case, the picture is on the background, so clicking on the page does not bring up the *Pictures* toolbar. Instead select *View / Toolbars / Pictures*.

- In the *Pictures* toolbar, click on the *Color* button, then select *Wash Out* (Figure 4.26).

- Save the page, and save the image as before.

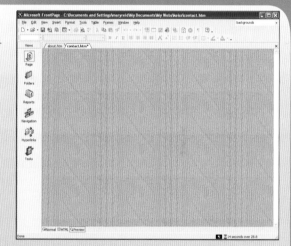

**Figure 4.24** *The photo tiled as a background*

**Figure 4.25** *The Wash Out button*

**Figure 4.26** *A washed out background*

## Hyperlinks

Hyperlinks can be used to link to:

- another position on the same page
- another page on the same website
- another website.

All web authoring packages allow you to convert text into a hyperlink. Usually the *Insert* or *Format* menu includes a *Hyperlink* item which opens up a dialogue.

You can also create links with images.

### Bookmarks

In a browser, a hyperlink can jump to an invisible bookmark placed elsewhere on a page. Using a page editor, bookmarks can be set anywhere on a page. In the HTML code, a bookmark is denoted with the <a> tag – standing for 'anchor' – which has a name attribute to identify it. In this example, a heading with the title 'By post' has been bookmarked so that a hyperlink somewhere else on the page can link to it.

```
<a name="By post">By post</a>
```

The text that is to become the hyperlink is then highlighted and formatted as a link. The HTML code for the hyperlink itself uses the <a> tag again and looks like this:

```
<a href="#By post">Contact us by post</a>
```

- **href**, standing for hyperlink reference, states the location that the hyperlink links to. In this case, 'By post' is the name of the bookmark that it links to, with the # used to identify it as a bookmark.

### Internal links

It is important that all the pages are linked together in some way. In a small website this usually means that each page is linked from each of the others. In a larger site you have to adopt one or other of the linking styles that were discussed on page 133.

The HTML code for a link to a page called *contact.htm* looks like this:

```
<a href="contact.htm">Contact us</a>
```

### External links

On the Web, the links between pages create one vast global network. An individual site will ensure that the visitor explores what the site has to offer by offering internal links to other pages on the same site, as well as external links to other sites.

A hyperlink can also link to a page in another website. In that case the full web address must be given:

```
<a href="http://www.1xtra/hiphop/">1Xtra Hip Hop</a>
```

## How to –

### Create links to bookmarks

- On the new page that you created, set up three sections, one for each of the methods of contact – By post, By email and By phone. Give each section a subheading. The links to these subheadings will be placed at the top of the page.

- To insert a bookmark, highlight the first subheading to be bookmarked (*By post*), then select *Insert / Bookmark*. This gives the bookmark the same name as the subheading. Click *OK*. A bookmark is displayed in *Normal* mode by a dotted underlining (as in Figure 4.27), but is invisible in *Preview* mode.

- Add bookmarks to the other subheadings.

- At the top of the page write 'Contact us by post'. This will act as the link to the first bookmarked subheading.

- Now highlight '*Contact us by post*', then select *Insert / Hyperlink*. In the dialogue box, on the left-hand side, under *Link To:*, click on *Place in this Document*. A list of the bookmarks on the page is given. Select the *By Post* bookmark, as in Figure 4.28.

- Add the text for the remaining links. Add the remaining hyperlinks.

- Now fill in the address and phone number in the relevant sections. We will be adding an email later.

- Try out the links in *Preview* mode (Figure 4.29).

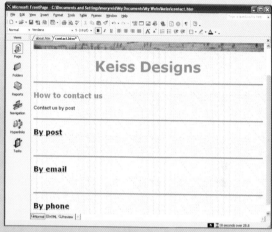

**Figure 4.27** *Creating a bookmark*

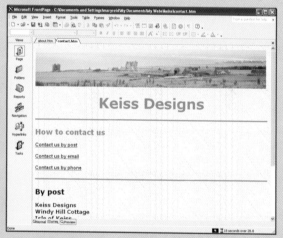

**Figure 4.28** *Setting up the link to a bookmark*   **Figure 4.29** *Links to bookmarks*

## How to –

### Add internal hyperlinks

- Close any pages that are open, then open the *about.htm* page in *Normal* mode.

- Write the text that is going to be used to link to the *contact.htm* page.

- Highlight the link text and select *Insert / Hyperlink*.

- In the dialogue box, check that *Existing File or Web Page* is selected in the left-hand column, under *Link To:*.

- Click on the name of the page. It will appear in the *Address* box. Click *OK* (Figure 4.30).

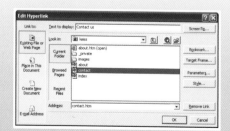

**Figure 4.30** *Creating an internal link*

Links to other sites can be added to any web page. Some sites provide no external links at all, because they do not want the visitor to leave the site once there. On the other hand, some sites contain very many links to other sites; where that is the main purpose, they are known as portal sites.

## How to –

### Add external hyperlinks

- Open the *about.htm* page in *Normal* mode.
- Highlight some of the text that is going to be used as a link.
- Select *Insert / Hyperlink*.
- In the *Address* box, enter the full address of the website, including the http://. For this example, it doesn't matter which website you link to.

- Alternatively, click on the *Browse the Web* button (to the right of the *Look in:* box), and find the correct website with your browser. When you switch back to FrontPage, the web address will be entered in the box.

### Email links

A hyperlink can also be used to send an email:

```
<a href="mailto://myname@example.com">Email me</a>
```

When this hyperlink is clicked, a new email window opens in the visitor's email client software, with the email address in the recipient field.

## How to –

### Add an email link

- Enter suitable text, such as 'Email Keiss Designs', in the *By email* section. Highlight the text, and then select *Insert / Hyperlink*.
- Under *Link To:* select *Email address*.

- In the *Email address:* box type in the email address.
- Use *Preview* mode to check that the link works correctly.

## Editing images

Normally you should manipulate images (change size, colours etc.) in a graphics package. FrontPage does have some simple image manipulation features built-in, but they have to be used with some care.

Most clip art, and many other images, have a white background, so the image look can look very odd on pages with coloured backgrounds.

You can make the background of the gif format images transparent so that the background colour of the page shows through. You can do this in any graphics package that generates gifs. Some web authoring packages allow you to do this to the image directly on the page.

How to –

### Use image manipulation in FrontPage

You can add clip art to a web page. In this case we will add a phone image next to the phone number.

- Click on the page where you want the clip art to appear. Select *Insert* then *Picture* then *Clip Art*, then choose the clip art image that you want. It will be inserted on the page.

The clip art image will probably have to be changed before it is right for your page (see Figure 4.31).

- Click on the image, and the *Pictures* toolbar will appear at the bottom of the window.

- You can use the buttons on the *Pictures* toolbar to rotate or flip the image. You can also change the brightness and contrast of the colours. Pass your mouse over the buttons on the toolbar to see what each one does.

- If you want to go back to the original drawing, click on the *Restore* button.

In this example, the background of the image is white and does not look right against the patterned image of the page background.

- Click on the image then click on the *Set Transparent Color* button in the *Pictures* toolbar. If the image was not already in gif format, you will

**Figure 4.31** *Clip art inserted on the page, with the Pictures toolbar*

get a message asking if it can be changed into a gif – click on *OK*. Chose the colour that you want to make transparent.

- If necessary, reduce the image as before, then click on the *Resample* button.

- Save the page. The image will be saved in the correct format. See Figure 4.32.

**Figure 4.32** *The clip art image after manipulation*

## Formatting layout

You can insert an image on a web page, but you will soon realise that it is not always easy to arrange items on the page where you would like them to be.

There are several ways of controlling the layout of text and images, including:

- using the picture properties
- using a table.

### Picture properties

Every image on a web page has a number of properties. These include the alignment of the image (left or right), the thickness of the border, and the horizontal spacing (to the sides) and vertical spacing (above and below) around it. The border and spacing properties are measured in pixels.

The width and height of the image are also properties. Do not use the picture properties to change the width or height properties of the image. If you want to change the size of an image then go back to your graphics software, or use the resampling facility in FrontPage, which was described earlier.

Once an image has been placed on a page, the HTML coding includes an <img> tag, such as:

```
<img border="0" src="images/sheep.jpg"
width="248" height="166">
```

Border, source (src), width and height are all **attributes** of the <img> tag. Attributes are HTML's way of listing the properties of the image.

- **src** is the filename of the image and its location relative to the page.
- **width** and **height** are the dimensions of the image in pixels; altering these values will distort the image but will not change the memory needed.

Images cannot be manipulated as simply as they can in DTP packages, but further attributes can be added to the <img> tag. Most web authoring packages provide an *Image properties* dialogue, usually accessed by right-clicking the image in *Page edit* mode, and this generates more attributes, such as:

```
<img border="2" src="images/sheep.jpg"
width="248" height="166" alt="Sheep on the
Island of Keiss">
```

- **border** values greater than zero draw a border around the image, with the given thickness measured in pixels.
- **alt** text appears as a screen label in a browser, when the mouse is held over an image (see Figure 4.33). This acts as a marker, if an image is slow to download, and it also provides a useful description to the visitor. Alt text is essential to make a site accessible to visually impaired visitors who use text readers to understand the content.

 How to –

## *Change the image properties*

- In *Normal* mode, right-click on an image and select *Picture Properties*. Any changes that you make to the properties of an image will be listed as <img> attributes in the HTML code.

- In the *Picture Properties* dialogue box, enter some descriptive text in the *Alternative Representations* text box. This is the 'alt' text for the image.

- Next, click on the *Appearance* tab. Do not alter the size properties, but alter the border thickness. All the values are in pixels.

- View the page in *Preview* mode. It should look like Figure 4.33.

**Figure 4.33** *Using the picture properties*

## Tables

Tables can be created on a web page, just as they can in a word processor. A table can be used for tabulation – to display data in boxes in the traditional way – but they are more commonly used on web pages as a way of arranging text and images on screen.

Web authoring packages provide dialogues for creating tables, usually from a *Table* menu.

It is useful to see how the HTML handles tables and their properties. The HTML code for a table has this basic structure:

```
<table>
  <tr>
    <td> </td>
    <td> </td>
  </tr>
  <tr>
    <td> </td>
    <td> </td>
  </tr>
  <tr>
    <td> </td>
    <td> </td>
  </tr>
</table>
```

This table consists of three rows each with a <tr> tag. Each row has two cells each with a <td> tag (for table data).

The table tag for the table in Figure 4.35 has these attributes:

```
<table border="1" cellpadding="5"
cellspacing="0">
```

- **border** fixes the thickness in pixels of the border around the perimeter of the whole table.
- **cellpadding** fixes the space in pixels between the border and the text.
- **cellspacing** is the space between one cell in the table and the next.

If the border is given a value of zero then the borders of all the cells disappear. This can be used to create an invisible structure for laying out items on a web page.

## How to –

### Create a table to display data

You can now create the Products page, which will hold information about the items that the company sells. You can copy the heading and background from the previous page.

- Look at your web in *Folders View*. Click once on *contact.htm*, then copy and paste the page.
- Rename the new page *products.htm*.
- Double-click on the page to open it in *Page view*. Delete any text and images that you do not need. Add any new text. You will add the images later.
- Click on the page where you want the table to appear.
- Select *Table*, then *Insert*, then *Table*.
- In the *Table* dialogue box, enter 3 as the number of rows, 2 as the number of columns.
- Set the *Alignment* to *Center*. Enter 1 as the border size and 5 as the cell padding. At this stage do not specify the width of the table, and leave the tick box blank (see Figure 4.34).
- An outline of the table appears on the page. Enter data in the table, as shown in Figure 4.35.
- Save the page.
- You can alter the alignment within each cell by right-clicking on it and seleting *Cell Properties*.

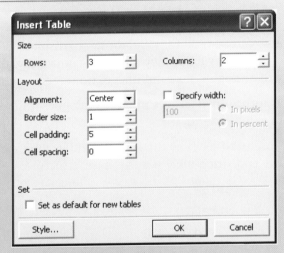

**Figure 4.34** *Setting up a table*

**Figure 4.35** *Inserting a table*

Individual cells in a table also have their own properties. Text and images can be aligned within each cell.

## Editing HTML

Throughout this section you have been shown the HTML code that is generated by the software. You can switch to the HTML editor at any time and modify the code. Each time you make a small change, switch to the preview mode to check that the page looks as intended. Save the page frequently.

One simple change that can be made is to add alt text to an image.

The code

```
<img border="0" src="images/keiss.JPG"
width="800" height="128">
```

can be changed to

```
<img border="0" src="images/keiss.JPG" alt="The
Island of Keiss" width="800" height="128">
```

by simply inserting the text in the HTML editor.

## Advanced techniques

### Buttons

An image can be used as a button instead of text for any of these links. The code will look like this:

```
<a href="news.htm"><img border="0" src="images/
newsbutton.gif" width="120" height="30">Latest
news</a>
```

If you have a suitable image, you can insert it on the page, then click on it and insert a hyperlink, just as you would for a text link.

Web authoring software usually provides tools that make it easy for you to create image buttons.

It is sometimes difficult to see which images on a web page act as buttons. To make this easier, a hover button is one that changes its appearance when the mouse moves over it.

## How to –

### Create buttons

The internal links that you have created so far look like those in Figure 4.35. FrontPage provides a tool to help you create hover buttons instead.

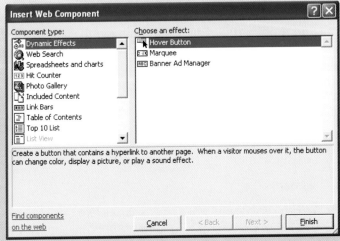

- Close all the pages, then open one of them. In *Normal* view, click where you would like to place a hover button.

- Select *Insert / Web Component*. In the dialogue box select *Dynamic Effects* on the left and *Hover Button* on the right (Figure 4.36). Click on *Finish* to open the *Hover Button Properties* dialogue.

- In the *Button text* box enter the text that will appear on the button on the first line. Then click on the *Font* button to format the font.

**Figure 4.36** *Creating a hover button*

- In the *Link to:* box enter the name of the page that you want the button to link to, including *.htm*, or click on the *Browse* button to find the right page (Figure 4.37).

- Make your choice of colours and effects. Click on *OK*.

- To see how the button works, first save the page, then select *File / Preview in Browser*.

- To make changes to the properties of the hover button, right-click on it in *Normal* mode.

**Figure 4.37** *Setting the properties of a hover button*

- Add more hover buttons to each of the pages. You can arrange these as either a horizontal or vertical navigation bar.

### Thumbnails

A thumbnail is a small image that links to a larger version. Thumbnails are often used to display high-quality photos on a website. The full-size photo may take some time to download, so a smaller image (thumbnail) is displayed on the page and the visitor can then choose whether to download it. Usually the thumbnail acts as a graphical button, and the visitor clicks on it to view the full size image.

FrontPage simplifies the process of creating thumbnails.

## How to –

### Create a thumbnail

You can add thumbnail pictures of products to the products page. You can use a normal-size photo, as FrontPage will create the small thumbnail for you.

First you can create a table to places the images on the page. In this case, we will make the border invisible:

- Click on the products page at the point where you want to insert the table that will hold the images.

- Select *Table / Insert / Table*. In the *Table* dialogue box, enter 1 as the number of rows, 2 as the number of columns.

- Set the *Alignment* to *Center*. Enter 0 as the *Border size* and 20 as the *Cell padding*. Leave the *Width* blank.

- In *Normal* mode, the position of the table is marked by a dotted line. This will not be shown in the browser. Add some text about two products to the cells. Change the cell properties (by right-clicking on a cell) to align the text as you like.

Now you can add a thumbnail.

- Click in the left-hand cell of the table. Select *Insert*, then *Picture*, then *From File*. Click on the folder icon and browse to the location of your photo.

- The full-size photo will eventually be replaced by a thumbnail, and the original photo will be displayed on a separate page. For the moment, the full-size photo appears in the position where the thumbnail will appear, so it may look a little odd. You may need to resize the full-size photo, but this is not necessary if it is already of a size that will fit into a single web page. Resample the photo if you resize it.

- Save the page and the photo before you go on to the next step.

- Click on the photo, then click on the *Auto Thumbnail* button in the *Pictures* toolbar. The full-size photo will be replaced by a thumbnail version.

- Save the page. You will be prompted to save the thumbnail image.

- You can change the appearance of the thumbnail by right-clicking on the image and selecting *Picture Properties*. Do not forget to add some 'alt' text.

- Use *File Preview in Browser*. See Figure 4.38.

- Click on the thumbnail, and the full size image should appear. See Figure 4.39.

**Figure 4.38** *A page with two thumbnails, viewed in a browser*

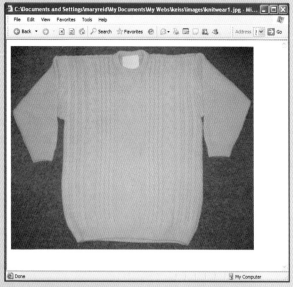

**Figure 4.39** *The full-size photo appears in the browser when the thumbnail is clicked*

# Combining information

On a website, you can use information derived from a number of different sources.

## Using a photo

You can either take a photo with a digital camera or scan in a photo print. These will normally be stored as bitmaps (*.bmp*), which is a non-compressed pixel format.

Sometimes the photos are stored in jpg format, but they will probably not be compressed sufficiently for use on a web page. If you take a photo from a photo CD that was supplied when a film was developed, the images will normally be in jpg format already.

Once you have transferred your photos to your PC, you can load them into a photo manipulation package, such as Microsoft Office Picture Manager, or Adobe PhotoShop.

Photo manipulation packages allow you to alter the colour, brightness and contrast of the picture. You can also crop it, which means cutting away parts of the image to the top, bottom and sides.

You can reduce the dimensions of a photo, which will also reduce the amount of memory that it takes up. For most web uses you will probably want to use a photo that is less than 100 pixels high and 300 wide.

Finally save the photo as a jpg. The package will offer you some choice over the level of compression. A more compressed photo will take up less memory, but will also display less detail. If you are asked to choose the **quality**, select 75%; on the other hand, if you are asked to specify the **degree of compression**, select 25%. These two choices have exactly the same effect as each other, but unfortunately software packages are not consistent in the way they ask the question.

Once you have saved a photo in a compressed jpg or gif format, try not to compress it any further, as you are likely to lose some quality.

Although you can manipulate photos and reduce their size in web authoring software like FrontPage, you will find you have more control over the result if you prepare the photos first in another package. FrontPage will also convert images from bitmap to either jpg or gif formats, but again you have more control if you use a graphics package.

## Using an image created in a graphics package

There are many ways of finding or creating images to use on a website. You can use a simple package such as Microsoft Paint, or a more sophisticated one such as Adobe Illustrator. You will be saving your image eventually in 256 colours as a gif, so you should use only the preset colours that are offered to you.

How to –

## Store and use photos in Windows XP

- Store photos in the *My Pictures* folder on your computer. You can create folders within the main *My Pictures* folder to keep your photos organised.

- You should be able to view all the photos in a folder as thumbnails. If not, then click on the *Views* button in the main toolbar and select *Thumbnails*.

- Pass your mouse over a photo to see its properties. Note the size in KB of any photos that you intend to use on a web page (Figure 4.40).

- Right-click on a photo, select *Open With* and then select *Microsoft Office Picture Manager*. This is a very useful application that offers you all the basic photo manipulation tools.

- In the *Picture Editor*, click on *Edit Pictures* to view the *Edit Pictures* task pane. Experiment with the tools. Try cropping a photo to remove parts that you do not want (Figure 4.41).

- You can zoom in and out of the photo, but this does not change the stored size of the image. To do that, select *Resize* from the *Edit Pictures* task pane. This offers you a number of options, including reducing the image by a fixed percentage, or making it fit inside a space, measured in pixels.

- Always save an amended photo with a new name, as you may want to go back to the original again.

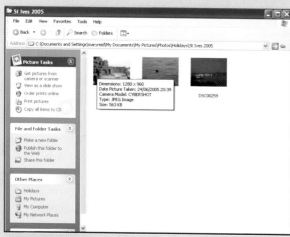

**Figure 4.40** *Using My Pictures in Windows XP*

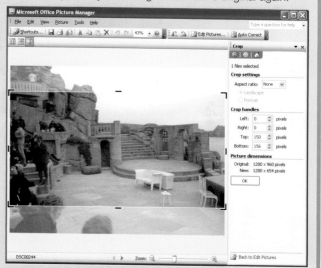

**Figure 4.41** *Using the cropping tool in Microsoft Office Picture Manager*

If you want to create a small image, it is sometimes helpful to design a larger image then reduce it in size. Once you have designed your image you should reduce the dimensions (number of pixels) to the exact ones needed on the web page.

You can also obtain an image from the Web. You should never simply copy images from existing websites, as the images will probably be protected by copyright; fortunately there are many sources of copyright-free web images online. In many cases the creators do ask you to acknowledge the source of any image you use. A search through a search engine will produce a bewildering choice. Go to www.heinemann.co.uk/hotlinks, insert the express code 2048P and click on the link to go to two example sites.

## How to –

### Create a small image for a web page in Microsoft Paint

- Launch Paint.
- Select *Attributes* in the *Image* menu. Set the width and height at 100 pixels by 100 pixels.
- Draw a simple image, like the mobile phone shown in Figure 4.42.
- Select *Stretch and Skew* from the *Image* menu. Reduce both height and width to the same percentage, such as 50%.
- Save the image. In the *Save as Type* box select *256 Colour bitmap*.
- Unlike some graphics packages, Paint does not allow you to make areas of the image transparent. When you insert the image on a page in FrontPage you will be able to make the background transparent and then it will be saved as a gif.
- The image can now be used as a small icon.

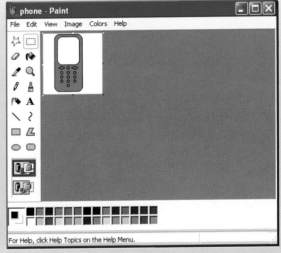

**Figure 4.42** *An image created in Paint*

### Headings

You will remember that you cannot just use any font that takes your fancy, as the characters will only be displayed in the font if the visitor already has that font installed on their system. To get around this problem you can create a heading in a graphics package and save it as an image. You can use any of the fonts that are available on your own system for this. You can also superimpose text on a photo or other graphic. See Figure 4.43 for examples of two alternative graphical heading styles.

**Figure 4.43** *Two alternative graphical heading styles*

### Hotspots (image maps)

You can create hotspots on an image. A hotspot is an area of an image that acts as a hyperlink. An image that has hotspots on it is known as an image map. Image maps can be used as highly graphical navigation bars. They can also be used to help the viewer identify items on a plan or geographical map of an area.

Web authoring packages usually provide an image mapping tool that you can use to develop them.

## How to –

## *Create an image map*

So far you have not used the index page, which is the first page that your visitor will see. You can create a large graphic on this page, which will have hotspots that act as buttons linking to the pages on the site.

- Create the image in Paint or another graphics package. It should be no more than 500 pixels wide. See Figure 4.44.

- Open the index page and insert the image. Save the page and the image.

- Click on the image and find the four hotspot buttons in the *Pictures* toolbar.

- Click on the *Rectangular Hotspot* button. On the map, draw a rectangle around the area that you want to act as a hotspot.

- When you release the mouse button, the *Insert Hyperlink* dialogue window appears. From the list, click on the page that it should link to. See Figure 4.45.

- Although you can see the border of the hotspot in *Normal* mode, it will not be visible in a browser.

- You can now create hotspots for the links to the other two pages.

- When you save the page you will be reminded to save the map in the *images* folder. Click *OK*.

- Select *File / Preview in browser* to check that the image map works correctly.

**Figure 4.44** *An image that can be used as an image map*

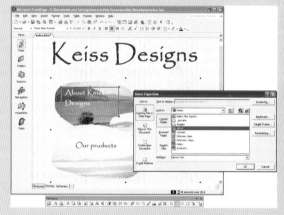

**Figure 4.45** *Creating an image map*

# Checking your website

You should always check a website, both before **and** after publishing it to the Web. Some things can only be checked when the site is online.

Both before and after publishing, check the web pages in a browser, not in the web authoring package that you have been using.

## Images

- Check that each image takes up the amount of space you intended and is positioned correctly.
- Select the properties of each image to check how much memory each uses. Do not forget to include any graphical buttons that you have used. Calculate the total memory used by all the images on each page. Aim to keep the total to under 100 KB per page.

- If you want to use a larger image (for example, if you want to offer your visitor the chance to see a full-size photo) you should warn the visitor before they follow the link that it will be a slow download.
- Check how long it takes to download each page, including all the images. You should, if possible, carry out this test on a number of different computers. In particular, try to check the download times on both slow dialup connections and fast broadband connections. This check can be carried out only after publishing.

## Colours

- Check that the colours of text and images appear as intended. After publishing, you should check this on a number of different computers.
- Try looking at the site on older monitors as well as new ones, on a smaller laptop screen as well as a desktop. If possible, check on screens that have been set to different colour depths.

## Links

- Check that all of the internal links on each of the pages load the correct pages.
- Check that any email links open a *New Message* window addressed to the right email address.
- Check that all external links go to the correct websites.

## Content

- Check that the content is appropriate on each page.
- Check that the text is correctly spelled and is accurate.

## Text

- Check that the text is the right size. You should check this on different browsers and on different sizes of screen.
- Check that you have used fonts that are widely available.

## Formatting

- Check that the contents are laid out as expected in the browser.
- Drag on the corner of the browser window to change its size and check that the page still looks acceptable.

## Reviewing your website

When you have checked your website you should review it. This means that you should go back to the original requirements and check that it meets them. You should ask two questions:

- Is the website appropriate for its purpose and target audience? You should go back to the section on Client Need, on pages 123 to 127, where you were looking at other people's websites. You should now review your work by applying all those questions to your own website.

- Are there any remaining problems? If your review indicated that there are still some problems, or elements missing, then you should list the problems and try to correct them.

Finally, if you were working for a real client, you should ask them to review the website and give you some feedback.

# Publishing a website

Once you have checked your site, you will then want to publish (upload) it so that others can visit it.

## Uploading files

You have two options. You could publish your website to the Web, in which case anyone in the world will be able to view it. Alternatively you could publish it to an intranet, such as one at your centre, which would restrict your visitors to those who have access.

When you upload a web you must transfer all the files and folders that have been created. This means, as a minimum, all the pages themselves and all the images that you have used. Web authoring packages like FrontPage also create additional files that need to be uploaded as well. If you have used FrontPage, in particular, you are advised to use the publishing tool that is included, which can be found in the *File* menu.

### Publishing to the Web

In order to make your website available to everyone on the Web, you publish it to a webserver. A webserver is a computer that is permanently connected to the Internet and which makes your website available to others.

To do this you must have some web space available for your use on a webserver. You will also be given a web address (URL) that identifies the web space.

If you are working on a network at your place of study then the network administrator will provide instructions on how to upload your site to the webserver.

If you are working from a standalone computer at home then your Internet Service Provider (ISP) should be able to offer you web space on their webserver.

Most web authoring packages provide you with a simple tool for uploading the web pages to the webserver. If you are using an HTML editor then you will have to use FTP (File Transfer Protocol) software, which can be downloaded free from a number of sites.

In both cases the following data is needed:

- domain name
- user name (as registered with the ISP)
- user password.

### Publishing to an intranet

Your network administrator will provide you with working space on the intranet, where you will be able to publish your site. You will also be given instructions on how to upload the pages to the site.

## Maintaining content

Few websites are completely static. Most need to be updated from time to time. Sometimes the contents will have to be amended because the organisation wants to give new information to visitors. Often, new pages will be added and links created.

When a website is first developed, the question of maintenance must be discussed and planned. In some cases the website is maintained by the person who designed the website, but often another person is given the task. That person needs to be trained in the use of the software so they can make any updates as they are needed.

## File management

Normally there will always be two copies of your website. One will be the working version on your computer and the other will be on the server where it will be accessible via the Internet or an intranet.

It is important that these two copies are identical. Usually the web authoring software checks for any differences between the two and uploads the latest version of pages. It will notice if files have been deleted or moved and will try to match the server version with the working version.

You can get into a muddle if you try to keep further copies of the site. This could happen if you want to work on your website from home as well as from your place of study.

All web pages should be given suitable filenames. If you are running Windows then you can create lengthy file names. But you should be aware that a server may be using a different operating system, which may not accept longer filenames, or names that include spaces or punctuation. You should check this with your network administrator. It is good practice to use simple short filenames without spaces or punctuation, as these will be acceptable on any server.

It is a good idea to use only lower case letters in a filename. Windows is not case sensitive – in other words, it will recognise the filenames *MyFile.doc* and *myfile.doc* as the same file. But some operating systems on servers are case sensitive, so you would be wise to use only lower case.

You can place web pages into folders (directories), and this is a sensible way of organising a large website. You have already seen that FrontPage places images in an image folder.

# Assessment tasks

The assessment tasks in this unit are based on the following scenario:

*The Big Blue Web Company have employed you as a junior web developer. They ask you to review some of the websites that they have already created for clients, both to check your understanding and to check whether you can suggest any improvements. Once you have demonstrated that you understand website design, you will be asked to create a multi-page website for one of their clients.*

> To work towards a Distinction in this unit you will need to achieve **all** the Pass, Merit and Distinction criteria in the unit and have evidence to show that you have achieved each one.

## How do I provide assessment evidence?

You can present your written findings as a report or using presentation software. You should include screen shots of any websites you refer to. If you make a presentation, include speaker's notes, and print off both slides and notes.

You should also provide evidence of the website that you create. This should also be a report about the creation and testing of your site, illustrated with screen shots and possibly supported by witness statements, observation records, tape or video evidence.

All your evidence should be presented in one folder, which should have a front cover and a contents page. You should divide the evidence into five sections corresponding to the five tasks.

## Task 1 (P1, M1)

The first section of this chapter describes a number of different purposes for which websites are created. Select four of these purposes.

For each:

- give at least one example of a website built for that purpose
- point out and describe the construction features used by each website
- explain how the construction features help the user to find and use the information on each website.

## Task 2 (P2, M2)

Select four websites, all of different types. You can use the websites that you used for Task 1, or you can add in websites that you have created.

- For each website, discuss whether they have achieved what they set out to do, by referring to the design features listed in this chapter. You can include screenshots of the sites to illustrate both good and bad points.
- For at least two of the sites, think about how the sites could be improved. Explain your ideas, using diagrams where appropriate.

## Assessment tasks continued

## Task 3 (P3, D1)

For this task you will create a multipage website. You should design this to match the needs of a client. The requirements will either be given to you by your tutor, or alternatively you can discuss with your tutor the needs of a real client.

- Design your website using the tools given in this chapter.
- Create your website using web authoring software.
- Check your website carefully, and give evidence of all the checks you have carried out.

> To work towards a Distinction you should discuss the construction features that you have used in your website. Explain in detail why you used them.

## Task 4 (P4)

For this task, use the website you created in Task 3.

- Upload the website to the Internet or to an intranet.
- Maintain the website by updating it on a number of occasions. Provide evidence of the website before and after maintenance activities.

## Task 5 (P5, M3, D2)

In this task you will describe some of the things you have learned in this unit. You can present the information in any appropriate way, but ensure that you provide enough printed evidence.

- Describe three different situations where you, as a web designer, could be in breach of the law.
- Many websites are interactive. Explain what this means and show how interactivity can be used on websites. Describe techniques that can be used to provide interactivity. Give examples of all the techniques you describe.

> To work towards a Distinction you should compare the generation of pages using wizards only, with using HTML. You should evaluate the benefits of learning and using HTML as well as the disadvantages.

# 6 Networking Essentials

## About this unit

This unit introduces you to the application of networks in organisations, and how these can enhance the activities carried out in organisations.

You will focus on two aspects: the improvements in communications that networks can bring to an organisation; and the increased efficiency that becomes possible in the use of resources. However, you will also consider the downside of networks: increasing complexity of computer systems; and the increased potential for unauthorised access to information.

You will look at different topologies of networks for both LANs (local area networks) and WANs (wide area networks) and gain an understanding of the function of individual hardware and software components, and how they interconnect within a whole system.

You will also gain some practical experience in setting up a network. This may be limited to the setting up of PC-based networks, but will demonstrate, on a small scale, the operation of all networks and allow you to make practical use of the theory of this unit.

▶ Continued from previous page

# Learning outcomes

When you have completed this unit you will:

**1** understand the use of computer networks

**2** understand the features and services of local and wide area network technologies

**3** understand network hardware and software components and how they are connected and configured

**4** be able to set up and use a simple local area network.

# How this unit will be assessed

This unit is internally assessed. You will provide a portfolio of evidence to show that you have achieved the learning outcomes. The grading grid in the specification for this unit lists what you must do to obtain Pass, Merit and Distinction grades. The section on Assessment Tasks at the end of this chapter will guide you through activities that will help you to be successful in this unit.

# Understand the use of computer networks

Computer networks are used to share information and resources. A network could communicate between two people, or, like the Internet, be accessible to millions of people.

You have most probably used a simple communications network at some stage in your life. A children's toy walkie-talkie (Figure 6.1) and the mobile telephone are both forms of communications network.

Computer networks are made by connecting one computer to another. One way of making the connection between two computers is to use a cable to link them. This is the simplest form of computer network, but they can involve hundreds, thousands, or even millions of connected computers.

If two computers in the same room need to be connected, it would not be a problem to link them using a cable. But if two computers at opposite ends of a country, or even in different countries, need to be connected, it would be impossible to link them using a single cable across so many miles. This is when other connections are needed, such as telephone lines and broadband connections. This unit looks at all the ways of connecting computers.

What does it mean?

*A **network** is a system that allows people to share information with each other.*

**Figure 6.1** *A walkie-talkie can be part of a simple network*

## Communication

Communication is an essential part of the day-to-day running of an organisation. Without the correct communication channels, organisations would find themselves missing information, holding out-of-date information and maybe even losing business opportunities.

Networks aim to help people with much of this communication. If electronic communications are in place, it can help to make communication easier, quicker, more reliable, less expensive and less stressful for those involved. Electronic communications and networks can also save paper, making this a more environmentally friendly method of communicating. For organisations today, a networked system can therefore be invaluable.

## What does it mean?

**Video conferencing** *is a meeting between two or more people where they can see and talk to each other through a computerised video link. The computer screen is the visual link and speakers are used for the sound link. A video camera attached to each computer sends the images through telephone lines, while a microphone captures the sound.*

For example, electronic communications in the form of **video conferencing** can save an organisation both staff time and travelling costs.

## Case study

### *Video conferencing*

Modern Mobiles, a mobile phone company, has offices in Australia, the USA and the UK, and needs to hold a meeting to discuss the launch of a new product: the Roam-a-fone. Each of the offices has a team of six people who have been involved in the design of this new product, and in its promotion, or will be involved in selling it.

Instead of hiring a venue, paying for flights and accommodation and other necessary expenses such

as car hire or meals, the organisation could set up a video conference.

Teams stay in their own countries, but meet at an agreed time in the video conference suite. The video link is then set up so that everyone present can see and hear each other.

This not only saves expense, but also saves time because no time is spent travelling. It can also be easier to set up than a face-to-face meeting.

## What does it mean?

*An* **electronic whiteboard** *is a shared work area in a window on the monitor of a networked computer. It is designed to be used while video or voice contact is taking place. More than one person at a time, in different locations, can see the window and can change drawings or documents that are on view.*

An **electronic whiteboard** can be used in each of the video conference suites so that all those present can look at and work on the same document at the same time. Any relevant documentation, for example an agenda, can also be sent, ahead of time, by email, saving on paper and postage costs.

Communication in an organisation is carried out at two levels: internally and externally.

## Internal communication

Internal communication does not involve any people outside the organisation. It can involve members within the organisation at any level, from a receptionist to a managing director. Internal communication has many uses: exchanges of information or ideas between staff members; internal orders for items such as stationery; meetings within departments to

## What does it mean?

**Internal communication** *is any communication within an organisation.*

discuss issues such as budgets; project meetings involving people from different departments; group presentations to show the latest sales figures; internal telephone calls; posting of company events on a notice board; or chats around the coffee machine.

### Communication between individuals

Individuals within organisations communicate constantly. They may just be having a chat between themselves about the latest sales figures, or it could be that someone in the Personnel department needs to know how many hours someone has worked the week before. Whatever the situation, individual communication happens when just two people are talking or sharing information and ideas.

### Communication within teams of people

In most organisations, teamwork is an important part of the working environment. For example, if an organisation is involved in the manufacture of mobile telephones, a team of people could be working together to design a new phone. This could be known as a 'project team' and it may be that the people within the team are not from the same department, building or even country. Project teams often include people who do not normally work together within an organisation on a day-to-day basis. Many organisations have more than one site in a country. Lots of organisations even have different sites spread around the world. It is important that communications systems are in place to enable these people to get in touch easily and quickly.

### Communication within functional areas

Functional areas need good communications systems to enable them to share information internally, and with other functional areas within the same organisation. For example, if a good communications system has been set up, someone in the Accounts department should be able to access a customer's record easily to see what the customer has ordered (input by the Sales department), whether the customer has received these goods or services ordered (input by the Despatch department), and whether payment has been made (input by the Finance department). This will make sure that the organisation does not wait too long for payment for the goods or services it has provided to that customer.

## External communication

There are lots of reasons why organisations need to communicate with people externally: placing orders with suppliers; taking orders from customers; dealing with government departments, e.g. on tax issues; ensuring the organisation is up to date with new legislation; and keeping an eye on competitors.

### Communication with customers

Good communication with customers is essential. It involves things like contacting the customer to see whether they were happy with goods or services. If customers feel that they are important to an organisation

### What does it mean?

*A* **functional area** *is the overall name given to each of the different departments within an organisation. For example, the Sales department would be the functional area for most jobs to do with sales within that organisation.*

### What does it mean?

**External communication** *is any communication that involves someone inside the organisation being in contact with anyone from outside the organisation.*

they are more likely to buy goods or services from that organisation again. Alternatively, an organisation wants to let their customers know about a special offer.

Whatever the reason for an organisation wanting to communicate with customers, it is important that the communication channels are easily accessible and that all information is up to date. If someone within an organisation were to ring a customer and use the wrong name, it would not be seen as professional. It is likely that the customer would not use that organisation again.

### The importance of public relations

Good public relations are important to organisations. If an organisation has a good reputation with their customers, this helps to ensure that customers trust the organisation and will buy goods or services from them.

If an organisation is easy to contact, has good customer services, and seems to care about their customers, then it is more likely that the organisation will be successful.

### Communications for research

There are a number of ways of conducting research, but using the Internet can usually provide the quickest route to information. This is one reason why good communications systems are important to organisations.

### What does it mean?

**Public relations** *is the overall name given to how an organisation is seen by its customers and how the organisation deals with customers.*

## Case study

### *Modern Mobiles product research*

Modern Mobiles has set up a project team to design the new Roam-a-fone telephone.

One of the first things that the project team will have to do is to look at all the mobile telephones that are currently available to customers, i.e. the competition. This is part of the initial research into the new product. There would be no point in producing a mobile phone that is identical in its design and functions to a mobile phone that is already available.

Two of the project team have been given the task of researching the mobile telephones currently available.

One team member is using leaflets from other mobile telephone companies and a telephone directory to talk to other mobile telephone manufacturers to see what is currently available. The other team member is using the Internet to search for mobile telephones currently available. Neither of these methods of research can guarantee that all currently available mobile phones will be found, but the team member who is using the Internet for research will be able to complete the task more quickly than the one using leaflets and making telephone calls.

## Information resources

Information resources are constantly used in one way or another by organisations. Information resources are obtained in different ways and come in different formats. Within an organisation these resources could include telephone directories, customer records, supplier records, sales invoices, order forms and supermarket loyalty cards.

All of these are sources of information for an organisation. The information that organisations collect from external sources is important, among other things, in building up a picture of their customer base. It is essential that any external resources used are accurate and up to date, as discussed in this next case study.

What does it mean?

*A **mailshot** is a leaflet, letter or brochure – or maybe an email – that is sent from an organisation to a wide range of customers. The listing of customers that are to be sent the mailshot will be collated by the organisation. All those on the listing will receive exactly the same message, although it may be personalised, for example starting Dear Mr X, or Dear Mrs Y. Sometimes organisations will target certain customers only. For example, if a new mobile phone has certain advanced functions, the organisation might send their promotional material only to those customers whose mobile phones do not yet have this additional functionality. To target customers so carefully, a database of information about individual customers and the products they currently own has to be maintained.*

## Case study

### Modern Mobiles mailshots

Modern Mobiles want to send a mailshot to inform people of the new mobile telephone product. They could buy a mailing list of the names and addresses of people who already own a mobile telephone from a market research company.
It would be important for this list to be up to date, so only reliable market research companies would be considered. The market research company, in turn, would be relying on communication with those on its mailing list to make sure it was up to date. If the data is not up to date, Modern Mobiles might waste money sending a mailing to someone who has moved, or who has died. And they would not send a mailing to someone who owns a mobile phone but, for some reason, is not on the list.

## Test your knowledge

1. Explain these terms: network, video conferencing, electronic whiteboard.

2. Distinguish between internal and external communications. Give two examples of each.

3. What is public relations? How can a network be used to improve public relations?

4. What is a mailshot? How can a network be used to build up a mailing list?

## Further research – methods of communication

In groups, research the methods of communication used within your centre of learning. Consider as many aspects as you can between you. For example, how is information passed between those teaching and those learning? How does the centre recruit new students? Think of more questions and share the research effort. Use the Internet where this is a sensible option.

Design a presentation to deliver to the rest of the class, reporting back on your research findings.

When you have seen all the presentations, compare your findings, and pool your best ideas.

## Standard ways of working

It is important that organisations have some control over the communication that takes place:

- Good team working is possible if members of staff are able to share information or resources easily, or can keep other members of the team informed about progress.
- It is also important to ensure that computers being used are secure and are not being used for anything that would be illegal or against the organisation's IT Security Policy.

A network can help communications with coordination, collaboration, keeping staff informed and enabling research:

- Coordinating communications in an organisation can be better managed by having a central server, where common folders for files can be held and accessed easily (as shown in the Case Study opposite).
- A network can help collaboration between employees and team members, for example in the setting of newsgroups (see page 191).
- A network can also be used to keep staff informed by email. There could be a **distribution list** of all team members set up on each user's email account. This would mean that if any team member needed to share some information, or let the team know about something, they could easily send an email to every member of the project team. The use of a distribution list of all staff would also help in keeping people informed of the current stages of work, ideas and information for the project.
- Access to the Internet (as seen in the Case Study on page 174) can speed up research.
- A network can also help with version control of documents that more than one person may be working on. When you are working on your portfolio, you may need to keep more than one copy of a particular

## What does it mean?

A **distribution list** is a collection of email addresses relating to the members of a group. Rather than having to complete the To: field for every member of the group, the sender can just refer to the group name. All those on the distribution list then appear in the To: field. The distribution list can be kept up to date by adding new members and deleting members, or amending their email addresses if these change.

file so that you can show where changes have been made, or material has been added. If your code your first version as V1, and then the next time you work on it you call it V2, you will know that this is the most recent version. When you work on it again you will be able to retrieve the most recent version.

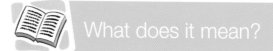

## What does it mean?

**Version control** *involves using filenames that indicate when the file was updated and/or what version of the file it is. All printouts of such files should include this same information, and the date it is printed.*

## Case study

### Modern Mobiles networking for project teams

The Modem Mobiles project team have a common folder for their research, design sketches and other information they require. By the use of version control they can ensure that any documentation they are retrieving from the folder is the most up-to-date version. This ensures that, even if more than one person is working on a design, for example, no one from the project team is looking at, or working on, out-of-date material.

The documentation within the folder is passworded, to ensure that the ongoing project is secure and that no one who should not be accessing the information has the ability to do so.

Using a common folder on a shared drive also helps with research. The two project team members who have been given the task of researching the mobile telephones currently available can access any information that has already been found, provided it has been stored in the common folder. In fact, any team member can look at it. Not only does this save team members from having to send photocopies of information found to the other team members, it also means that the team members are not wasting time by searching for the same information. They can access the folder, see what has already been found, and know which mobile telephone companies the other person has already researched.

## Test your knowledge

5   What is a distribution list?

6   What is version control?

## Further research – naming files

Think of different ways of naming files that will help you to control the versions of your work. Save some dummy files to illustrate your method.

Compare your method with others in your group. Decide on what you consider to be the best method, and adopt this for all future work.

# Managing resources

When an organisation is using a network system, it is important that all aspects of that system are correctly managed.

Organisations need to ensure that their systems are not being overloaded with information and documentation that is not required. They also want to know that the data is held as securely as possible and that any hardware and software are being used correctly. Sometimes, there might be legal issues to take into consideration.

Most organisations employ someone to manage the network overall. Their role includes aspects concerning information, network hardware and software, overall administration of the network, security and legal issues. This person usually has the job title of Network Manager. In large organisations, there may also be other people employed for specific jobs that result from the organisation having a network computer system.

## Information resources

When users log into a network system, they must enter a user ID and a password. This tells the network administrators which person is using which workstation, what hardware and software he or she is using, and even which websites are being accessed and if any information is being downloaded from these websites. Access rights can be set up individually by programming the access rights against the user login.

## Hardware

The hardware that is connected to a network is likely to be shared for some, if not all, of the time. It is important to manage hardware, such as printers, storage devices and scanners, to make sure users do not encounter problems.

Shared hardware, such as printers, can be controlled using a **queuing system**. When a user sends a document to the printer, that document may not be first in the queue. It may not print out immediately, even if the printer appears to the user not to be busy. It is important that users know whether any hardware is on a queuing system; otherwise, they might think that their instruction has failed, and try resending the document. This can result in the same document being printed out lots of times. Most network systems have an icon or a facility in the *Start* menu to enable a user to check the print queue. From here, users can see that their instruction has been sent, but that they will have to wait to get their printed document until they are at the front of the queue. Figure 6.2 shows a printer queue.

## Software

When a network system is set up in an organisation, the management of software is important.

Most organisations have different types of software available on the network for different types of job. For example, someone working in the Accounts department might need to use a financial management package but it is unlikely that he or she will need to use a desktop publishing package. However, someone working in the Marketing department might need to use a desktop publishing package but would not have much use for a financial management package.

**Figure 6.2** *A printer queue*

The network can be set up so that, after logon, the person in the Accounts department has access to the financial management package and the person in the Marketing department has access to the desktop publishing package (but not vice versa).

There are two main reasons for the organisation restricting who uses the packages held on the system:

- When you buy a software package for use on a network, you have to buy more than one licence for it. By restricting who has access to the package, the organisation needs to buy fewer licences (at lower cost) and yet be certain that the number of users does not exceed the number of licences.
- Software packages that require a lot of memory to run can slow down the system. If you allow only those people who need to use a package to access it, there should be fewer problems with the network system.

Another reason that software needs to be managed on a network is to make sure that there is no illegal software on the system. When the network is set up, programming can be used to allow only certain people to install software. This way, a member of staff cannot install any software that the organisation is not licensed to use.

## Staffing

When a network is installed, it is usual for an organisation to appoint a Network Administrator or Network Manager who is someone responsible for monitoring the network and its resources. The job involves many aspects of monitoring the network:

- making sure the network is running smoothly
- recognising sources of potential problems
- fixing any problems that occur

- making sure the network is performing to its maximum capability
- backing up data
- setting policies on the use of the network and all its resources
- providing security for the network and the data held on it.

One important aspect of managing personnel in an organisation is to have an **IT Security Policy** and to make sure that all staff are aware of the policy. Most organisations ask their staff to sign a copy of the IT Security Policy, stating that they will comply with the rules that the organisation has laid down about using its network system. Then, having set up access rights through user logins and passwords, an **audit trail** can be used by the Network Administrator to keep track of what each user is accessing on the network.

## Legislation

Software and data must be protected from unauthorised access.

- The Computer Misuse Act (Unit 2, page 109) makes hacking a criminal offence.
- The Data Protection Act (DPA) (Unit 2, page 107) sets out principles that registered data users are expected to adopt.

The Data Controller in each organisation must ensure that data is kept secure, and that the DPA is applied.

On a network, one potential problem could be in the way that software is shared. In your centre of learning you might have software available for certain courses that is not licensed for everyone to use at one time. Although this software might be available on every workstation, it would be breaking the law if more people than the licence covered were to access it at the same time. Someone therefore needs to keep track of software usage, and make sure that licences are obtained.

**What does it mean?**

An **audit trail** can be set up using an audit trail program. This is used not just for keeping track of individual users, but also, for example, to trace transactions as they go through a system. The audit trail can tell the network administrator where a transaction is in the system at any time, or where a user is logged on and what he or she is accessing, downloading or printing.

**Further research – software licences**

Look again at Unit 2 and refresh your knowledge of relevant legislation such as the Data Protection Act. Prepare a leaflet explaining the data protection principles.

Find out what licences are applicable to the computers you use in your centre of learning or place of work. How does the organisation make sure that the terms of these licences are not broken?

# Disadvantages of networks

As well as saving the organisation money and time, networks can also create problems. However, most of these potential problems can be addressed:

- **Response times.** If your centre of learning or place of work had a small server to run the network, the people in charge of the IT facilities would need to be careful that not too many people tried to use the system at the same time. This could result in the server running very slowly, and users becoming frustrated. It could even result in a system crash, so that no one could use the system until the problem had been dealt with.

  This can be avoided by having sufficient resources (memory and fast processing speed) and a sophisticated enough operating system to handle the intended number of workstations at peak times.

- **Complexity and costs.** A networked system is necessarily more complex than the same number of standalone computers. The interconnection of all the hardware, and the installation of the operating system, adds to the overall complexity – and cost – of the system.

  This problem needs to be addressed by careful design of a network topology (page 183) that suits the intended use of the network.

- **Skill levels.** Users of a network need slightly higher skills than those using standalone computers. However, this can be provided through training in how to log on, the importance of passwords, sharing files and using work areas.

- **Security issues.** Imagine that all the people in your class could access your personal record from their workstations. There may be information stored there that you do not wish to share with anyone. For example, you do not wish others to have your home address and telephone number, unless you choose to give it to them. You might not be happy if everyone in your class could access that information.

  The problem of unauthorised access to data, and possible loss of data, needs to be addressed by the control of access rights (pages 188–190).

## Test your knowledge

7   How might a queuing system be used on a network?

8   What is a software licence?

# Understand the features and services of local and wide area network technologies

## What does it mean?

*A **LAN** consists of computers connected across a small geographical area.*

*A **WAN** consists of computers connected across a large geographical area.*

## Features of LANs and WANs

There are two basic types of computer network that are used today: local area networks (LANs) and wide area networks (WANs).

Two computers in the same room could be connected to form a LAN (Figure 6.3).

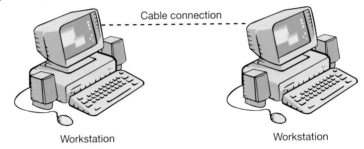

Figure 6.3 *A simple LAN connection*

In both LAN and WAN connections, the workstations (page 196) are usually connected to a server (page 197) that holds the hardware, software, information and resources that the computers can share.

WANs have to be connected in a different way to LANs because of the problems (or sometimes impossibility) of connecting nodes through a simple cabling system. The best known WAN is the Internet.

## Case study

### Modern Mobiles network needs

Modern Mobiles have offices in more than one location: there is an office in London and another in Birmingham. Because of the distance between these two offices, it is not possible to connect computers between the offices by using a simple cable connection. The organisation needs to use other types of connection, such as a telephone line, to connect the computers. Their solution is shown in Figure 6.4.

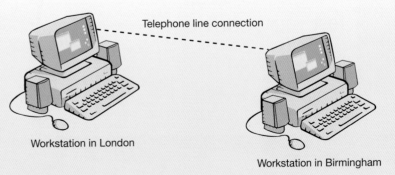

Figure 6.4 *A simple WAN connection*

## Network topologies

There are many different network topologies, but the most common ones are called bus, star and ring.

### Bus topology

In the bus topology (Figure 6.5) all the nodes are connected to a central cable. It works in a way similar to how a bus would follow its route on the road. This central cable is not joined up, so the 'bus' has to travel backwards and forwards along the length of the cable to let data on and off the bus. When data is sent from one computer, it is carried by the 'bus', visiting each node in turn, until it reaches the correct destination.

*The **topology** of a network is the way in which the **nodes** – the workstations, servers and peripherals – are connected, and how information travels around the network.*

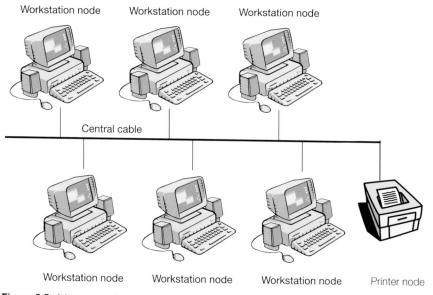

Figure 6.5 *A bus network*

With a bus topology, there is no main computer and there is no level of priority between the nodes. All nodes have equal status for transmitting data. For this reason, if the central cable is busy elsewhere, other transmissions have to wait their turn.

The main problem with a bus topology is that only one node at a time can send or receive data. For this reason, bus topologies are normally used for small LANs, where not many workstations are connected to the network. If, as the organisation grows, more workstations are added, the network topology may need to be changed. If too many workstations are connected to a bus topology, the system will become very slow and the work rate will not be efficient.

The main advantages of a bus topology are as follows: it is easy to set up; it is a reliable network connection; and – because only one main cable is required – it is not as expensive to set up as other network topologies.

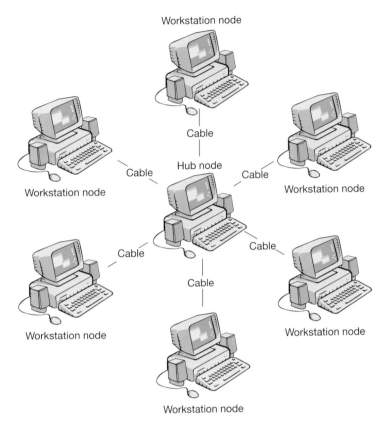

**Figure 6.6** *A star topology*

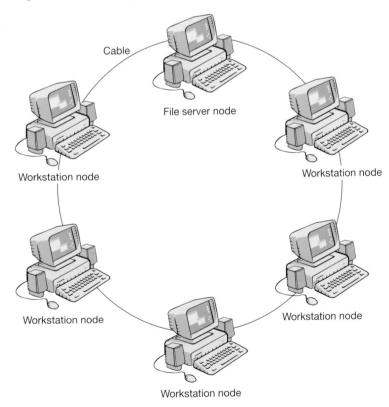

**Figure 6.7** *A ring topology*

## Star topology

The star topology consists of a central controlling computer, connected to nodes by individual cables (Figure 6.6). The central computer is called the **hub node**, and is responsible for controlling the flow of data between the other nodes. Each workstation user can send data to and receive data from the central computer when required, without having to wait their turn. This means that it is a faster network than the bus topology.

One of the disadvantages of a star topology is that, if the hub node has a problem or crashes, the entire network is affected. It is likely that no one will be able to work. However, as each node is connected by its own cable, if one of the nodes has a problem then the rest of the network will be unaffected.

## Ring topology

In the ring topology (Figure 6.7), all the nodes are connected together in a loop. There is no one controlling computer; all workstations have equal status. One computer, the server, holds all the files for the network, including all the programs and software that are required.

Data is transmitted in a ring topology using 'tokens'. These tokens travel around the ring and a node needs a token before it can send data. The node waits for the token to reach it, captures the token and then sends its data with the token. The token then passes around the ring, holding the data, until the correct destination is reached. The data is then downloaded, releasing the token so that it can continue passing around the ring waiting to be used again.

In a ring topology, if one node has a problem, then it affects the whole network. Also, if nodes need to be added or removed, or new hardware or software put on to the network, then the whole network will be unusable while this is being done.

However, because all nodes have equal status and can use a token as it passes around the ring, no one user should hold up the other users.

## Test your knowledge

9 What is the difference between a LAN and a WAN?

10 Distinguish between bus, star and ring topologies.

## Network types

There are two basic types of local area network: peer-to-peer and client-server. Since client-server networks are most common, these are considered first.

### Client-server networks
In a client-server network (Figure 6.8), one computer holds most of the information, resources and software. Other computers that are networked to it can access what they need, without having the software or hardware installed on hard disks.

What does it mean?

*A **server** is a networked computer used to manage software and/or hardware resources for all users (clients).*

Consider how you access documents and software at your place of learning. Maybe there is a computer in the classroom that you have to log on to. Having logged on, you can access work that you have stored on the hard disk in your own work area. You will not be able to access work that someone else has stored on the hard disk in another work area. This is because you are not accessing the hard disk of the computer you are physically using, but the hard disk of the server computer.

The computer you are using may have its own hard disk. This can be used to store things temporarily during the session, to install software that is needed only within that classroom, or to process information you are working with. However, when you save something during your lesson, you are not saving it to the computer you are working on, but to the server computer.

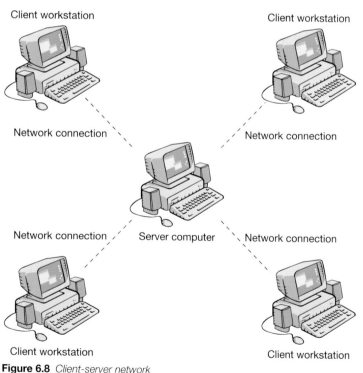

**Figure 6.8** *Client-server network*

### Peer-to-peer networks

In some smaller organisations, where there are not many workstations that need to be networked (usually less than 20), it is sometimes preferable not to have a single server. This means that, if there are problems with the server, they will not affect other workstations and the majority of people can carry on working. A network can still be set up between the workstations but, because they each have an individual

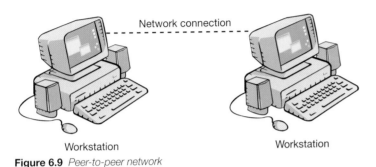

server, they are all equal. For this reason, this type of network is known as peer-to-peer (Figure 6.9). The workstations can still share resources, but can also each use printers and store files individually without having to pass the data and/or instructions through a central server. In other words, each workstation manages its own section of the network.

**Figure 6.9** *Peer-to-peer network*

Peer-to-peer networks do not cost much to set up and run, as only ordinary workstations are needed. Organisations will not need to invest in a powerful server. However, it must be remembered that a peer-to-peer network is suitable only for a small number of workstations, as the system can run very slowly if more than one person tries to access the hard disk at the same time.

## Test your knowledge

11  What is a server?

12  What is a client-server network? How does it differ from a peer-to-peer network?

## Case study

### Creating a network

Vital Comics creates and sells comic books, and needs to network its computer system. It has an office in Manchester and another in New York. The company's basic requirement is that some members of staff, in both offices, need to use and update the same data. It is vitally important that the data is up to date. (Assume that there is an unlimited budget.)

Look at the different types of operation for networks that could be used, i.e. peer-to-peer, client-server.

Give a recommendation for a network for the company to install, and justify your choice.

Write a short report for Vital Comics, detailing how the installation of a networked computer system could help them in the following areas: improving internal communication; improving external communication; management of their information; and security of their information.

## Network access methods

A network access method is chosen to stop nodes from attempting to gain access at the same time, which would result in a 'collision'. There are two main network access methods: token passing and CSMA/CD.

### Token ring networks

In ring topology (page 184), a 'token' is used to carry the data around the network, and a workstation must have use of a token before it can transmit any data. The token then carries on around the ring and stops at the correct destination for the data to be passed to another workstation or node, before the token is released and ready for use again.

### Further research – types of token ring access methods

ARCNET is a network that uses tokens. Use the Internet to research into ARCNET to see how it differs from other token ring networks.

If you would like a real challenge, summarise your findings and create a one-page handout on the topic of 'token rings'.

### CSMA/CD

With Carrier Sense Multiple Access (CSMA), devices attached to the network cable can 'listen' to sense if the network is busy. The network sends a certain sound, known as a 'carrier tone', when it is in use. Unlike the token ring access method, this means that users do not have to wait their turn for the token, but can transmit data across the network when they know the network is free. This is a bit like looking both ways to check the road is clear before crossing.

Collision detection (CD) works in conjunction with CSMA. Because CSMA is a multiple access method, more than one node might sense that the network is clear for use and try to send data at the same time. This can cause a collision of data on the network. When this happens, the nodes stop trying to transmit the data and wait a random amount of time before trying again. Collision detection, with random times for trying to send data again, prevents the network from failing completely.

However, if the network is constantly busy, the collision detection aspect could slow the network down dramatically. Nodes could be randomly trying to send data for a long time after their initial attempt. In this scenario collision detection means that the nodes are no longer 'listening' to find out when the network is free, but 'repeatedly and randomly' trying to send their data.

**Network access methods** *are ways in which users can gain access to the network without interfering with other users on the network.*

**CSMA/CD** *stands for carrier sense multiple access with collision detection.*

## Test your knowledge

13 Explain these terms: network access method, token ring, CSMA.

14 Explain how collision detection works.

15 What are the advantages of using CSMA/CD?

## Further research – network access methods

Produce a short report detailing the differences between the two network access methods: token ring and CSMA/CD. Include a diagram for each method to show how it works.

### What does it mean?

*The **data transfer rate** is calculated on the basis of the amount of data transmitted through a channel per second. Analogue transmissions are measured in cycles per second. Digital transmissions are measured in bits per second.*

## Data rates

Data rates are the speed of transmission over the network.

Factors that determine data rates include **bandwidth** and **delays**.

Delays can affect the speed of a system, and may be caused by a variety of factors:

- the distance that the transmission has to travel
- errors occurring during transmission and error recovery programs running to deal with these
- the amount of 'traffic' on a network, i.e. the congestion factor
- the processing capabilities of the systems involved in the transmission.

In a network situation, **throughput** takes into account possible delays, and then measures system performance, including these delays.

### What does it mean?

**Bandwidth** *is the capacity that an information channel has, i.e. how much data can be carried at one time.*

## Test your knowledge

16 Explain these terms: data transfer rate, bandwidth, throughput.

17 Give *four* examples of what might result in delays that can affect the throughput of a network.

### What does it mean?

**Throughput** *is the amount of work done by a system.*

## Security

One way to make sure that only the people who are allowed to see information held on the system actually see it, is to set up **access rights**. These depend on a logon procedure, which identifies the user; from that, the access rights establish what can or cannot be done on the system by that person. This also enables an organisation to make sure that certain information is not altered by anyone who is unauthorised to do so.

There are several different levels of access rights that can be applied to files:

- **Read-only.** Users are allowed to view the information held on the system, but cannot alter it in any way. It also means that users with read-only access cannot delete information. For example, once the product information leaflets for Modern Mobiles have been issued, the organisation will not want anyone to be able to delete or alter them, unless they are authorised to do so. By making the file a read-only file, Modern Mobiles knows that only someone with the correct access rights can update the leaflet.

- **Write.** Authorised users are allowed to alter the information held on the system, e.g. the person mentioned above who is allowed to update a product leaflet. He or she can call up the leaflet, update it, and save it back to the location it was downloaded from.

- **Create.** Authorised users are allowed to create new files, folders or directories on the system. Looking at the example of the product leaflet, it may be that Modern Mobiles will want only one person to be able to produce a new product leaflet. This will save duplication and confusion. Anyone who does not have the correct access level of 'creating' within that location will not be able to do this.

- **Erase.** Authorised users are allowed to erase files, folders or directories on the system. For example, if a mobile telephone became obsolete for Modem Mobiles, it would not be wise still to have the product leaflet available to everyone, so the person with the correct access rights could delete it to ensure that no one was recommending that product to a customer.

- **Modify.** This is where someone is allowed to change the names and attributes of files, folders and directories. As an example, Modern Mobiles could have a folder for their product leaflets that is named 'Product Leaflets'. When a product becomes obsolete, they might not want to delete the leaflet from the system completely but keep it on the system somewhere for future reference. Someone with the correct access rights could change the name of the existing folder to 'Current Product Leaflets', and create a new folder called 'Obsolete Product Leaflets' to store the old product leaflet in.

- **Copy.** This is where someone is allowed to copy work from one area to another, or from the hard drive to a disk. For example, a person from Modem Mobiles who has been given the task of creating a new product leaflet might want to take a product leaflet template home to work on it over a weekend. If the correct access rights have been set up, the person can copy the template to a disk for this purpose.

## Test your knowledge

18 What are the functions of access rights?

19 Explain the difference between a 'read-only' file and one other access type of your choice.

# Services

These are several possible reasons for setting up a network:

- It may be to facilitate communication. We have already discussed, on page 172, one important use – video conferencing. This is a cost-effective solution to meetings for organisations that have offices and staff located in a number of different places. Depending on the network setup, various other services can be used (as discussed below).

- A network may also be set up to allow transfer of files. For example, a chain of shoe shops may need to send details of takings and stock movements every day to allow the head office to plan when to send replacement stock.

- A network may be set up to allow many users to access the same data from one database. For example, criminal records are shared by all police forces in the UK.

## Communication

An organisation that has a LAN in place, rather than a WAN, has the capability of sharing information and resources internally. There are many ways in which this can be done:

- Setting up a drive to store shared files lets people access the drive from their own workstation, and use whatever resources are required. For example, a folder on the shared drive could hold product leaflets or brochures, which could then be easily accessed by any member of staff to look at or print off the information needed.

- Setting up software, such as word processing, on the LAN means it can be shared throughout the organisation. For example, in the templates of the word-processing package the organisation could have outline documents, such as sales invoices, that could be called up on individual workstations and used. Once completed, these could be saved into a common folder on the shared drive so that records of the sales invoice are kept.

- A network can house an **intranet**. The main purpose of a company intranet is to share organisational information confidentially; no one from outside the organisation can access it without access rights being set up. An intranet can be used to provide easy access routes to any organisational data that needs to be accessed by more than one individual, e.g. the organisation's IT Security Policy.

### What does it mean?

*An **intranet** is a type of website that is accessible only within the network in which it has been set up.*

- An intranet can enable the sending of private messages by individuals, allowing functional areas to communicate electronically within the organisation. For example, if the Accounts department were planning a meeting, a message could be sent to all their staff to let them know in advance and invite them to attend.

- If a **bulletin board** is set up, notices can be posted on it, and these can then be accessed by anyone with the correct access rights. Bulletin boards are best used to post information that a wide range of individuals may need to know. For example, if there is to be a fire drill, or a works Christmas party, the date and time of these events could be posted on the bulletin board to save the organisation sending individual notes to each person.

- If a **newsgroup** is set up, users with appropriate access rights can communicate in real time. A newsgroup differs from a chat room; the discussion topics on a newsgroup can normally be viewed after the discussion has taken place, as well as in real time. Newsgroups are usually set up to discuss a specific subject area so that like-minded people can join in; this can then be used for groups of people to communicate electronically and brainstorm their ideas. For example, a newsgroup might be set up for the project team that is designing a new mobile telephone. This would provide a way for them to keep in touch and up to date with the progress of the project. It could also be used to discuss ideas or problems, without having a physical meeting.

When an organisation needs to communicate externally on a regular basis, it is likely that, as well as an intranet, access to the Internet may be arranged, and the organisation may have a website. This enables the organisation to use extra facilities to help with external communication needs:

- Providing staff with access to external websites means they can carry out research, check on competitors, and access other external websites, e.g. government websites to ensure they are up to date with new legislation. The project team member researching currently available mobile telephones could also search competitors' websites to see what is available, including designs, functions and features.

- Provided the website is kept up to date and looks professional, having a website could help an organisation to gain and maintain a good reputation with its customer base. Existing or potential customers can access this site to look for products, and to find out more about the organisation. They can also be given the option to contact the organisation easily through the use of forms, email buttons etc. For example, Modern Mobiles could decide to have a customer feedback form on its website, so that valuable comments from their customers can be collected.

- Having **EDI facilities** available would enable an organisation to send orders to suppliers electronically and to take customer orders electronically. For example, Modern Mobiles could have a customer order form on their website, which would save the customer's time in

What does it mean?

*A **bulletin board** is like an electronic notice board.*

What does it mean?

*A **newsgroup** is an interactive area on a network, where users can communicate in real time. Each user is accessing and using information simultaneously, and can respond immediately to something that someone else is typing.*

What does it mean?

**EDI** *stands for electronic data interchange.*

ordering products. The orders would be received much quicker than if being sent by normal postal services, and could be actioned immediately by the organisation to give a good customer service.

- Using the email facilities available via the Internet, an organisation could send mailshots to customers and keep in touch with both customers and suppliers. For example, if Modern Mobiles had a special offer on a new product, information about this could be emailed automatically to a distribution list of existing customers. This is considerably cheaper than sending out printed mailshots, thereby saving the organisation money. Email can facilitate internal communications too. Emails can have attachments; so, after any meeting, the minutes could be emailed, as an attachment, to anyone who needed a copy.

- Creating newsgroups that can be accessed from the organisation's website provides another source for information exchange. For example, Modern Mobiles could create a newsgroup for their customers, whereby customers could find out information on products from people already using them. If someone was thinking about buying a new mobile telephone, they could go to the newsgroup and type up a message to see what other users thought of the product they were thinking of buying.

- Creating bulletin boards that can be accessed from the organisation's website is yet another option – for example, Modern Mobiles could set up a bulletin board for its customers. They could post information about new product ranges, special offers etc. instead of sending email mailshots.

## Test your knowledge

20  Suggest three reasons for setting up a network.

21  Explain these terms: intranet, bulletin board, newsgroup, EDI.

## File transfer

On a network, resources can be shared; this includes files.

Transferring files from one node on a network to another node on another network needs to be done in a way that is secure and as quick as possible. A special protocol (FTP, see pages 193 and 205) is used.

Transferring large files can take time and so may slow down a network for other users. To minimise this problem, files may be zipped and, for example, large image files may be compressed.

## Further research – file compression

Find out what facilities you have to zip files. If you would like a challenge, compare the sizes of files before and after zipping.

Research the Internet to find out the options for compressing image files. If you would like a further challenge, identify two methods of image compression: lossy and lossless. Find examples of formats for each compression method.

**What does it mean?**

**Zip** *is a file compression format, commonly used prior to data transfer.*

## Test your knowledge

22  What does FTP stand for?

23  What happens when a file is zipped? What is the purpose of zipping a file?

## Databases

Some data needs to be accessed by a lot of people scattered over a wide area. So that everyone has access to the most up-to-date information, a network can be set up, with a database linked to it, so that all those that need access can have access.

Many websites are linked to databases. For example, a website offering books and CDs for sale might be linked to a database giving information about the products, who else has bought them and how long it might take for one to be delivered to you.

## Further research – information held in databases

Find out what information is held by the Criminal Records Bureau, and who might need to access this information.

Find *two* websites that rely on databases to provide information for visitors. How is data that is personal to a particular visitor kept private from other visitors?

## **Protocols**

Groups of protocols – such as TCP/IP – usually work together for different types of networks. One of the main protocols used for LANs is called Ethernet. This uses a bus topology and CSMA/CD, for its access method (see page 187).

**What does it mean?**

*A* **protocol** *is a set of rules that determines how data is transmitted between computers.*

Protocols have been produced to manage data transmission in a common way. This reduces the likelihood of errors during transmission. The protocol will tell the computers, which are trying to communicate, when to send and receive data. The protocol also needs to understand addresses so that it can direct the data to the correct destination.

## Test your knowledge

24  What is a protocol?

25  What does TCP stand for?

## Further research – network protocols

Look at the information given above concerning the purpose of network software protocols. Think about what could go wrong if the protocols were not followed.

If you cannot think of anything, then research network software protocols further to give you a better understanding.

If you would like a challenge, prepare a brief scenario of how a business could be affected when sending data through a network that has not set up a correct protocol. One or two paragraphs are enough.

## Data security issues

One of the disadvantages of a network is the increased risk of security breaches. However, measures can be taken to minimise this risk:

- **Access control.** The greatest risk comes from unauthorised access. Physical security barriers (Unit 15, page 25) are a first line of defence. Then user IDs and passwords are used to set access privileges. See also page 189 for details of access rights that can be set on a file.
- **Virus protection.** Viruses can damage files, but may be prevented by installation of virus protection software (Unit 2, pages 106 and 110; Unit 17, pages 17–19) and through appropriate procedures, for example, not allowing employees to use diskettes that they bring from home.
- **Backup and recovery.** Just in case disaster strikes, it is essential that adequate backups (Unit 2, page 110; Unit 17, pages 24–26) and a recovery procedure are in place (Unit 17, pages 9–10).
- **Hacking** is the act of breaking into a computer system. It is a criminal offence under the Computer Misuse Act (Unit 2, page 109). Hacking is best prevented through installation of a firewall (discussed below).

## Firewalls

If someone tries to hack into your network system from outside your organisation, a firewall will detect this and, hopefully, prevent it from happening. Firewalls are usually a combination of a piece of hardware and some software to monitor and manage the firewall.

Firewalls work by putting an invisible wall between your network file server and the external network. When someone tries to connect to your network server, the firewall will check to see whether the person is authorised to access the network. Any attempts at connection which the firewall does not recognise as being from an authorised user are just ignored and the user trying to connect is thrown off the system.

All communications in and out of the network system are checked by the firewall. This means that, if you are trying to connect to a network that the organisation does not want you to visit from their network, this can also be blocked. Users within the organisation will usually receive a message telling them that they are not going to be allowed to access this site.

On another level, firewalls can be programmed to block only part of an access or retrieval process. A good example of this is that a lot of organisations will let people access most websites, but will block the network system from letting cookies into the system.

Firewalls are a good way of organisations easily keeping control of what is coming into and going out of their network system.

You will need a firewall software package, and maybe some firewall hardware, to install a firewall on your network. There are two main types of firewall:

- **Network-level firewalls** are usually built into a **router** (page 199) and can be used to check the content of incoming/outgoing data, whether the correct protocols are being used for data transfer, which port number is being used to transfer data and whether it is the correct one, and what the address is of the sender of the information.
- **Application-proxy firewalls** act as a proxy for the connection, translating the data before allowing it into or out of the network system, rather than just running a standard set of checks.

### What does it mean?

A **firewall** *is a type of security system, used primarily to protect networks from external threats.*

### What does it mean?

A **cookie** *is a small file that records information about your visit to a particular website. It stores personal information such as your password, so you do not have to re-key this data every time you visit the same site.*

## Test your knowledge

26  What is a firewall?

27  What does a cookie do?

28  Distinguish between network-level firewalls and application-proxy firewalls.

# Understand network hardware and software components and how they are connected and configured

## Hardware and technologies

Some hardware components for LANs are needed no matter which type of network is set up on the system. Just as in any type of computer system, the main hardware components required for LANs are the hard disk, monitor and keyboard. There are then other components and technologies:

- network cards
- workstations
- servers
- modems
- broadband technologies
- peripherals
- routers
- hubs and switches
- uninterruptible power supplies.

This section now looks at each of these components in turn.

### Network cards

**What does it mean?**

**NIC** *stands for network interface card.*

To be able to access the network, each workstation requires a network adaptor – often referred to as a network card or NIC (Figure 6.10). This is installed into an expansion slot inside the computer and acts as an interface for connection to the network. The type of network card used depends on the network topology being used.

Figure 6.10 *A network card*

### Workstations

**What does it mean?**

*A* **workstation** *is a computer that is linked to a network.*

To be able to access the network, each workstation requires its own NIC.

Some types of network do not require all their workstations to have individual hard drives, but other types of network use both the server and individual hard disks for each workstation. So, a workstation may or may not have its own hard disk; and, in some types of network, the workstation is just a monitor and keyboard.

Workstations that are linked to a network can use the hardware and software of the computer that is acting as a server on the network.

Once these basic components are present, cabling is required to connect the workstations to the network, though wireless links may also be used.

## Servers

There can be a number of servers on a network:

- Servers that house all the software and data are called **file servers**.
- Servers often manage and prioritise the use of peripherals that workstations can share, such as printers; these are called **print servers**.

The server then 'serves' any other user, i.e. the **clients**, with any resources needed.

## Modems

A modem is required if data has to be transferred between two computers over links, such as telephone lines, which will accept only analogue signals. When the digital signal leaves the computer, a modem converts it to analogue. A modem at the receiving end reconverts the signal to digital before passing it to the second computer (Figure 6.11).

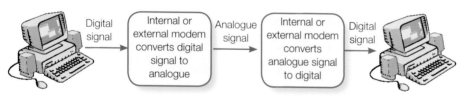

**Figure 6.11** *How data is sent between computers using modems*

## Broadband technologies

Broadband is becoming more popular as a network connection, as it usually provides a permanent connection. Most broadband technologies work through a digital signal, so it is also a fast way of connecting to a network because no conversion of analogue data is required. Broadband technologies are capable of using a wider bandwidth than other connection technologies. The most commonly available broadband technologies are ISDN and ADSL:

- ISDN converts voice to digital and sends data and voice over the standard telephone system with a bandwidth of 2 Mbit/s in both directions; **there are no limits on distance, or numbers of voice/ data links within the bandwidth.**

**Broadband** *is the name now given to any communication method that has a faster transmission rate than that of the fastest telephone line.*

**ISDN** *stands for integrated services digital network.* **DSL** *stands for digital subscriber line.* **ADSL** *stands for asynchronous DSL, which just means higher rates in one direction, i.e. for downloading data.*

**ISP** *stands for Internet service provider.*

*A* **peripheral** *is a hardware component that is connected to a computer, e.g. a printer.*

- DSL/ADSL was primarily developed for home use, allowing data to be sent over the copper telephone cables using unused frequency capacity on the line (separated out electronically in the home). **Voice continues to be analogue and limited to one per line.** Much higher data rates are possible than ISDN, up to 24 Mbit/s on ADSL. Hence, some businesses now use it, especially for internet access, using non-ISDN lines. **However, subscribers have to be within about 2 km of the telephone exchange.** It is normally offered by telephone companies, although some **ISPs** can supply an ADSL.

## Test your knowledge

29 Explain these terms: NIC, workstation, server, client.

30 Why might a network have more than one server? Give two examples of servers.

31 What does a modem do?

32 What is broadband?

33 Explain these terms: ADSL, ISDN, ISP.

## Further research – network connections

In groups, prepare a short presentation showing the differences between using a modem and using broadband technologies to connect to a network.

Include diagrams, where appropriate, for examples of the different types of cabling used in broadband technologies.

## Peripherals

Just as a standalone computer is likely to have a mouse as an additional data capture component, on a network of computers there may be data capture devices other than a normal keyboard, depending on the nature of the organisation. Supermarkets, for example, normally have a **bar code scanner** as an input device, as well as a type of keyboard known as a **concept keyboard**.

If peripherals are to be a shared resource on the network, then a server may be needed to manage this hardware resource.

A **bar code scanner** is an input device that reads a series of lines of different thickness and shading. The scanner is passed over the bar code on a product and a light on the scanner is read. The bar code is then processed automatically and converted to a code. It is this code that identifies the product. If you look at a bar code on a product, you will see that, because scanner systems are not 100% reliable, the code that the bars represent is also printed underneath the pattern of lines to enable manual data entry.

A **concept keyboard** has different keys from that of a QWERTY keyboard. For example, a concept keyboard may be attached to the weighing scales in the greengrocery section of a supermarket. The customer places produce on the scales and presses a button to say what type of food is being weighed, e.g. carrots, potatoes, mushrooms. The food is weighed and the cost calculated, based on the weight and the price per kilo of the produce. A ticket is then printed, and this is stuck on the bag ready for the checkout assistant. Some systems are designed to do the weighing at the checkout.

## Routers

In networks such as the World Wide Web, many millions of computers can be linked, and there may be more than one route from any one computer to another (Figure 6.12).

A **router** is used to connect networks. It decides what route the file or message will take towards its destination.

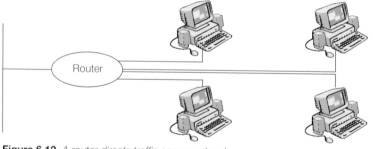

**Figure 6.12** *A router directs traffic across networks*

## Hubs and switches

Depending on the type of network being installed, you may also need a **hub**.

A hub can give workstations some independence from the other connected workstations. This is useful if, for example, one computer on the network develops a problem. With the use of a hub, other workstations can carry on working normally, unaffected by the problem.

Other hardware components can be used in networks:

A **hub** is a type of electronic switching box, and its purpose is to control the traffic flow around the network.

- **Repeaters** are electronic devices that boost signals before sending them along the network. They are also used to connect two cables together in a LAN if the cable needs extending.
- **Bridges** are used to extend a network by linking two LANs together.

## UPS

There are two principal types of UPS, both of which contain batteries to power the computer system if the mains power supply fails:

- In a **stand-by UPS** the computer system operates using the mains until there is a cut, when the UPS switches over to a battery, converting its stored energy to alternating current. It is cheap and silent but offers only limited filtering against 'spikes' on the mains.
- **Inline UPS** is more expensive but isolates the computer from the mains at all times, using it to charge a battery, then reconverting this stored energy to alternating current to power the computer system. Hence, the computer always receives a 'clean' waveform.

For more information about why a UPS might be needed, see Unit 17 (page 27).

## Test your knowledge

**34** Give *two* examples of peripherals that might be connected to a network.

**35** Explain these terms: router, hub, UPS.

## Connectors and cabling

This section considers the connectors and cables needed to link all the components of a network, and the options available, e.g. using leased or dedicated lines (page 202).

There are a variety of cabling options:

- Fibre optics relies on light signals.
- Other cabling, such as UTP, STP and coaxial (often referred to as coax) is made from wires.

However, networks today do not have to be physically linked by cables but can use wireless links, using a combination of satellite, infra-red or microwave communications. Mobile telephones are a good example.

One of the main problems with wireless technology is that the connection is not as fast at the moment as when using cabling. Also, wireless connections are not as reliable as cabled connections.

However, the use of wireless connection for LANs is becoming more popular. This is because a wireless connection is easier to install, as cables do not need to be laid. This can often make it a cheaper alternative.

For example, many supermarkets use wireless technology when stock checks are being carried out. Staff carry portable devices with keypads. These terminals have a wireless link to a central computer. The stock checkers count the number of items on the shelf, entering codes and quantities into the terminal. This information is then sent, through the wireless LAN, to the central computer.

Having determined the basic method of connection, usually there will be some inclusion of telephone lines, and this can introduce a mix of digital and analogue transmissions. All these issues are considered in this section.

## Further research – standards for network protocols

There are several groups of people that are helping to set up protocols and to standardise the use of wireless technology. These include Bluetooth, the Infrared Data Association (IrDA) and HomeRf. Research each of these groups and make notes.

If you would like a real challenge, prepare a short presentation, outlining how each is involved in wireless technology.

## Fibre optics

Fibre optic cables consist of glass or plastic fibres (Figure 6.13). They carry a digital signal and can have a very high transmission rate. They are also one of the most secure ways of networking, as fibre optic cables do not give off any electromagnetic radiation so remote sensing equipment cannot detect them.

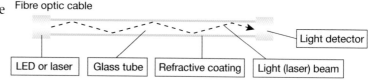

Figure 6.13 Fibre optic cabling

## Microwave and satellite technologies

**Microwave transmissions** use a short-wavelength signal, an electromagnetic radio transmission that operates at an ultra high frequency.

One problem with using microwave technology for networking is that data can be sent over only fairly small distances, up to about 50 km. This is because the nodes require 'line of sight' to be able to transmit to each other. So both the 'sender' and 'receiver' components must be able to 'see' each other, and the Earth's curvature can affect this line of sight.

With **satellite communications** technology, the communication is over a two-way transmission beam via a satellite. Satellites in the Earth's orbit receive and retransmit data that has been sent from a device on Earth. The signal being transmitted to the satellite is called an 'uplink'. Once the satellite has read the destination address, the signal can be sent back down to the correct location on Earth. This retransmission of the data is called the 'downlink'.

Because the satellite is above the Earth, the transmission can be made over many thousands of miles – there is always a line of sight between the sender and receiver.

The main disadvantage of using satellite communications is that, because the data has to travel to the satellite and then back again, the connection is not always reliable and there is a noticeable time delay.

## Cabling

Different types of cables and wires are required, depending on the type of network that is being set up. Fibre optic cabling could be used, but the main type of cable used for networking is made of copper wire (Figure 6.14):

Unshielded twisted pair

Coaxial cable
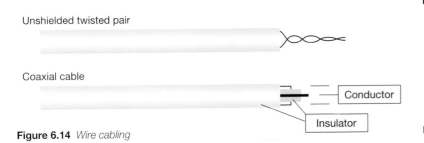

**Figure 6.14** *Wire cabling*

- In UTP cable, the wires are insulated and twisted together in pairs, held together by a plastic covering. STP is similar but has a metal sheath, usually copper braid, inside the outer plastic covering.

- Coaxial cable has a straight copper core surrounded by an insulator and outer metal sheath, usually copper braid, inside a plastic covering. You are most likely to have seen it used for connecting television aerials.

## Leased and dedicated lines

A leased line is usually leased on the basis of how often and for how long the user connects to the WAN. Users normally pay a monthly or annual fee for the use of the line, and will probably pay extra each time they connect to the WAN.

In a switched-connection leased line situation, an ordinary telephone line is used. By using an adaptor, you can connect both a telephone and a modem to the same line. When you want to use the Internet, the modem will connect to the telephone line, and when the modem is not connected the line can be used for the telephone.

The main disadvantage of this is that you cannot use both the telephone and the modem at the same time. So, if you are on the Internet for long periods of time, people will not be able to reach you on that telephone number. You can buy gadgets nowadays that will let you know if someone is trying to telephone you when you have your modem connected, so that you can still take your telephone calls without having to pay for an extra line to be installed.

Dedicated lines are usually still leased and the users pay to be able to use them. The biggest advantage is that it is much quicker than using a switched line. Your telephone will never be engaged just because you are using the Internet.

**What does it mean?**

**Coaxial** *means that the parts of the cable share the same axis. Thus, when you cut through the cable, they appear as a series of rings around the central core.*

**What does it mean?**

*A **leased line** is a permanent or switched connection that links a user's computer to a service-provider's WAN.*

## Digital and analogue lines

Digital and analogue are two different types of transmission system. Data cannot be sent directly between them unless an analogue-to-digital converter is used.

Computers cannot deal with analogue signals, and some types of cabling cannot deal with digital signals. For this reason, when a node is transmitting data via an analogue line, it is converted from digital to analogue (using a modem, page 197) before travelling along that line. However, the user at the other end of the network would not be able to read the analogue signal, so the analogue has to be converted back to digital again (using another modem) before entering the computer system.

Digital technology is quicker and more reliable than analogue technology and, hence, is one of the fastest growing areas within the communications sector.

**What does it mean?**

**Dedicated lines** *are those where a permanent connection to a WAN is set up.*

## Test your knowledge

36  How does infra-red communication work?

37  Explain these terms: Bluetooth, IrDA, HomeRf, uplink, downlink.

38  What is the main disadvantage of microwave transmission?

39  Describe how UTP cabling is constructed.

40  What are leased lines? How do they differ from dedicated lines?

41  Give one example of an analogue signal, and one example of a digital signal.

## Further research – setting up a network

Write a short report explaining the differences between cabled networks and wireless networks. Make sure that you include clear indications of the advantages and disadvantages of each.

Produce a diagram showing the hardware components that will be needed to set up a simple LAN between two workstations. Include any peripherals that you think may be required. Clearly label each piece of hardware and show, through the use of arrows, how the hardware will connect to the workstation, and which way the data will flow.

# Software

This section looks at Internet browsers, firewalls, email, FTP software and network operating systems.

## Internet browsers

An Internet browser is a package that displays pages that have been created in Web format. The two most common Internet browsers available are Microsoft Internet Explorer and Mozilla Firefox.

Internet browsers run on **TCP/IP** networks and transfer the HTML coding, used to create web pages, into a user-friendly front end. They are capable of presenting the information to the user in many formats as well as text, including animation, graphics and videos.

The choice of Internet browser should not be dictated by the computer and network you are accessing the Internet from. There is a standard way of developing websites that can be fully viewed and accessed, whichever browser you are using. However, different browsers offer different functions and features, and this might be relevant when deciding which one to install.

## Further research – network browsers

Research the features and functions that are available for the Microsoft Internet Explorer and Mozilla Firefox browser software.

Produce a table showing what is available from each and give a brief explanation of what the feature or function provides for the user.

## Firewalls

A firewall serves to protect a network from attack. This is covered in some detail in the section on Data Security Issues (page 195).

## Email

Email is an electronic communication system for sending messages from one user to another through an email client. On a computer, files of any format can be attached, e.g. a simple document or a jpeg graphic.

A subject or title for the email is entered, the message is typed, and the sender specifies the email address of where the message is to be sent. When the sender presses Send, the message is moved to the 'outbox' of the sender. Immediately or later (depending on the set up), the message is processed through the network connection telephone line or cabling, passing through different servers until it reaches its destination. It is placed into the 'inbox' of the person it has been sent to, and that person can access the message next time he or she logs on.

**What does it mean?**

**TCP/IP** *stands for transmission control protocol / Internet protocol. This protocol dictates the way in which networked computers are named and addressed, how different networks can be connected together and how messages are sent across a wide variety of networks that are linked together to make up the Internet.*

**What does it mean?**

**Email** *is an abbreviation for 'electronic mail'.*

Most email packages have several functions available as standard. For instance, there is usually a 'reply' button; you can click on this and the email address you want to send the message to is automatically set up in the email message. Similarly you can forward email messages.

To use email facilities, you may decide to install an email client software package. If your computer has a browser loaded, you may already have an email package installed: Microsoft Internet Explorer uses an email client called Outlook Express; Mozilla Firefox uses an email client called Mozilla Thunderbird. There are other email clients available, and they will usually work with the most common browser software.

*An **email address** is a string of characters that identify a user. It will enable the user to receive email. For example, hp123@example.com could be the email address of user hp123 who works for a company with the domain example.com.*

## Further research – choosing an email client

Research commonly available email packages. Find *three* different ones.

What differences are there between the email packages? Do they all offer the same facilities?

## FTP software

FTP software enables you to download information on to your computer from other computers that are within the same network. The most common use of FTP is in loading web pages on to a server so that they are accessible over the Internet.

**FTP** *stands for file transfer protocol.*

You will need an FTP client, such as CuteFTP, to enable you to connect to FTP sites. There are many FTP clients available, some of which can be downloaded free from Internet sites. A quick search on the Internet for FTP clients will show you what else is available.

TCP/IP is used to download from an FTP site. When you start up your FTP client and connect with an FTP server, a connection is opened between your computer and the computer that you are accessing. This connection remains open until you give the 'close' command. There is another connection that is open when you request a file transfer, but this one will automatically close when the file's data has finished being transferred. For each file that you transfer, a different connection is opened. So, if you request more than one file to be transferred, there could be more than two connections open at one time between your computer and the computer you are accessing.

## Further research – FTP

Search on the Internet to locate three FTP clients.

Compare what is on offer and the costs involved.

If you would like a challenge, prepare an oral presentation explaining the options available for FTP.

## Network operating system

When you turn on your computer, it is the operating system that kicks into action and controls the interface – i.e. what you see on screen – and then obeys your commands to load and run software applications.

The network operating system (NOS) is software with special functions that let you connect computers and other devices to create a LAN. This software also helps you to manage the users that you will allow on your LAN.

Some operating systems (such as UNIX and the Mac OS) have networking functions built in. However, the term NOS is generally reserved for software that enhances a basic operating system by adding networking features. Novell Netware, Artisoft's LANtastic, Microsoft Windows Server are all such examples of an NOS.

## Test your knowledge

42    Explain these terms: TCP/IP, HTML, FTP, NOS.

43    What is a firewall?

44    Give one example of an email address and explain the parts of it.

45    Give three examples of a NOS.

# Be able to set up and use a simple local area network

This section focuses on the practical activity of setting up a network.

## Preparation

As with all activities involving computers, you should make sure you know what you are planning to do, and have everything to hand, before you begin.

It helps to write notes – a bit like a recipe, showing the ingredients (the components) and each step that you plan to follow during installation of your network.

### Collect components

The components that you will need to collect, ready for setting up your network, are the workstations, the NICs, cabling and all relevant software. If you are creating a star network, with the PCs connected to a central point, you will also need a hub (Figure 6.15).

You will need some tools:

- a screwdriver to open the PC casing so that you can install the network card
- a multimeter in case the network does not work and you need to test a cable's connectivity.

**Figure 6.15** *A hub*

You may also need a copy of installation guides and any manuals supplied with the components. Read these carefully before starting.

### Check software licensing

Before installing software on a workstation, you should check that you have the necessary licence to do so. This gives you the authority to use the software. Attempting to copy software to save buying new is a criminal offence.

During software installation you may be asked to key in a product code, which is proof that you have purchased the software. The software then has to be registered online, and the vendor can check that you have not used a product code that has already been allocated to another computer. This product code will be on the licence.

## Test your knowledge

46 What hardware will be required to set up a basic LAN between two workstations?

47 Apart from the use of cables, what other ways are there of networking computers?

## Set up

The process of setting up can be broken into two sections: physically connecting the hardware, and then installing the software.

### Hardware

The hardware – as collected in the Preparation stage – needs to be connected:

- The network card has to be installed.
- The cabling has to be connected.

The network cards have to be installed first, because the cabling connects to the cards! There are several options for a NIC as shown in Figure 6.16.

- You can install a NIC in an open expansion slot on the motherboard and then connect the cabling to the NIC port.
- The PC can be connected through a device, such as a modem, attached to the USB port.
- You can use a PC card as a network card for a portable computer, i.e. a laptop or notepad.

Note that the NIC connectors will determine the type of cabling that can be used on the network and vice versa.

If the card is to be installed in a vacant slot inside the PC casing, the type of NIC card has to match the type of slot.

**Figure 6.16** *NIC options*

## How to –

### Add/remove a NIC

- Check that you know which slot you are going to use, and that you have the correct NIC board for your PC (Figure 6.17).

- You may need to set a DIP switch or a jumper for the NIC card, so check the documentation.

- Be careful to handle the card by its non-connecting edges. Otherwise, you may leave traces of grease or dirt from your fingers.

- Gently place the NIC card into the slot and press it into place.

- To remove a board, release the locking mechanism, and then slide the board gently out of its slot.

**Figure 6.17** *A NIC with its connectors*

## Software

The NOS to be installed will depend on the **platform** that you are using.

Having identified the platform, this will limit the options as to which NOS can be supported. However, having decided on the NOS, installation is straightforward.

The vendor will supply the software on CD, and full instructions will be provided as to how this is to be installed. You should follow these exactly!

Then you will need to set up users, decide on what access you will allow to the various resources and make some resources, such as a printer (Figure 6.18), available to all users. The methods to be followed will be explained in your software documentation.

## Health and safety

It is important to be aware of the dangers to your health, and the risks to the safety of the equipment you are handling. Unit 2 (page 95) gives general advice on sensible procedures to be adopted when handing computers.

### What does it mean?

*The **platform** is the underlying operating system, for example, Mac OS or Windows.*

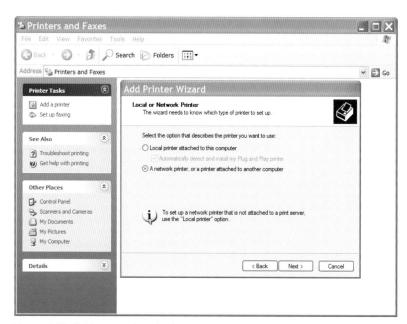

**Figure 6.18** *Setting up a shared printer*

To avoid electrocution, you must switch off all electrical equipment before opening the computer case and installing the network card. However, when installing hardware, you should be aware of an additional source of harm to the equipment: ESD.

ESD can happen when two things (you and the computer) connect. To prevent ESD, you need to make sure that the static charge between you and the hardware you are about to touch is equalised. One way is to wear an antistatic wrist strap (Figure 6.19).

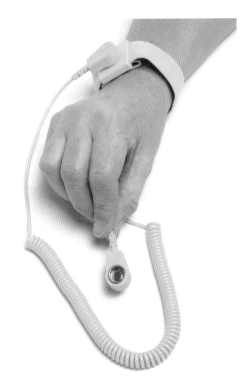

**Figure 6.19** *An antistatic wrist strap*

## Escalation

When working on a computer, installing hardware or software, or testing it, if you hit a problem that you cannot solve then the sensible option is to ask for help. Your friends or colleagues may be able to help, or you might need to ask your teacher or a technician.

## Testing

When new equipment or software is installed, it is essential to test that the system still works; this applies to not only the new functions installed, but to whatever the system used to do before the change.

### Functionality

Setting up a network will upgrade a number of standalone workstations into a system that should allow communication between the workstations and sharing of hardware and software resources. You should test that this is indeed the case.

### User interface

Once a number of standalone computers have been linked to form a network, and the NOS has been installed, the user interface ought to recognise this and require each user to log on. You must check that the user interface works as anticipated.

## Use

Part of the process of setting up the software for the network includes allocating users and their rights, and allocation of file space to individual users.

### Communication

Users will expect to be able to communicate with each other, so you will need to set up email addresses for users. Additional tasks include allocation of file space, allocating users and their rights (pages 188–189) and transfer of files.

### Transfer files

If your network is to be used to maintain the organisation's website, you will need to set up an FTP link to the host of the website. Then, as pages are amended and tested locally, they can be uploaded to the website.

## Test your knowledge

**48** Give two examples of a platform.

**49** What is ESD? How can it be avoided?

**50** What is escalation? When should you resort to escalation?

## Assessment tasks

The assessment tasks in this unit are based on the following scenario:

*MAGIC, a small marketing company, employs 35 people, most of whom need access to information that is currently held on a number of standalone computers.*

*Most of the marketing work is done on computers. Customers are contacted by telephone, but the customer details are called up from a large database. Mailshots are sent out on a regular basis to a mailing list held on a computer. Leaflets and questionnaires are designed in-house to be sent in mailshots. The company administration tasks, e.g. the company payroll, are performed on computer.*

*MAGIC has decided that it needs to network the computers. They have made some decisions already:*

- *They are going to employ a Network Manager and one Network Administrator.*
- *They do not want to spend a lot of money on setting up their network system.*
- *They are willing to purchase a central controlling computer, if this is felt necessary.*
- *The company holds personal information on members of the public. So security is important for them.*

# Assessment tasks continued

> To work towards a Distinction in this unit you will need to achieve **all** the Pass, Merit and Distinction criteria in the unit and have evidence to show that you have achieved each one.

## Task 1 (P1)

Prepare a poster describing how the use of networks can improve communications for an organisation such as MAGIC.

## Task 2 (P2)

You will attend a structured workplace visit. Following this visit, prepare an oral presentation, describing how a network is used by an organisation to manage its resources. Include how networks allow sharing of information, hardware, software and staffing. Plan your talk to last at least four minutes.

## Task 3 (M1)

Referring back to your material for Tasks 1 and 2, prepare an online report comparing the benefits that networks offer to communication and managing resources with non-networked alternatives.

## Task 4 (P3)

Create a visual presentation, listing and describing the advantages and disadvantages of networks. Include slowing down of response times, unauthorised access to information, increased complexity and costs, selection factors, staff skills and security issues.

## Task 5 (P4, M2, D1)

Create a visual presentation describing the features and services of local and wide area network technologies. The network technologies chosen should be complex enough to involve features, services, protocols and data security issues as detailed below, and can be based on the MAGIC case study.

- Features should include topologies, peer-to-peer, client-server and network access methods. Services should include communications, file transfer and online databases.
- Protocols should include their purpose and function, with an example.
- Data security issues should include access control, virus protection, backup, hacking and firewalls.

Include time in your presentation planning for a group discussion, so as to involve your audience.

Building on your presentation, create a handout of at least 500 words, explaining how security risks can be minimised in a network. Include accurate explanations on how access control, virus protection, backup, recovery and firewalls can be set up.

> To work towards a Distinction, when building on your presentation and handout you should create a poster to compare and evaluate the features and services provided by a local and a wide area network.

## Assessment tasks continued

### Task 6 (P5)

Prepare a report that lists and describes network hardware and software components. Include hardware and technologies (network cards, workstations, servers, modems, broadband technologies, peripherals, routers, switches and UPS), connectors and cabling (fibre optics, microwave and satellite technologies, cabling, dedicated lines, digital and analogue lines) and software (internet browsers, firewalls, email, FTP software and a network operating system).

### Task 7 (P6, D2)

For this task, you will be observed setting up, using and testing a simple LAN. You may be given a checklist to work through, and you may be working on the same equipment as others in your class. Follow the instructions given to you.

> To work towards a Distinction you should write a report explaining how the network you set up in Task 7 could be extended to add functionality and additional services. You will need to consider reconfiguring the network and what additional purchases might be needed to extend the system.

### Task 8 (M3)

Prepare a troubleshooting guide for a local area network, including symptoms of problems and possible solutions. You may word-process your guide, or prepare a web-based guide.

# 7 Software Design and Development

## About this unit

While not every IT practitioner is a programmer, an understanding of the process by which programs are written is important. This unit covers all the main steps in software development: understanding the customer's requirements, designing a program to meet those requirements, writing a program using the design, documenting the solution, and testing that the program meets its requirements.

Throughout this unit, we will use a case study on Modern Carpets. This is a small company with several shops selling carpets and floorings. We will see how a program is developed for them, from understanding their requirements to developing a solution to meet those requirements.

▶ Continued from previous page

# Learning outcomes

When you have completed this unit you will:

**1** understand the software development process

**2** be able to design and produce a software component using an appropriate programming language and environment

**3** be able to debug and test a solution

**4** be able to document the solution.

# How is the unit assessed?

This unit is internally assessed. You will provide a portfolio of evidence to show that you have achieved the learning outcomes. The grading grid in the specification for this unit lists what you must do to obtain Pass, Merit and Distinction grades. The section on Assessment Tasks at the end of this chapter will guide you through activities that will help you to be successful in this unit.

# The software development process

## What is a computer program?

A computer program is a series of instructions that tells the computer's processor what to do. Programs are what make computers powerful. Unlike typewriters or fax machines, which have only one function, computers must carry out many different tasks: programs make this possible.

Computers, however, can understand only machine code instructions in the form of binary codes (see Unit 2, page 70). Although programs for the very first computers were written using these binary codes, they are very difficult for people to understand. Because of this, **programming languages** (sometimes called **high-level languages**) were developed.

## Solving problems

Computers are often used in business to solve problems. For example, a computer program might be written for any of the following reasons:

- to help a shopkeeper to place orders by keeping track of stock levels
- to allow a sales manager to record customer details in such a way that they can be found quickly
- to provide the doctors and nurses in a health centre with a diary of appointments.

Because the programs are normally written by a programmer, not by the person who has the problem, the first step in solving the problem is for the programmer to spend time understanding the exact nature of the problem.

## Development procedures

### User need and problem requirements

Before a piece of software can be designed, the person designing it must have a clear idea of what the software should do. Software developers usually write software to solve other people's problems – unless the developers understand those problems in detail before they start to write code, the resultant software is unlikely to be successful.

It is important that the developers discuss the problem in detail with the customer. The result of this process should be a document thoroughly explaining the problem. It may take several attempts to produce a document that the customer and developers agree explains the problem correctly and in sufficient detail to act as the basis for the design of a solution to that problem.

**What does it mean?**

*A **programming language** has instructions that are written in English-like statements, which are easier for people to understand than binary codes. These English-like statements are converted into the binary codes that the computer understands using a piece of software called a **compiler**.*

When determining the requirements for a software component, you need to consider the following:

- what **input** the component will have; in other words, what data will be passed to it by the user or other software components
- what **output** the component will have; this includes files that the component will create, reports that it will print, anything displayed to the user and any messages that are sent to other software components
- the internal **data structures** and **processes** that the component will have (although these can mostly be left until the design stage).

## Writing good requirements

The following is a list of criteria to be considered when writing requirements, with examples of poorly defined (✘) and well defined (✓) requirements in each case. Good requirements should be:

- **unambiguous** – wherever possible, a requirement should be written in such a way that it has only one reasonable interpretation and includes all of the necessary information
    - ✘ The software shall allow the user to view reports.
    - ✓ The software shall allow the user to view a report that has previously been saved to disk. Only a single report shall be viewable at any one time.
- **concise** – requirements should be as short as they possibly can be while still conveying all of the required information
    - ✘ It shall be possible to view on the screen what the report would look like if it were to be printed.
    - ✓ The software shall include print preview for reports.
- **consistent** – you must take care that requirements do not contradict one another (directly or by omission)
    - ✘ The software shall automatically download updated data files from the Internet every day.
    - ✘ The minimum hardware requirements shall be 25 MB free disk space and 256 MB RAM.
    - ✓ The minimum hardware requirements shall be 25 MB free disk space and 256 MB RAM. An Internet connection shall be needed if data files are to be updated automatically.
- **possible** – some things simply cannot be done; if a requirement is impossible then no satisfactory software solution can be produced
    - ✘ The software shall include a complete index of the Internet.
    - ✓ The software shall generate an index of any website entered by the user.
- **verifiable** – requirements must be worded in such a way that the software can be tested to see whether its requirements have been met
    - ✘ The software shall never crash.
    - ✓ The software shall be accepted only after it has been running for fourteen consecutive days on the client's site without crashing.

- **high-level** – requirements should state what the problem is, not how the solution will be implemented
    - ✗ The software shall use the quicksort algorithm for sorting customer records.
    - ✓ The software shall be able to sort 10,000 customer records by up to three fields in less than five seconds.

## Further research

Look at the examples above very carefully and make sure you understand why one is poor and the other better.

## Investigation of requirements

Most commercial programs are written to solve some kind of problem or to take advantage of an opportunity. Clearly, it is necessary to understand the nature of the problem or opportunity before you can write a program that will achieve what is required. To gather the requirements of the system, you must ask questions such as:

- What are the aims of the new system?
- How does the current system work?
- What other systems does it need to interface with?
- What is the scope of the system?
- What are the boundaries of the system?

We shall look at each of these questions in turn, with the help of a case study.

## What does it mean?

*The **scope** of a software system is the set of features that will need to be inside the system itself. Other features may be recorded in the requirements document, but noted as **out of scope** if they are not in the direct control of the software system. For example, a requirement may be that the system's log files do not exceed a certain size; if it is the system administrator's responsibility to archive the log file before it reaches that size then this requirement will be **out of scope** (although there may be an **in scope** requirement to alert the administrator when the log file reaches a certain size).*

## What does it mean?

*The **boundaries** of a system are the points at which it interacts with the end user or with another system. For example, the user interface will be a boundary, as will any components that need to perform networking or printing.*

## The problem faced by Modern Carpets

Customers who come in to Modern Carpets' shops want to know how much it would cost to buy the carpet for a particular room in their house. To calculate this, they need to know not only how large the room is (its length and width) but also how much the carpet costs per square metre. They also need to add in the cost of the carpet underlay (a foam sheet that goes under the carpet to protect the floor) and the cost of fitting.

John Dixon, the company's sales manager, thinks it would be a good idea for each shop to have a program on its computers which the sales people could use to demonstrate to customers how much different carpets might cost. Modern Carpets buys all of its computers and software from a company called Small Business Solutions (SBS). John has a chat with Rajesh Khah,

their support manager at SBS, and asks him whether what he has in mind is possible. They discuss using a spreadsheet but decide that a simple Visual Basic .Net program would provide a neater solution with an easier-to-use interface.

Rajesh will need to find out exactly what John wants, so he can work out how much time it will take him, and from that how much it will cost. John will have to make sure about what, exactly, Rajesh is going to provide them with and how much it will cost. John will then need to go and see Modern Carpet's managing director, Sue Francis, and justify the expenditure to her.

Rajesh and John decide that the best way to persuade Sue is to put together a document that will describe the system they have in mind.

### What are the aims of the system?
It is important to get the aims of the system clear from the start because sometimes, during the course of developing the software, people can lose track of the original reason why the software was required.

## Modern Carpets' aims

John makes a list of the aims of Modern Carpets' cost calculator program:

1 To provide sales assistants with a simple way of showing customers how much different carpets would cost.

2 To improve the service provided to customers, giving a competitive advantage over other carpet shops in the area.

3 To encourage potential customers to purchase a carpet by quickly providing them with accurate information about the costs involved.

### How does the current system work?
In many cases, the software to be developed will replace an existing system. It may be a manual system (using people instead of computers) or it may be an old computer system that has outlived its usefulness. In any case, it is important that the current system be thoroughly understood so that the new software can preserve its essential elements and its good features and avoid the problems that it now suffers from.

## Case study

### The report for Modern Carpets

John needs to explain in his report what currently happens, so that Sue can clearly see why the new system will be better. Currently, if a customer asks how much a carpet would cost, the sales person needs to go through the following steps:

1   Find out the size of the room by multiplying its length by its width.

2   Find the cost per square metre of the chosen carpet.

3   Find out whether the customer wants economy or luxury underlay.

4   Multiply the cost per square metre of the carpet by the area of the room.

5   Multiply the cost per square metre of the chosen underlay by the area of the room.

6   Multiply the cost of fitting by the area of the room.

7   Add together the cost of the carpet, underlay and fitting.

While none of this is particularly difficult, it can be quite time-consuming. If a mistake is made during the process then the customer may not be very happy when the mistake is discovered, especially if this means an increase in the cost of the carpet.

What other systems does it need to interface with?
No system works in isolation. All systems take input – from the user or another computer system – and produce some kind of output. Part of understanding the system to be developed involves defining what these inputs and outputs are. At this stage there is no need to go into a lot of detail about these inputs and outputs – this will come later.

## Case study

### Inputs and outputs for Modern Carpets

John's list of inputs and outputs looks like this:

*Inputs* – the customer using the system will enter the length and width of the room and the price of the chosen carpet.

The cost of the underlay and the fitting are the same whatever carpet is chosen. At Modern Carpets, economy underlay costs £1.75 per square metre, while luxury underlay costs £2.15 per square metre. Fitting costs £2.00 per square metre.

*Outputs* – the system will show the total price of the carpet, including fitting and underlay.

To help develop their understanding of the system, Rajesh draws up a diagram (Figure 7.1) showing the inputs and outputs the system has.

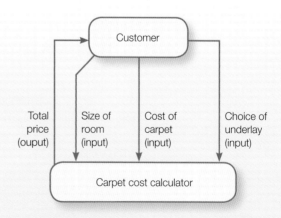

**Figure 7.1** *Diagram showing the inputs and outputs*

**What is the scope of the system and what are its boundaries?**
The question being asked here is really 'what will the system do, and what won't it do?' This may be an obvious question, but it is an important one. Computers are very powerful machines and there are many facilities you could include in the software you are developing, if you had endless time and money. In some cases you may want to decide what the most important features are (referring back to the aims of the system) and develop the first version of the software with those features, putting the rest on a 'wish list' for future versions.

The investigation stage should result in a document that draws together all of the information that has been collected, and puts the case for developing the software. It should also describe the costs involved. Before the project can go ahead, this document will be presented to the manager responsible for authorising the expenditure. The decision on whether or not to proceed will probably be a commercial rather than a technical one: in other words, the manager will need to decide whether the cost can be justified and what the return on investment will be.

## Test your knowledge

1  What should be the first step when developing a piece of software?

2  How can the required information be gathered in the first step?

3  What questions does a programmer need to ask during the initial investigation of the problem?

## Design

The design stage builds upon the requirements, and it is now that you must think *how* the software is going to work.

The first step may be to break the problem down into components, particularly for large, complex software.

Once the general structure of the solution has been decided (what the components are and how they interact), each component can be designed in detail.

There are many different tools available to software designers: storyboards, pseudocode, narratives, action lists, flow charts, and so on. These are discussed on pages 234–240.

## Preparation

Before starting to write the software, it is a good idea to make sure that the development environment is thoroughly prepared. This means creating a suitable folder structure on disk for holding the project files, making sure that back-up procedures are in place, and checking that anti-virus packages are installed and up to date.

Professional software developers keep every version of the software components that they create. This makes it easy to roll back to older versions if a change is made in error, and can pinpoint when erroneous code was first introduced into the build. You will probably not have access to software that automates this (called **version control** software), but you should decide how you are going to manage this process manually, e.g. by creating a copy of your development folder at the end of each day.

## Creation of software components

The creation (or **implementation**) stage is when the program is written. Programmers follow the design and refer back to the requirements to help them; if implementation highlights any problems with the requirements or design then these documents should be updated appropriately.

Software developers often find writing the code to be the most enjoyable stage of a project. When planning for, and working on, your own software development projects, be sure to allocate a fair proportion of your time to the requirements and design stages (which will save you time overall) and to the testing and documentation stages (which will improve the quality of your software product).

## Testing

All non-trivial software contains bugs. This might sound harsh, but it is true. In this sense, writing software is like writing a book: try as you might to avoid spelling mistakes, poor grammar and factual errors, some inevitably slip through the net.

Software developers use testing (just as publishers use editors and proofreaders) to minimise the severity and number of errors as much as possible.

If the requirements have been carefully written then many of the tests will flow directly from these.

For a large software project, each component is tested individually – these tests are called **unit tests**, and may be run manually or written as extra software that can be run automatically. Further tests, called **integration tests**, check that the components work properly together.

## Documentation

Each stage of the software development process results in the creation of one or more documents. The requirements investigation stage culminates in a formal requirements specification. During the design stage, various charts and documents are produced to record the design decisions that have been made. Even the implementation and testing stages generate internal documentation in the form of program comments and test plans and logs.

What does it mean?

**Integration** *is the process of bringing together software components, perhaps written by different development teams, into a single piece of software.*

Often, additional time must be put aside to formalise the internal documentation (e.g. ensuring that the design documents are up to date) and to prepare any customer documentation, such as a manual.

## Maintenance

Software maintenance is rather like car maintenance. After a car has been manufactured, it still needs regular tune-ups to keep it performing well; it may even be taken to a mechanic for an upgrade, such as fitting satellite navigation. In the same way, software bugs that are discovered after release will need to be fixed, and users may request that developers add new features to the software.

One measure of the success of a software product is the length of time for which it remains in use. Some software in use today has gone through many versions over the course of years, or even decades. Because of this, over the lifetime of a software product, the maintenance stage is likely to last the longest and take the most effort. If the earlier stages have been rushed or performed carelessly (e.g. if the design documentation is poor) then the maintenance stage will be heavy going, difficult, inefficient and mundane. If care has been taken, though, the maintenance stage can be as interesting and productive as the implementation stage.

# Programming languages

## Examples of programming languages

Since computers first came into general use, many different programming languages have been developed. Some of these have been aimed at particular applications, such as Fortran for science and Ada for work in the defence industry.

Today, the most popular languages are suited to general use. Languages such as C, C++ and Java have been used to write any software you could imagine, from systems to manage bank accounts to the latest video games.

In this unit, you will be developing software using Microsoft Visual Basic 2005. This language is well suited to developing small to medium applications that will run on Microsoft Windows. The following section provides an overview of Visual Basic and some of the other languages you might choose to learn. If you intend to develop software professionally then you should learn at least two or three different programming languages, so that you can choose the most appropriate one for each new project.

### Visual Basic

The original language BASIC dates back to 1963. BASIC stands for 'Beginner's All-purpose Symbolic Instruction Code', and it was developed as a language suitable for teaching computer programming to beginners. It became very popular, being included as standard with many of the early home computers. The very first Microsoft product, written by a young Bill Gates, was a version of BASIC.

Once Windows became the dominant desktop operating system, a new language was needed that would make it straightforward for programmers to create programs that could take advantage of the rich graphical interface that Windows provided. Microsoft wrote Visual Basic to fulfil this need. Visual Basic has since been extended to work with Microsoft's .Net framework.

### C

C is the oldest language we will be looking at; it was designed in the early 1970s by Dennis Ritchie at AT&T Bell Labs. Although C is a high-level language, it is very powerful and allows programmers to control their hardware at a much lower level if they so wish. It is even possible to embed machine code instructions directly into a C program.

C is a very powerful, flexible and popular language. C compilers are available for almost every combination of computer hardware and operating system. This is good news if you want to write one program and then be able to run it on various different types of computer.

### JavaScript

Although standalone JavaScript interpreters do exist, this language is most commonly embedded in web pages. In this way, a higher degree of user interaction is possible; for example, a web page can check that a user has filled in a form correctly before they will be allowed to send it.

JavaScript is also becoming popular as a language for customising existing programs. For example, you can write OpenOffice.org macros in JavaScript.

### Pascal

Pascal is rather like BASIC, in that it is suitable for beginners. (Similarly, Borland Delphi is a Pascal-like language for Windows, in the same way that Visual Basic is a BASIC-like language for Windows.)

In general terms, Pascal is slightly more powerful than BASIC, but is less widely used.

## Further research – programming languages

1   There are many different programming languages, but which are currently the most popular in the IT industry? One way you can gauge the popularity of different languages is to check the number of programmer jobs that are advertised looking for each language. Get hold of one of the weekly IT magazines, such as *Computing* or *Computer Weekly*, and check the jobs section. Alternatively, search on the Internet for programming jobs.

If you would like a challenge, try this:

2   Create a table listing the popular languages from the first question. For each language, research it on the Internet and rate it out of five on the following criteria: ease of learning, power, speed and flexibility. Explain why you have chosen these ratings.

*The **syntax** of a programming language defines the rules which govern how programs are constructed in that language.*

## Programming language features

This section describes the features that are common to all programming languages (although the syntax used to express them does vary between languages). A simple Visual Basic .Net example is given for each.

### Constants

A constant is a container for a value that does not change.

```
Const SOFTWARE_VERSION As String = "v1.1"
Const PI As Double = 3.1415926535
```

### Variables

A variable is a container for a value that does or may change.

```
Dim changeMe As Integer
changeMe = 27
changeMe = 41
' The following writes "changeMe is 41" to the console
Console.WriteLine("changeMe is " + changeMe.ToString())
```

### Keywords

Keywords are sequences of characters with special meaning in the language, such as `Dim`, `Integer` and `WriteLine` in the example above. You cannot use a keyword as the name for your constants or variables.

## Advantages and disadvantages

Table 7.1 lists some advantages and disadvantages of four popular programming languages: Visual Basic, C, JavaScript and Pascal.

| Language | Advantages | Disadvantages |
|---|---|---|
| Visual Basic | Quick to create graphical user interfaces (GUIs)<br>Relatively easy to learn<br>Good tool support | Not as powerful as C for intensive data processing applications<br>Not portable to non-Microsoft operating systems |
| C | Good performance (programs run quickly)<br>Highly portable between operating systems | Not the easiest language to learn |
| JavaScript | Typically embedded into web pages to interact with the user | Not ideal for creating general tools that are not on the Web |
| Pascal | Easy to learn | Not often used in commercial software development |

**Table 7.1** *Advantages and disadvantages of four popular programming languages*

## Constructs

This section describes the three basic constructs (building blocks) that can be used to control computer programs: sequence, iteration and selection. A simple Visual Basic .Net example is given for each.

### How to –

#### *Compile and run simple programs*

**1** Start Visual Basic 2005. (If you do not already have this software, you might be able to download it. At the time of writing, Microsoft was offering Visual Basic 2005 Express Edition as a free download from their website.)

**2** On the *Start* page, click the *Project... link* next to *Create*. The *New Project* dialogue will appear.

**3** Select *Console Application*, give it a name and press *OK*.

**4** Type the code you want to test between `Sub Main()` and `End Sub`.

**5** Add the following three lines just before `End Sub`. These will keep the console window open.

```
Console.WriteLine()
Console.Write("Press ENTER to
close")
Console.Read()
```

**6** Select *Debug*, *Start Debugging* from the menu (or press F5). Your program should run.

### Sequence

A sequence is the simplest programming language construct, i.e. instructions are followed one after another in sequence.

```
' Write the string "Hello world!" to the console
Console.Write("Hello ")      ' Do this first...
Console.WriteLine("world!")  ' ... then do this.
```

### Iteration (loops)

Iteration is where instructions are repeated, either a certain number of times or until some condition becomes true. For example, you might loop through a list of numbers adding each in turn to the total. Alternatively, you might keep prompting a user for input until they enter an acceptable value.

```
Dim total As Short = 0       ' Initialise the total to 0
For num As Short = 1 To 10   ' Start of loop
    total = total + num      ' Add the number
    Console.WriteLine("total is " + total.ToString())
Next                         ' Go back to start of loop
Console.WriteLine("Final total is " + total.ToString())
```

```
        Dim input As String
        Do
            Console.Write("Continue (Y/N)? ")
            ' Get input from user's keyboard
            input = Console.ReadLine()
        Loop While input <> "Y" And input <> "N"

        ' Ask again if not OK
```

Selection (branching)

Selection is where a choice is made as to which set of instructions to carry out. For example, the following code can perform the four basic arithmetic functions based on the value of the supplied op variable.

How to –

## Build this code

If you want to test the following code for yourself, you will need to add it between the **End Sub** and **End Module** lines of your program. You will also need to add a call to the function somewhere inside your **Main()** subroutine, for example:

```
Console.WriteLine(Arithmetic(2.0,
"plus", 3.5))
```

which should print 5.5 to the console.

```
    Function Arithmetic(ByVal first As Double, _
                        ByVal op As String, _
                        ByVal second As Double)
            As Double
        Dim result As Double
        If op = "plus" Then
            result = first + second
        ElseIf op = "minus" Then
            result = first - second
        ElseIf op = "multiplied by" Or op = "times" Then
            result = first * second
        ElseIf op = "divided by" Then
            result = first / second
        Else
            ' For any other operator, display an error message
            MsgBox("Unknown operator " + op + " in Arithmetic()")
        End If
        Return result
    End Function
```

## Data structures

Often it is necessary to work with a set of related data. The basic data types (such as `Integer`) can contain only a single item. To keep many items together, it is necessary to put them in a data structure.

### Arrays

The simplest data structure is the array. An array is like a group of variables lined up next to each other, where each one can be written to, or read from, according to its position in the line-up. The following Visual Basic example demonstrates how this works:

```
Dim myArray(3) As Integer
' Create an array with 3 elements
myArray(3) = 5
myArray(1) = 2
myArray(2) = 3
Console.WriteLine(myArray(1))
' This writes 2 to the console
```

Figure 7.2 shows what the array looks like after this code has run.

| myArray | | |
|---|---|---|
| Element 1 | Element 2 | Element 3 |
| 2 | 3 | 5 |

**Figure 7.2** *An array data structure*

### Other data structures

There are many other data structures. Lots of these use pointers, which is a topic beyond the scope of this book.

## Further research

Search for `System.Collections` in Microsoft's online help to find out about the other types of data structure you can use (such as lists, queues and hash tables).

If you would like a challenge, try using reference books or the Internet to find out about pointers. What is a pointer? Which popular programming languages support pointers, and which do not? Why are pointers useful in data structures?

# Organisational standards

## Organisational specific standards

A **standard** is a document that explains in detail the rules that must be followed when creating or modifying something. For example, there are safety standards for car seatbelt design and HTML standards describing the acceptable structure for web pages.

Some standards are written by governments or multi-national organisations. We will concentrate on the types of standard written by smaller companies and organisations to control the structure and content of the software products they produce.

### Design standards

There are many different ways to design software. Organisations may have a preference for certain tools and techniques for software design. If so, they will set these out in a design standard, and make sure that their employees are trained in these tools and use them in a consistent way.

### Coding standards

Organisations often use coding standards. These lay down the style that programmers must use for all of the software they develop. Coding standards try to share best practices, and provide a common look and feel to the code so that working on code produced by other people within the organisation becomes easier.

## Further research

For an example of a coding standard for Visual Basic, look at one of the following books:

- *Practical Guidelines and Best Practices for Microsoft Visual Basic and Visual C# Developers*, Giuseppe Dimauro and Francesco Balena, Microsoft Press; ISBN: 0735621721
- *The Visual Basic Style Guide*, Tim Patrick, Prentice Hall PTR; ISBN: 0130883611

### Documentation standards

Organisations often have their own standards for the many types of documents that they produce. In a software development environment, such documents might include manuals, test specifications and result logs, technical notes, help files and release notes.

## Case study

### *Template for this book*

When we were writing this book, we used a template that the publisher provided, and followed instructions about the style and tone of writing. The template had pre-defined styles for the different types of headings and boxes. By all following the same template and using a similar writing style, each of us could ensure that our work was consistent, and the task of bringing it all together into a cohesive whole was much simplified. Another benefit is that this book fits in with the others in the series, which looks more professional and makes it easier for readers who are familiar with the series to find their way around.

If a document is worth writing, it is worth writing well. Documentation standards provide a consistent framework to use when writing new documents, and help to ensure that important things are not left out by mistake.

Standards are not set in stone: they should just represent the best practice at the current time. If you find things in the standard that you disagree with, or can identify things that you think should be added, then there should be a way for you to submit a change request. By improving the standard, all future documents created from it will also be improved.

## Further research

If you would like to see a comprehensive style guide for technical documents, take a look at the following book:

- *Read Me First!: A Style Guide for the Computer Industry*, Sun Microsystems, Prentice Hall, Second Edition (2003). ISBN: 0131428993

## The need for standards

Standards are rather like requirements documents (see pages 217–222). They provide a common understanding of how something should be done, ideally with reasons why it should be done that way.

Large organisations may have very many software development projects happening at once. By applying the same standards to each, the organisation sees the following benefits:

- Products for the customer will appear more professional if they have been produced according to standards. For example, a manual will be less likely to have important sections missing, and will look similar to other manuals produced by the same organisation.
- Software code is easier to understand if you are not distracted by its formatting. If an organisation has coding standards, all of its developers will get used to the same type of style. This also makes it easier to reuse software components between projects.
- Coding standards can encourage developers to write better code by outlawing unsafe programming practices.
- It is easy to move staff between projects, because they will not have to learn a whole new way of doing things.
- If one of the projects comes up with an improvement to an existing process, this can be added to the standards so that all of the other projects benefit too.

# Design and produce a software component

## Software components

Having completed the investigation stage and received the go-ahead from management, developers can move on to the next step: producing a design. The system design provides more detailed information about the internal working of the software. Much of what is done at this stage involves taking what has already been decided at the investigation stage and adding more detail to it. There are a number of things that need to be designed and planned, such as how the program will look to the user, what data the program will need to store and how that data will be processed.

As you already know, programs take some kind of data as input, perform some kind of processing on that data (perhaps a calculation) and produce some kind of output. At the design stage, software developers must add more detail to what they have discovered about what is to be input, how it will be processed and what will be output.

Where the problem is large and complex, consideration also needs to be given to how it can be split into manageable sections. The key to deciding how to split a problem up into sections is to choose sections that can be as self-contained as possible. Clearly, when dividing a system into different sections (or **modules**, as they are often called), these modules will need to communicate with each other (probably by passing values, often called **parameters**) to a certain degree. However, this should be kept to a minimum, with each module having a clearly defined purpose and as little interaction with other modules as possible.

Where several programmers are working on the same software development project, dividing the system up into modules is necessary so that each programmer can work on an individual module. Dividing a program into modules also makes the testing easier, because developers can test each module as it is completed rather than having to wait until the whole program is complete.

### Types of software component

When designing a new piece of software, or adding new features to existing software, it is important to choose what type of component you will create. Most new applications are standalone programs, although it may be possible to achieve the functionality you require by adding a new module to a larger system.

#### Standalone programs
A standalone program is one which is delivered as a whole, and which can be extended only by modifying the source code and recompiling it.

Most software is in this category, although modular programs (see below) are becoming more popular.

A simple example of a standalone program is Notepad, the text editor that comes with Windows. Notepad exists as a single executable file (*notepad.exe*), and, although it contains enough features to load, edit and save text files, there is no way to add extra features to it (unless Microsoft chooses to make changes to the source code and release an updated version of the compiled program). See Figure 7.3.

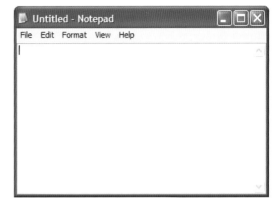

A standalone program is often suitable for simple applications, and we shall be developing the example application in this unit as a standalone program. Sometimes, however, a modular system can provide greater flexibility.

**Figure 7.3** *Notepad is an example of a standalone program*

## Modular programs

There are two aspects of a modular program: a framework built to work with modules, and the modules themselves.

A good example of a modular program is Firefox. This program provides a web browser with the fundamental features that most users need: loading web pages, viewing different types of file, printing, saving, and so on. But Firefox has been designed so that developers can easily write extensions that plug into it and provide additional features. See Figure 7.4.

**Figure 7.4** *Extensions installed in Firefox*

Modular software often takes on a life of its own, with new developers writing extensions to add features that the original developers never dreamed of. This makes more people want to use the software. The extension developers also benefit, because they are able to concentrate on writing software to solve specific problems without having to engineer all of the framework code for basic functions – they get this for free!

## What does it mean?

**Closed source software** *is software that is distributed in only binary (compiled) form. Companies using this business model usually make most of their money from selling the software.*

**Open source software** *is freely available for anyone to look at and modify. Companies using this business model make their money from paid support instead of from charging for the software.*

Modular software is becoming more popular in open source projects, although there are also ways of extending closed source software in a modular way. For example, Microsoft Office supports both add-ins and macros. For some problems, it can be more efficient to create a spreadsheet with custom macros than to write a program in a programming language.

## Further research

1  You can try out Firefox. To download it go to www.heinemann.co.uk/hotlinks, insert the express code 2048P and click on this unit. You will also find there a list of extensions to Firefox.

2  For another example of a modular framework for software development from the Eclipse foundation go to www.heinemann.co.uk/hotlinks, insert the express code 2048P and click on this unit.

If you would like a challenge, try this:

3  Do some research on the Internet to find out about the pros and cons of **closed source software** and **open source software**. Suppose you work for a small software consultancy. When might you choose to produce closed source software for a client? When might you choose to produce open source software for a client?

## Component content

A software component will contain one or more of the following:

- **code** – program code to control the processing
- **data structures** – containers for the data held by the component
- **interfaces** – functions with which other software components can communicate with this one
- **visual components** – any forms, toolbars, menus, icons etc.

## Design tools

### Designing the user interface

In Visual Basic, one or more **forms** are used to provide the user with a way of running the program (the **user interface**). The design of the form is a good place to start because it can help you to visualise how the program will work. The Visual Basic form editor makes creating forms quite easy, but you must remember that they need to be neat and clear. As far as possible, they should also be intuitive; it should be obvious to the user what they are expected to do with the form.

Most forms will contain the following types of object:

- **labels** to inform the user what to do
- **text boxes** for the user to enter (input) information, and for the program to output information

- **list boxes** for the user to make choices
- **buttons** for the user to click to perform various actions.

The documents created in the investigation stage should list the inputs and outputs for the program; these provide a guide to which user interface objects are required.

## Case study

### *Designing the form for Modern Carpets*

Using the information from the investigation stage, we can see that the form will need the following:

- text boxes for users to input the length and width of the room
- a text box for users to input the price of the carpet
- a way for the user to select the type of underlay
- a button for the user to click to perform the calculation
- a text box for the program to output the calculated cost.

The initial design for the form is sketched out (see Figure 7.5). A type of list box called a **combo box** has been used to allow the user to select the type of underlay. A combo box is a combination of a drop-down list box and a text box: the user can make a selection either by typing or by selecting an option from the list.

Whenever you add a new object to a form, Visual Basic assigns it a default name. It is tempting to just keep these default names but, as these names give no clue about what each object is used for, it is better to give the objects meaningful names. You can do this by modifying the `Name` property for each object.

The names given to the objects in this example are shown in Figure 7.5. So that it is clear what type of object the name belongs to, text boxes have been given names beginning with *txt*, combo boxes with *com* and command buttons with *cmd*.

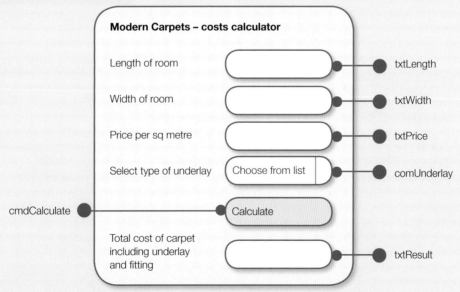

**Figure 7.5** *Completed form design with object names shown*

## What does it mean?

*A **variable** is an area of memory that a program uses to store a value while it is running. Variables have names, so that they can be referred to in the program, and a data type, which sets the type of data that the variable can hold, such as text or numbers (see page 226).*

## What does it mean?

*A Visual Basic form contains various objects, such as text boxes and buttons. These objects have **properties** that control aspects of their appearance and behaviour. When you click on an object in the Visual Basic environment, its properties are displayed in the Properties window in the bottom-right of the screen. You can change properties by modifying them in the Properties window or by setting them in the program's code.*

### Creating a variable list

The next thing to decide is what data the program will need to store. Programs store data in variables. At this stage, the developers must decide which variables to create, what to call them and what their data types will be.

In Visual Basic, every text box on every form will need a variable to hold its input or output value.

## Case study

### *Variables for Modern Carpets*

Rajesh begins work on the data design for the program. By looking at the form he can see that the following variables will be required:

- length of the room
- width of the room
- price per square metre of the carpet
- total cost of the carpet.

| Variable name | Data type |
|---|---|
| roomLength | Single |
| roomWidth | Single |
| carpetPrice | Single |
| totalCost | Single |

**Table 7.2** *Variables identified so far*

These variables are shown in Table 7.2. The data type **Single** stores a single-precision floating-point number.

However, this isn't a complete list of the variables needed. In order to work out what other variables will be required, Rajesh needs to think in more detail about the processing.

### Designing the processing

So far, we have been thinking mainly about the input and output that a program requires. This has helped us to complete the form design and also to identify some of the variables that the program will need. We shall now consider the processing that has to be done. The starting point for the design will probably be the manual processing that is currently done, which should have been identified at the investigation stage. There are a number of techniques that can be used to design the processing steps required in a program. We will look in detail at a simple technique called **flowcharting** and then have a quick overview of some other design tools.

Drawing a flowchart

As the name suggests, a flowchart is a diagram that shows the steps that must be taken to carry out some task. Flowcharts can be used to design all sorts of processes, not just programming ones.

Flowcharts use a variety of symbol shapes, each of which represents a type of step. These symbols are linked by arrows, which indicate the direction of flow of the process through the chart. All flowcharts start with an oval containing the word **Start** and end with an oval containing the word **Stop**.

Normal processing steps (a 'sequence' building block), such as doing a calculation, are represented by a rectangle containing a brief description of the step. The rectangle has one arrow entering (from the previous step) and one leaving (to the next step), as shown in Figure 7.6.

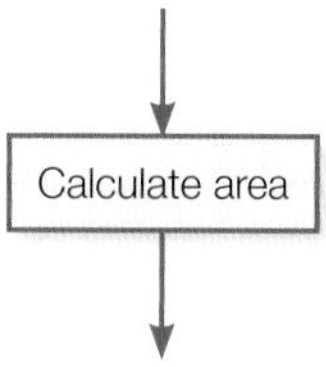

**Figure 7.6** *Flowchart processing step*

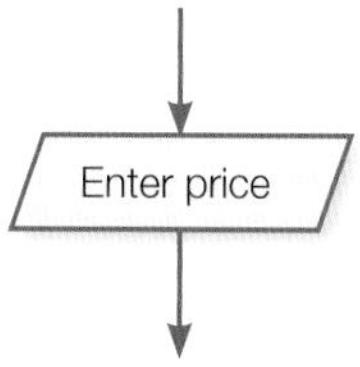

**Figure 7.7** *Flowchart input box*

A processing step that involves some input is represented by a parallelogram, as shown in Figure 7.7.

An output step, on the other hand, is represented by a box that is meant to look like a torn-off piece of paper (Figure 7.8).

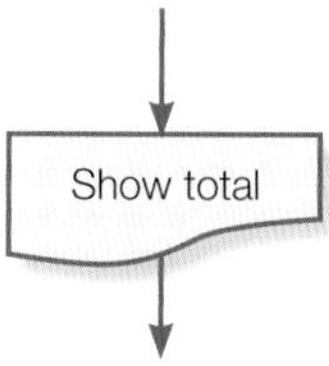

**Figure 7.8** *Flowchart output box*

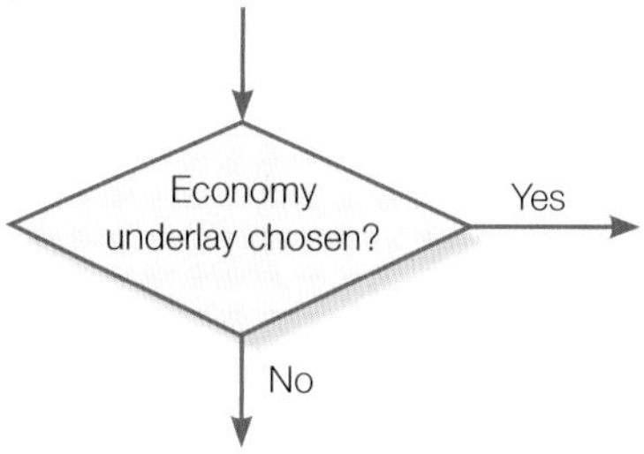

Where a choice or decision needs to be made (a 'selection' building block), a diamond shape is used. The diamond contains a question that describes the choice. Only one arrow enters the shape, but two arrows leave it: one of these shows the route taken if the answer to the question is Yes; the other if the answer is No.

**Figure 7.9** *Flowchart decision box*

Flowcharts are a good introduction to program design methods. However, they are not good for complex problems, as the flowcharts themselves can become complex and difficult to follow.

## Further research – flowcharting skills

Practise your flowchart drawing skills by creating some simple flowcharts for well-known tasks, such as making a cup of tea or getting ready in the morning.

## Case study

### Flowchart and design process for Modern Carpets

In order to develop the process design for the program, Rajesh refers back to the manual process that the sales people currently go through. This is listed in the document that John produced earlier (see page 221):

- Find out the size of the room by multiplying its length by its width.
- Find out the cost per square metre of the chosen carpet.
- Find out whether the customer wants economy or luxury underlay.
- Multiply the cost of the carpet by the area of the room.
- Multiply the cost of the chosen underlay by the area of the room.
- Multiply the cost of fitting by the area of the room.
- Add together the cost of the carpet, underlay and fitting.

These steps are shown as a flowchart in Figure 7.10.

On looking at the flowchart, it becomes clear that more variables will be needed to hold the results of the calculations, such as the following:

- area of room
- underlay cost
- fitting cost.

Rajesh should add these to the variable list he started earlier. The updated variable list is shown in Table 7.3, with the new variables highlighted in bold.

| Variable name | Data type |
| --- | --- |
| roomLength | Single |
| roomWidth | Single |
| carpetPrice | Single |
| totalCost | Single |
| **roomArea** | Single |
| **fittingCost** | Single |
| **underlayCost** | Single |

**Table 7.3** Variables identified so far

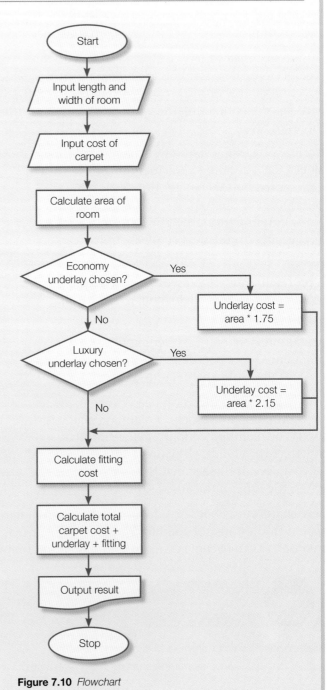

**Figure 7.10** Flowchart

# Other design tools

## Storyboards

A **storyboard** is a sequence of illustrations used to show something changing over time. Storyboards are widely used in the film industry to show the sequence of the action and the camera angles that will be needed.

Storyboards can be used in the same way to show what will appear on the screen when the user performs a particular sequence of actions. An example is shown in Figure 7.11.

Step 1: The user clicks the Browse button

Step 2: File dialogue appears and user selects a directory

Step 3: The chosen location appears in the Options dialogue

**Figure 7.11** *An example storyboard used in software design*

---

**Changing the default save location**

1 The user selects *Tools*, *Options* from the menu.

2 The *Options* command loads the *Options* dialogue box. This shows the currently selected *Default save location*.

3 The user presses the *Browse* button.

4 The *Browse* button loads the *Location* dialogue box.

5 The user navigates to a new folder.

6 The user presses the *Open* button on the *Location* dialogue box.

7 The *Location* dialogue box updates the *Default save location* box in the *Options* dialogue with the value that the user selected.

8 The *Location* dialogue box closes.

9 The user closes the *Options* dialogue.

**Figure 7.12** *An example narrative used in software design*

## Narratives

A **narrative** is, essentially, a storyboard in word form. A narrative may be more appropriate than a storyboard when the visual aspect of the process being described is not that important or if the number of steps is very large. An example narrative used in software design is shown in Figure 7.12.

## Pseudocode

It is generally a bad idea to write any software at design stage. However, sometimes the easiest way to explain a proposed design is to sketch out the code framework that it will use. This is generally done in **pseudocode**, which is typically based on the language that will be used for implementation, but showing just enough detail to get the design ideas across. Examples are shown in Figure 7.13, which shows the pseudocode

```
function MergeSort(unsorted as List)
    Dim left, right as List
    if length(unsorted) <= 1
        return unsorted
    else
        middle = length(unsorted) / 2
        for each x in unsorted up to middle
            add x to left
        for each x in unsorted after middle
            add x to right
        left = mergesort(left)
        right = mergesort(right)
        return merge(left, right)
    end if

function Merge(a as List, b as List)
    Dim result As List
    Dim i, j As Integer = 0
    if length(a) = 0
        return b
    if length(b) = 0
        return a
    while (i < length(a)) and (j < length(b))
        if a[i] <= b[j]
            add a[i] to result
            i = i + 1
        else
            add b[j] to result
            j = j + 1
    while i < length(a)
        add a[i] to result
        i = i + 1
    while j < length(b)
        add b[j] to result
        j = j + 1
    return result
```

**Figure 7.13** *Pseudocode used in design*

```
Function MergeSort(ByRef unsorted As List(Of _
Integer)) As List(Of Integer)
    Dim left, right As New List(Of Integer)
    If unsorted.Count <= 1 Then
        Return unsorted
    Else
        Dim middle As Integer = unsorted.Count \ 2
        left.AddRange(unsorted.GetRange(0, middle))
        right.AddRange(unsorted.GetRange(middle, _
unsorted.Count - middle))
        left = MergeSort(left)
        right = MergeSort(right)
        Dim result As New List(Of Integer)
        result = Merge(left, right)
        Return result
    End If
End Function
Function Merge(ByRef a As List(Of Integer), ByRef b _
As List(Of Integer)) As List(Of Integer)
    Dim result As New List(Of Integer)
    Dim i As Integer = 0
    Dim j As Integer = 0
    If a.Count = 0 Then Return b
    If b.Count = 0 Then Return a
    While (i < a.Count) And (j < b.Count)
        If a.Item(i) <= b.Item(j) Then
            result.Add(a.Item(i))
            i = i + 1
        Else
            result.Add(b.Item(j))
            j = j + 1
        End If
    End While
    While i < a.Count
        result.Add(a.Item(i))
        i = i + 1
    End While
    While j < b.Count
        result.Add(b.Item(j))
        j = j + 1
    End While
    Return result
End Function
```

**Figure 7.14** *Corresponding real code created during implementation*

used in design, and Figure 7.14, which shows the corresponding real code created during implementation.

### Action lists

An **action list** (or **event list**), as the name suggests, is a list of actions that the user can perform (such as 'user presses the big red button') and relevant events that can occur (such as 'an email arrives in the user's inbox').

An action list will be useful both in the implementation stage and to form the basis for an event testing plan (see page 252).

## Conclusion

The design process described here involved taking the understanding of the system, which the investigation stage provided us with, and developing that understanding using a form design, flowchart and variable list. The end result is a design from which the programming code can be written. Flowcharts are not the only diagrammatic programming design technique; there are quite a number of alternative techniques available. They all have broadly the same purpose, which is to assist in the development of a detailed design for the system.

The system design is normally produced as a document that describes the design of the system and includes all of the diagrams that have been produced. The document is important because the designer of the system may not be the person who is going to write the program.

## Test your knowledge

4. What are the three building blocks used in program writing?

5. Why is it better to give objects on a form names other than the default ones (Text2, Command1, and so on)?

6. How can the design form help you to create a list of variables?

7. When designing the processing steps, where should you look to find the information about the steps needed?

8. In a flowchart, what shape symbol is used for the following:

   - inputs
   - outputs
   - processing
   - decisions?

9. In a flowchart, what is different about a decision box, apart from its shape?

10. Why is it important that all the information about a program design be written down in a formal document?

11. What criteria should be used when splitting a large program up into modules?

12. Why does splitting a large program up into modules make the testing easier?

# Development environment

## Editor

Figure 7.15 shows the Visual Basic 2005 Integrated Development Environment (IDE). If you choose to write your software using the Visual Basic .Net programming language this is the environment in which you will work.

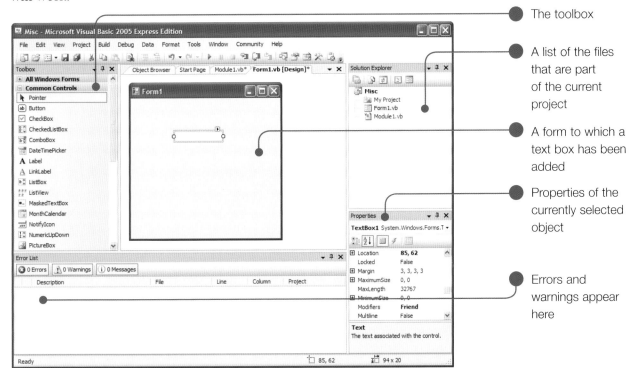

- The toolbox
- A list of the files that are part of the current project
- A form to which a text box has been added
- Properties of the currently selected object
- Errors and warnings appear here

**Figure 7.15** *The Visual Studio 2005 IDE*

## File management

The Visual Basic IDE makes it easy to keep track of the various files that make up your software project. Nevertheless, it is a good idea to make sure that all of the files that you create are held within the same directory on your disk, since this will make it easier to create backups.

The IDE will handle most of the file management tasks, such as creating new files, for you. It is useful to have a working knowledge of additional file management tools, such as Windows Explorer, in case you need to make changes manually.

Another aspect of file management is saving multiple revisions of files. Professional developers use version control systems to automate this. You may choose to manually create copies of your files each time they reach a stable state.

What does it mean?

*An **IDE** (integrated development environment) is a program that includes an editor where you can type the programming code, a compiler for converting the code into binary codes understood by the computer, and a tool called a debugger, which can help you to find errors in the program (see page 246).*

## Other development environment tools

There are separate tools in the development environment, but the IDE brings them all together:

- compiler
- debugger
- GUI component designer.

## Coding the solution

Following a considerable amount of time spent on the design, in theory at least, the program writing should be fairly straightforward. The more detailed the design, the easier the programming should be. However, nothing in life is simple: some inadequacies and omissions in the design are likely to be revealed at this stage or when the program is tested. The more complex the system, the more likely this is to be the case.

The steps in creating the program are as follows:

- Create the program's forms, if this has not already been done as part of the design.
- Declare the variables required.
- Write the code for the event procedures.
- Test the program to ensure it works correctly.

### Syntax and constructs

Before you can start typing away, it is important that you understand the syntax (formal rules) and constructs (ways of controlling the path taken through the program) of the programming language you have chosen. You can follow through the case study to pick these up for Visual Basic .Net, although you should consider getting a reference guide as well; some recommended reference books are listed on page 245.

### Pre-defined functions

A function is a section of code that can be called from somewhere else, and which returns a value. All programming languages contain pre-defined functions to perform common tasks. You will be expected to make use of these in your software component, so this is another reason to invest in a reference guide.

## Case study

### *Writing the code for Modern Carpets*

Code needs to be written for one or more events that occur on the form. The most obvious of these is the click event for the command button `cmdCalculate`. When this button is clicked, the total cost will be calculated.

Before writing the code, Rajesh needs to have the design documents to hand:

- the form design (Figure 7.5)
- the flowchart (Figure 7.10)
- the completed variable list (Table 7.3).

As the first step, Rajesh sets the options `Strict` and `Explicit` to `On`. These options will help him to avoid introducing bugs due to automatic conversions between data types, but mean that he will have to specify each of the necessary conversions by hand.

```
Option Strict On
Option Explicit On
```

Because the costs will need to be updated over time, Rajesh decides to declare them all as constants at the top of the file. By giving them meaningful names, he will make the code easier to understand as well as being easier to maintain.

```
Private Const EconomyUnderlayCost
PerSquareMetre As Single = 1.75
Private Const LuxuryUnderlayCostPer
SquareMetre As Single = 2.15
Private Const FittingCostPerSquare
Metre As Single = 2.5
```

Rajesh then writes the variable declarations, using the variable list as a guide:

```
Dim roomLength As Single
Dim roomWidth As Single
Dim roomArea As Single
Dim carpetPrice As Single
Dim underlayCost As Single
Dim fittingCost As Single
Dim totalCost As Single
```

He then looks at the boxes on the flowchart and works out what code is required to carry out each of the identified processing steps.

The first box in the flowchart is labelled 'Input length and width of the room'. This step involves transferring the contents of the text boxes on the form into the variables. He knows the names of the variables from the variable list, and he gets the names of the text boxes from the form design. So the code he writes is as follows (where `CType(..., Single)` converts the supplied object to a single-precision floating-point number):

```
roomLength = CType(txtLength.Text,
Single)
roomWidth = CType(txtWidth.Text,
Single)
```

The next box on the flowchart is labelled 'Input cost of carpet'. Again he knows the names of the text box and variable, so he writes the following:

```
carpetPrice = CType(txtPrice.Text,
Single)
```

The next box is labelled 'Calculate area of room'. This is the length multiplied by the width:

```
roomArea = roomLength * roomWidth
```

The next part of the flowchart involves making a choice between the two types of underlay. This requires an `IF` statement, which will simply check which option has been selected in the `comUnderlay` combo box.

```
If comUnderlay.Text = "Economy" Then
    underlayCost = roomArea * Economy
    UnderlayCostPerSquareMetre
Else If comUnderlay.Text = "Luxury"
Then
    underlayCost = roomArea * Luxury
    UnderlayCostPerSquareMetre
End If
```

Then the calculation for the price of the fitting is done, so the code is as follows (where `CSng` converts the result from a double-precision floating-point number to a single-precision one):

```
fittingCost = CSng(roomArea *
FittingCostPerSquareMetre)
```

The final calculation works out the price of the carpet (area of the room multiplied by the price per square metre of the carpet) and adds the fitting and underlay costs previously calculated:

```
totalCost = (roomArea *
carpetPrice) + fittingCost +
underlayCost
```

The last box on the flowchart is labelled 'Output result'; this simply involves transferring the total, calculated in the last step, into the text box on the form. Rajesh decides to use the **Format** function to format the result as currency.

```
txtResult.Text = Format(totalCost,
"currency")
```

The complete code for the **cmdCalculate** button is shown in Figure 7.16.

Users will choose between economy and luxury underlay using the **comUnderlay** combo box. This combo box, when the user drops it down, must display these two words so that the user can select

the required one, as shown in Figure 7.17. The words 'Choose from list' are set using the text box's *Text* property and the choice of values is supplied using the *Items* property.

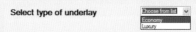

**Figure 7.17** *List of underlay types in the comUnderlay combo box*

Figure 7.18 shows the result of running the program with some sample values.

**Figure 7.18** *Total price calculated from the supplied information*

```
Option Strict On
Option Explicit On

Public Class Form1

    ' Define constants for the prices of underlay and fitting
    Private Const EconomyUnderlayCostPerSquareMetre As Single = 1.75
    Private Const LuxuryUnderlayCostPerSquareMetre As Single = 2.15
    Private Const FittingCostPerSquareMetre As Single = 2.5

    Private Sub cmdCalculate_Click(ByVal sender As System.Object, ByVal e As System.EventArgs) Handles cmdCalculate.Click
        Dim roomLength As Single
        Dim roomWidth As Single
        Dim roomArea As Single
        Dim carpetPrice As Single
        Dim underlayCost As Single
        Dim fittingCost As Single
        Dim totalCost As Single

        ' Read data from input text boxes
        roomLength = CType(txtLength.Text, Single)
        roomWidth = CType(txtWidth.Text, Single)
        carpetPrice = CType(txtPrice.Text, Single)

        roomArea = roomLength * roomWidth

        If comUnderlay.Text = "Economy" Then
            underlayCost = roomArea * EconomyUnderlayCostPerSquareMetre
        ElseIf comUnderlay.Text = "Luxury" Then
            underlayCost = roomArea * LuxuryUnderlayCostPerSquareMetre
        End If

        fittingCost = CSng(roomArea * FittingCostPerSquareMetre)

        totalCost = (roomArea * carpetPrice) + fittingCost + underlayCost

        txtResult.Text = Format(totalCost, "currency")
    End Sub
End Class
```

**Figure 7.16** *The code for the cmdCalculate button*

## Test your knowledge

**13** Give an example of a text box property. What is the property used for?

**14** What are the three attributes of a variable?

**15** Why is `Account Number` not a valid variable name?

**16** Which of the programming building blocks is normally created using an `If` statement?

**17** Give an example of a statement that can be used to start a loop.

**18** What function can you use to test whether a value is numeric?

**19** What is the `Dim` statement used for?

**20** What previously created document is used as a guide when writing program code?

**21** What function can be used to display a numerical value as currency?

## Producing an executable version of the program

Once the coding for the program is complete, you will want to create an executable version of your program. At the moment, the program can be run only from the Visual Basic IDE. When you create an executable version, a file is created that you can run simply by double-clicking on it. You can place the file in any folder, or on the desktop. You can also copy the file to any Windows computer, where it will run without needing the Visual Basic IDE.

To create an executable version of your program, use the *Build* menu in the Visual Basic IDE. This contains two options: *Build* and *Publish*. For a simple project, it will be sufficient to choose *Build*. This will generate some files under your project's `/bin/release` directory, and you will be able to run these or copy them to another location. The *Publish* option creates a more professional (but more complicated) installation file, which automates things such as adding a shortcut to the *Start* menu and allows the program to be uninstalled via *Add/Remove Programs* on the *Control Panel*.

## Further research

You will probably need a reference book in order to write your own software in Visual Basic 2005. Some possibilities are as follows:

- *Visual Basic 2005 in a Nutshell*, Tim Patrick et al, O'Reilly; ISBN: 059610152X
- *Programming Visual Basic 2005*, Jesse Liberty, O'Reilly; ISBN: 0596009496
- *Visual Basic 2005 Step by Step*, V. Halvorson, Microsoft Press; ISBN: 0735621314
- *Beginning Visual Basic 2005*, Willis T and Newsome B, Hoboken NJ, Wrox Press; ISBN: 0764574019

# Debug and test a solution

## Debugging

Figure 7.19 shows a program being debugged in the Visual Basic 2005 debugger.

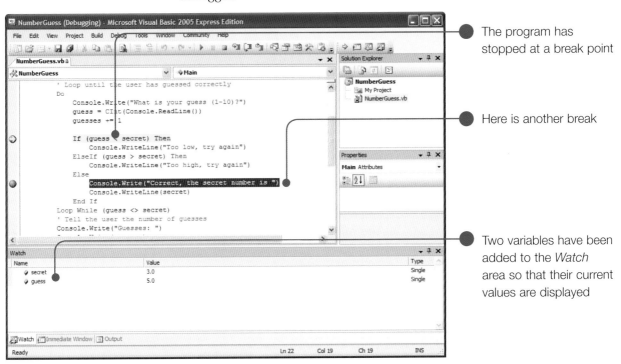

The program has stopped at a break point

Here is another break

Two variables have been added to the *Watch* area so that their current values are displayed

**Figure 7.19** *Debugging a program*

### Breakpoints

When you debug a program, you usually want it to run at full speed to a certain point and then stop so that you can take a closer look. To do this, you set a breakpoint on any lines where you want the debugger to stop.

In Visual Basic you can set a breakpoint by clicking in the grey column to the left of the line; a red circle appears to show that the breakpoint has been set. Figure 7.19 shows two breakpoints: one on the If line (the arrow shows that the debugger is currently stopped here) and one on the first line after the Else.

### Watches

When you stop at a breakpoint, you are usually interested in the value of one or more of the variables. By setting a watch on a variable, its value will be displayed in the debugger until you decide to remove the watch. Figure 7.19 shows two variables being watched: secret (with a value of 3.0) and guess (with a value of 5.0).

## Traces

A trace is a record of the steps that have been taken through a program. This can be useful for finding the location of an error without having to step slowly through the debugger.

Visual Basic 2005 supports traces using the `Trace` class. Here is an example of how it could be used, printing messages whenever the program enters or leaves a particular subroutine:

```vb
Sub myTracedSub()
    ' Set up the trace to print to the console
    Trace.Listeners.Add(New TextWriterTraceListener
    (Console.Out))
    Trace.AutoFlush = True
    ' Indent the output so that it stands out
    Trace.Indent()
    ' Write some output
    Trace.WriteLine("Entering myTracedSub")
    ' ------------------------
    ' Do actual processing here
    ' ------------------------
    Trace.WriteLine("Exiting myTracedSub")
    ' Go back to the original indentation
    Trace.Unindent()
End Sub
```

# Types of error

## Compile-time errors

Compile-time errors are mistakes in the code that prevent the compiler from understanding it.

### Syntax errors

A syntax error occurs when the rules governing the structure of the language have been broken.

```vb
' Example of a syntax error
Dim myName = "Matthew" As String
' The correct order is as follows
Dim myName As String = "Matthew"
```

### Typos

Sometimes a slip of the finger during typing can lead to an error.

```vb
' Example of a typo
Dim length As Integer = 0
lenght = 5   ' Spelled wrongly
Console.WriteLine(length)
```

This code will cause different things to happen depending on whether Option Explicit is on or off. If it is on, the typo will result in an error because all variables must be declared before they are used. If it is off, a second variable – called lenght – will be created automatically on the third line, so the value written to the console will be 0, whereas the programmer probably wanted it to be 5. This is why you should always set Option Explicit to On in your programs.

## Run-time errors

Run-time errors are mistakes that cannot be detected by the compiler, but which cause problems when the compiled code is running.

### Infinite loops

The programmer wanted the following code to print the numbers 1 to 10. By forgetting to increment the variable, the programmer created an infinite loop: the program just prints the number 1 again and again.

```
' Infinite loop
Dim i As Integer = 1
While (i <= 10)
    Console.WriteLine(i)
    ' The programmer wanted this to loop ten times
    ' but forgot to add the code to increment i
End While
```

### Array bounds errors

An array has a fixed number of elements, referred to by their index numbers (see page 229). Code that tries to access an element with an index less than one, or more than the size of the array, will cause an error at run time.

### Division by zero errors

In most computer programming languages, dividing a number by zero causes an error. However, in Visual Basic, variables can have the special

```
' Array out of bounds error
Dim array(5) As Integer
' There are only 5 elements in the array, so trying
' to set a value for the sixth causes a run-time error
array(6) = 47
```

value Infinity.

```
' Divide by zero
Dim cost As Double = 100.0
Dim months As Double
```

```
Console.WriteLine("How many months would you
like to pay over? ")
months = CDbl(Console.ReadLine())
' The following line will divide by zero if
' that is what the user has typed
Dim monthlyPayment As Double = cost / months
Console.Write("Monthly payment is £")
Console.WriteLine(monthlyPayment)
```

If you run this and type 4 when prompted, the program will display the following:

```
Monthly payment is £25
```

However, if you type 0 the result is as follows:

```
Monthly payment is £Infinity
```

This is quite expensive, but only what you would expect if paying over zero months! It would be far better to check that the user enters a sensible Months value before using it in any sort of calculation, particularly division.

## Testing for errors

Testing is a vital (though often unpopular!) part of software development. The users of the software would not be very impressed if the program produced the wrong answers, nor would they be happy if the program kept crashing while they were using it. Testing is the process of checking that all the functions of the program work as they should, and give the correct results. The definitions of terms like 'work as they should' and 'correct results' need to come from the original program specification, which was agreed by the users and the developers before the program was written.

As well as checking that the program works correctly when used correctly, the software developer also needs to check that the program is robust and can stand being used incorrectly without crashing. This is important because the users of the program are unlikely to be expert computer users. They may misunderstand how the program is supposed to be used; they may also make mistakes when using the program, such as pressing keys or clicking buttons in error or making inappropriate entries in a text box (text instead of a number, for example).

Making sure a program works correctly may sound like a fairly simple task, but software testing, except for the simplest of programs, is a complex and involved task, which requires planning.

Testing a program is often split into data testing and event testing. Data testing checks that the program can deal correctly with the data that is input by the user, and that it produces the correct output. Event testing checks that all the different options, such as button and menu options, produce the expected results. We shall look at data testing first.

## Data testing

The first step in data testing is to produce some test data. This involves choosing some input values and then manually working out what output the program should produce if it is supplied with these input values. The program is then run using these input values and the expected outputs are compared with the actual ones the program produces. If they are different then the program has failed the test and will need to be modified so that the actual and expected values match.

The choice of input values is important. A range of values needs to be chosen in each of the following categories:

- **Normal values** – realistic expected values that the program is likely to need to deal with regularly.
- **Extreme values** – the minimum and maximum values that are valid input. For a number, these would be a very small number and a very large number. For text, this would be a very short string and a very long string. For example, in a text box where someone's name is to be entered, two extreme values might be 'Ng' and 'Fotherington-Thomas'.
- **Abnormal values** – incorrect entries, e.g. 32/10/06 as a date, 205 for someone's age, or a text value where a numeric one is expected.

## Case study

### *Data testing the program for Modern Carpets*

Rather than testing the program himself, Rajesh asks one of his colleagues, Amy Weston, to test the carpet cost calculator. It is a good idea to get someone other than the original programmer to test a new program. The original programmer may be too 'gentle' with his or her creation. Also, another person may have fewer preconceived ideas about how the program should work.

Amy needs to produce a test plan for data testing the cost calculator. For some of the categories in extreme and abnormal test data, Amy needs to check back in the specification to see how it says these values should be dealt with.

She needs to know the following:

- Is there a maximum length and width of room that the program needs to deal with?

- Is there a maximum price of carpet that the program should accept?

She looks these questions up in the specification and discovers that 100m is the largest length and width and £50 per square metre is the highest price the program should accept.

Amy produces a table showing the input data and accepted outputs, shown in Table 7.4. Notice that the form includes spaces for her to record the software version and the date on which the tests were run. This could be useful information when looking back on test results later (e.g. if a later change causes one of the tests to fail then it will be easy to find out when it was last known to have run successfully, which might make it easier for the developers to track down the problem).

In order to check that the program is calculating carpet prices correctly, Amy manually works out the correct results for the normal and extreme data where the result should not be an error message. She fills in all the expected results on the test data table and then tries out each of the test calculations on the program, entering the actual results the program produces in the last column. If the entries in the expected and actual columns match then the program has passed the tests. If they are different then there is a problem.

Amy discovers that the program passes the tests with the Normal data, but there are problems with both the Extreme and Abnormal data tests. She makes a list of the problems:

■ *Extreme data* – the program works as it should with test data items 5, 6, 8 and 10 but it does not

produce an error message with test data items 7, 9, 11, 12 and 13. The calculations are done despite the fact that the input data is beyond the ranges listed in the specification.

■ *Abnormal data* – the results are worse with this data. Tests 14, 15, 16 and 17 all cause the program to crash as they contain non-numeric data.

Amy passes the results of her tests back to Rajesh, who is not very happy! When Rajesh wrote the program he forgot that the specification listed maximum values for the room size and carpet price. He also forgot to include code in the program to check that the data entered by the user was numeric before attempting to do anything with it. Fortunately, neither of these problems is difficult to fix, but it is important that they were spotted before the program was handed over to the users.

| Test data | | | | Software version | | Date | | |
|---|---|---|---|---|---|---|---|---|
| Test no. | Length | Width | Underlay | | Price | Expected result | Actual result | |
| **Category: Normal** | | | | | | | | |
| 1 | 2.5 | 3.4 | Economy | | 2.50 | £57.38 | | |
| 2 | 5.2 | 4.5 | Luxury | | 5.99 | £248.98 | | |
| 3 | 1.4 | 6.2 | Luxury | | 3.50 | £70.74 | | |
| 4 | 6.5 | 6.8 | Economy | | 7.25 | £508.30 | | |
| **Category: Extreme** | | | | | | | | |
| 5 | 0 | 0 | Luxury | | 0 | £0.00 | | |
| 6 | 100 | 5 | Economy | | 5 | £4,625.00 | | |
| 7 | 101 | 5 | Economy | | 5 | Error Msg | | |
| 8 | 6 | 100 | Luxury | | 3 | £4,590.00 | | |
| 9 | 4 | 101 | Economy | | 7 | Error Msg | | |
| 10 | 5 | 7 | Luxury | | 50 | £1,912.75 | | |
| 11 | 6 | 3 | Economy | | 51 | Error Msg | | |
| 12 | -1 | 5 | Economy | | 5 | Error Msg | | |
| 13 | 5 | 5 | Economy | | -1 | Error Msg | | |
| **Category: Abnormal** | | | | | | | | |
| 14 | Five | 2.3 | Economy | | 2.99 | Error Msg | | |
| 15 | 4.5 | Three | Economy | | 5.99 | Error Msg | | |
| 16 | 2.5 | 4.6 | Luxury | | Three fifty | Error Msg | | |
| 17 | Blank | Blank | Choose from list (Blank) | | Blank | Error Msg | | |

**Table 7.4** *Test data table*

## Further research

How could Rajesh fix these problems? Try this yourself by modifying the code and running it.

## Event testing

Event testing checks that the program responds correctly to events such as mouse clicks on buttons and the selection of menu options. These can simply be tested by making a list of all the events that the program is supposed to respond to, and describing what the correct response to each event is. Once the list is made, each event on the list can be tried on the program.

Our case study example is very simple – the only notable event is what happens when the user presses the 'Calculate' button, and this has effectively already been tested during data testing.

## Making modifications

Once the tests are complete, the program will need modifying to fix the errors that have been found. Details about the modifications made should be kept, along with the original test data and event table, in the technical documentation for the program. The program should then be retested, just to check that the modifications really have been successful and no other errors have been introduced accidentally.

## Test your knowledge

22  Why is it important to test a program?

23  Why do you need to check the original specification when testing a program?

24  What is test data? How is it used?

25  Suppose a program asks the user to input a number between 1 and 10. Give two examples of each of the following that could be used to test the software: normal values, extreme values, abnormal values. Can you think of any more abnormal values that should be tested?

26  What is the difference between data testing and event testing?

27  Why is it a good idea for the tester not to be the author of the code being tested?

# Document the solution

Simply handing over a completed program on disk is not sufficient. People need to know how to install the program, how to use it and how to deal with problems that may arise. The completed program must be supported by documentation. Developers need to produce two types of documentation:

- **Technical documentation** – this describes the internal workings of the software.
- **User documentation** – this explains to the users how they should use the program.

As you would expect, the contents of these two types of documentation are rather different.

## Technical (internal) documentation

Technical documentation is written for support staff and programmers. Software is very rarely static: throughout its life it is constantly changing as new features are added and bugs are fixed. Some errors may surface only after the software has been in use for many years. The programmers who originally wrote the software will probably have moved to new projects or perhaps to different companies. Technical documentation is therefore needed so that the people who need to modify or correct the program can understand how it works.

If the programs are written well in the first place, using meaningful variable names for example, certain aspects will be self-documenting. Also, if the programs follow the design closely then the design documents can be used to understand the working of the program.

### Meaningful identifiers

Figures 7.20 and 7.21 show two functionally identical sections of code, the first without and the second with meaningful identifiers. The second is longer, but easier to understand and to maintain.

### Hungarian notation

Hungarian notation is a method of encoding the data type of a variable in its identifier by prefixing it with lower case letters. For example, a variable might be named `sName`, where `s` signifies that it is a string variable. Other examples are shown in Table 7.5. There are two schools of thought about the use of Hungarian

```
Function DOMT _
        (ByVal d As Integer, _
        ByVal m As Integer, _
        ByVal flag As Boolean) _
As Integer
    Dim lim As Boolean
    Select Case m
        Case 2
            If flag Then
                lim = (d = 29)
            Else
                lim = (d = 28)
            End If
        Case 9, 4, _
            6, 11
            lim = (d = 30)
        Case Else
            lim = (d = 31)
    End Select

    If lim Then
        Return 1
    Else
        Return d + 1
    End If
End Function
```

**Figure 7.20** *Section of code without meaningful identifiers*

## What does it mean?

*An **identifier** is the string of characters used to identify a particular variable, constant or function. For example, in the code* `widgets = 3`, *the identifier is* `widgets`.

### What does it mean?

**Hungarian notation**

*was originally developed by Charles Simonyi. Because he was originally from Hungary, and code written in this style is not plain English, Simonyi's co-workers at Microsoft christened this style Hungarian notation.*

notation: some people think that it makes it easier to find and prevent bugs, and can make programs easier to understand; other people think that it makes code cluttered and difficult to read.

```
Enum Month
    January = 1
    February = 2
    March = 3
    April = 4
    May = 5
    June = 6
    July = 7
    August = 8
    September = 9
    October = 10
    November = 11
    December = 12
End Enum

Function DayOfMonthTomorrow _
        (ByVal dayOfMonthToday As Integer, _
        ByVal monthOfYearToday As Month, _
        ByVal isLeapYear As Boolean) _
As Integer
    Dim isLastDayInMonth As Boolean
    Select Case monthOfYearToday
        Case Month.February
            If isLeapYear Then
                isLastDayInMonth = (dayOfMonthToday = 29)
            Else
                isLastDayInMonth = (dayOfMonthToday = 28)
            End If
        Case Month.September, Month.April, _
            Month.June, Month.November
            isLastDayInMonth = (dayOfMonthToday = 30)
        Case Else
            isLastDayInMonth = (dayOfMonthToday = 31)
    End Select

    If isLastDayInMonth Then
        Return 1
    Else
        Return dayOfMonthToday + 1
    End If
End Function
```

**Figure 7.21** *Same section of code with meaningful identifiers*

| Data type | Prefix | Example |
|-----------|--------|---------|
| Boolean | b | bIsFinished |
| Floating point number | f | fAverageHeight |
| Integer | n | nDaysInDecember |
| Long integer | l | lWorldPopulation |
| String | s | sCapitalOfEngland |

**Table 7.5** *Examples of Hungarian notation*

## Comments

A comment is a part of a computer program that is ignored by the computer – it is there entirely for the benefit of the programmer. Programmers use comments to document their programs: to explain what a particular module or function is for, to highlight anything unusual or incomplete, and generally to act as reminders. However well you think you understand a computer program you have written, when you come back to it months or years later it will no longer be fresh in your mind, and you might have to work hard to understand how it works. The same difficulty occurs when you look at programs written by other people, or they look at your programs. If you use comments liberally in your programs, this will make them easier to understand.

The proportion of a program that should be 'comments' is open to debate. Some programmers have a naturally terse style, and believe that the use of meaningful identifiers is enough to make programs 'self-documenting'. Other programmers write more comments than lines of code. You should avoid either of these extremes; use comments wherever they add extra useful information about the program.

In Visual Basic, comments must begin with a single quote mark (') so the computer knows they are not program code.

Examples of pointless comments

```
' Temporary function
Dim count as Integer ' The count
total = first + second ' Calculate the total
```

Examples of useful comments

```
' Calculates the number of seconds between two
times.
Dim count as Integer ' Number of apples eaten
so far
total = first + second ' Unsafe if first or
second is too large
```

An important point is that you should write comments as you go along, not just at the end. Often, explaining a problem in clear English will help you to find a solution. If you think of a useful comment then add it straight away – if you delay, you are likely to forget to add it at all.

Sometimes it is useful to use comments to mark bug fixes in the code, perhaps by commenting out the original lines of code but keeping them in the program together with a comment about the change. Comments should probably only be used in this way where there is a likelihood that programmers might otherwise put the code back to its original state in future maintenance. Too many such comments will become unwieldy – they are no substitute for a proper **version control** system.

## Indentation

Many programming languages ignore the spaces and tab characters (collectively known as **white space**) between keywords. As a result, programmers can choose how to space out their code. It is a good idea to indent blocks of code at the same level (e.g. everything inside a loop), since this makes it easier to see the structure of the program.

What does it mean?

**Version control** (or **revision control**) is the management of multiple versions of software components. Software tools, such as Microsoft Source Safe, allow programmers to inspect old versions of their programs, e.g. to see when a particular bug was fixed (or introduced). Every professional software development team should use version control software.

What does it mean?

The **Tab key** is situated above the Caps Lock on the left-hand side of your keyboard. The character it produces, known as a **tab**, is used to create columns of text. A tab character is not a fixed width; instead it expands to fill up to the next **tab stop**, defined in terms of a number of characters.

| So, for example | might appear as | |
| --- | --- | --- |
| Name[tab]Age | Name | Age |
| Bill[tab]50 | Bill | 50 |
| Jennifer[tab]35 | Jennifer | 35 |

There are no universal rules about the number of spaces to use for each level of indentation (typically three or four), or indeed whether to use tab characters or spaces. Programmers often have strong preferences about which styles of indentation and spacing should be used on a project. Rules for indentation and spacing are often given in coding standards. If no rules are given then you should follow the style already used for existing programs on your team. Sensible and consistent use of indentation and spacing will make the programs you write easier to understand and more pleasant to read.

## Further research

1   If you do not believe that these things are all that important, go and look at some of the entries in *The International Obfuscated C Code Contest*. Go to www.heinemann.co.uk/hotlinks, insert the express code 2048P and click on this unit. This is an annual competition where programmers deliberately try to produce the most complex and unmaintainable C code that they possibly can. The programmers deliberately use obscure identifiers, remove comments and play about with indentation (for example, producing code in the shape of a Christmas tree). By seeing these things taken to extremes, you should understand the value of good internal documentation.

If you would like a challenge, try this:

2   Create a simple program, but deliberately make it as difficult to understand as possible by not using comments or meaningful identifiers. Swap your program with someone else. Can you work out what their program does? Try modifying their program so that it is easier to understand.

## What the technical documentation should include

The technical documentation should include the original design documents (variable lists, flowcharts, pseudocode etc.) that the program was written from. Diagrams should also be included that describe how the different modules in the program interact. Any special features or complex calculations should be explained.

For each procedure or module in the program, the following should be included:

■ a listing of the program code, either fully commented or with annotations
■ a printout of any forms, including the object names.

Full details of the testing carried out on the program should be in the technical documentation, including the completed test data plan and event testing plan. Notes listing the modifications, made as a result of errors uncovered during tests, should also be included.

The documentation should also include details of the operating systems and versions that the program will work with, as well as the disk space required and any other hardware requirements. Instructions on how to install the software should also be included.

When improvements or corrections are made to the program, details of these changes should be added to the technical documentation.

## User documentation

### User instructions

User manuals, 'quick start' guides and other documents written for users are fundamentally different from the types of document that software developers write for other software developers. Users often have a wide range of skills and knowledge levels, so user instructions need to be simple enough for inexperienced users to follow, while having sufficient detail to allow more advanced users to get the most out of the software.

When you write user documentation, try to avoid technical jargon. If some technical jargon is unavoidable, you might consider adding a glossary that explains the terms you have used.

### 'Quick start' instructions

When a user first receives a new piece of software, they may want to start using it straight away. If they are familiar with previous versions of the software then they will not want to wade through a detailed manual before installing and using the new version. Various 'quick start' instructions are often supplied to bring users up to speed as quickly as possible.

Perhaps the most common 'quick start' instructions are the **readme** files that are often supplied on the same disk as the new software. These files contain the information that people need to know before they use the software for the first time. Readme files often contain an installation guide, release notes, and a list of known bugs.

An **installation guide** provides instructions about how to install the software. It guides users through the necessary steps, and explains any potential problems with the process (such as whether old versions of the software must be manually uninstalled before the new version is installed). Even if a program does not need to be installed (that is, it can be run from any directory), the user should be told how to start the program (where it is installed and how to run it) and how to exit again.

**Release notes** explain what changes have been made to the software since the previous version. This document will list any major bugs that have been fixed and any new features that have been introduced. Release notes for previous versions of the software are often kept for the benefit of those users who do not upgrade to each new version – they can look lower down the document to find out what changes were made in all of the versions that they skipped.

A **list of known bugs** is sometimes included, perhaps with estimates of when patches or fixed releases will be available. This list is usually limited to major bugs, and any known workarounds to avoid the problems are usually given.

What does it mean?

*A **patch** is a change to a larger program to fix a problem. In Windows, patches are usually executable files that modify or replace software components that have already been installed on the computer. A good example of this is 'Patch Tuesday': on the second Tuesday of each month, Microsoft makes security patches available, which can then be downloaded and installed by the Microsoft Update software.*

The 'quick start' instructions can also be a convenient place to add a **frequently asked question (FAQ)** list. In such lists, the questions and answers tend to be quite short, such as:

*'Can I get help by email?'*

*'Yes. If you have a problem, please email support@example.com'.*

A FAQ list is a good place to mop up any questions that are not answered in the manual, help files or online help.

## General instructions

Once users have installed and started a software application, they need to know how to use it. Programmers usually supply these instructions in the form of a printed manual or an electronic help file (or both).

There are two ways to document how to use a piece of software: command-based instructions or task-based instructions. Take a manual for a word processor as an example. A command-based manual would go through each of the menu options one by one and explain what they do (Figure 7.22). A task-based manual would select a task that the user is likely to want to do, such as changing the margins, and then explain how to achieve this (Figure 7.23).

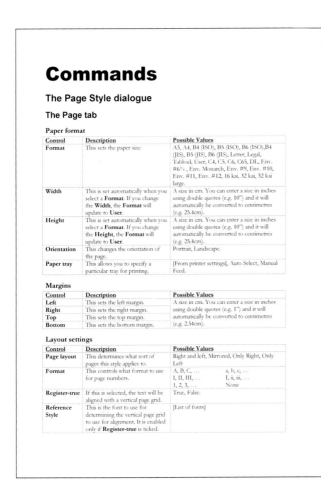

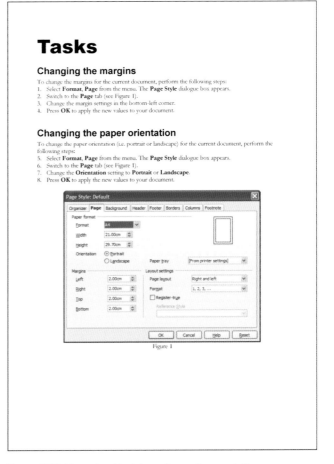

**Figure 7.22** *Example of command-based user documentation*

**Figure 7.23** *Example of task-based user documentation*

Of course, there is no reason why the two approaches should not be combined; for example, a task-based manual could have a concise command-based reference guide as an appendix.

Whichever style is chosen, appropriate use of screen shots is a useful technique. A well-chosen screen shot can show information much more concisely than a text description, and is more difficult for readers to misinterpret. Screen shots also help to break up the text; page upon page of type would put many users off reading the manual at all!

The instructions should explain how to use each of the program's features. This should include details of what the buttons, text boxes, list boxes and any other objects should be used for. The instructions should also explain how to use any menus and shortcut keys.

The user documentation must be written in a way that the target audience can understand. Therefore, technical jargon needs to be avoided and the manual must be relevant to the way the program will be used in the workplace; e.g. by using realistic examples.

### Troubleshooting guide

A troubleshooting guide is often just a simple, short list of the problems that people have reported in the past and the ways that users can overcome them. See Figure 7.24. These problems are often to do with the unpredictable environment in which the software might end up being used; for example, problems may occur when using a modern software package on an old machine with limited amounts of memory and free disk space.

The troubleshooting guide is often a convenient place to add a list of all the error messages that a program can produce, what they mean, and what the user must do when these messages occur. The guide should also include details about what to do if something goes wrong or the program crashes, such as who to contact (you!).

# Troubleshooting

### Known problems

| Problem | Workaround |
|---|---|
| Print Preview always uses portrait orientation, even if the page has been set up to be landscape. | This is scheduled for fixing in the next release. For now, use PDF export instead of Print Preview when working with landscape documents. |
| Opening large files causes the application to stop responding. | This can occur on machines that have Acme Memory Manager installed. Please disable AMM before attempting to open a large file. |

### Error messages

| Message | Description |
|---|---|
| Fatal disk error occurred when writing log. | The software cannot save the log file to disk. Check that you have sufficient free disk space. |
| Unable to allocate widgets. | A widget request could not be fulfilled. This is usually because there is insufficient memory – try closing any programs you are not using. |
| Unknown user. | The user name and/or password you used is incorrect. |

### Further help

If you encounter some other problem with the software, please email help@mysoftwarecompany.co.uk for assistance.

**Figure 7.24** *An example of a troubleshooting guide*

## Other forms of user documentation

Although the term 'documentation' tends to suggest a printed book of some kind, it is increasingly popular to do away with the expense of producing user documentation in the form of a book and provide online help instead. The Microsoft Windows operating system provides a way of producing help files in a standard format, with search and index facilities already built in. It is beyond the scope of this chapter to explain how to create these files, but you should at least be aware that the option exists to create them. As well as being cheaper than manuals, help files are easier for developers to update and easier for users to search.

Companies that produce software for a large number of users often set up websites and mailing lists to provide support. These services help customers and developers communicate with one another, providing a simple way for customers to report any problems they find with the software, and for developers to keep the customers up to date about new versions of the software.

# Maintenance documentation

Maintenance documentation is written for support staff and programmers. Throughout the life of a program, changes or improvements may need to be made, and it may be the case that, despite careful testing, some errors surface only after many years of use. The programmers who originally wrote the software will probably have moved to new projects or perhaps even to different companies. Maintenance documentation is therefore needed so that the people who need to modify or correct the program can understand how it works.

## Technical description

The technical description is written by programmers for programmers, and should include all of the necessary information to allow other people to understand and modify the software. This should include all of the documentation that was produced during the design, which should be updated to reflect any changes that have since been made. A data dictionary (see below) can be useful, particularly for applications that interact with databases.

Special care should be taken to explain any unusual or complex parts of the program, since these are the areas that are most likely to cause difficulties for the future maintainers.

The maintenance documentation should also include full details of the testing carried out on the program, including the completed data-testing plan and event-testing plan. Notes listing the modifications made to fix errors uncovered during tests should also be added.

## Data dictionary

A **data dictionary** is a precise description of the data held within a computer application. Data dictionaries are typically used to document the structure of databases, and should include all of the information that would be necessary to recreate an empty database. For simple databases, a data dictionary might just consist of the name, data type and description of the fields in each of the tables. A **table** is the part of a database in which the data is stored. A table consists of **rows** (or **records**) made up of **columns** (or **fields**). Each field stores a single item of data, such as a telephone number.

## Evaluation of the solution

At the end of a project, or even after a release part way through a project, it can be useful to look back at how it has gone. If everything has gone well then it is worth recording what tools and techniques you used, so that other people can benefit from your experiences (for example, if you believe that an automated testing tool saved time during development then it is worth recording this for whoever ends up maintaining the software). Similarly, if some things went badly then it is well worth recording what went wrong and why; this will help people to avoid such problems in future.

Your evaluation should include an assessment of how well the final product satisfied the customer's requirements, details of any unexpected events that affected the project (such as the customer adding extra requirements at a late stage, or a power cut causing work to be lost), and recommendations for improving the software development process in future (such as more time spent gathering initial requirements, or a better method of making backups of work in progress).

### Evaluation of the process

Learning to program is not easy. It may well be that your first experiences of programming have been difficult and confusing. Evaluating your experiences can help you to understand where you went wrong and where your strengths and weaknesses lie.

One of the most difficult things about software development can be developing a design for a program that makes it possible to produce the program relatively easily. To do this requires a good understanding of programming techniques in general as well as specific knowledge about the programming language you are using. This, of course, is something that at this stage you probably do not have. It is worth remembering that, in industry, the people who produce the system design (often called **systems analysts**) normally work for many years as programmers before moving on to the more senior role of systems analyst.

Here are some questions you might like to ask yourself:

- Which parts of the software development process did you understand well?
- Which parts of the software development process do you still not understand well? These are the areas you may need to go over again. Developing a good understanding of the whole process will take time.
- Did the program development process go according to your plan? If not, which parts of the process took more or less time than you planned?

### Evaluation of the program

As well as evaluating your experiences in developing software, it is important to check that the program you have produced meets its original aim.

It is possible, in the excitement and relief of finally getting a program working properly, to forget its original aims. You need to look at the investigation you did and see whether the program you developed solves the original problem. In particular, you need to decide whether the aims of the system that were identified in the investigation have been met.

When evaluating a program, it can be difficult to be objective about your own work. One effective method of obtaining constructive feedback about your program is to let other people try it out and comment on it.

Here are some questions you might ask them to answer about your program:

- Is the layout and labelling of the forms neat and clear?
- Does the program do what you would expect?
- Does it match the program as it was originally specified?
- Does it work properly?
- Is there anything missing from the program?

The result of the evaluation stage should be a report. In the report, you need to describe your experiences in developing the software, what the other people who evaluated your program thought about it, and your views on how closely the program you wrote met the original requirements.

## Case study

### *User testing the program for Modern Carpets*

The real test of a program is to give it to the users. After all, they are the people who have to use the program on a day-to-day basis.

Rajesh installs the carpet cost calculator at Modern Carpets' shops and shows the staff how to use it. They find it a useful aid in their negotiations with customers but it is not long before they start to think how it could be made better. This begins another software development process. Rajesh needs to investigate what improvements and additions they would like, then design how these changes can be done, and so on through implementation and retesting.

This is why you will sometimes hear the term **software development cycle**. Just as the software development appears to be complete, the process starts again with the development of the next, improved version of the system.

## Future development

It is also important to record ideas for future development of the software. This may include bugs that were not fixed, aspects of the customer's requirements that have not been completely fulfilled, or new features that would improve the software.

## Test your knowledge

28 What are the main aims of user and maintenance documentation?

29 For whom are the user and maintenance documentation written?

30 What sort of information will be included in the maintenance documentation?

31 What are program comments and why are they important?

32 What are the two main approaches used when writing user documentation?

33 List some of the advantages of online documentation.

34 Why is it useful to include screen dumps in user documentation?

35 What does the term FAQ mean?

## Assessment tasks

The assessment tasks in this unit are based on the case study of Modern Carpets, referred to throughout the unit.

> To work towards a Distinction in this unit you will need to achieve **all** the Pass, Merit and Distinction criteria in the unit and have evidence to show that you have achieved each one.

## How do I provide assessment evidence?

Your evidence can be presented in any suitable form, such as written reports, visual or online presentations, leaflets or posters. Evidence of your design can be presented in the form of storyboards, pseudocode, narratives, action lists, flowcharts or structure diagrams. Evidence of the creation of your software component is expected to be in the form of a printout of the code with either an observation record or screen shots of the running program.

All your evidence should be presented in one folder, which should have a front cover and a contents page. You should divide the evidence into ten sections corresponding to the ten tasks.

## Task 1 (P1)

Your tutor will provide you with a software development procedure. Describe the software development procedure and the need for organisational standards.

## Task 2 (P2(1))

Identify a problem that can be solved by writing a program. If possible, choose a real-life problem, perhaps a program that you can write for a friend, or organisation you know. Beware of choosing a problem that is too complex. You will need to investigate the problem, finding out as much as you can about it. Create a requirements document explaining the problem.

## Task 3 (P3)

Produce a detailed design for the program you will write.

Break your problem down into manageable sections. Design input and output screens or reports and produce a list of the variables that will be required. Use an appropriate tool (such as a flowchart) to design the processing that will be required, and justify your choice of design tools.

## Task 4 (P2 (2), M1)

Read the overviews of Visual Basic 2005 available on the internet. Go to www.heinemann.co.uk/hotlinks, insert the express code 2048P and click on this unit. Write a summary of these articles, highlighting any features that you think will be particularly useful in your program. Justify the choice of Visual Basic 2005 for this project.

# Assessment tasks continued

## Task 5 (P4, M1(1), D2)

Implement the program, following the design you created in Task 3. You might consider producing an early prototype with limited functionality, and getting feedback from your customer before implementing the full version. You might also need to rework your requirements and design in response to this feedback (if so, remember to keep every version of these documents, because they provide useful evidence of how you developed the software). Demonstrate how you have complied with organisational standards when producing your software.

> To work towards a Distinction, you should evaluate how you applied development procedures to produce your software component.

## Task 6 (P5 (1))

Write test plans for your software, covering both data and event testing. Create a log of the tests that you perform.

## Task 7 (P5 (2), M3)

Investigate the errors identified in the testing of the program and document the modifications you make to correct the program. Demonstrate your understanding of the debugging facilities, for example by creating screen shots when you are debugging.

## Task 8 (P5 (3))

In a group, look at one another's test plans and logs. Discuss whether you think sufficient debugging and testing has taken place. Write a summary of any improvements you could make to your debugging and testing in your next software development project.

## Task 9 (M2 (1))

Demonstrate that the program meets the original requirements. For example, you could demonstrate the program to your client and ask them to fill in an observation report to confirm which of their requirements have been met.

## Task 10 (P6, M2 (2), D1)

Provide full technical and user documentation for the program (your tutor will provide you with organisational standards, which you must follow). Also include details of the problem areas and what went according to plan. Demonstrate compliance with organisational standards for the content and formatting of the document you produce.

> To work towards a Distinction, your maintenance documentation must be complete with technical description, data dictionary, evaluation of solution and future development for the software component identified. Your user documentation should include a troubleshooting guide. You must consistently make correct usage of specialist terminology.

# 8 Customising Applications Software

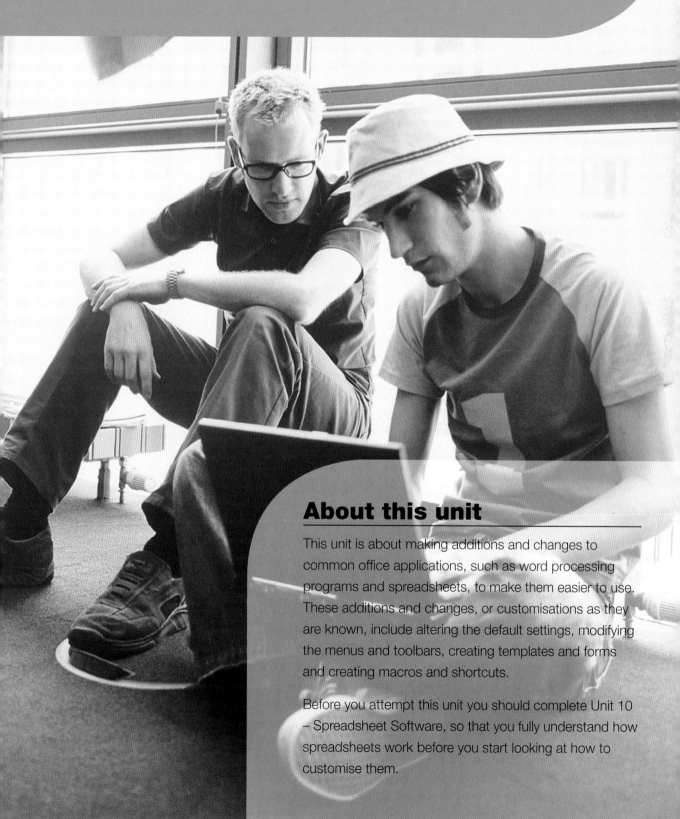

## About this unit

This unit is about making additions and changes to common office applications, such as word processing programs and spreadsheets, to make them easier to use. These additions and changes, or customisations as they are known, include altering the default settings, modifying the menus and toolbars, creating templates and forms and creating macros and shortcuts.

Before you attempt this unit you should complete Unit 10 – Spreadsheet Software, so that you fully understand how spreadsheets work before you start looking at how to customise them.

▶ Continued from previous page

# Learning outcomes

When you have completed this unit you will:

1 understand why applications software is customised

2 be able to customise applications software

3 be able to create templates in applications packages

4 be able to create macros and shortcuts in applications packages.

# How is the unit assessed?

This unit is internally assessed. You will provide a portfolio of evidence to show that you have achieved the learning outcomes. The grading grid in the specification for this unit lists what you must do to obtain Pass, Merit and Distinction grades. The section on Assessment Tasks at the end of this chapter will guide you through activities that will help you to be successful in this unit.

# The purpose of customising applications software

Word processing, spreadsheet and database applications provide a wide range of facilities that enable many common tasks to be completed easily. This may make us wonder why we should need to customise the applications for a particular purpose. However, the 'office' software we are considering is designed to be a 'jack of all trades', which means that it is not likely to be ideally suited to a particular application. Hence, there are a number of reasons why we might want to customise applications software:

- to improve the ease of use of a particular feature, perhaps to meet the needs of a novice user
- to enable a complex task to be quickly and easily completed with the minimum of user input
- to improve the accuracy of data entered, by adding validation to help ensure data is correct.

As future IT technicians you may well be called upon to customise office software to meet particular user needs. Throughout this unit we will be using Microsoft Office 2003 and the Windows XP operating system for all the examples. What you see on your screen may differ slightly, depending on your operating system or the way your system is set up.

## Types of customisation

There are a number of different ways that office applications can be customised:

- **Changing default settings.** Default settings control the way an application works, and are set when it is installed. However, these settings may not be the best for all users and changing them may make the application easier to use.

- **Modifying menus and toolbars.** As with the default settings, the layout of the various toolbars and menus are set at installation time; but, depending on the facilities used most often, it may be more convenient to change this arrangement by, for example, having different toolbars displayed when the application starts.

- **Creating templates and forms.** Templates save time when creating standard documents like memos and business letters. They are also used to ensure consistency across many employees in the same company (e.g. all memos and letters can have the same layout). Forms created in a Word document or Excel spreadsheet provide an easy way for users to enter data. The form can be locked so that the user can enter data only in the required fields and cannot edit the rest of the document. Features such as list boxes and check boxes make the form easy to complete.

### What does it mean?

**Defaults** *are the settings that are selected by the program maker, and the ones used unless the program user changes them.*

### What does it mean?

*All office software has* **Toolbars**, *which are groups of icons used to control the functions of the program. The default setting for toolbars places them at the top of the program window under the menu bar. However, toolbars are 'floating' and can be dragged into any position in the program window. Different toolbars can be displayed if required, using the Toolbars option under the View menu.*

**What does it mean?**

*A **Macro** is a method of automating a series of functions within an office application.*

- **Macros.** These allow regularly used functions to be automated. A task that might take several keystrokes or menu selections can be simplified by creating a macro that carries out the task with a single mouse click.

- **Creating shortcuts.** Many professional IT users find it slows their work down if they have to take their hands off the keyboard to use the mouse to select commands from toolbars or menus. Using and customising keyboard shortcuts means commands can be selected from the keyboard.

**What does it mean?**

*A **keyboard shortcut** is a key combination that runs a certain command. For example, the built-in short cut Ctrl+S will save a document in most office applications.*

## Case study

### *Using a form to capture lesson observations*

Phillip Jones, IT manager at Northgate College, has produced a Microsoft Word form on which to record lesson observations. 'I produced the form in response to a request from the Staff Training Department' he says. 'They needed a standardised way for lesson observations to be recorded. Previously a standard Word document was used, but this caused problems. Some of the lesson observers were not all that skilled at using Word and sometimes messed up the document, which created problems for us. Also there is some data that needs to be completed on the form where the possible answers need to be selected from a restricted list. For example, there is a question about the type of contract the lecturer is on; full-time, part-time or hourly paid are the only possible answers. With a Word form we can create a drop-down box, so the observer can only choose one of those valid responses. Making sure the data entered in the form is valid made things easier for the Training Department, as it reduced to number of errors on the forms.'

Using a form has solved some problems but it has also created some other ones. 'We have had some difficulties using the form', says Phillip. 'At first the lesson observers took time to get used to the Word form, and the fact they could type in certain fields only, as some of them had never come across a Word document like this before. Also we had a major problem because, on the first version of the form, spell checking was disabled inside the text boxes where the observers had to type their comments. Many of them found this difficult, as they were used to Word highlighting their errors for them. However, we were able to resolve this problem by writing a macro that spell checks the text in the form field.'

1   What problems did using a Word form overcome?

2   What problems did using a Word form cause?

3   Does your centre of learning or place of work use any Word forms? What are they used for and why are they used? Do the people who use them find they are easier or more difficult to use than a standard Word document?

## Advantages of customised applications software

There are a number of potential advantages to customising applications:

- **Ease of use.** This is one of the main benefits. Customisation can make complex procedures easier for novice users.

- **Speed.** Customisation can make features within an application quicker to use by reducing the amount of keystrokes or mouse selections required. This is particularly important when a commonly used task requires a quite complex series of user inputs.

- **Accuracy.** Where applications such as Excel or Access are used to enter data, it is important that the data entered is accurate and, as far as possible, invalid entries are rejected. By adding customised data-entry facilities, which validate the input data as far as possible, the likelihood of incorrect data being entered is reduced.

- **Consistency of style.** Many organisations like to maintain a corporate image, which includes things like their logo and contact details being used in a consistent way (e.g. by being in the same position in the document and using the same font and point size) on all the documents they produce. This can be done by using standard templates throughout the company for common documents such as business letters.

**Consistency** *in relation to documents means that there is obvious similarity that enables you to recognise that they come from the same source.*

## Disadvantages of customised software

There are, of course, disadvantages to customising software. The main ones are as follows:

- Users require training on customisations that are added to the standard packages. This takes time and money.

- The customisations produced need supporting. Since the customisation is unique, commonly used sources of support, such as the Microsoft website, are not of any help. Support probably needs to be provided by the person or team that wrote the customisation. Since people may leave the company or move to other jobs, it is important that sufficient documentation is provided to allow other people to support the customisation.

- Increased complexity. The more complex an application becomes, the more likely something is to go wrong and the more difficult it can be to fix. Customising existing applications may cause technical problems and may make the application more unreliable.

Despite the disadvantages, customisations are often made to office software to make things easier for users. This is particularly the case for users who make heavy use of applications such as Word and Excel. The Word document I am typing into right now for this book is based on a template that provides all the styles for the headings and other features, such as the 'what does it mean?' and 'test your knowledge' boxes. This template was developed by Heinemann for all the authors writing for this book. It helps ensure consistency between the authors and helps us get an idea of how the book will look when it is complete.

## Test your knowledge

1. List two reasons why you might want to customise software.
2. Describe four basic types of customisation that can be applied to software.
3. List three advantages of customising applications software.
4. List three disadvantages of customising applications software.

# Customising applications software

Having understood the types of customisation and their benefits and drawbacks, we now need to look at how to make simple changes, such as modifying default settings, changing the user interface and altering how certain tools and functions work.

## Default settings

Most applications have a wide range of settings to suit different user requirements. Some of them relate to the country you are living in.

### Printer settings

The default size of paper for word processing documents will need to be set to A4 for people who live in Europe. However, in the USA the standard size paper is known as 'letter', which is slightly smaller than A4.

### How to –

### Set the paper size and default printer

Paper size is set by opening the *Page Setup* dialog under the *File* menu. This also allows you to set other characteristics for printing, such as margins and page orientation (portrait or landscape).

Many office users have access to more than one printer, such as a networked laser printer and a local colour inkjet. The default printer is the one that documents are printed on if you click the *Print* icon in the *Standard* toolbar. It is also the first one listed in the *Print* dialog box. You can change the default printer, to be used by all applications, by going to *Start* then *Printers and Faxes*. This will open the *Printer and Faxes* dialog, as shown in Figure 8.1.

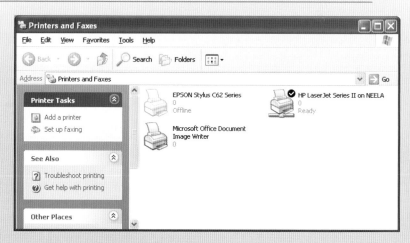

**Figure 8.1** *The Printer and Faxes window*

The default printer is the one with the tick above it. To change the default, right-click on the printer and choose *Set as default* from the menu that pops up.

## Text settings

You can also change default settings for the text font and size used in Word. This is set to **12 point Times New Roman** when you install Word, but you might prefer another size and font. Rather than changing it every time you type a new document, you can set a different default.

## How to –

### Change default font and size used for text in Word

Go to to the *Format* menu and choose the *Font* option. This will display the font dialog box on your screen as shown in Figure 8.2.

Choose the default font you would like all new documents to start off in, then click the *Default* button. You will then see the message shown in Figure 8.3. This is reminding you that you are changing a default setting that will affect all new documents. The default settings for every new Word document are held in a template called *Normal*. We will look at templates in more detail later.

**Figure 8.3** *Warning message*

**Figure 8.2** *The Font dialog box*

You can also set the default for a number of page layout options.

## What does it mean?

**Margins** *are the gaps between the edge of a piece of paper and where the text starts.*
**Page orientation** *defines how print will be displayed on the paper: with the long side along the top it is known as* **landscape** *orientation; with the short side on the top (the normal setting for letters etc.) it is know as* **portrait**.

## How to –

### Set the default for page layout options

Select the *Page Setup* option under the *File* menu. This displays the *Page Setup* dialog box. Here, in the *Margins* tab you can set the page margins and page orientation for the current document by selecting the margin sizes you want and clicking *OK*; or, if you click the *Default* button rather than *OK*, the changes will apply to all new documents.

## Further research

There are a number of other settings on the *Page setup* dialog box. Use the help system to find out what they are used for. For example, what is a 'gutter' used for? Also on the *Layout* tab of the *Page Setup* dialog, what is a 'section' and what is it used for?

If you would like a real challenge try using **styles** as another way of setting up default text and paragraph formatting. Find out what styles are and how to use them.

## Further research

A colleague asks you to set up their Word program so that their **default** settings reflect the page and text settings they like to use, which are as follows:

- Page settings: A4 paper, landscape orientation, 2 cm top margin, 1.5 cm bottom margin and 1.8 cm left and right margins.
- Text settings: Arial font, 11pt.

Set up these as your default settings. Create a new document and check that it is using these settings as default. Then change the settings back to the standard ones.

## File locations

You can also change the default folder where files are saved in Word. Normally when you save a new document, the default folder, shown in the *Save as* dialog box, is *My Documents*. However, you can change this and also change other default file locations for both saving and opening files.

## How to –

### *Change default file locations*

Go to the *Tools* menu and choose *Options*, then select the *File Locations* tab, as shown in Figure 8.4.

To change the default location, first select the file type, then click the *Modify* button and select the folder you want.

For example, you might want to change the default location that is displayed when you insert a picture, as all your pictures are located in a particular folder. Choose the *Clipart pictures* file type in the *Options* dialog, click the *Modify* button, then select the folder where your pictures are located. Now if you select *Insert / Picture / From file* from the menu, the folder that will be selected on the *Insert picture* dialog will be the one you have previously chosen.

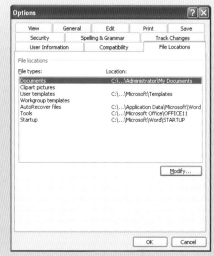

**Figure 8.4** *File Locations tab and Options dialog*

## Interfaces

The 'human interface' is what users see on their screen as they interact with the computer. It has many aspects: windows, menus, dialog boxes and so on. Some of these aspects can be customised to suit a user's particular needs.

### The desktop

You probably already know that you can customise the Windows desktop to your tastes.

## How to –

### Customise your desktop

Right-click on the desktop and choose *Properties*. This will bring up the *Display Properties* dialog box, as shown in Figure 8.5.

**Figure 8.5** *The Display Properties dialog box*

This is a tabbed dialog box with the following tabs:

- **Themes.** This allows you control the overall look of the windows display. Most people choose the *Windows XP* theme, but some users prefer a look similar to older versions of Windows (such as Windows 2000) and choose the *Windows classic* theme.

- **Desktop.** Here you can change the desktop background picture.

- **Screen Saver.** You can control the type of screen saver and related settings.

- **Appearance.** This allows you to further customise the look, colour and size of windows.

Generally these settings are purely a matter of user preference, although people with eyesight problems may find that changing the size or colour of the window items is beneficial.

## Further research – desktop settings

What other desktop setting and themes are available? Use the help facility and the Microsoft web site to find out what other options you can set.

If you would like a real challenge, try to find out what sort of desktop settings would suit people with poor eyesight or other disabilities. Look on the RNIB (Royal National Institute for the Blind) web site for advice on settings that suit people with eyesight problems. Go to www.heinemann.co.uk/hotlinks, insert the express code 2048P and click on this unit. Also check the accessibility options on the Windows *Control Panel*, and search on the Microsoft web site for 'Accessibility' to see what options you can set. Create Windows desktop settings and Word default text settings that would suit someone with eyesight problems. If you know someone with poor eyesight you could ask them to evaluate the settings you have chosen. Remember, different setting will probably suit different types of eye problem.

## How to –

### Modify which toolbars are visible and their locations

In Word go to the *View* menu and choose *Toolbars*. The drop-down menu that appears allows you to choose the toolbars that are visible. Those with a tick next to them are currently visible. Clicking on these will remove them from view, while clicking on the toolbars without a tick will bring them into view.

Toolbars that are currently displayed can be moved around the screen to different locations by clicking and dragging on their control bar, as shown in Figure 8.6. They can be 'snapped' into place at the top, bottom, left or right of the Word window or float anywhere inside the window.

**Figure 8.6** *Moving toolbars*

## How to –

### Modify which buttons are visible

You can also control the buttons that appear on a particular toolbar. To do this you need to go to the *View* menu and choose *Toolbars* again. This time, select *Customize* from the bottom of the drop-down menu. Alternatively, choose the *Customize* option from the *Tools* menu. Either of these methods will display the *Customize* dialog box as shown in Figure 8.7.

**Figure 8.7** *Customize dialog box*

You can drag buttons that you do not want off any toolbar that is visible. Having dragged an icon, you can drop it anywhere in the Word window that is not on a toolbar and the icon will disappear.

As well as removing icons you can also add additional ones. Any menu item can be used as a toolbar icon. First make sure you have the *Commands* tab of the *Customize* dialog box showing. On the left-hand side of the *Customize* dialog box the categories of commands are listed; these are equivalent to the main menu options. So for example if you wanted to add a *Close* toolbar button to the Standard toolbar you would choose the *File* category (since *Close* appears under the *File* menu). In the left-hand list box (labelled *Commands*) you should see an icon labelled *Close* (you may need to scroll down the list box to see it). Drag this icon from the dialog box to the place in the toolbar where you want the button to be. See Figure 8.8.

If you want to return a toolbar to its original configuration, i.e. as it was before you started adding or removing buttons, you can select the *Toolbars* tab of the *Customize* dialog box, select the toolbar you want and then click the *Reset* button.

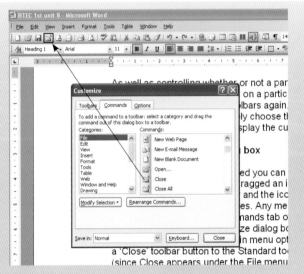

**Figure 8.8** *Adding a Close button to the Standard toolbar*

## How to –

### Create new toolbars

As well as adding and removing buttons from toolbars, you can create your own new toolbars if required. To do this go once again to the *Customize* option under *View*, *Toolbars*. Then, with the *Toolbars* tab selected on the *Customize* dialog box, click the *New* button to display the *New Toolbar* dialog box, as shown in Figure 8.9.

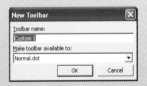

**Figure 8.9** *The New Toolbar dialog box*

The new toolbar will have a default name of *Custom1*. This is the name that appears in the title bar of the toolbar when it is floating, and also in the *Toolbar* menu. You should probably change this name to something more descriptive.

You can also select the template that this toolbar is associated with. The default setting of the *Normal* template will mean this toolbar appears whenever you create a standard new document. Templates are explained in more detail later but, for now, leave this set as it is.

When you click the *OK* button on the *New Toolbar* dialog box, a new empty toolbar is created. You can now swap to the *Commands* tab of the *Customize* dialog box and start adding icons to the new toolbar, just as you did when you added buttons to an existing toolbar. The new toolbar will automatically grow to accommodate the new icons you drag on to it. See Figure 8.10.

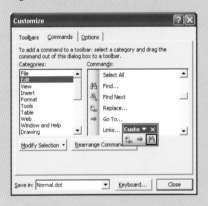

**Figure 8.10** *Creating a custom toolbar*

## How to –

### Delete toolbars

Having experimented with a new toolbar you may decide you want to delete it. Note that, if you close a floating toolbar by clicking it, this does not permanently delete it and it will still be listed in the *Toolbar* menu.

To delete it permanently, return to the *Customize* dialog box, make sure you have the *Toolbars* tab selected,

then scroll to the bottom of the list of toolbars, select the custom toolbar you have created then click the *Delete* button and click *OK* on the confirmation message. Remember that the tick in the check box next to each toolbar indicates whether the toolbar is visible or not.

## Customising menus

As well as dragging commands for the *Customize* dialog box on to a toolbar, you can also drag the commands into any menu.

## How to –

### Customise menus

Simply drag the command from the list in the *Commands* tab of the *Customize* dialog box on to the menu where you want to place it. The menu will then

automatically drop down and you can then drag the command into the desired position.

## Further research

Carry out a small survey amongst your fellow students and find out which toolbar buttons they regularly use in Word and Excel. Then, based on the results of your survey, create a new custom toolbar that contains only the most commonly used commands.

## Mouse and keyboard settings

Further examples of how you can change the user interface are the mouse and keyboard settings. The mouse and the keyboard are as much a part of the user interface as the information that appears on the screen.

## Change mouse and keyboard settings

Open the *Control panel* window by choosing *Start*, *Control panel*, then choose the *Printers and other hardware* icon and then the *Mouse* link. This will display the *Mouse Properties* dialog, as shown in Figure 8.11.

This tabbed dialog box allows you to customise a number of aspects of the way the mouse works. For example, if you find double-clicking quickly a bit tricky you can reduce the speed at which you need to click for it to be recognised as a double-click. You can also adjust the look and behaviour of the mouse pointer.

Using the link to the *Keyboard Properties* dialog you can set the character repeat delay (how long you have to press on a key before it repeats) and the repeat rate (how fast the character repeats) as well as the cursor blink rate.

**Figure 8.11** *The Mouse Properties dialog box*

## Tools and functions

Modern software, such as Microsoft Office, comes with many sophisticated features designed to make the user's life easy. However, to get the most out of these features, the settings that control how they work can be customised. Let us look at some examples in Word.

### Spelling and grammar options

Word offers facilities to carry out checks on the spelling and grammar you use when writing a document. There are a number of options, including letting Word highlight possible errors as you type.

## Set spelling and grammar options

Open the *Tools* menu and select the *Spelling and Grammar* option, then click the *Option* button on the dialog box that appears. See Figure 8.12. This dialog box lets you control the way the spell checker works.

However, Word contains several dictionaries against which it checks spellings, including ones that allow for the different ways that we and the Americans spell the same words. To make sure that you are using the correct dictionary, go to *Tools*, *Language*, *Set language*, choose *English (UK)* and then click on *Default*.

**Figure 8.12** *The spell and grammar check options dialog*

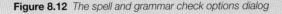

The spell checking facility is particularly useful. However, it can only accept the spelling of words in the dictionary you have selected. Other words, such as people's names or the names of companies, which may be correctly spelt, will be rejected by the system unless they are added to the custom dictionary. For example, suppose you had a friend called Hasmita. Her name will be shown as a spelling error as it is not in the dictionary. However, if you right-click on her name and choose *Add to dictionary*, the name will be added and no longer shown as an error.

## Further research

There are a number of other spelling and grammar settings that you can change under *Tools / Spelling and Grammar / Options*. Find out what these settings do and consider why you might want to use them.

If you would like a real challenge then find out why, when you add entries to your spelling dictionary, they are not added to the main dictionary, but are instead added to your **custom dictionary**. There are a number of things you can do with custom dictionaries. Find out more about them and how to modify your custom dictionary and how and why you might want to add new ones. Start by clicking the *Custom Dictionary* button on the *Spelling and Grammar* option dialog box. Use the help system to assist you.

### Automatic text insertion and correction
### *AutoText*

Some commonly used names and phases are already provided for you in Word in an AutoText list (e.g. 'Thank you'). These can be automatically inserted using the AutoText feature. When Word detects that you have started to type something in the AutoText list it displays a message, telling you to press Enter to complete the text, as shown in Figure 8.13.

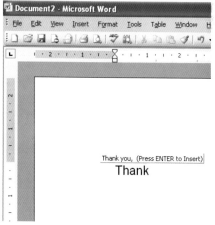

**Figure 8.13** *AutoText entry*

## How to –

### *Add AutoText*

Open the *Tools* menu and select *AutoCorrect options*, and then the *AutoText* tab. See Figure 8.14.

New entries can be inserted by typing them in the box above the list of existing entries and then clicking the *Add* button.

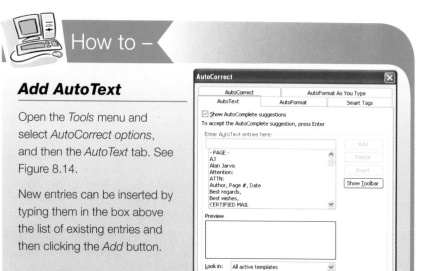

**Figure 8.14** *The AutoText tab*

**Figure 8.15** *Adding AutoCorrect entries*

*AutoCorrect*

This feature automatically corrects certain types of spelling errors as you type. Quite a number of corrections are already included within the Word program but you can add more if you require them. For example, if you find you often type 'clikc' rather than 'click', then you can add this to the AutoCorrect entries, as shown in Figure 8.15.

You must be careful when adding AutoCorrect entries, because the word you enter to be corrected must not be a real word, otherwise you would never be able to type it. Word would keep changing it to the 'correct' spelling. So, for example, you could not use AutoCorrect if you often type 'form' rather than 'from', since 'form' is a real word. This kind of error can be corrected only by proofreading your work.

AutoCorrect also carries out a number of formatting modifications, such as correcting two initial capitals to one, and capitalising the names of days.

## Further research

Think about the mistakes you commonly make when typing. For example, you might often make the mistake of typing 'clikc' as described above. Make a list of the most common mistakes, then check to see if they are automatically corrected by AutoCorrect. Check carefully that the incorrect word you type is not another real word (such as the 'form' and 'from' example above) and, if it is not, create AutoCorrect entries to correct these errors. Test that AutoCorrect works properly by typing the incorrect spellings and seeing whether they are corrected.

## Test your knowledge

5   Give two examples of default printer settings you might need to change.

6   Where would you go to change the settings that affect how the mouse works? What settings can you change?

7   When you type your name (or a friend's name) in Word, it is highlighted as a spelling error. How can you prevent this happening?

8   What must you check (and why) before adding an AutoCorrect entry?

# Creating templates

Templates are a useful way of customising applications. They not only help make sure documents within an organisation are consistent, but they also save time by avoiding the need to retype the same text and set the same formatting repeatedly. Templates are most often created in Word and Excel, although they can be created for other applications too.

## Word templates

Word comes with a number of built-in templates. Although we need to know how to create our own ones, it is worth having a look at how to use the built-in ones first.

## How to –

### *Use Word templates*

Choose *New* from the *File* menu (click the *Expand* arrows at the bottom if it is not shown on the menu). The *New Document* task pane will appear and, if you click the *On my computer…* link under the *Templates* section, the *Templates* dialog box will appear, as shown in Figure 8.16.

Then, supposing you want a memo, you would choose the *Memos* tab on the dialog box then select the type of memo you require, and click the *OK* button. This will create a new, unnamed document containing the text and formatting that is included in the memo template, as shown in Figure 8.17.

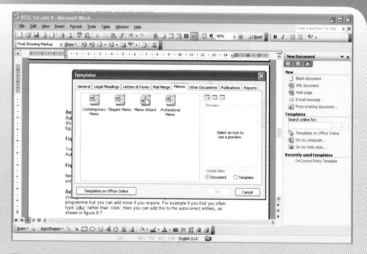

**Figure 8.16** *The Templates dialog box*

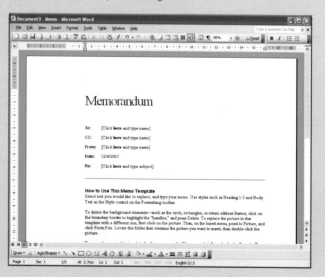

**Figure 8.17** *The memo template in use*

Creating your own templates is quite straightforward. A template is simply a Word document that is saved as a template rather than a standard document. Therefore the first step in creating a template is to create the text and formatting required. However, before you start on the task of creating the template, consideration needs to be given to its design.

## Further research

Word and Excel are not the only programs that come with built-in templates. For example, PowerPoint has a slide template. Find out how to use these templates and how to create your own.

## Designing a template

### User requirements

The first stage in designing a template is to find out what the user requires. On this course, the work you do is only for your own benefit. However, in the future you may be working as an IT technician and most of the work you do will be in support of users of the IT system. You must therefore learn ways to identify user requirements and design solutions that meet them.

Identifying user requirements may sound like a fairly easy task: you just go and ask the users what they want! However, in reality it is usually more complex than that. There may be many different users to consider, and issues such as company standards for document layout and formatting that you have to take into account. You need to find out some basic details:

- What type of document is required?
- What logos and other graphics are required on the document?
- What is the layout of any existing documents that the template should replace?

Once this information is collected you should then be in a position to produce a draft version of the template. This should be shown to the users, and other interested parties, to see if it meets their needs.

## Creating a simple template

## How to –

### Create a simple template (part 1)

To create a template you simply need to type the text you require. Remember that you need to leave out anything that will change each time the template is used, although you might include some instructional text such as 'type name of sender'. An example of a memo template is shown in Figure 8.18.

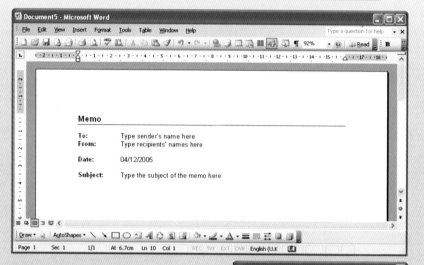

**Figure 8.18** *A memo template*

You should not type the date into the template, but insert an updating date field instead. To do this go to the *Insert* menu and choose *Date and Time*. This will display the dialog shown in Figure 8.19. Choose the date format you want, then click the check box marked *Update automatically*, and then click *OK*. This date will automatically update to the current date whenever the template is used.

**Figure 8.19** *Automatic updating of the date*

## Further research – fields

There are a number of other fields that you can insert in a template or any other document. You can see the list of them by choosing the *Field* option under the *Insert* menu. Find out what some of these fields can be used for, using the help system to assist you.

## How to –

## Create a simple template (part 2)

Having completed the text of the memo, the most important step to make sure you have created a template for future use is to save it as a template rather than a normal document. To do this go to the *File* menu and choose *Save As*, then in the dialog box that appears select *Document Template* from the *Save as type* drop-down list.

Notice that the *Save* location is automatically set to a folder called *Templates*. This folder resides in *C:/ Documents and Settings/[current user]/Application Data/Microsoft/Templates* where *[current user]* is the name of the current logged-on user. Make sure that you give your template a meaningful name, such as *Memo*. See Figure 8.20.

Once you have saved the template, it is ready to use. To do this choose *New* from the *File* menu as

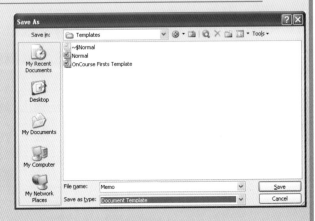

**Figure 8.20** *Saving a template*

before and click on the *On my computer* link in the *New Document* pane to display the *Templates* dialog. Templates you create yourself are listed under the *General* tab.

## Modifying a simple template

Whenever you use a template in this way, you get a copy of the document, not the original. So how can you edit and modify the original?

## How to –

## Edit and modify a template

When you open the *File Open* dialog you can select *Document templates* in the *Files of type* drop-down list, but this does not select the correct folder for you. Hence, to find the template, you will need to use the *Look in* drop-down list at the top to navigate to the *Templates* folder.

Having found your template, you can then modify it in any way you want. However, when you save your changes, make sure that you have selected the file type *Document Template* again, otherwise you may find that you have just saved a new Word document *Memo.doc* instead and your template is unchanged!

## Further research – templates

Create a template for an assignment front sheet for your course. Your teacher or tutor should be able to help you decide what information needs to be included in the template.

# Forms

## Form fields

The templates we have looked at so far have really just been normal documents saved in a special location. When a user opens a template, all that happens is that they get a copy of the original document. One disadvantage of this is that the user can edit all parts of the document. This can be a problem with some types of documents, such as more complex forms, as the user may mess up the format or layout of the document, especially if they are inexperienced at using Word. To avoid these problems, the *Forms* tools can be used to create a locked form in which the user can enter data only in certain fields.

## Creating a form

Forms such as questionnaires or surveys can be quite complex, and you may find it easier to sketch out a hand-drawn version before attempting to create it in Word. You also need to consider which of the form input controls would be most suitable for each entry. Forms support text fields, check boxes and drop-down fields. Text fields are best where it is difficult to predict what input the user will make (such as a name); check boxes should be used for responses where only yes or no is allowed. List boxes can be used where the response can be selected from a limited list of options, such as a title (e.g. Mr, Miss, Ms, Mrs).

Having decided the basic layout of your form you can now start work on the actual document.

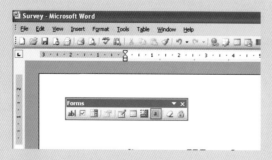

How to –

### *Create a form in Word*

In order to create a form you need to bring the *Forms* toolbar on to the screen. To do this go to the *View* menu, choose *Toolbars* then select *Forms*. The *Forms* toolbar allows you to insert text fields, check boxes and drop-down fields into your document. It also allows you to protect the document, so the user can type only into the fields you have created and cannot

edit the rest of the document. The toolbar is shown in Figure 8.21.

Clicking on the *Text field* button will insert a grey box into your document at the cursor position. You can then set options for the text field by clicking the *Properties* button on the toolbar. This will display the *Text Form Field Options* dialog, as shown in Figure 8.22.

This dialog allows you to set the following options for the text field:

- **Type of text.** This drop-down list allows you to select various different types of text, such as regular text (i.e. any combination of text and numbers), numbers or dates and times. If you select numbers or dates then a valid entry must be made in the field otherwise an error message will result.

**Figure 8.21** *The Forms toolbar*

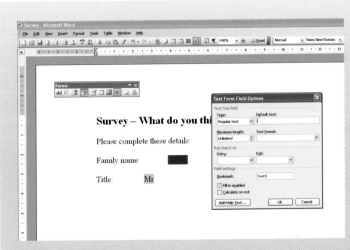

**Figure 8.22** *Inserting text field options*

- **Default text.** This is text that appears in the field as a default. It can of course be deleted by users and replaced by their own entry. You can use this to make the form easier to use if the text used is the most common entry in the field.

- **Maximum length.** Use this to control the maximum number of characters that can be entered. The default setting is 'unlimited' but, in some situations, you might want to limit the number of characters to help ensure a valid entry is made.

- **Format.** This changes depending on the type of text you have chosen; so, if you choose *Regular text*, it shows a list of text formats, such as *All lower case* and *Initial capitals*. If you choose *Number*, it shows various number formats and if you choose *Date* it shows various date formats. Once the form is locked, the user's entry will be converted to the correct format. So, for example, if you choose a date format of DD/MM/YYYY and the user enters 5/3/05 it will be converted to 05/03/2005. If an entry is invalid then an error message will appear.

- **Macros and other settings.** You can specify a macro to run when the user enters or exits the field; there are also a number of other settings, but these are beyond the scope of this unit.

The options available for a check box are fairly simple. The most important is whether the box should initially be checked or unchecked. Drop-down boxes are a little more complex, as you need to enter the items listed in the box when it drops down. Figure 8.23 shows the *Drop-Down Form Field Options* dialog box, with some entries already made.

Items that are to appear in the drop-down list are typed into the *Drop-down item* box and the *Add* button is clicked to add the item to the list. To remove an item from the list, click on it and then click *Remove*. The *Move* buttons can be used to move items up or down the list.

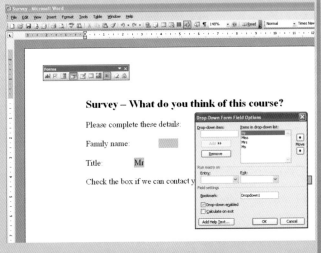

**Figure 8.23** *Drop-Down Form Field Options dialog box*

## Testing and saving a form

Once you have completed the form, you need to test that it works as you expect.

### How to –

#### *Test and save a form in Word*

First lock the form by clicking the *Protect Form* button in the *Forms* toolbar. Having locked it you should try out all the input controls to check they work as you expect. Note that with the form locked you can move between the fields by pressing the Tab key. You should not be able to type anywhere except in the fields you have created.

Once you are happy with the form you can save it. Save it while it is protected so that, when a user opens the document, the form will be ready to use. You can save it as a template so that each time it is opened a new copy is created.

### Further research – forms

Create a questionnaire using a Word form to find out information from your fellow students, such as which football team they support or what music they like.

### What does it mean?

*An **invoice** is a request for payment for a sale of goods or services that has been made.*

## Excel templates

Like Word, Excel comes with a number of built-in templates, and you can create your own in a similar way.

One of the benefits of using templates in Excel is that you can build formulas into them. This means that the templates can be used by people who may not know how to create formulas; all they need to do is to enter the numbers and the formulas will automatically do the calculations. This can also avoid errors caused by users entering formulas incorrectly. However, you must check carefully that the formulas you put in the template are correct.

We shall look at an example of how to create a template for an invoice in Excel.

### Creating an Excel template

The spreadsheet shown in Figure 8.24 is an example of how an invoice template could be designed. The formulas have been entered to calculate the total for each item (quantity times unit price), the net total (total before VAT), the amount of VAT, and the grand total.

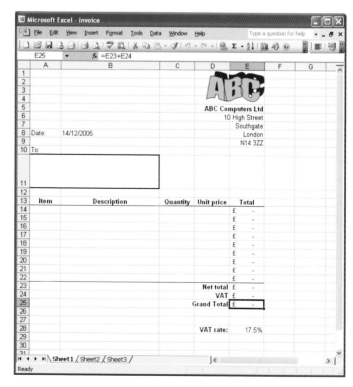

**Figure 8.24** *Invoice template*

Once the formatting and formulas of the invoice template spreadsheet are complete you need to save the sheet as a template. This is done in the same way as a Word template. Simply choose *Template* from the *Save as type* list box in the *Save* dialog box.

As always, before the template, is ready for use it must be tested carefully. As mentioned earlier, this is important: if there are errors in your formulas, everyone who uses your template will suffer those same errors.

## Testing an Excel template

To test the template properly, you need to think up some test invoices. The quantities, unit prices, total prices, VAT etc. for these test invoices first need to be calculated independently from your template. This is known as test data. You could, for example, type the details into a Word table, then do the calculation by hand or with a calculator, but check the results carefully to ensure they are correct. You should come up with a minimum of six different invoices, some with a small number of items and quantities, others with larger amounts. See Figure 8.25 for an example.

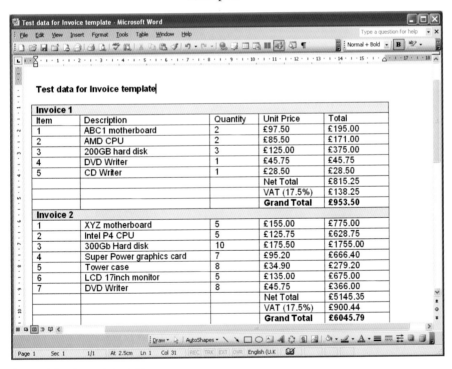

**Figure 8.25** *Example test data*

Once you have completed the test data you should use the template to create invoices with the same items, quantities and prices as your test data. As you complete each invoice using the template, compare the results with the calculations you did manually on the test data. If you find there are differences in the results, then there must be an error, either in the formulas you have used in the template (if every template is wrong) or in the calculations you did manually (if just one or two are wrong). You need to identify the error and correct it, if necessary editing and saving your template again (Excel templates are saved in the same folder as Word ones).

## Further research – Excel templates

Create a spreadsheet template for an assignment action plan.

## Test your knowledge

9   Explain the purpose of the Word document template called Normal.

10  How can you include a date in a template so that it is always correct whenever the template is used?

11  What is the most important thing you must do to make a document a template rather than just a standard document?

12  What is the difference between a locked and an unlocked form document?

# Creating macros and shortcuts

## What does it mean?

*A **Macro** is a method of automating a series of functions within an office application.*

## Macros

Templates are a simple and effective way to customise an application, but macros are much more powerful.

Once a macro has been created you can also create a shortcut (which we will cover later in this section) using key combinations, or toolbar buttons that allow the user to run the macro. You can create macros in most of the Microsoft Office applications, but we will look only at Excel.

### Creating a macro

There are two ways you can create a macro:

- Use the macro recorder facility.
- Write program code.

The simplest way is to use the macro recorder facility by switching on the macro recorder then carrying out the tasks you wish to automate (select text or cells, choose menu options etc.). When you have completed the sequence of tasks, the macro recorder is switched off. You can then replay your recorded macro whenever you want.

## What does it mean?

*A **footer** is text which prints at the bottom of every page, often used for things like page numbers. A **header** is text that prints at the top of every page.*

The other method is to write the program code using the **Visual Basic for Applications** programming language. While the first approach may seem the simpler of the two, there are a quite number of restrictions on what you can record in a macro. However, editing the Visual Basic macro code is beyond the scope of this chapter.

Let us look at recording a simple macro. Suppose you would like to record a macro to add a footer to an Excel sheet. Rather than having to set up a footer each time you use a new worksheet, the macro will automatically do it for you.

## How to –

### *Record a macro*

To record the macro you have to carry out the steps required to set up the footer with the macro recorder switched on. First open Excel and use either a new worksheet or one that does not already have a footer set up. Then go to the *Tools* menu and choose *Macro*. From the drop-down menu, choose *Record New Macro* and you will see the dialog box shown in Figure 8.26.

There are a number of things you must enter in this dialog box:

- **Macro name.** Each macro must have a name, and Excel will have inserted a default name of *Macro1* (if this is the first macro you have recorded); this is not a very good name, since it does not tell you anything about what the macro does. You should,

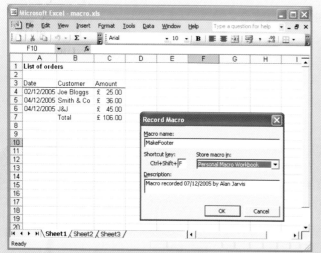

**Figure 8.26** *The Record Macro dialog box*

therefore, change its name to something more meaningful, like *MakeFooter* in Figure 8.26. Note that you cannot have a space in a macro name.

■ **Shortcut key.** You can assign a shortcut key to the macro, so you can run it by pressing the Ctrl key along with another key of your choice. In this example the 'F' key has been chosen (for 'Footer'). Note that this is a capital F (i.e. Ctrl+Shift+F), because lowercase f is already allocated to a shortcut, which is used to open the *Find* dialog box.

■ **Store macro in.** The default setting in this drop-down box is the current workbook, which would mean the macro was only available in this workbook. This might be the correct choice for a macro that was specific to a particular workbook but, if we want to be able to use this macro in any workbook, the drop-down box should be set to *Personal Macro Workbook.*

■ **Description.** The default information, entered by Excel, is shown here; you can add more information if you wish.

Once you have made the required entries in the dialog box you can click *OK*. Be careful because, once you do this, the macro recorder is on and everything you do will be recorded in the macro – make sure you only do things that you want in the macro. Also remember that, at the end, you must stop the macro recorder by clicking the *Stop* button that appears in a small floating toolbar which should come on to your screen when you start the recorder.

To create the footer macro, go to the *View* menu, then choose *Header and Footer*, which will display the *Header and Footer* dialog on your screen. On that dialog box, click the *Custom Footer* button, which should then display the dialog box shown in Figure 8.27

In this example, the *Date* button has been used to insert the code for an updated date (i.e. it changes to the current date) in the left side of the footer, the user's name has been typed into the centre section and the word 'Page' followed by clicking the automatic page number button has been entered in the right section.

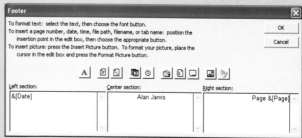

**Figure 8.27** *The Custom Footer dialog box*

Once you have the footer as required, click the *OK* button, which will return you to the previous dialog box (you should see a preview of the footer you have set up) then click *OK* on this dialog to return you to the worksheet. Then click the *Stop* button on the macro recorder toolbar, as shown in Figure 8.28. Your macro is now complete and the toolbar will disappear.

Click here to stop recording the macro

**Figure 8.28** *The Macro toolbar*

You cannot really test out your macro on the current worksheet, since it now has a footer. Therefore you need to move to a new worksheet by using the worksheet tabs at the bottom of the Excel window. Then press the Ctrl+Shift+F shortcut key combination that was set for the new macro. You will not see anything on the screen, but, if you now go to the *View* menu and choose *Header and Footer*, you should see that this sheet now has a footer, set by the macro.

## Further research

Record another macro that adds a header to a spreadsheet. The header can contain information such as your centre of learning or place of work and the name of the course you are on.

## Defining user needs

As with the templates we looked at earlier, as an IT professional you may be asked to create a macro for a particular user or group of users. The term macro may not, of course, be used – you may just be asked to help users with a particular problem they have, or something they find difficult or time consuming to do. After investigation you may decide a macro would provide a good solution, but you will need to carry out a number of steps first:

- **Thoroughly investigate what the problem is.** Sometimes technicians can be tempted to jump very quickly to a solution without fully understanding the users' problem. This can lead to a solution that does not fully meet the need. You must talk to the users, get them to show you what they are having difficulties with and ask questions to gather as much information as you can.
- **Look for alernative solutions.** Remember there are disadvantages to customising software, so first you should look for a solution that does not require writing macros. Perhaps some of the simpler solutions would be suitable, such as using AutoText or AutoCorrect, or creating a template.
- **Choose a solution and write up a specification.** Having looked at the different possibilities, you should select the one you think is most suitable and write up a specification that describes the problem and how your solution will deal with it.
- **Check your chosen solution with the users.** Discuss your specification with the users to check if it meets their requirements.

Of course, as a student, it is not really possible to carry out these tasks for real. However, your fellow students, family and friends might be able to act as your 'users' and provide you with a problem that some kind of customisation might solve.

## Further research

Discuss among your fellow students, family and friends what tasks they regularly carry out using Word or Excel. Find out as much detail as you can about the task and select one that can be carried out more easily using a template or macro. Using the steps described above, create a template or macro to meet the requirements they have described to you.

## Assigning a macro to a toolbar button

We have seen that a macro can easily be assigned to a shortcut key, but you might want to assign the macro to a toolbar button instead.

## How to –

### Assign a macro to a toolbar button

Go to the *View* menu and choose *Toolbars*, then select *Customize* from the bottom of the drop-down menu. This will display the *Customize* dialog box. Choose the *Commands* tab, as shown in Figure 8.29.

Scroll down to almost the bottom of the *Categories* list box and click on *Macros*, then drag the *Custom Button* (with the smiley face icon) from the list that appears on the right up into the toolbar and location of your choice.

Once the smiley face icon is in place in one of the toolbars, right-click on it and, from the bottom of the menu that appears, choose *Assign Macro*. See Figure 8.30.

The *Assign Macro* dialog box will appear, and you can choose the macro you have created from the list, as shown on Figure 8.31. Click *OK* to close the dialog box.

**Figure 8.29** *The Customize dialog box*

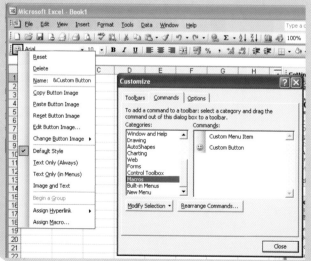

**Figure 8.31** *The Assign Macro dialog box*

**Figure 8.30** *The right-click menu for the Custom button*

The macro is now assigned to the new toolbar button and every time you click it the footer will be set on the worksheet (or whatever action the macro you have assigned to the button carries out).

## Assigning a macro to a menu item

As well as assigning toolbar icons to macros you can assign them to menu items.

### How to –

## Assign a macro to a menu item

Open the *Customize* dialog box as before (*View / Toolbars / Customize*), and scroll to the *Macro* category. This time choose *Custom Menu Item* from the box on the right and drag it to the required place in the menu of your choice. Figure 8.32 shows it added at the bottom on the *View* menu.

However, *Custom Menu Item* is not a very meaningful name, so the first thing we need to do is change it. Right-clicking on the menu item displays a further menu of options, shown in Figure 8.33.

First change the text of the menu item by editing the text in the *Name* box of the right-click menu (in the example it has been changed to 'Add standard footer'). The ampersand (&) is placed before the character that will be used as the shortcut key to select the item.

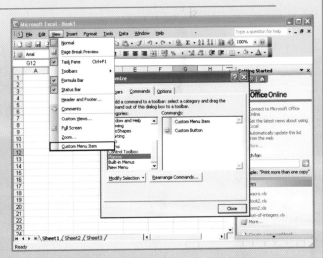

**Figure 8.32** *New menu item located in the View menu*

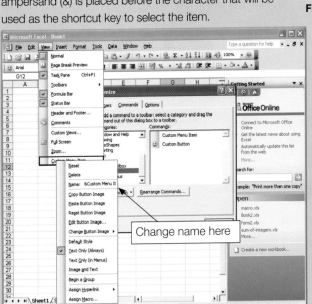

**Figure 8.33** *New menu item options menu*

Then click the *Assign Macro* option on the right-click menu and assign the macro as before. The completed menu item is shown in Figure 8.34.

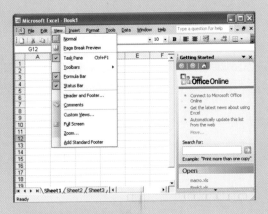

**Figure 8.34** *Completed new menu*

## Further research

Using a macro you have previously created, assign it to a toolbar icon and a suitable menu.

## Testing a macro

Having created your macro, you need to test it to ensure it works properly. Although simple macros may not need very detailed testing you should consider carefully if there are any situations in which your macro might not work properly. Just doing one test of your macro is not sufficient.

If the macro is designed to work with any worksheet (like the *MakeFooter* macro created earlier) you should try it with different worksheets to check that it really does work with any worksheet. For example, you might be temped to just try it on a couple of small spreadsheets but, since it contains page numbers, you need to check it with a multi-page worksheet to see if the numbering still works correctly.

Also, the *MakeFooter* macro contains a date, so you should try it on different days to make sure the date updates automatically. You should also try out some situations that might cause problems, such as:

- What happens if you use the macro on a worksheet which already has a footer?
- What happens if the spreadsheet is set for landscape printing rather than portrait?

To do the testing properly you need to create a list of the tests you will do and record the results of the tests along with evidence (such as screen prints or paper printouts). The list of tests is known as a test plan. An example test plan for the *MakeFooter* macro is shown in Table 8.1.

| Test plan | | | | |
|---|---|---|---|---|
| Macro name: | MakeFooter | Tester: | | Alan Jarvis |
| Date: | 15–16 Dec 2005 | | | |
| **Test number** | **Description** | **Result** | | **Action needed** |
| 1 | Test with small worksheet | | | |
| 2 | Test with large multi-page sheet | | | |
| 3 | Test on two different days | | | |
| 4 | Test on sheet with footer already | | | |
| 5 | Test on sheet set for landscape printing | | | |

**Table 8.1** *Test plan for the MakeFooter macro*

The Result column is completed when you actually carry out the test. If the test went as you expected you can just enter 'OK' in this box or perhaps something more descriptive such as 'page numbers printed OK on all pages'. However, if you do not get the result you are expecting and you need to make some modification to the macro to correct the problem, then you need to make an entry in the Action needed column, such as 're-record macro to solve this problem'. No entry is needed in this column if the test went as expected.

## Case study

### *Using a macro to speed up creation of new worksheets*

Neela Soomary is a training manager. She needs to keep track of the results of various exams (key skills, ECDL etc.) that her learners do on a month by month basis. She uses a spreadsheet with an individual worksheet for each month. Each worksheet has the same layout, with number of learners, exams taken and numbers who passed. Neela found creating each new month's worksheet a bit fiddly. 'I had to insert a new sheet, copy the previous month's sheet contents into the new one, delete the previous month's data and then adjust the column sizes. I had to be careful which worksheet I selected before inserting a new one, otherwise the new sheet would end up in the wrong place. Then a colleague showed me how I could record a macro that did all these tasks. Once the macro was recorded we created a button on the toolbar to run the macro. Now when I need a new month's worksheet I just click on the button and the sheet is created for me. The only thing I need to do is type the name of the month at the top of the sheet.'

1 What are the benefits of using a macro to create a new worksheet?

2 Is there a way you could automate the task of inserting the month name at the top of each worksheet?

## What does it mean?

**Touch typing** *is using the keyboard with all your fingers without looking at it (you look at the screen not the keyboard). Professional typists touch type and achieve very high typing speeds.*

# Keyboard shortcuts

We have already seen how toolbars and menus can be customised. However, to many users, especially those who are touch typists, taking their hands off the keyboard to move the mouse is time consuming and frustrating.

For these users keyboard shortcuts can be very useful, as they allow commands to be selected using the keyboard only. Office programs have many built in shortcuts using the Ctrl (Control) key, such as Ctrl+S to save or Ctrl+B to make text bold. However, you can also create your own shortcuts, which you can assign to commands, macros, fonts, AutoText, styles, or symbols. You need to exercise some caution in assigning your own shortcuts, as Word comes with a large number of keyboard shortcuts and you will need to find key combinations that are not already assigned.

# Creating and assigning keyboard shortcuts

How to –

## Create and assign keyboard shortcuts

Choose the *Customize* option from the *Tools* menu to display the *Customize* dialog box. Then click the *Keyboard* button on the bottom of the dialog box. The *Customize Keyboard* dialog box will appear as shown in Figure 8.35.

**Figure 8.35** *The Customize Keyboard dialog box*

Using this dialog box you can select from *Categories* on the left, then *Commands* on the right. If the command you select already has a keyboard shortcut set, then it will appear in the *Current keys* box. You can see in Figure 8.35 that the *FileSave* command has been chosen, and several shortcuts are already assigned to it by default.

You would probably want to set up shortcuts only for commands that do not already have a shortcut, such as *FileClose*. In doing this you are faced with a problem since you need to choose a shortcut that is not already assigned, but how do you know what shortcuts are available? The answer is to look in Word Help under 'keyboard shortcuts'.

To do this, choose *Microsoft Word Help Topics* from the *Help* menu to open the *Help* pane. Then enter 'keyboard shortcuts' in the search box and click the *Start searching* button. You should get a list of topics as shown in Figure 8.36.

**Figure 8.36** *List of help topics*

If you select *Keyboard shortcuts for Word* from the list then a help page will open, which, if you click the *Show all* link at the top right, will display a complete list of all the keyboard shortcuts. The problem with the list is that it is very long, so it will take a while for you to search through to find if the key combination you have in mind is already used. For simplicity it might be best to experiment with the key combinations Ctrl+7, Ctrl+8 and Ctrl+9, which are not already assigned.

If you enter a key combination that is assigned, the *Customize Keyboard* dialog box will tell you and show you what it is assigned to. For example, you might decide that Ctrl+C is a good shortcut to close a document. However, if you enter this combination, the dialog box will show you that it is already assigned to the Copy command. See Figure 8.37.

**Figure 8.37** *Shortcut already assigned*

Note that you can assign this shortcut to your chosen command, but then you could no longer use Ctrl+C for Copy. If you choose an unassigned shortcut, such as Ctrl+7, then it will show as unassigned in the dialog box and you can click the *Assign* button to assign that shortcut to the command. See Figure 8.38.

**Figure 8.38** *An unassigned shortcut*

## How to –

### *Remove keyboard shortcut assignments*

Open the *Customize Keyboard* dialog box. Select the command and key combination to be removed and then click the *Remove* button.

You can also reset all the shortcuts to their default settings by clicking the *Reset All* button.

## Testing keyboard shortcuts

Testing keyboard shortcuts is very simple – just press the key combination and see if the command you have assigned to the shortcut is carried out!

Collecting evidence for your course assignment, to show that you have successfully assigned the shortcut, is probably best done by taking screen shots of the *Customize Keyboard* dialog box, with the shortcuts you have created showing. To do this press the *Print Screen* button on your keyboard when the dialog box is displayed, then close the *Customize* dialog box, return to a suitable Word document and click the *Paste* button in the toolbar (or use the shortcut key Ctrl+V).

## Further research

Think of two commands that you regularly use in Word and would like to create shortcuts for. Create shortcuts for them using the Ctrl+8 and Ctrl+9 shortcut key combinations.

## Test your knowledge

**13** List the basic steps for recording a macro in Excel.

**14** List three different ways that you can run a macro.

**15** You have been asked to write a macro for a novice computer user. What steps should you follow to investigate what the user requires?

**16** Explain the steps you should take when creating a new keyboard shortcut in Microsoft Word.

# Assessment tasks

The assessment tasks in this unit are based on the following scenario:

*You work as an IT support technician at your centre of learning or place of work. From time to time administration and teaching staff ask you to provide customisations to their application programs. The following tasks are examples of some of the customisations you have been asked to do.*

> To work towards a Distinction in this unit you will need to achieve **all** the Pass, Merit and Distinction criteria in the unit and have evidence to show that you have achieved each one.

## How do I provide assessment evidence?

Your evidence can be presented in any suitable form, such as written reports, presentations or verbal explanations, together with the documents that you create for tasks. These can be supported by other documentation, such as printouts, screen shots, witness statements, observation records and transcripts of conversations.

All your evidence should be presented in one folder, which should have a front cover and a contents page. You should divide the evidence into four sections corresponding to the four tasks.

## Task 1 (P3, M1, D1)

Create two templates, one for Excel and one for Word as described below:

Create a 'paper saving' Excel template. This template should have narrow margins (about 0.7cm along the top, bottom, left and right) and the page orientation set to landscape. Add a footer to the template with your name and page numbers.

Create a Word template using a form to generate a questionnaire. The subject of the questionnaire should be your fellow students' opinion of this unit. The questionnaire should record basic information such as their name, gender and age. Example questions should include:

- Do they think this is an interesting unit?
- Did they learn many new things?
- Do they think the unit has sufficient practical content?

Rather than just expecting yes or no answers you can use a numerical scale from 1 to 5, where 1 is 'very much agree' and 5 is 'completely disagree'. Use check boxes or drop-down lists to allow the person filling in the questionnaire to make their selection for each question.

> To work towards a Distinction you should evaluate the way templates can be used to capture and present information. Using the Word questionnaire you have created, consider the benefits of completing this on the computer rather than printing it out. Also consider other types of templates you have created and describe what benefits their use may bring. You should also consider any disadvantages there may be in using templates.

## Assessment tasks continued

### Task 2 (P4, D2)

Write an Excel macro to add the following formatting to the current cell (or selected cells): bold text, blue colour text and bottom border.

Test that the macro works correctly and then assign the macro to a keystroke combination, a toolbar button and a menu option. Demonstrate to your teacher or tutor that the different ways of running the macro work.

> To work towards a Distinction you should evaluate the ways that macros can aid productivity. For example, you could time how long it takes to carry out the tasks you have recorded in a macro manually, then compare how long it takes to run the macro. You would also need to consider how long it originally took to record the macro. This way you can estimate how many times you would have to use the macro to save more time than it took to record it. You should also consider any possible disadvantages of using macros.

### Task 3 (P2, P5)

Create Word AutoText entries for the names (first name and family name together) of all the students in your class, so that Word will automatically complete their names when you start typing them. Also create custom spelling dictionary entries for all the names that are not in the standard dictionary (you can easily find out which ones are not in the standard dictionary by typing in all the names and seeing which ones come up as spelling errors).

Create three keyboard shortcuts to carry out functions in Word that you commonly use. Test that they work correctly and demonstrate them to your teacher or tutor.

### Task 4 (P1, M2, M3, M4)

Write a report describing the reasons why applications software is customised, explaining what possible disadvantages there might be. You also need to explain:

- the ways in which a template could benefit an organisation, using the templates you have created as examples
- the benefits of customising at least two different functions or tools (e.g. AutoCorrect, spell checker etc.), using the customisations you have done as examples
- the benefits of the different techniques used to assign macros (e.g. keystroke combinations, a toolbar button and a menu option).

# 9 Database Software

## About this unit

Databases are very widely used today. It is important that you understand not only what they can do but how they are structured. You will then be in a position to decide whether a database is the most appropriate way in which to store specific data.

The person who sets up a database is known as a database developer. The person who uses the database is always referred to as the user. So even if you are creating a database for yourself you will always have to think of yourself as two separate people – the developer and the user.

In the first section on database basics you will be looking at databases from the point of view of a user. In the rest of the chapter you will be learning how to create them as a developer.

▶ Continued from previous page

# Learning outcomes

When you have completed this unit you will:

1 understand the structure and principles of databases

2 be able to create a simple database to meet user needs

3 be able to create database queries, forms and reports

4 be able to document a database.

# How is the unit assessed?

This unit is internally assessed. You will provide a portfolio of evidence to show that you have achieved the learning outcomes. The grading grid in the specification for this unit lists what you must do to obtain Pass, Merit and Distinction grades. The section on Assessment Tasks at the end of this chapter will guide you through activities that will help you to be successful in this unit.

# Structure and principles of databases

## Database basics

Databases are organised collections of data. They are widely used in organisations to store information and to help them carry out their business. In this unit you will be learning about and creating single-table databases.

Many software packages include simple database features. For example, your email client software will include an address book, in which you can store details of people and organisations. The address book is a very simple single-table database, and each entry is a **record**. The email address book stores the data in categories, such as the name of the person and the email address; these categories are known as **fields**. If you use an address book that can be linked to other packages then it may contain other fields, such as telephone number, fax number and postal address as well.

A database management system (DBMS), such as Microsoft Access, offers a much wider range of facilities than a simple database. In this unit you will be looking at the features that a DBMS offers.

### Uses of databases

You will be able to find many examples of databases used in industry. Many of them are more complex, with several tables linked together. Here are some examples:

- **Banking accounts.** All banks and building societies run accounts for customers. A bank account database will have details of the account holder, and then data about each of the transactions (withdrawals and deposits). If the customer has set up standing orders or direct debits then these will be recorded in the database as well. Some of this information can be read by a customer at an Automatic Teller Machine (cash machine).

- **Personnel records.** All businesses keep information about their employees, including their names, addresses etc., their qualifications and training, plus their departments and job titles. This information is also linked into the payroll system, which works out how much each person should be paid each week or month, and then sends out instructions to the bank and payslips to employees.

- **Telephone directories.** These are very large but simple databases, which are used both in the printed form (in telephone books) and also online for directory enquiries. They contain names and addresses of subscribers, with their telephone numbers.

### What does it mean?

*A* **database** *is a collection of data. It is organised so that different kinds of information can be retrieved from it by the users.*

### What does it mean?

*A* **single-table database** *is a database in which all the data can be written down as a single list or table.*

- **Stock control.** The database in a shop stores all the data about all the items that the shop sells. It will include stock codes and descriptions of the items, as well as up to date information about how many items are in stock, how many have been sold, and how many should be re-ordered from the supplier.
- **Booking systems.** Customers can book tickets for entertainment venues, for flights or for holidays, either by phoning or visiting an agency. These systems depend on complex databases that keep a record of all the seats or vacancies and allocate new bookings. It is very important that these databases are up to date, to the minute, to avoid double-booking.

 ## Further research – exploring databases

You may like to share this out between the members of a group.

Find out one example of each of the types of database listed above. As this is not a complete list, you may find others as well. In each case, try to speak to someone who uses it.

Ask these questions:

- How is the data input into the database?
- How is the information displayed on screen?
- What data is printed out?
- How can the data be searched?

## Advantages and disadvantages of computerised databases

Computerised databases replace paper filing systems. Here are some advantages of using a computer database:

- The data is organised and easy to use.
- The user is able to search all the data for specific information.
- The database takes up very little physical space.
- The database can be shared between several users at the same time.
- The database can be transferred from one system to another.

And some disadvantages:

- A database cannot be accessed if the computer system is malfunctioning.
- Like all computer data it is at risk of unauthorised access, illegal changes and virus attacks.

## Database objects

A database consists of data together with some objects that work with the data. The main objects are tables, forms, reports and queries.

### Tables

Databases are usually displayed on screen or printed out as tables. Each row of the table is one record, i.e. information about something in the real world. For example, in a database containing information about people in an organisation, all the data about a particular individual would be held in one record. See Figure 9.1.

**Staff : Table**

| Staff ID Code | First Name | Last Name | Address | Post Code | Phone extension | Sex | Date of birth |
|---|---|---|---|---|---|---|---|
| BAT386 | Christopher | Bathurst | 1 Station Road | KM4 2DF | 1591 | M | 06/05/1977 |
| FIT752 | Jenny | Fitzgerald | 49 George Street | KM4 9YS | 1504 | F | 13/02/1949 |
| KIM980 | Jin-Ho | Kim | 45 Foxglove Close | KM3 9RT | 2315 | M | 14/09/1967 |
| PAT319 | Derek | Paterson | 103 Victoria Street | KM7 2GH | 2373 | M | 21/12/1954 |
| PAT504 | Meena | Patel | 14 Oaktrees Crescent | KM9 4FG | 1642 | F | 13/04/1972 |
| PRY123 | Michelle | Pryce | 37 Harrison Grove | KM3 5TH | 1590 | F | 01/07/1983 |

Record: 1 of 6

**Figure 9.1** *A table*

The data in each record is divided into separate categories, known as fields. For example, the fields in a database about people could include name, address, phone number, sex etc.

The headings at the top of the columns are the fieldnames. The data in a field in a particular record is sometimes referred to as a value. (Note that the term value is not limited to numbers.)

### Forms

Databases allow you to view and browse through the data, and also to add, delete or amend individual records. As a developer you will be able to view the data in a table. But the user will normally view the data through a much more friendly form.

A form can present the data one record at a time. See Figure 9.2. The user can then use the form to make any changes to the existing data, to add new records or to delete records. A form will have helpful headings and other information for the user. Buttons can be placed on a form that link to other forms or carry out specific actions.

In general, the raw data in a table should usually be hidden away from the user, and the user should always access the data through a form.

### Queries

Databases can be searched (or queried, or interrogated) for data using a query. The query might be searching for all the records with data in one particular field that matches some criterion. The criterion could specify some text that the data has to match; e.g. it could search for all the names with the surname Jones. Alternatively, it could search for data

**Staff**

| | | | |
|---|---|---|---|
| Staff ID Code | BAT386 | Phone extension | 1591 |
| First Name | Christopher | Date of birth | 06/05/1977 |
| Last Name | Bathurst | | Sex M |
| Address | 1 Station Road | Post Code | KM4 2DF |

Record: 1 of 6

**Figure 9.2** *A form*

that meets a condition; e.g. a search could be made in the Date of Birth field to find all the records of people born after a specified date. More complex searches can be carried out that check the data in several fields. See Figure 9.3.

**Staff Query : Select Query**

| | First Name | Last Name | Date of birth |
|---|---|---|---|
| ▶ | Michelle | Pryce | 01/07/1983 |
| | Christopher | Bathurst | 06/05/1977 |
| | Meena | Patel | 13/04/1972 |
| * | | | |

Record: ◀◀ ◀ 1 ▶ ▶▶ ▶* of 3

**Figure 9.3** *A query has selected those people born after 1970 and displayed only three fields*

**Staff**

| Staff ID Code | First Name | Last Name | Address | Post Code | Phone extension | Sex | Date of birth |
|---|---|---|---|---|---|---|---|
| PRY123 | Michelle | Pryce | 37 Harrison Grove | KM3 5TH | 1590 | F | 01/07/1983 |
| KIM980 | Jin-Ho | Kim | 45 Foxglove Close | KM3 9RT | 2315 | M | 14/09/1967 |
| BAT386 | Christopher | Bathurst | 1 Station Road | KM4 2DF | 1591 | M | 06/05/1977 |
| PAT504 | Meena | Patel | 14 Oaktrees Crescent | KM9 4FG | 1642 | F | 13/04/1972 |
| PAT319 | Derek | Paterson | 103 Victoria Street | KM7 2GH | 2373 | M | 21/12/1954 |
| FIT752 | Jenny | Fitzgerald | 49 George Street | KM4 9YS | 1504 | F | 13/02/1949 |

**Figure 9.4** *A report generated in Access*

## Reports

You can usually print out the data in a file. Any printout like this is known as a report. A report can list all the data in the database or can use a query to select specific records and to present data in certain fields only. See Figure 9.4.

## Data types

When a database is set up, the data type for each field is defined.

The main data types are:

- **Text.** (Also known as a 'string'.) The user can enter up to 255 characters in a text field.
- **Memo.** (Also known as 'text' in some DBMS.) This is simply a longer text field and can include thousands of characters.
- **Number.** You usually have a choice of number types.
- **Date/Time**. You can usually specify which format the date should appear in, such as 12/05/05 or 12 May 2005.
- **Logical.** (Also known as 'Yes/No'.) This can simply hold one of two values – 'yes' or 'no'. As alternatives to 'yes' and 'no', the words 'true' and 'false', or 'on' and 'off' may also be used.

The data type of a field determines two things:

- How many bytes of storage are allocated to each item of data.
- What kinds of functions can be carried out with the data. For example, you can carry out calculations only with data that has a Number data type.

In Figure 9.1 the first five fields all use the text data type, while the 'Phone extension' is a number. When the data is keyed in, the database will not allow the user to enter data that is of the incorrect data type. So if words are entered in the 'Phone extension' field by mistake, the software will display an error message.

## Size of database

The size of a database is measured in KB. You can check the size of one that you have created from its listing in a directory or folder. In Windows you can find this information by right-clicking on the filename.

The size of a database depends on a number of factors, but the most crucial one is the number of records that it contains and the size of each record. A method for estimating this is given on page 319, in the section on data storage requirements.

# Database structures

As a database developer you will have to decide on the structure of the tables that you create.

## Tables

A table is built around a number of fields. A table definition is a list of all the fields in a table. You will be creating a database that contains information about the books in a library. The table definition is given in Table 9.1.

| Books table |
| --- |
| Title |
| Author |
| Publisher |
| Year published |
| ISBN |
| Notes |
| Star rating |

**Table 9.1** *The Books table definition*

## Fields

You will give each field a fieldname and a data type. In addition, each field may have some field properties. These might include the maximum length of the data in the field and the specific format, e.g. for a date.

## Records

The records hold the data that is stored in the database. A record consists of several separate data items, each entered in a different field.

A field in a record can often be left blank if the data is not available. But you may decide that a particular field must contain data in each record, and the field properties for that field can be set up to force the user to enter data.

Data is normally entered by the user, not by the developer, although the developer will have to enter test data to check that the database works as intended.

## Primary key

Often a single-table database will have one field, the primary key field, which uniquely identifies each record. Examples of primary key fields would be membership number in a database of club members, account number in a customer account at a bank, or stock code in a file of stock held in a shop.

Each table should have a primary key field. In nearly all companies each staff member is given a number which is unique to them and is used for things such as paying their salary. So, as shown in Figure 9.1, the Staff ID Code is the primary key field for the table, and BAT386 is the primary key for Christopher Bathurst. The ISBN (International Standard Book Number) is a number given to each title that is published in the world. You will usually find it on the back cover of the book. As this number is unique to each book it can be the primary key field in a database of books.

The primary key field is always underlined in the table definition, as shown in Table 9.1.

Sometimes it is difficult to decide which field should be the primary key field. Often, a new field can be created to do the job. For example, a table may hold a list of people's names and addresses. Some people may have the same name, so the name cannot be used as the record key field, as the data would not be unique for each record. And more than one person could live at the same address, so again address could not be used as the primary key field. So a new field would have to be created as the primary key field. This could simply number the records.

## What does it mean?

*A **primary key field** is the field in which the data uniquely identifies each record. The data in a primary key field in one record is known as the primary key (or record key) for that record.*

## Further research – primary key fields

In each of these examples, is there a field which can be the primary key field? If not, suggest a new field that could be created for this purpose.

1. A list of the stock held in a warehouse for an online shop, which includes for each item the stock code, a description of the item and the quantity in stock.
2. A list of students at a college consisting of name, address, course studied and the date a student started.
3. Entries in a telephone book.
4. Mobile phone account details including name, address and phone number.

# Data integrity

It is very important that the data stored in a database is correct. Data can be incorrect for four reasons:

- The original data may have been wrong.
- The original data may have been correct, but it may have been entered incorrectly into the database.
- The facts in the real world may have changed since the data was first entered but the data may not have been amended to match.
- The data may have been changed by mistake since it was first entered.

## Data accuracy

The original information for a database could have come from a number of sources, such as paper-based lists or old databases, any of which could have been incorrect. It is important that the user checks the accuracy of the information.

The information for a database is often collected on a paper form. When this is keyed into a database, the user should always read back the data after it is entered to check that it has been entered accurately. This kind of accuracy check is referred to as **verification**.

Sometimes a company will collect details over the phone, for example when selling tickets for an event. In this case, the user who is entering the data straight into the database should read the details back to the customer to verify that they have been entered correctly.

## Consistency of data

Some data will have to be changed from time to time. For example, when a person moves house, the new address should be entered on any databases that contain their personal details. Other data, such as exchange rates, interest rates and tax rates fluctuate, so should be amended whenever necessary.

Keeping data consistent with the real world is an ongoing problem.

## Validation

When data is entered into a field, validation checks can be carried out by the DBMS to make sure that the data is as expected for that field. The rules for each field are either set up automatically by the database, or are created by the developer. If the user enters data that does not match the rules then an error message will be displayed.

Validation will not guarantee that the data is accurate, but will at least exclude some obviously wrong data.

**What does it mean?**

**Data integrity** *means ensuring that the data correctly matches the facts.*

**What does it mean?**

**Validation** *is a process carried out automatically by a database. It checks that data entered into a field matches rules laid down for that field.*

There are several ways in which data can be validated, including:

- **Data type checks.** The data is checked to see whether it matches the data type for a field. For example, if you try to enter text in a date field it will report an error.
- **Lookup lists.** The data is checked against a list of acceptable values in a reference table. For example, if you are asked to enter your title (Mr, Mrs, Ms etc.), you could be given a drop-down list from which to choose. This would prevent you from entering an invalid title like George.
- **Default values.** Some fields may have data already in them. The default value is the data that is used in this field unless the user changes it. For example, if you are asked whether you have any criminal convictions, the default value may be 'No', since most people do not.
- **Upper or lower limits.** The data is checked to make sure that it is less than a value (the upper limit), greater than a value (the lower limit), or between two values. This can be used for numerical fields and also for dates and times. For example, if you are asked to enter your date of birth it could check that the year is after, say, 1900, and warn you if you try to enter an invalid year.

## Test your knowledge

1  What data will be kept on a ticket booking system for a football cllub?

2  In the context of a database system, what is a form and why are forms used?

3  Why is it necessary to define the data type for a field?

4  What is a primary key?

5  Give three examples to illustrate how data in a database could be incorrect.

6  Describe two ways in which data can be validated.

# Create a simple database to meet user needs

A piece of applications software known as a database management system (DBMS) holds all the data, as well as all the forms, queries and reports in a database. It organises the data on the hard disk, and controls access to the data by users.

Individual users are not really aware of the complexity of the database; the DBMS hides much of it away from them. Users are only aware of the data that they require, which will often appear to them to be a simple single-table database (or flat file). Different users in the company will want to use different mixes of data within the database, and a DBMS handles all these needs.

Microsoft Access is a well known DBMS, which is used by professionals to create complex databases. It was originally intended for use on standalone systems, so that users could create their own small databases. This meant that some end users found that they became database developers as well, even though they did not have the skills in database design that you will be learning in this unit.

There are other database management systems on the market that are designed for network use, and these do require specialist professional skills. Examples of these are Oracle Database and Microsoft SQL Server.

This section and the next contain case studies in the use of Access to build databases. The notes all refer to Access 2003. You may find some minor variations if you are using a different version.

## Using a wizard

You may use any of the wizards provided by Access. These include:

- **Form, query and report wizards.** Always create a form, query or report using the wizard to begin with. You can then customise them if necessary in *Design* view.

- **Table wizard.** This is not particularly useful, and you would be wiser to create your tables from scratch in *Design* view.

You may come across templates for complete databases in Access. You may like to explore these, but you should never use a template to create the solution to a problem that you are set as part of your course. It will be very obvious to the assessor that you have used a template, and it is very unlikely to match the requirements of the problem.

# Constructing a simple database

Whenever you carry out a software project, there are several steps that you must take:

- Identify the problem.
- Design the database.
- Build (implement) the database.
- Provide documentation.
- Evaluate the database.

In this section and the next you will learn how to design and build a database for a problem that has already been identified for you. The final section deals with documentation.

How to –

## Set up a single-table database

We will set up a single-table database with information about books that you have found useful for your work. You can view the books on screen, add notes about them, and print out lists for your portfolios.

- Launch Microsoft Access. If the task pane is visible on the right of the window then click on *Create a New File*. Otherwise, select *New* from the *File* menu.

- Select *Blank database*. See Figure 9.5.

- You will be prompted to save your database straightaway. All Access databases are given the file extension *.mdb*. Call the database 'Bibliography'. Click *Create*.

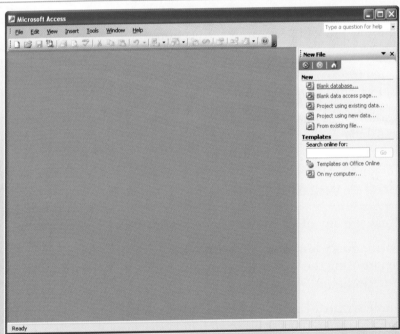

**Figure 9.5** *Blank database in Access*

- The database window appears. Note the list of objects to the right. We will be using *Tables*, *Queries*, *Forms* and *Reports*.

Access will prompt you to save your work whenever you add a new object.

# Creating tables

## Selection of fields

You should start by:

- listing all the fields you will need
- deciding on the data types for each field
- identifying the primary key field.

## Choice of data types

The data types that can be used in Access are as follows:

- **Text.** (Also known as a 'string'.) This allows the user to enter up to 255 characters in a field. Text can include numerical digits, but the database will not be able to calculate with them as it will treat them just like letters. Each character takes up one byte of memory.
- **Memo.** (Also known as 'text' in some DBMS.) This is simply a longer text field and can include thousands of characters – in fact, up to 65,536 characters.
- **Number.** You usually have a choice of number types, including:
  a. **Byte.** Holds an integer (whole number) in the range 0 to 255.
  b. **Integer.** Holds an integer between –32,768 and 32,767.  Use this for most integer fields unless the data is likely to be very large.
  c. **Long integer.** Holds an integer in the range -2,147,483,648 to 2,147,483,647.
  d. **Single.** (Also known as 'single precision real' or 'floating-point'.) Holds a number with a decimal point. Use this for most decimal number fields.
  e. **Double.** (Also known as 'double precision real'.) Holds large decimal numbers.
  f. **Decimal.** Holds a positive or negative number with a decimal point. This should not be used unless a high degree of accuracy or extremely large numbers are needed.
- **Date/Time.** You can usually specify which format the date should appear in. Do not forget that American dates are written in a different order from UK dates, so that 5/10/03 is 10th May 2003 in the USA, and 5th October 2003 in the UK.
- **Yes/No.** (Also known as 'logical'.) This can simply hold one of two values – 'yes' or 'no'. As alternatives to 'yes' and 'no', the words 'true' and 'false', or 'on' and 'off' can also be entered.

The table definition for the Books table is repeated in Table 9.3, with data types.

| Books table | Data types |
|---|---|
| Title | Text |
| Author | Text |
| Publisher | Text |
| Year published | Number |
| ISBN | Text |
| Notes | Memo |
| Star rating | Number |

**Table 9.3** *The Books table definition with data types*

You use a Text data type for the ISBN field because the character X is sometimes used in the rightmost position.

The Memo data type for the Notes field will allow the user to enter lengthy comments on each book.

## Field properties

Once the data type has been defined for each field you can decide whether to use some additional field properties.

### Field size (or length)

The field size is the maximum amount of space that is allowed for the field. In Access, text fields are initially set with a maximum of 50 characters. This can be changed for any particular field to anything from 1 to 255 characters.

You will probably want to leave the field size at 50 for the Title, Author and Publisher fields. But an ISBN consists of exactly 10 characters, if you leave out any spaces or dashes, so you should set the field size to 10. This will prevent anyone from entering more than 10 characters and will also make the database more efficient.

You cannot change the field size for a memo field, but its maximum size is 65,536 characters so that should be enough for all users.

Whatever the field size, a text or memo field actually only uses one byte of memory for each character that is entered.

The field size of a number field is expressed as a byte, integer etc., as shown in the list on the previous page. The 'Year published' field is best set up as an integer instead of a long integer, as this will save some storage space. The 'Star rating' can be set up as a single byte as the numbers entered will be small.

### Format

A number field can be formatted with a fixed number of decimal points, or as currency, as a percentage or in scientific notation.

There are several options for the formats for date and time fields. For example, the date 29th July 2006 can be written 29/06/2006, 29 July 2006 or 29-Jul-06.

Default value
There is a default value for the field size for most data types, which is used unless you change it. The default values are 50 for a text field and Long Integer for a number field.

## How to –

### Create a table

■ The database opens in the *Tables* window (Figure 9.6). Select *Create Table in Design View*.

**Figure 9.6** *The Tables window*

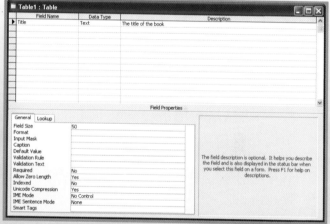

**Figure 9.7** *Adding a field*

■ Enter this information about the first field, exactly as shown. See Figure 9.7.

| Field Name | Data Type | Description |
|---|---|---|
| Title | Text | The title of the book |

When you later come to enter some data, the description will appear at the bottom of the window to remind you what the field contains.

■ Add these fields:

| | | |
|---|---|---|
| Author | Text | Author — surname first |
| Publisher | Text | The name of the publishing company |

■ The next field will be a number:

| | | |
|---|---|---|
| Year published | Number | The year the book was first published or revised |

For the *Data Type*, click on the down arrow and select *Number*. At the bottom of the window you will see the *Field Properties* for this field. Select *Integer* for the *Field Size*.

- The ISBN field is entered next.

  ISBN                Text          International Standard Book Number — enter without spaces or dashes

  Look at the *Field Properties* at the bottom of the window, and change the *Field Size* to 10.

- Finally you can add the Notes and Star Rating fields.

  Notes              Memo        My notes on the book
  Star rating     Number     Enter a value from 1 (poor) to 5 (very useful)

  Set the *Field Size* for Star Rating to *Byte*.

- The table must have a primary key, which in this case will be the ISBN. Click anywhere on the row containing the *ISBN* field name. A pointer will appear at the beginning of the row. Now click on the *Primary Key* button in the toolbar (it looks like a door key). See Figure 9.8.

- Close the window. When prompted to save your table, name it 'Books'. You will see the 'Books' table listed in the *Tables* window.

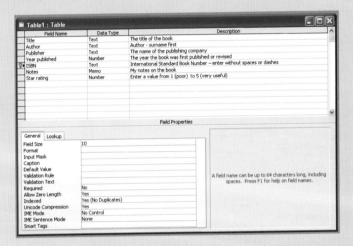

**Figure 9.8** *Completed fields with primary key defined*

## How to –

### Enter data into a table

- From the *Bibliography* database window, select *Tables*. Click once on the *Books* table and click on *Open* (in the toolbar in the *Tables* window). This opens the table in *Datasheet View*, which allows you to enter data.

- Enter your own choice of data for a few books. See Figure 9.9.

| Title | Author | Publisher | Year published | ISBN | Notes | Star rating |
|---|---|---|---|---|---|---|
| How to be a geek | Entwhistle Y | Almond Harrison | 2004 | 0707804031 | | 3 |
| Imaginative PC assembly | Lewis A et al | Greatham | 2003 | 0435454697 | | 4 |
| Finding your way through project management | Rice S & Jam K | Lost Books | 2004 | 0735615190 | | 5 |
| Finding your way through web design | Selby T & York F | Lost Books | 2003 | 076454074X | | 2 |
| Cabling, connections and ports | Stamp H P | Almond Harrison | 2003 | 0764541738 | | 2 |
| When all else fails: troubleshooting for beginners | Bracket K | Jones & Jones | 2004 | 1904467786 | | 4 |
| | | | 0 | | | 0 |

**Figure 9.9** *Data entered in Datasheet View*

- You can make the window wider if you like. You can also drag the edges of the fields to give more room.

- The data is automatically saved as you go along.

## Validation

It is easy for the end user to make a mistake when entering data. Well-written database software has built-in tests that check whether the data 'makes sense' when it is input. These tests are known as validation checks.

Access automatically checks that the data you enter is of the correct data type. You will have noticed that a number of data types can be selected, including text and number.

You can add some further validation checks by checking that data falls within acceptable ranges.

Validation checks help to make the database user friendly, as well as increasing the accuracy of the data.

### How to –

## Check the data type

- Open the *Books* table in *Datasheet View*.

- Enter a new record, but enter a letter instead of a number into the *Year* field, then press the *Enter* key. You will get an Access error message. See Figure 9.10.

| Title | Author | Publisher | Year published | ISBN | Notes | Star rating |
|---|---|---|---|---|---|---|
| Imaginative PC assembly | Lewis A et al | Greatham | 2003 | 0435454697 | | 4 |
| How to be a geek | Entwhistle Y | Almond Harrison | 2004 | 0707804031 | | 3 |
| Finding your way through project management | Rice S & Jam K | Lost Books | 2004 | 0735615190 | | 5 |
| Finding your way through web design | Selby T & York F | Lost Books | 2003 | 076454074X | | 2 |
| Cabling, connections and ports | Stamp H P | Almond Harrison | 2003 | 0764541738 | | 2 |
| When all else fails: troubleshooting for beginners | Bracket K | Jones & Jones | 2004 | 1904467786 | | 4 |
| Finding your way through networking | Hill V & Dale T | Lost Books | K | | | 0 |
| | | | | | | 0 |

**Microsoft Office Access**

The value you entered isn't valid for this field.

For example, you may have entered text in a numeric field or a number that is larger than the FieldSize setting permits.

OK

Record: 7 of 7

**Figure 9.10** *A data type error message*

- Correct the data, then close the table. The new data will be saved automatically.

### How to –

## Add a validation rule

- From the *Bibliography* database window, select *Tables*. Click once on the *Books* table and click on *Design* (in the toolbar in the *Tables* window). This opens the table in *Design View*.

- Click somewhere in the Star Rating row. In *Field Properties*, click in the *Validation Rule* box and key in : <6 This means that only numbers less than 6 will be considered valid.

- In the *Validation Text* box key in: **Please enter a star rating from 1 to 5** This is the message that will appear if an invalid Star Rating is entered.

- Note that the Default value is 0 (see Figure 9.11). That is the number which will appear in the Star Rating field if you do not enter a rating. It means that the book has not yet been rated.

- Close the table. You will be warned that the new validation (or data integrity) rule may make some existing data invalid. Click on *Yes*.

- Open the table in *Datasheet View*. Add a new record with an invalid Star Rating (e.g. 9) to see how it is handled. See Figure 9.12.

- In future you should always add validation rules before entering any data.

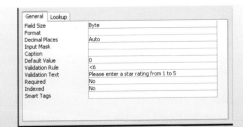

**Figure 9.11** *Validation rule and text in the Star Rating field*

**Figure 9.12** *Validation text appears in an error box when the validation rule is broken*

## Improving efficiency through shortcuts

You can improve your efficiency as a database developer by learning a few keyboard shortcuts that you can use. Some are shown in Table 9.4.

| Shortcut | Action |
|---|---|
| Ctrl+S | Save a table or other object |
| Ctrl+P | Print out a table or other object |
| Ctrl+F | Find data in a table |
| F7 | Check spelling |

**Table 9.4** *Keyboard shortcuts for database development*

You can also help your users by providing on-screen shortcuts for them. These will be in the form of buttons that they can click. You will learn more about these later.

## Naming

The objects that you create in a database should have meaningful names. For example, tables called 'Mytable' or 'Project' are not very explicit, whereas 'Items in stock' or 'Contacts' are much clearer.

If you progress to more advanced database design on another course, you will find that objects are usually given names without spaces or punctuation. Also, each fieldname may be given a prefix that identifies the data type. For example, the fieldname 'txtSurname' might be used.

# Data storage requirements

You can work out how much memory space the data in a database is going to need by a simple calculation.

Look at the field properties for each field in a table. If the field is a number field then you can work out how many bytes it needs from the list in Table 9.5.

| Number type | Bytes used |
|---|---|
| Byte | 1 |
| Integer | 2 |
| Long integer | 4 |
| Single | 4 |
| Double | 8 |
| Decimal | 12 |

**Table 9.5** *Bytes used by each number type*

Text and memo fields only use as many bytes as they need to hold the characters. So you will have to estimate the average number of characters that will be entered in the field across all the records. You need to add in at least one further byte per field as an 'overhead', i.e. for the system to store information about the field.

Add up the bytes to find the total for each record. An example is shown in Table 9.6.

| Field | Data Type | Field size | Average number of characters | Number of bytes |
|---|---|---|---|---|
| Title | Text | 50 | 25 | 25 |
| Author | Text | 50 | 15 | 15 |
| Publisher | Text | 50 | 20 | 20 |
| Year published | Number | Integer | | 2 |
| ISBN | Text | 10 | 10 | 10 |
| Notes | Memo | | 100 | 100 |
| Star rating | Number | Byte | | 1 |
| | | | Overheads | 7 |
| | | | Total number of bytes per record | 180 |

**Table 9.6** *Example calculation for number of bytes per record*

Next, estimate how many records will be entered into the database, and multiply that number by the number of bytes per record.

Number of records (estimate) = 30

Number of bytes required = 30 × 180 = 5,400 bytes

Hence the memory storage required for the data is around 5 KB.

In practice the memory taken by this database, developed in Access, will be very much larger. The forms, reports and queries will all be added to the data making a total of several hundred KB.

However this calculation is particularly important if the database is very large. Suppose the list of books was used in a library with 100,000 volumes. The amount of memory for the data alone would be:

100,000 × 180 = 18,000,000 bytes, that is, around 18 MB.

## Test your knowledge

7   What is a DBMS?

8   Explain the differences between these numerical data types: integer, long integer, decimal.

9   Why is it good practice to define the size of a field?

10  Calculate the number of bytes per record that are needed for a database that you have created.

# Create database forms, reports and queries

## Forms

Tables, in both *Design* and *Datasheet View*, are used by the database developer (i.e. you) when constructing a database. The user should not need to see anything you have worked on so far. Instead, you, as developer, should design forms that will give the user a simple, non-technical view of the database.

### Automatic creation of forms

#### Wizards

The form, report and query wizards are all useful in Access. You can start by using the wizard then customise the result afterwards.

### How to –

#### *Use a wizard to create a form*

- Open the Bibliography database.

- In the database window click on *Forms*, then click on *Create form by using wizard*. See Figure 9.13.

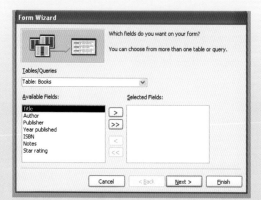

**Figure 9.13** *The form wizard*

- Note that the name of the table 'Books' appears in the top box, and fields in this table are listed in the *Available Fields* box. Click on the >> button to select all the fields. (You could select individual fields by clicking on the > button). Click on *Next*.

- Select *Columnar* layout and click on *Next*.

- Select *Standard* style. We will add colour later. Click on *Next* then *Finish*.

- A form appears with all the fields in it. Use the navigation buttons at the bottom of the form to browse through the records. Find out what each navigation button does.

- The form has some shortcomings. For example, some of the text boxes are not wide enough to display all the text, but you will fix those in the next case study.

- Change the data in one or two fields of existing records.

- Click on the navigation button marked with * to add a new record. Add data in the first field, then use the right cursor (arrow) key on your keyboard to move from one field to the next, and the left cursor key to move back. You can also use the Tab key (to the left of Q on the keyboard) to move to the next field.

- Use the form to add a few new records. This is how the end user will enter data. You can add notes on some of the books you have read. See Figure 9.14.

- Close the form.

**Figure 9.14** *A form produced by the form wizard*

**Figure 9.15** *Switching between Design View and Form View*

## Formatting forms

The wizard is a quick and easy way to create a form. But you probably want to customise the form further.

In Access a table can be displayed in *Design View* or *Datasheet View*. In the same way a form can be displayed in *Design View* or *Form View*. *Form View* is the version that the end user will see, but you need to make any changes to the form in *Design View*.

When you have opened a form in either *Design View* or *Form View* you can switch between them by clicking on the icon at the left end of the main toolbar. See Figure 9.15.

How to –

## *Format a form*

- In the Bibliography database window, click on *Forms*, then click once on *Books*. Click on *Design*.

- The floating toolbox will have appeared. You will be using this later.

- Enlarge the form by dragging the right-hand edge to the right of the text boxes. See Figure 9.16.

- Notice the bar with the words *Form Footer*. To stretch the form downwards, click the top edge of this bar and then drag down.

- Each field on the form has two objects – the label and the text box. The label is on the left. The text box is known as a control because it controls the way the user can access the data. The text box displays the actual data in *Form View*.

- Click on the *ISBN* label. Now click on the *ISBN* text box. You will note that they are linked. As you move

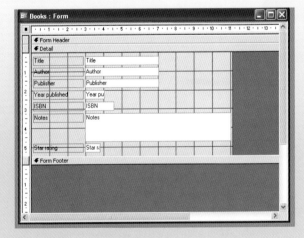

**Figure 9.16** *Formatting a form*

the cursor over the label and it changes to a full hand (with all the fingers showing) you can drag the label and text box together to another position.

- When the cursor changes to a pointing finger you can move the label or text box independently.

- When the cursor is positioned over the resizing handles it also allows you to resize the label or text box. You will probably want to enlarge some of the text boxes.

- After you have rearranged the form, close it.

- Back in the *Bibiography* database window click once on *Books* then click on *Open* to open it in *Form View*.

## Labels

At first the label contains the fieldname that you used when you designed the table. You can alter the words to make them more meaningful to the user.

## Change the wording on a label

- Open the 'Books' form in *Design View*.

- Click inside the *Title* label. The cursor changes to an I-bar. Click again and you can edit the words. Change the label to read 'Title of book'.

- Close the form and open it in *Form View* to see your changes. See Figure 9.17.

- You can also switch directly between *Design* and *Form View* by using the button at the left end of the main tool bar.

**Figure 9.17** *Some improvements to the form*

## Titles

You can place any other information you like on the form by adding extra labels. This can help the user to decide what to do. You can also use a label as a title for the form.

## Add a title and other information to the form

- Open the 'Books' form in *Design View*. You may want to enlarge the window so that you can see all of the form.

- Notice the *Form Header* and *Detail* bars at the top of the form. You can open the *Form Header* area

by clicking on the line where the two bars touch and dragging down. You will create a label as a heading for the form.

- Click on the *Labels* button in the toolbox. See Figure 9.18. (Move your mouse over the buttons in the toolbox to identify them.) Then click on the *Form Header* where you want the label to appear, and start typing. Press the *Enter* key when you have finished.

**Figure 9.18** *Form design floating toolbox*

**Figure 9.19** *Use of fonts on the form*

- You can change the font style in any label. Click on the label so that the handles appear, then use the font buttons in the toolbar at the top of the screen. Note that all the text in one label will have the same style. See Figure 9.19.

## Data entry order

The data entry (or tab) order is the order in which the user is guided to enter data on to a form. The user presses either the Enter key or the Tab key to move to the next field. The fields will be visited in the same order as they appear in the original table – in our case Title, Author, Publisher etc.

If you have rearranged the fields in the form, as in the example above, then you will want to change the tab order so that the user is taken from one field to another in a sensible sequence.

How to –

### Change the data entry order (tab order)

- Open the 'Books' form in *Design View*.

- Select *View* from the main menu, then *Tab Order*, then follow the instructions.

## Colour and images

You can change the colours of any component on a form. It is best to be fairly subtle with colours, as too many conflicting colours can be distracting. It is better to use no more than two contrasting colours.

You can also add images, but again you should be careful not to take the eye away from the main function of the form, which is to display the data.

## How to –

### Add colour and images to the form

- In *Design View* click anywhere on the background of the form. Then use the *Fill* button on the toolbar to change the colour.

- You can also change the text colour and the fill colour of any label, and add borders. Just click on the label and then use the buttons in the toolbar. See Figure 9.20.

- To insert a picture, click on the *Image* button in the floating toolbox. Click on the form in the position

**Figure 9.20** *Buttons on the toolbar for fill colour, text colour and borders*

where you want the image to be placed. Find and select the picture as you would in other software packages.

## Buttons

A button is a type of shortcut that you can create to help the user work efficiently.

The end users should be able to carry out all their tasks from the form. They can already add a new record, and change data in a record. You should now add a button to the form to let them delete a record.

## How to –

### Add a button to delete records

- Open your form in *Design View*.

- In the floating toolbox, make sure that the *Controls Wizard* button is depressed. Click on the *Command Button* button, then click on the form in the position where you want the button to be placed.

- The button wizard will guide you through the next steps.

- In the *Categories* box click on *Record Operations*. In the *Actions* box click on *Delete Record*, then click on *Next*.

- You can choose whether to have text or an icon on the button. Make your choice, then click *Next*, then *Finish*.

- Switch to *Form View* to test the button.

- Close and save the form. See Figure 9.21.

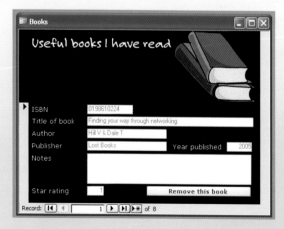

**Figure 9.21** *A customised version of the form*

## What does it mean?

*A **sort key field** is the field that is used to sort the data into alphabetical or numerical order (including date order).*

## Sorting records on a form

A form automatically sorts the records before displaying them for the first time. It uses the record's primary key field as the sort key field. But the user can change the order in which records are displayed at any time.

### How to –

### Change the order in which records are displayed

The books are normally sorted in ISBN order. You can change this to sort the books by author, or by any other field, such as title.

- Open the form.
- Right-click on the data in the *Author* field, and select *Sort Ascending*.
- Click through the records to check that they have been sorted. The next time you open the form, the data will be sorted in the new order.

# Reports

A report is a printed record of data in the database. Access gives you a number of style options when formatting a report; the simplest is a list of all the data set out in columns.

## Automatic creation of reports

The report wizard, like the form wizard, is a good way to start off a report, which you can then customise.

### How to –

### Create a report

- Close any tables or forms that are open.
- In the *Bibliography* database window click on *Reports*, then select *Create report by using wizard*.
- Select all of the fields, except Notes, by clicking on the > key for each field. Then click on *Next*.
- Click on *Next* in the following two windows. For the layout select *Tabular*, and *Landscape*, then click on *Next*.
- Choose the style you want for the report, then click on *Next*, then *Finish*.

- You will then view a preview of your report. Print it out or close the window. See Figure 9.22.

### Books

| Title | Author | Publisher | Year published | ISBN | Star rating |
|---|---|---|---|---|---|
| How to be a geek | Entwhistle Y | Almond Harrison | 2004 | 0707804031 | 3 |
| Imaginative PC assembly | Lewis A et al | Greatham | 2003 | 0435454697 | 4 |
| Finding your way through proje | Rice S & Jam K | Lost Books | 2004 | 0735615190 | 5 |
| Finding your way through web | Selby T & York F | Lost Books | 2003 | 076454074X | 2 |
| Cabling, connections and ports | Stamp H P | Almond Harrison | 2003 | 0764541738 | 2 |
| When all else fails: troublesho | Bracket K | Jones & Jones | 2004 | 1904467786 | 4 |
| Finding your way through netw | Hill V & Dale T | Lost Books | 2005 | 0198610224 | 1 |
| Listen to the problem | March Q | Greatham | 2006 | 1861976123 | 3 |

**Figure 9.22** *A report listing all the books*

The report wizard can produce reports in a number of styles. But you may want to make some changes to the appearance and layout of a report. For example, you might want to alter the width of some of the fields in the report, or change the wording of the column headings.

Reports can be viewed in two views – *Preview* and *Design View* – and you can switch between them using the icon on the left of the main toolbar.

## Selection of appropriate layouts

When you use a wizard to create either a form or a report you are asked to choose between a number of layouts. You can experiment with them all. The three most useful ones are:

- **Columnar layout.** This arranges the data in pages, one for each record. The labels are placed to the left of the data. This layout is ideal when there is a significant amount of data in each record. On a form you can navigate between records using the navigation buttons at the bottom of the screen. See Figure 9.14, page 322. On a report, each record is laid out with the fields under each other, and you can print only a few records on each page.
- **Tabular layout.** This arranges the data in a familiar table. This layout can be used for forms and reports if the amount of data in each record will fit comfortably on the screen or page. See Figure 9.22.
- **Justified layout.** This displays the data, as in the columnar layout, one record at a time. The appearance is a formal boxed style, which fits neatly across the page, with the labels for each field above the data. It makes efficient use of the space.

## Appropriate labels and titles

When you use a wizard to design a report, the fieldnames are used as the labels for each field. In fact, you can change these labels in *Design View* to make them more understandable to the user. As we saw in the section on naming, if you use more advanced database techniques you may have to use fieldnames, such as 'txtSurname', that will mean very little to your user.

The title that you choose in the report wizard is used for a number of purposes:

- as the filename of the report
- as the name in the title bar of the window when you open the report
- as the heading in a report.

Note you can change the heading in *Design View* without changing the filename of the report. A report heading can be longer and give more information than the simple name of the report.

# How to –

## Change the design of the report

- In the Bibliography database window, click on *Reports*, then click once on *Books*. Click on *Design*. See Figure 9.23.

- Notice that the report is divided into four sections:

  a. The Report Header appears only on the first page of the report.

  b. The Page Header appears on every page, and gives the headings for each of the fields.

  c. The Detail section formats all the records that will be displayed in the report.

  d. The Page Footer appears on each page and contains the date the report was printed and the number of pages.

- The heading 'Books' in the Report Header is a label. Click on this once, then make any changes you want to the text. You can also use the formatting toolbar at the top of the window to change the font, font size, font colour etc.

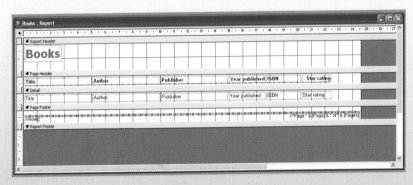

**Figure 9.23** *The report in Design view*

- If you want to add any more information to the Report Header you can use the toolbox to create a new label.

- To change the appearance of one of the lines, click once on it then use the *Lines/Borders* button in the toolbar. You can use the toolbox to create a new line.

- If you decide to make the field columns narrower or wider, do this with care, and make sure that the fieldnames in the Page Header line up with the data in the Detail section.

## Special fields

The report wizard places two important special fields in the footer. It uses an **expression**, which is a coded instruction that is recognised by the database system. You have already used one expression, when you set up <6 as the validation rule for the Star Rating field. Expressions often begin with =.

- **Date/time.** The expression for today's date is =Now() (i.e. a pair of brackets with nothing between them). Notice the effect of this in the footer of the report.

- **Page number.** Another useful expression is the one that displays the page number. Of course, it is a little redundant if you only need one page to print out the report, but it becomes very useful with larger databases.

You do not need to know how to construct expressions to do either of these. Simply open a form or report in *Design View*, then go to the *Insert* menu and select *Date and Time* or *Page Numbers*.

### How to –

### *Allow the user to print a report*

You need to add a button to the form that allows the user to print the report.

- Open the form in *Design View*. Use the button wizard as before. Select the *Report Operations* category, and the *Preview Report Action*.

- In the next window, select the '*Book*' report.

- Select text rather than a picture, and use the words 'Print out the full list of books'.

- Switch to *Form View* to see how the button operates. See Figure 9.24.

**Figure 9.24** *The print button on the form*

## Further research – creating a CD catalogue database

A friend of yours has an extensive collection of CDs. You have been asked to create a database that catalogues them all. Before you use Access you should do these three things:

- Decide on a suitable set of fields for recording information about the CDs, e.g. record label, singer, style of music, when released, single or album.
- Choose meaningful names for the fields. In some database software you are not allowed to have spaces in a fieldname, so you might have to use TypeOfMusic as a field name. Access does permit spaces.
- Decide what validation rules you could use.

When you go into Access you should start a new database, because the data in the new database is unrelated to the Bibliography database. If a database is already open then close it. Create your own database by following the steps used to create the Bibliography database.

## A database with more advanced features

In order to understand some more advanced functions of databases, we will set up a new database with some additional features.

This next database will contain a membership list for a gym in Kingsmond, called King Gym. The database will be used for a number of purposes, including printing out lists of members.

## How to –

### Create a new database to handle membership lists

If a database is already open then close it. You should always start afresh for a new database.

- Select *File / New Database*. Click on *Blank Database*, then click *OK*.
- You will be prompted to name your database. Call it 'King Gym'.
- Use *Create table in design view* to design a table with these fields and data types:

| Membership number | Autonumber | The Membership Number will be allocated by the system |

This is the primary key field. *Autonumber* will automatically allocate a number to each member in sequence. Make *Membership Number* the primary key.

| Surname | Text |

Choose suitable *Field Sizes* for this and all the other text fields.

| Forename | Text |

Names should usually be divided into Surname and Forename (or Initials). We often sort names by surname, so it needs its own field and should not be buried in a Name field.

| Address | Text | The first line of the address |

Add a description for any fields where it will help the user.

| Town | Text |

Since most of the members live in Kingsmond, we can save the user a lot of typing by making Kingsmond the default value. In the *Field Properties* enter Kingsmond as the default value. The user can still type in another town if necessary.

| Postcode | Text |
| Phone | Text |
| Sex | Text | Enter M or F |

The *Sex* field needs a validation rule. The rule is ="M" OR ="F" and the validation text is 'Please enter either M or F'.

| Junior | Yes/No | Tick the box if this is a Junior member |
| Over 60 | Yes/No | Tick the box if this member is over 60 |
| Subscription paid | Number |

In the *Field Properties*, click in *Format*, then select *Currency*.

| Date subscription | Date/Time paid |

In the *Field Properties*, click in *Format*, then select the date format that you would like to use. The user can enter the date in any format but it will be displayed in the chosen format.

- Close and save the table as 'Members'.

## Further research – use of numbers in databases

Telephone numbers are always given the text data type. Why?

A full phone number in the UK has eleven digits. We should normally store the whole of the number, including the dialling code for a landline number. Mobile phone numbers all begin with 07 and landline numbers all begin with 01 or 02.

Find out what happens if you try to store a number that begins with zero, such as 0123. You can try this out on a calculator to see the result.

You should ensure that, wherever possible, data is validated on entry. You can use validation rules, and you can also set up a lookup list.

## How to –

### Create a lookup list

You will create a lookup list for the *Subscription Paid* field. The annual subscription rate is normally £300, but £100 for concessions, i.e. Juniors and the over-60s.

- Open the *Members* table in *Design View*.

- In the *Subscription paid* row, click in the *Data Type* column, and then select *Lookup Wizard,* which is at the bottom of the list of data types.

- In the first screen of the wizard, select *I will type the values that I want.* Click on *Next*.

- For the number of columns, leave this as 1.

- Under *Col1*, type in 300 in the first row, then 100 in the second row, then 0 in the third row. Click on *Next*. See Figure 9.25.

- In the final screen simply click on *Finish*.

- Switch to *Datasheet View*. Start adding records. In the *Subscription Paid* field use the lookup list to choose the value.

**Figure 9.25** *A lookup list*

You should always provide your user with one or more user-friendly forms, so that they can interact easily with the database.

## How to –

### Set up the main form

- Create a form based on the *Members* table using the wizard as before, and save it.

- Rearrange and customise the form in *Design View*.

- Open the form in *Form View* and use it to enter details of at least twelve members. Do not enter anything in the *Membership Number* field. You have set the *Data Type* for this field to *Autonumber,*

so the system will give each record a unique membership number.

- Include both males and females, juniors and over-60s, and two or three members who do not live in Kingsmond.

- Close the form.

# Queries

Users often want to select data from a database. For example, in the King Gym database you may want to see a list of all the members who have paid their subscriptions, or you may want to find all the female junior members. This is carried out by setting up a query or a filter within the database.

Another kind of query is one that displays all the records but gives data only in specified fields. For example, you might want to list just the names and addresses of members.

## Creating a query to select fields for display

We will now set up a query that selects all the records in the *Members* table but will only display certain fields. We will then use it to create first a form and then a report which gives a simple list of all members, giving their names and membership numbers.

How to –

### Create a query that selects certain fields only

- Close any tables or forms that are open.

- In the *King Gym* database window click on *Queries*, then select *Create a query by using a wizard*.

- In the *Available Fields* box click on *Membership number*, then click on the > to transfer it to the *Selected Fields* box. See Figure 9.26.

- Repeat with the *Surname* and *Forename* fields, then click on *Next*.

- For the title of the query, which will also be the name it is saved under, enter Names Query. Click *Finish*.

- The query will run and generate a new table, which will be displayed in *Datasheet View*.

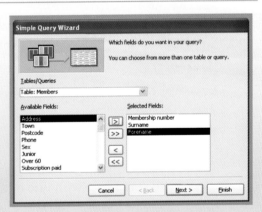

**Figure 9.26** *Selecting fields for a query*

## Creating forms and reports based on queries

As a database developer you should not allow your user to view the queries directly. Queries are part of the engine of a database, and they should be used to generate new forms or reports.

## How to –

### Use a query to create a form

Your user should be viewing the output from a query in a form rather than in Datasheet View.

- Use the form wizard. In the first window go to the *Tables/Queries* text box, and select the *Names Query*. Select all three fields using the >> button.

- We want to present the information as a list on screen, so in the next window select *Tabular* layout, then work through the rest of the wizard. Enter Names Form as the title for the form.

- Switch to *Form View* to see what the form looks like. See Figure 9.27.

| Names Form | | | |
|---|---|---|---|
| Membership number | Surname | | Forename |
| 1 | Jones | | Michael |
| 2 | Patel | | Vina |
| 3 | Harris | | Jenny |
| 4 | Leung | | Chi |
| 5 | Hinton | | Sam |
| 6 | Russell | | George |
| 7 | Russell | | Amy |
| 8 | Russell | | William |
| 9 | Russell | | Charlotte |
| 10 | Russell | | Alexandra |
| 11 | Park | | Tracey |
| 12 | Park | | Michael |
| (AutoNumber) | | | |

Record: |◄ ◄ [ 1 ] ► ►| ►* of 12

**Figure 9.27** *The Names form with tabular layout*

## How to –

### Use a query to create a report

The *Names Query* can also be used to print a simple membership list.

- Use the report wizard. As with the form, in the first window go to the *Tables/Queries* text box, and select the *Names Query*. Select all three fields using the >> button.

- The next window asks about grouping records. This is only useful for complex reports, so click *Next*.

- The user is not able to choose the sort order for the report so you must do so now. In *box 1* select *Surname*, and in *box 2* select *Forename*. This means that the records will be sorted first by *Surname*, then, if the *Surname* is shared by more than one member, those records will be sorted by *Forename*. You may need to add some more records later to see the effect of this.

- In the next window select *Tabular*.

- Next choose your style.

- In the final screen, the title of your report will appear in the header of the report itself, so choose something explanatory like *List of Names*.

- Preview the report and decide whether you want to print it. See Figure 9.28.

## List of Names

| Surname | Forename | Membership number |
|---|---|---|
| Harris | Jenny | 3 |
| Hinton | Sam | 5 |
| Jones | Michael | 1 |
| Leung | Chi | 4 |
| Park | Michael | 12 |
| Park | Tracey | 11 |
| Patel | Vina | 2 |
| Russell | Alexandra | 10 |
| Russell | Amy | 7 |
| Russell | Charlotte | 9 |
| Russell | George | 6 |
| Russell | William | 8 |

**Figure 9.28** *The report showing the sorting (note how the Russell family has been sorted)*

## Creating a query to select records

A query can be used to select just some of the records in the database, according to rules known as criteria. For example, the query might be used to pick out all the members with the surname Patel. This uses one criterion: Surname = "Patel". Note that you should put double quote marks around the text.

You can also create criteria on number and date fields, such as Date subscription paid = #01/01/05#. Note that you should place the hash symbols to identify a date.

Criteria can also be used with other operators, such as <, > or Not.

Each criterion is applied to just one field. Here are some examples:

- **Equals.** To check whether the data is exactly the same as that required. Examples: Surname="Patel", Subscription Paid = 100, Junior=yes (for a yes/no field).
- **Less than (<).** This can be used with numbers. It can also be used with dates where it means 'before', or with text where it means 'alphabetically before'; e.g. Subscription paid < 300, Date subscription paid < #01/01/05#, Surname < "Morris".
- **Greater than (>).** Can also be used with numbers, dates or text.
- **Not equals (Not).** This can be used to find fields that do not match the data, e.g. Town Not "Kingsmond".

How to –

### *Use a query to select records*

This query will only select the female members.

- Close any tables, queries or forms that are open and use the query wizard as before.

- In the first window make sure that *Table:Members* is displayed in the *Tables/Queries* box.

- Select all the fields using the >> button.

- You may see a screen asking you whether you want detail or a summary; if so, select *Detail*.

- In the last screen, name the query Female Members Query then select *Modify the query design* (because we have not yet told it to pick out the female members). Click *Finish*.

- The query now opens in *Design View*. The window shows the *Members* table at the top, and the query design grid below. You can enlarge the top part of the window by dragging down on the line above the query design grid. You can then enlarge the table to show all the fields. See Figure 9.29.

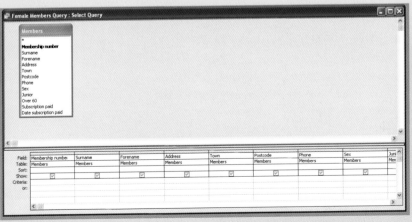

**Figure 9.29** *Query window with table at the top and query design grid below*

- You may need to scroll horizontally through the query design grid to find the *Sex* field. Click on the *Criteria* row in the *Sex* column and key in: ="F". See Figure 9.30.

**Figure 9.30** *Setting up a criterion*

- You do not have to type in the equals sign; if you leave it out, it just assumes that is what you mean.
- Switch to *Datasheet View* and check that only female members are listed.
- When you close the query make sure you save the amended version.

## How to –

### Use other operators in queries

Start a new query for each of these activities.

- Close any tables, queries or forms that are open.
- Use the query wizard as before.
- When the query opens in *Design View* enter one of the criteria given below.
- Switch to *Datasheet View* and check that the correct records are listed.

  **1** This query will select the junior members. In the *Junior* column, key in:Y

**2** This query will select members who have paid a subscription greater than £50. In the *Subscription Paid* column key in: >50

**3** This query will select members who paid their subscriptions before 31st August 2005. In the *Date Subscription Paid* column key in: <#31/08/05#

## Further research – creating queries

Can you create queries to do each of these tasks?

**1** Select only those members who have paid their subscriptions since the beginning of the year.

**2** Select those members who are not Juniors.

**3** Select those members with surnames that come after Jones in the alphabet.

## Create queries using multiple criteria

You can combine two or more criteria by using AND or OR. These are known as multiple criteria.

## How to –

### Select records using AND criteria

This query will select only the junior male members; i.e. those members who are both male AND junior.

- Use the query wizard as before.
- Select all the fields in the *Members* table using the >> button.
- In the last window name the query 'Male Juniors Query' then select *Modify the query design*. Click *Finish*.
- In *Design View* click on the *Criteria* row in the *Junior* column and key in: Yes

- Click on the Criteria row in the Sex column and key in: ="M" (see Figure 9.31).
- Switch to *Datasheet View* and check that only male junior members are listed. If you get no results then that is simply because none of your records match the criteria. Try adding some more records.

| Sex Members | Junior Members | |
|---|---|---|
| | ☑ | ☑ |
| ="M" | Yes | |

**Figure 9.31** *Setting up AND criteria*

## How to –

### Select records using OR criteria

This query will select members who are either juniors or over 60. Both types of member pay the subscription at a concessionary rate.

- Use the query wizard as before.
- Select all the fields in the *Members* table using the >> button.
- In the last window, name the query 'Concessions Query'; then select *Modify the query design*. Click *Finish*.

- In *Design View*, click on the *Criteria* row in the *Junior* column and key in: Yes
- *Notice that the row below the Criteria row is labelled OR*. Click on the OR row in the *Over 60* column and key in: Yes (see Figure 9.32).
- Switch to *Datasheet View* and check that the correct members are listed.

| Junior Members | Over 60 Members | Su Me |
|---|---|---|
| ☑ | ☑ | |
| Yes | | |
| | Yes | |

**Figure 9.32** *Setting up OR criteria*

As a general rule, AND queries appear on the same row in the query grid, and OR criteria appear on different rows.

## Further research – using multiple criteria

Can you work out how to do each of these queries?

- Select all the members who are female and over 60.
- Select those junior members who live in Kingsmond.

## Creating forms and reports based on queries with multiple criteria

You can create forms and reports based on any kind of query, whether they use single or multiple criteria.

## Sorting results

You saw earlier that the default sort key is the primary key. You can also specify the sort order for a report.

Users can sort the data in any order they like, but you can help by setting up the sort order in a query.

This can be used on any kind of field:

- **Date order.** You can sort dates ascending, i.e. from earliest to latest, or descending.
- **Numerical order.** You can sort any number field in ascending or descending order.
- **Alphabetical order.** You can sort any text field ascending in alphabetical order (from A to Z) or descending (from Z to A).

## How to –

### *Set the sort order in a query*

- Open the *Names* form. You will see that the data is sorted by the primary key; i.e. the membership number. Close the form.

- Now open the *Names Query* in *Design View*. This was used to produce the *Names* form.

- In the query design grid note the *Sort* row. Under *Surname*, click in the *Sort* row, then select *Ascending*. Next, click on the *Sort* row under *Forename* and select *Ascending*. See Figure 9.33.

**Figure 9.33** *Sorting data in a query*

- Switch to *Datasheet View* and you will see that the list has been sorted. In our example, the Russell

family have been sorted by *Forename* as well. *Surname* is the first-level sort because it appears first on the query design grid.

- Now close the query and open the *Names* form again. You will find that the data has been sorted in line with the underlying query. See Figure 9.34.

| Membership number | Surname | Forename |
|---|---|---|
| 3 | Harris | Jenny |
| 5 | Hinton | Sam |
| 1 | Jones | Michael |
| 4 | Leung | Chi |
| 12 | Park | Michael |
| 11 | Park | Tracey |
| 2 | Patel | Vina |
| 10 | Russell | Alexandra |
| 7 | Russell | Amy |
| 9 | Russell | Charlotte |
| 6 | Russell | George |
| 8 | Russell | William |
| (AutoNumber) | | |

Record: 10 of 12

**Figure 9.34** *Sorted data in a query*

## Completing the database

The database should be easy for the user to use. Normally you will have one main form with options that link to other forms. In the examples, the *Members* form is the main form.

You can create forms based on any of the queries you have created. You should decide which ones will be useful to the user then add buttons to the main form that link to these.

Once the user has looked at one of these forms they may want to print out the data, so you can add a button that links to the report.

 How to –

### Add buttons to link to forms and reports

You can add a button to the *Members* form to let the user view the *Names* form.

- Open the *Members* form in *Design View* and use the button wizard. Select the *Form Operations* category, and the *Open Form Action*.

- In the next window, select *Names Form*.

- Then select *Open the form and show all the records*.

- Select text rather than a picture, and use the words 'View alphabetical list of members'.

- Switch to *Form View* to see how the button operates.

- You will now add a button to the *Names* form to give the user the option of printing the list once they have viewed it.

- Open the *Names* form in *Design View*. We will put the button in the footer of the form. Drag down the lower edge of the form to open up the *Form Footer*.

- Use the button wizard and click in the *Form Footer*. Select the *Report Operations* category, and the *Preview Report Action*.

- In the next window, select *List of names*.

- Select text rather than a picture, and use the words 'Print alphabetical list'.

- Switch to *Form View* to see how the button operates.

## Check

A database is not ready for use until you have checked that it works properly.

Although you have included a number of validation checks, you should still check that any data that you have entered is correct. You should also look carefully at all the forms and reports, and try out any buttons.

### Check data

There are several ways in which you can check the data itself.

- **Check against the original data.** If the data was copied from a paper document, then you should read it through and make sure the data on screen matches the original. Sometimes it is helpful to have another person with you, so one of you is reading the document and the other is checking the screen.

- **Spellcheck.** You can spellcheck any of the data in the *Datasheet View* of a table or on a form. Highlight the data you want to check, then click on the *Spellcheck* button on the main toolbar. If you want to spellcheck a whole table in *Datasheet View*, select *Select All Records* from the *Edit* menu then click on the *Spellcheck* button. On a form you can check a field by highlighting the data, or the whole record by selecting *Select Record* from the *Edit* menu, or all the records at once by selecting *Select All Records* from the *Edit* menu.
- **Sorting.** You can often spot data entry mistakes by sorting the records. It is easiest to spot duplications or omissions in *Datasheet View*. For example, you may have entered the same record twice, but if you sort the data on, say, the *Surname* field, you will find that the two records appear next to each other.

## Check layout and output of reports and screens

You should check each form and report by asking these questions:

- Are the right fields displayed?
- Are the correct records displayed?
- Can the labels for each field be read easily?
- Is all the data visible? Sometimes the width of the textbox or column is too narrow and some of the data remains hidden.
- On a form, is the data entry order sensible?
- On a form, do the buttons work as expected?
- On a report, is there useful information in the header and footer?

## Using a test plan

You should formally record all these checks in a test plan. The test plan could look like Table 9.7.

| Object tested | Test | Expected result | Actual result |
|---|---|---|---|
| Members form | Check the presence of fields | All fields displayed from members table | |
| Members form | Is it clear what each textbox and button is for? | All components are suitably labelled | |
| Members form | Check correct data entry order | Cursor moves across and down the form in a natural sequence | |
| Members form | Check validation rule for Sex | Validation text appears when letter other than M or F is entered | |

**Table 9.7** *Example database test plan*

This should be drawn up before you start the testing and the actual results entered as each test is done. At the end of this process you should comment on any results that are not as expected, and on what can be done to deal with the problem.

# Document the database

## Technical documentation

When you, as a developer, have finished creating a database, you must remember that someone might need to work on it again. For example, some errors may be discovered in the future, or the user might want some new facilities added. You could be asked to carry out the upgrade yourself, or the job could be given to another person. In either case, there needs to be full information about the development of the original database. Even an experienced developer can forget how they created a particular database. So you have to write technical documentation as evidence of what you have done.

The technical documentation should include descriptions and evidence under these headings.

### Fields

You should list the fields in a table definition. For each field, the following information is needed:

■ **Fieldnames.** Explain why you have chosen the fields, and also the choice of fieldnames.

■ **Field descriptions.** Describe what each field contains. This could be used for the field descriptions when the table is designed.

■ **Field properties.** For each field give the data type. Then describe the field properties that are used for each field, such as field size, validation rule, validation text. Describe any lookup lists that have been used and why.

The primary key field should be identified in the table definition. You should explain why you chose it as the primary key.

You can produce a screen shot of the table in *Design View* as evidence that you have created it as described.

### Forms

You should provide a screen shot of each form. This can be labelled to describe what each component (label, textbox, button) is for.

### Reports

You can print out each report, then annotate it to explain what the data is and how it was selected.

### Queries

You can take screen shots of each query in *Design View*. If you have used multiple criteria (in AND and OR queries), then make sure that all the criteria are visible.

You should then show what effect each query has, by providing evidence of the whole set of data, then evidence of what is selected by the query. This evidence could be screen shots of tables in *Datasheet View*. Alternatively, you could print out reports based on each query as evidence.

## Validation

You should describe all the validation techniques that are used in your database. These will include:

- type of checks carried out automatically by the software
- validation rules that you have created
- lookup lists that you have created.

For each kind of validation, give screen shots to provide full evidence of the checks and how they work.

## Assessment tasks

Here is an example database development scenario. All of the tasks in this unit could be based on this scenario, or on an alternative provided by your tutor.

*Jones & Smith Ltd is a new estate agency in your local town. They have hired you to investigate and create a computerised database to hold details of all the properties they have on their books. They expect to have about 100 properties on the market at any one time, but also want to keep records of old properties that they have sold (together with the asking price and selling price) or which have been withdrawn from sale. They expect to sell or remove about 25 properties a month and to list an equivalent number of new ones. You can store old and current properties in a single table, but Jones & Smith need some way of generating a report listing just the properties currently for sale. They will also need to generate a report to compare the asking prices and sale prices of all of the properties that they have sold in the last three months.*

> To work towards a Distinction in this unit you will need to achieve **all** the Pass, Merit and Distinction criteria in the unit and have evidence to show that you have achieved each one.

### How do I provide assessment evidence?

You can present your written findings as a report. Alternatively, you could discuss the topics with your tutor, who can provide observation records.

You should also provide evidence of the database that you created. This should also be a report about the creation and checking of your database, illustrated with screen shots and printouts and possibly supported by witness statements or observation records.

All your evidence should be presented in one folder, which should have a front cover and a contents page. You should divide the evidence into four sections corresponding to the four tasks.

# Assessment tasks continued

## Task 1 (P1)

You have been working with computer-based databases. Before these came along, databases were stored in paper files. Explain the advantages and disadvantages of computer-based databases. Give some examples to show what you mean.

## Task 2 (P2, P3, P4)

You will create a simple database based on a scenario offered by your tutor. You should:

- Design your database. You should use at least three different data types in your table.
- Check the number of records that will be required and estimate the storage requirements.
- Create the database using suitable database software.
- Make sure that you have used a number of validation techniques.
- Create a data entry form based on the table. Use it to enter data into the database.
- Create at least two queries to select data for specific needs.
- Produce a form based on one of the queries.
- Produce at least two reports. At least one of these should be based on a query. The other could be based on the original table or on another query.
- Include at least one shortcut on your forms.
- Check the database, as explained in this unit.

## Task 3 (P5, M1, D1)

You should now write about the database that you created in Task 2.

- Explain your choice of fields, data types and primary key.
- Produce technical documentation.

> To work towards a Distinction you should recommend improvements that could be made to your database. Justify all the points that you make.

## Task 4 (M2)

- Explain why, in general, data integrity is important in a database.
- Show how data integrity is maintained in a specific database. This could be the one you created in Task 2, or it could be one provided for you.

# 10 Spreadsheet Software

## About this unit

The spreadsheet and the word processor were the business applications that started the personal computer revolution and they remain the most popular and useful applications. The popularity of spreadsheets came from the ability to allow financial calculations to be done with ease, but the software is very versatile and, as well as financial and mathematical uses, it can also be used for a number of other applications such as:

- maintaining simple lists and databases
- presenting data as charts and graphs
- creating complex tables of text and numbers.

This unit links closely with Unit 8 'Customising applications software', where improving spreadsheets and other applications software with templates, shortcuts and macros is discussed.

▶ Continued from previous page

# Learning outcomes

When you have completed this unit you will:

1 understand what spreadsheets are and how they can be used

2 be able to create complex spreadsheets that use a range of formulae, functions and features

3 be able to use spreadsheets to present, analyse and interpret data

4 be able to check and document a spreadsheet solution.

# How is the unit assessed?

This unit is internally assessed. You will produce a spreadsheet to meet a user requirement supplied by your teacher or tutor. It will use various simple and complex formulas and functions, charts, appropriate data types and formatting. You will need to create, check and document the spreadsheet.

The grading grid in the specification for this unit lists what you must do to obtain Pass, Merit and Distinction grades. The section on Assessment Tasks at the end of this chapter will guide you through activities that will help you to be successful in this unit.

Throughout this unit we will use Microsoft Excel 2003, which is part of the Microsoft Office 2003 package. It works in a very similar way to earlier versions of Excel, and most other spreadsheet software shares the same basic concepts.

# What are spreadsheets?

## Their nature and purpose

A spreadsheet is made up of tables known as worksheets, with rows and columns making up individual cells. This is shown in Figure 10.1.

The columns are labelled with letters of the alphabet and the rows are numbered. Each cell therefore has an address, which is its column letter and row number.

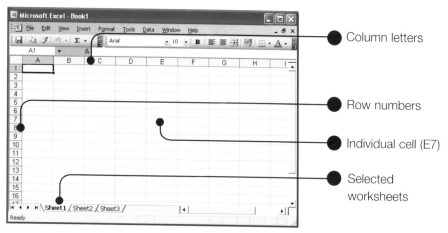

Column letters

Row numbers

Individual cell (E7)

Selected worksheets

**Figure 10.1** *A worksheet*

## Further research – spreadsheet size and quantity

What happens after column Z? How many rows and columns does a worksheet have? How many cells does this provide?

If you want a real challenge, find out what other limits there are in Excel; e.g. how many different worksheets can you have in one spreadsheet file?

By default, a spreadsheet has three worksheets, but you can add more if required. A single spreadsheet can therefore hold a very large amount of data.

There are basically three things you can enter in a worksheet cell:

- **Text** (sometimes called labels). Text can be formatted in a variety of ways, e.g. you can change its font, size or colour.
- **Numbers**. Numbers can be formatted to suit their purpose. For example, by default the currency format will display a number with a currency symbol in front (£ in the UK) and two digits after the decimal point. You can also format the appearance of numbers in the same way as you can text. We shall look at formatting in more detail later.
- **Formulas**. Formulas are what make spreadsheets really useful. A formula carries out a calculation on numeric values in other cells. We shall also look at formulas in more detail later.

Many people also use spreadsheets as simple databases, storing flat file data, i.e. single database tables.

## Further research – uses in industry and commerce

Do you know anyone who uses spreadsheets in their business? Find out what they use them for. Perhaps your teachers use spreadsheets for a variety of purposes. Look into how staff at your school or college use spreadsheets and find some examples of the spreadsheets they use.

# Uses of spreadsheets

Spreadsheets are very flexible and are used for all sorts of applications. They are most commonly used for storing, manipulating and analysing numeric data. The table structure of the worksheet makes it ideal for

## Case study

### NEAL training

NEAL training are a small private training company who carry out vocational training for job seekers under contract to local Job Centres. They need to keep track of their learners' attendance and punctuality, and meet the targets set by the organisations that fund the training. Neela Soomary, the training manager, uses a spreadsheet to keep track of this data, an example of which is shown in Figure 10.2.

The spreadsheet uses formulas to calculate the weekly percentages for attendance and punctuality for each of the training programmes that the company runs. It also uses an IF function to highlight those programmes with below-target attendance or punctuality. Charts are drawn from the data to help identify trends and problem areas.

Neela comments about the spreadsheet: 'Although in some ways this kind of data might be better suited to a database application, it is quicker and easier to set it up using Excel. Also my director prefers me to

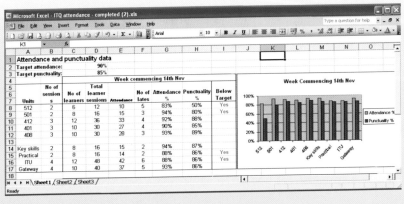

**Figure 10.2** *Weekly attendance and punctuality spreadsheet*

use spreadsheets to record information because he understands them well. The charts are useful as they make it easy to see at a glance where the serious problems lie.'

1 What reasons does Neela give for preferring to use a spreadsheet rather than a database?

2 What disadvantages might there be to using a spreadsheet rather than a database in this application?

3 Does your teacher or tutor collect or use statistics on attendance and punctuality? How do they store and present that data?

storing values that represent something such as the number of sales made in each month of the year, or a student's mark in an assignment.

Large quantities of data can be stored in a spreadsheet but lots of numbers can be difficult to interpret, making questions such as 'are the value of sales we make each month increasing or decreasing?' difficult to answer. Therefore spreadsheets provide tools, such as charts and graphs, to enable you to present data in different ways, making interpretation easier. It is much easier to see trends and to identify relationships between data when looking at a graph than it is by looking at 'raw' figures.

Spreadsheets are also useful for carrying out calculations repetitively and, as long as the initial formulas are correct, the spreadsheet can be relied upon to be accurate. This can be useful in applications such as monthly payroll calculations.

The ability to manipulate large lists of data is also one of the spreadsheet's strengths. Facilities such as sorting and filtering allow items in the list that match certain criteria to be easily identified.

# User need

In your future career as an IT professional you may well need to create spreadsheets, not just for your own use but also for use by other people, i.e. computer users rather than IT professionals. As with many of the services you will provide to computer users, you will need to find out what they require in order to provide them with an effective solution. You will need to find out their requirements in three main areas:

- **Input required.** This is the data that will be put into the spreadsheets. You will need to find out where it comes from (paper based sources, copied from another program etc.), what format it is in (numbers, text, dates etc.) and the range of values that is to be expected. You might also find out what input would be valid and invalid for each type of data.
- **Output required.** You need to discover what type of output the user needs. This might be in the form of a printed result or the data displayed on screen, perhaps as a chart.
- **Processing required.** This covers the calculations or other manipulation to convert data that is input to the required outputs.

When developing a spreadsheet for a computer user you will need to formalise this information with a design document that describes the spreadsheet. The input data will need to be listed in some kind of table that describes the key information about the data. You will also need to draw (either by hand or using a computerised method such as a word-processed table) a basic layout of the spreadsheet that shows where data will be input and where the output results will be displayed. Any intermediate results (such as subtotals) should also be shown. As part of the layout you will also need to indicate where calculations are done and what these calculations will do.

Case study

# Developing a design document

The following is an example of part of the design document for a simple spreadsheet which is used to keep track of the number of games in stock at a shop.

## Spreadsheet Design

| | |
|---|---|
| Spreadsheet: | Games Store Stock List |
| Designer: | Amil Khan |
| Version: | 1.1 |
| Date: | 21/2/06 |

### Layout (with example data)

| Game | Price | Quantity | Value | Reorder |
|---|---|---|---|---|
| Need for speed | £31.50 | 5 | £157.50 | Reorder |
| Call of Duty | £26.99 | 8 | £215.92 | |
| FIFA 06 | £28.99 | 12 | £347.88 | |
| The SIMS 2 | £26.50 | 4 | £106.00 | Reorder |
| | Totals | 29 | £827.30 | |

### Input data

| Column heading | Data type | Description |
|---|---|---|
| Game | Text | Name of the game |
| Price | Currency | Price of the game |
| Quantity | Number (zero decimal) | Number of copies of the game in stock |

### Output data and formulas

| Column heading | Data type | Description | Formula |
|---|---|---|---|
| Value | Currency | Total value of the games in stock | Price x quantity |
| Reorder | Text | Displays a message if the quantity in stock is below 6 | If (quantity < 6, "Re-order", "-") |
| Total Quantity | Number (zero decimal) | The total number games in stock | Sum(quantity) |
| Total Value | Currency | The total value of the games in stock | Sum(value) |

The completed spreadsheet is shown in Figure 10.3. Creation of this spreadsheet is described in the section on the *Sum* function.

1   What other details need to be added to the design of this spreadsheet?

2   What sort of problems might occur if the design is not discussed and agreed with the user before work is started on creating the spreadsheet?

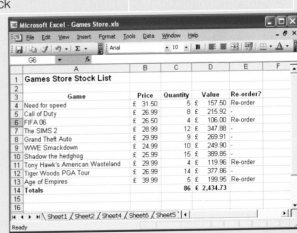

**Figure 10.3** *The completed spreadsheet*

## Test your knowledge

1   Name four different things you can do with a spreadsheet?

2   What are the three things you can enter in a worksheet cell?

3   When identifying a user's requirements for a spreadsheet, what are the main areas that you need to investigate?

4   How are the rows and columns of a worksheet identified?

## Creating spreadsheets

### Simple formulas

Formulas provide the real power in spreadsheets. The key thing to remember is that, if you want to enter a formula in a cell, it must begin with an equals sign (=). Let us look at a simple example. The following formula will add together two numbers:

=6+8

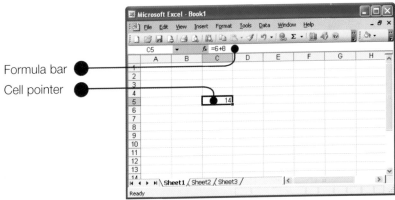

**Figure 10.4** *The Formula bar*

If you type that formula into a spreadsheet cell, the cell will display the number 14. Note that the cells in the worksheet will display the result of the formula; the formula itself will be displayed in the formula bar when the cell pointer (the thick black box around a cell) is located on that cell. See Figure 10.4.

The cell pointer can be moved by the mouse, by clicking in the cell where you want it located, or by using the cursor keys one cell at a time.

Entering actual values in a formula is fine, but to move it it is much more useful to be able to enter cell addresses instead. Suppose we entered the value of 6 in cell B5 and changed our formula to:

=B5+8

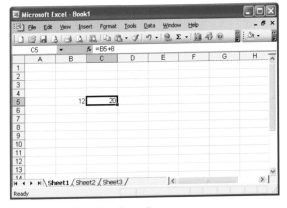

**Figure 10.5** *Formula using cell address*

Note that you can edit the formula by clicking in the formula bar, deleting the number 6 and typing the cell address B5. The result of the formula (in C5) remains the same. However, if we make a change to the value in B5, e.g. entering 12 rather than 6, the formula in C5 automatically recalculates the new result. Figure 10.5 shows the modified formula.

As well as adding, you can also subtract, divide, multiply etc. The symbols are shown in Table 10.1.

| Symbol | Meaning |
|--------|---------|
| + | Add |
| - | Subtract |
| * | Multiply |
| / | Divide |
| ^ | Raise to power |

**Table 10.1** *Arithmetic symbols*

## A financial spreadsheet

Let us have a look at a simple example of how a spreadsheet can be used. Suppose you were saving money to buy a car that costs about £1500. You want to buy the car in about 9 months' time but you do not know how much you will need to save to reach your target of £1500. The spreadsheet shown in Figure 10.6 shows the basic layout.

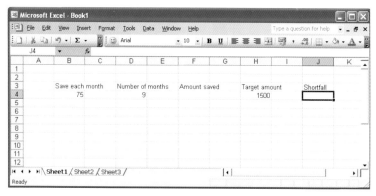

**Figure 10.6** *'Buy a car' spreadsheet*

The amount saved each month in B4 is a number, as is the number of months in D4. These two amounts need to be multiplied together to give the total amount saved, so a formula is needed in F4, which is =B4*D4. The target amount in H4 is entered as the value of 1500, while the shortfall (or surplus) is the difference between the amount saved (in F4) and the target amount in H4. The formula =H4-F4 will calculate this. Figure 10.7 shows the spreadsheet completed, with example values in cells B4 and D4.

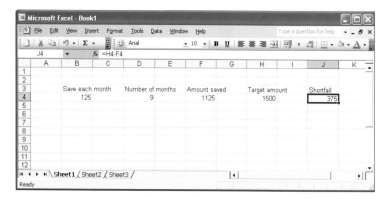

**Figure 10.7** *Completed spreadsheet*

This spreadsheet demonstrates one of the big benefits of spreadsheets: as the formulas are constantly recalculated we can vary the amount saved each month (in B4) and the number of months (in D4) to investigate different possibilities. This kind of spreadsheet is sometimes called a 'what if' spreadsheet, since we can use it to answer questions such as:

- What if you could only save £75 a month? Changing the number of months shows it will take 20 months to save for the car.
- What if you choose a cheaper car, say £900? Keeping the number of months to 9, you will need to save £100 each month.

## A budget spreadsheet

Another common type of spreadsheet is the budget spreadsheet. In this type, columns of figures representing income or outgoings, to or from various sources, are totalled up. Using the car example again, suppose we wanted to estimate the monthly cost of running a car over four months. Figure 10.8 shows a spreadsheet set up to calculate monthly costs. Note that the values entered have been formatted as currency. You can do this either by entering a £ sign in front of each value as you type it or by highlighting all the cells with the cell pointer (by dragging across them with the mouse pointer) and clicking the *Currency* button in the *Formatting* toolbar. See Figure 10.8.

Currency button

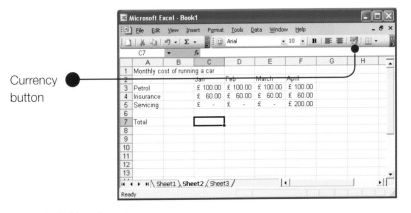

**Figure 10.8** *Monthly cost spreadsheet*

Since the costs of petrol and insurance stay the same each month, you can enter the value once, then copy and paste it into the other cells. If you highlight all the cells where you want to paste the value, you can then paste multiple copies in one go.

## Relative addressing

To add up the costs for the month of January we could enter the formula =C3+C4+C5. Once this formula has been entered it can be copied as well. However, when you copy formulas something very important happens. Normally when you copy and paste something it stays the same, but not with spreadsheet formulas. Instead, the cell addresses change relative to the cell into which they are copied.

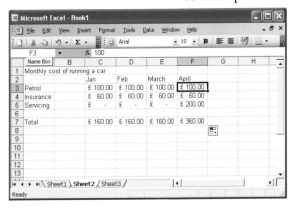

**Figure 10.9** *The completed spreadsheet*

So, since we copy this formula along the columns (i.e. into columns D, E and F) the column letters in the formula change, although the row numbers remain the same. In this case this is exactly what we want to happen, so the formula adds up the correct values for each month. The effect is known as **relative addressing**. Later in the unit we will look at situations where you do not want the cell addresses to change when you copy a formula. Figure 10.9 shows the completed spreadsheet.

What does it mean?

**Relative addressing** *is a cell address that changes when it is copied to a different cell.*

Because spreadsheet software allows you to copy both values and formulas easily, it makes it easy to create large spreadsheets as well, especially since the addresses in the formulas are automatically adjusted as you copy them, so that they have to be entered only once. Many financial budget spreadsheets include figures for a whole 12 months, i.e. one year. Having to enter a formula once to add up a monthly total, rather than 12 times, obviously saves a lot of time.

## Mathematical precedence

Mathematical precedence is an important concept that you need to understand, as it governs the way complex formulas are calculated. Take, for example, the following formula:

=5+2*2

You might imagine that the result would be 14, because 5+2 is 7, then multiplied by 2 is 14. However, calculations in spreadsheets are not done left to right. They are done based on the order of mathematical precedence, and multiplication is done before addition. So the result would be 2 multiplied by 2 is 4, then add 5 is 9. The order of mathematical precedence is shown in Table 10.2.

| 1 | Brackets () |
|---|---|
| 2 | Raise to power ^ |
| 3 | Divide / |
| 4 | Multiply * |
| 5 | Add + |
| 6 | Subtract - |

**Table 10.2** *The order of mathematical precedence*

Note that anything in brackets is done first, so to get the answer of 14 from the previous example the formula would need to be:

=(5+2)*2

Let us look at a spreadsheet with a complex formula and several stages to demonstrate the importance of this concept. Figure 10.10 shows a spreadsheet used to work out weekly wages. The standard hourly rate for up to 35 hours is £7. For every hour worked over 7 hours an additional overtime bonus payment of £3 is made.

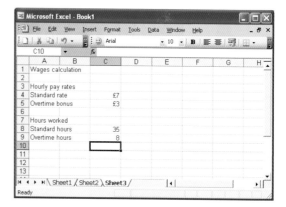

**Figure 10.10** *Wages calculator*

To calculate the total wages for the hours shown, we might enter the following formula:

=C4*C8+C4+C5*C9

We might think that this formula would multiply the standard rate in C4 (£7) by the standard hours worked in C8 (35) giving 245; then add the standard rate (£7) to the overtime bonus rate in C5 (£3) giving £10; then multiplying this by the overtime hours in C9 (8) giving 80; making a grand total of £325. However, we would not get this answer, because the multiplication part of the formula is done first; instead we would get £276. To get the correct answer we must ensure that the overtime bonus

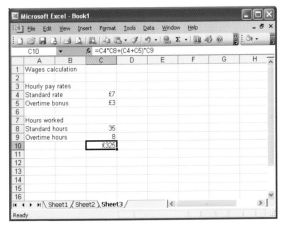

**Figure 10.11** *Wages calculator with correct formula*

rate is added to the standard rate before it is multiplied by the overtime hours. This is done using brackets, like this:

=C4*C8+(C4+C5)*C9

The wages calculator with the correct formula entered is shown in Figure 10.11.

Clearly, getting formulas correct is important. Imagine the problems that would be caused if you underpaid your workers by £49 per week! Whenever you have formulas that use several stages, you must check that the calculation will be done in the required order, using brackets where necessary to modify the order.

# Functions

As well as the arithmetic operators we have used so far, formulas can also include functions that carry out a wide range of mathematical calculations. Excel has hundreds of functions, but we shall look at only a few.

## The **Sum** function

The *Sum* function is one of the most widely used functions. It is used to add up a column or row of values, and is so often used that it has an *AutoSum* button on the toolbar to automatically create a formula using the *Sum* function. First let us look at how to use it manually, so that we can understand how it works before looking at the automatic version.

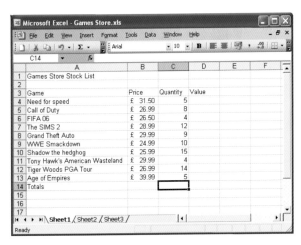

**Figure 10.12** *Games store spreadsheet*

Suppose you had a spreadsheet like the one shown in Figure 10.12.

This spreadsheet might be used by a games shop. It lists all the games they have, their price and the number in stock. Note that column A has been widened to allow the names of the games to be displayed. This can be done by moving the mouse pointer into the grey title bar of the columns, between the column you want to widen and the next one (A and B in this case) until the two-headed arrow mouse pointer appears, then dragging to the right to widen column A.

To add up the total number of games in stock, we could enter a formula in C14 that added each cell one by one, but this would be rather long-winded. The *Sum* function is much easier to use, since we need only to enter the starting cell in the list to be added (C4) and the ending cell (C14) separated by a colon, like this:

=SUM(C4:C13)

However, using the *AutoSum* button in the toolbar means we don't have to type anything. Simply click in the cell where the formula should go (C14) and click the button. Excel looks for a row or column of numbers above or to the left of the currently selected cell and creates the formula using the *Sum* function for you (see Figure 10.13). It displays the formula for you to check, and when you press the *Enter* button it completes the automatic creation of the formula.

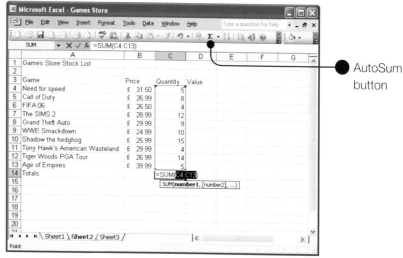

AutoSum button

**Figure 10.13** *The AutoSum button*

Further research – using the *Autosum* button

Column D on this spreadsheet is meant to display the value of the games in stock (the price multiplied by the quantity). Enter the correct formula in D4 and copy it down to D13, then use the *AutoSum* button to calculate the total value of the games in stock.

## The *Min*, *Max* and *Average* functions

These statistical functions work in a similar way to the *Sum* function, but there is no toolbar button to create them automatically. To find the maximum price of the games you would enter the following formula:

=MAX(B4:B13)

The *Min* function works the same way and displays the minimum value in the range, while the *Average* function displays the average value (or mean) across the range.

## Further research – finding minimum, maximum and average values

Enter the formulas to calculate the minimum, maximum and average prices for the games. When complete, the spreadsheet should look like Figure 10.14.

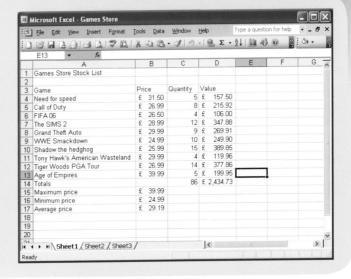

**Figure 10.14** *Spreadsheet with minimum, maximum and average prices*

## The *Count* and *Countif* functions

*Count* is another simple statistical function. As the name suggests it counts the number of cells within a range that contain numbers. For example, if we use the Games Store spreadsheet shown above and enter the formula =COUNT(C4:C13) we will get the result of 10, since there are 10 cells in the range that contain a number (all of them in this case). Note that the *Count* function counts the cell only if it contains a number; if it contains text then it will not be counted.

The *Countif* function adds the ability to count only the values in a range that meet certain criteria. The criteria can be a single value (such as 3), a text value (such as "Yes") or an expression using a comparison operator (such as ">10"). Note that expressions are enclosed in double quotation marks.

Table 10.3 shows the comparison operators you can use.

| | |
|----|----------------------------|
| =  | Equal to                   |
| >  | Greater than               |
| <  | Less than                  |
| >= | Greater than or equal to   |
| <= | Less than or equal to      |
| <> | Not equal to               |

**Table 10.3** *Comparison operators*

For example, suppose in our Games Store we need to reorder games where the quantity in stock has fallen below 6. We could show the number of games that need reordering using the following formula:

=COUNTIF(C4:C13,"<6")

## Further research – identifying excess stock

The Games Store manager is thinking of discounting the prices of games where there are more than 10 in stock. What formula would tell you how many games that applies to?

## The *If* function

The *If* function is more complex than the statistical functions we have looked at so far, but it is also more powerful, as it gives you the ability to change what the spreadsheet does depending on the outcome of some kind of test. So, for example, if the value in a particular cell is greater than 10 then you can display a message or do a calculation; whereas, if it is less than 10, you can display a different message or do a different calculation.

First let us look at the basic structure of the *If* function. This has three parts within the brackets that follow the function name:

=IF(*test, action if test is true, action if test is false*)

The test can simply be comparing the contents of a cell with some value or text, such as:

C4=10 (think of this test as 'does C4 contain 10?')

C4="Yes" (think of this test as 'does C4 contain the text Yes?')

Or it can be some kind of expression using the comparison operators we have already come across with the *Countif* function. For example:

C4>10  (think of this test as 'is C4 greater than 10?')

The next two parts of the function describe what to do if the result of the test is true or if it is false. These actions can also be a simple value or some text, such as:

=IF(C4>10,"Too much","Not enough")

In this example, if the value in C4 is greater than 10 then the text "Too much" is displayed in the cell that contains the *If* function. If the value in C4 is not greater than 10 then the text "Not enough" is displayed.

These actions could also be a calculation, such as:

=IF(C4>10,C4+2,C4-2)

Here if the value in C4 is greater than 10 then that value has 2 added to it and the result is placed in the cell that contains the *If* statement; if it is less than 10 then 2 is subtracted.

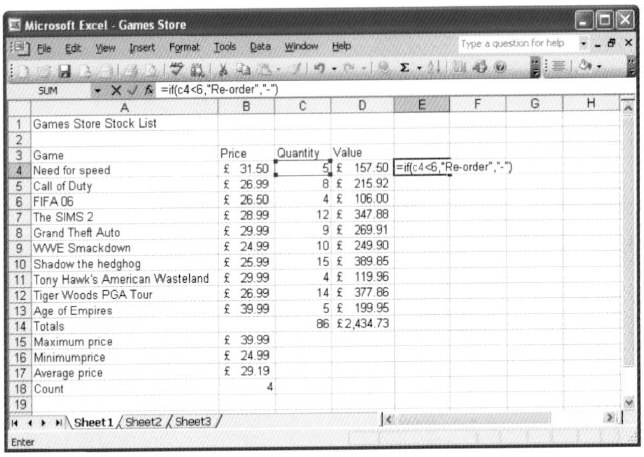

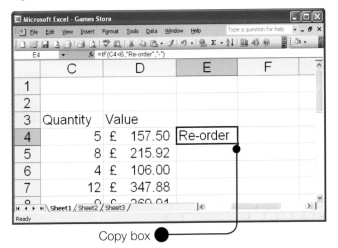

**Figure 10.15** *The formula using the If function*

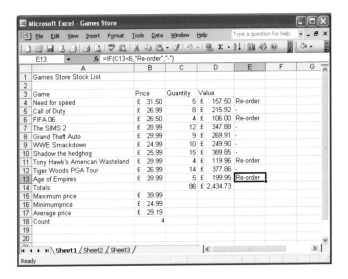

**Figure 10.16** *The cell pointer copy box*

Now let us look at a real example of the *If* function in use. Remember the Games Store spreadsheet we have used to demonstrate the other functions. The last example used the *Countif* function to show the number of games that needed reordering because the quantity in stock had fallen below 6. However, this function does not tell us which games need reordering, only how many there are. With the *If* function we can display a message next to the game telling us to reorder it.

We start off by entering the formula using the *If* function in cell E4. The test is 'is C4 (the quantity) less than 6?' The action, if the test is true (i.e. C4 is less than 6), is to display the text 'Reorder' and, if the test is false (i.e. C4 is 6 or more), is to just display a dash. The formula is shown in Figure 10.15.

Once the formula has been entered in E4 it can be copied down through cells E5 to E13. You can do this by copying and pasting or you can use the copy box on the current cell pointer. This is the small black box on the bottom right corner of the current cell pointer, as shown in Figure 10.16.

When you move the mouse pointer over the copy box it changes to a black cross. If you drag down through the cells that you want to copy into (E5 to E13) with the black-cross mouse pointer, the formula will be copied for you. The completed spreadsheet is shown in Figure 10.17.

**Figure 10.17** *The completed spreadsheet*

## Using AND and OR

The *If* function we used in the previous example was able to test only one cell (C4), but there might be situations where you want to test the values in two or more cells and do something if both the tests are true.

Let us look at an example. Suppose we wanted to discount (reduce) the price of any game that cost over £26 if we had 10 or more in stock. Here we have two tests (>£26 and >=10). Because we only want to discount the game if both the tests are true, we use the AND logical operator. Figure 10.18 shows the modified *If* function.

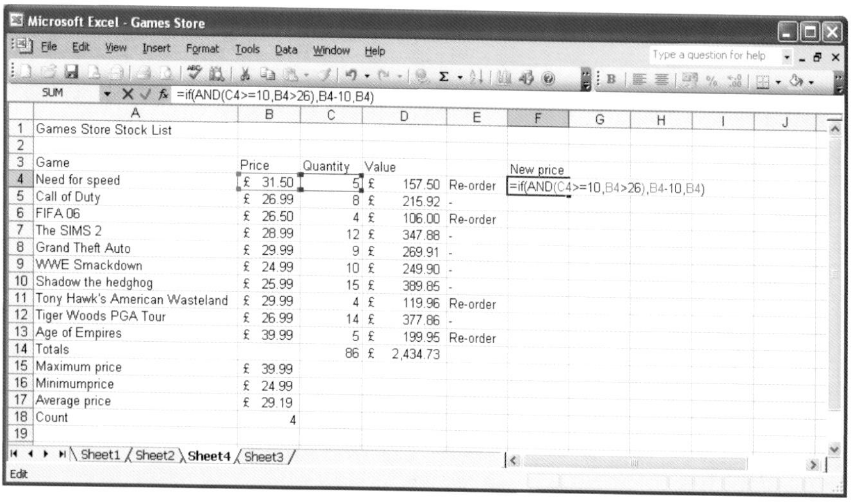

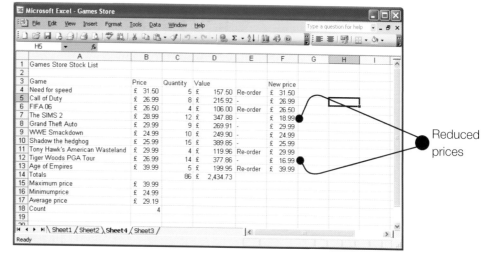

**Figure 10.18** *If function using AND*

The tests are now preceded by AND, like this:

AND(C4>=10,B4>26)

If the test is true (i.e. we have more than 10 in stock and the price is over £26), then the price in B4 has £10 subtracted from it, otherwise the price is kept the same. The complete formula looks like this:

=IF(AND(C4>=10,B4>26),B4-10,B4)

Once the formula is complete you can copy it down the rest of the column. If you check carefully, you should see that the prices have been reduced on the games that meet the two test criteria, as shown in Figure 10.19.

Using the AND logical operator means that both tests must be true for the true action to be carried out. However, if you use the OR logical operator then the true action will be carried out if either of the tests is true. If we modify the formula just entered to use OR, then the price of the game will be

**Figure 10.19** *The new reduced prices*

Reduced prices

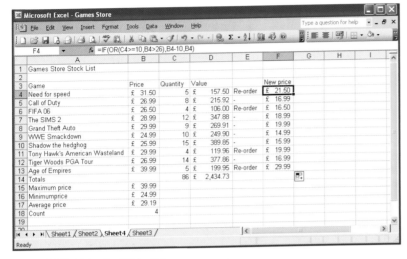

**Figure 10.20** *Using the OR logical operator*

reduced if there are 10 or more in stock or if the game costs over £26. This is shown in Figure 10.20. Note that now the prices of all the games are reduced, since they all meet one or other of the test criteria.

## Further research – other worksheet functions

Excel has many more functions than the few we have looked at here. Find out more about the other functions by searching in Help for 'list of worksheet functions'.

If you want a real challenge, find out how these worksheet functions can be used and create example spreadsheets that use them:

- Today
- Vlookup
- Rand
- Weekday

# Entering and editing data

## Absolute and relative cell addressing

We have already introduced the concept of relative addressing. This is the way cell addresses in formulas change when you copy them. However, there are some situations when you do not want the cell address in a formula to change when you copy it. An example will demostrate why this might be.

We will use the games store spreadsheet again, although for simplicity we will leave out the various *If* function formulas we recently added. This time we want to have a sale and reduce all the prices by between five and fifteen per cent but we want to do a bit of 'what-if' experimentation to see how different percentages will affect the total value of our stock. Figure 10.21 shows the modified version of the spreadsheet with an example percentage reduction

**Figure 10.21** *Games store sale spreadsheet*

already entered in B16. To enter a value as a percentage, simply type the % sign after the number.

We need to enter a formula in E4 to reduce the existing price in B4 by the percentage in B16. If we simply multiply these two values together we will get 10% of the current price (£3.15), so we need to subtract that from the current price to get the correct answer. Hence, the formula is:

=B4-B4*B16

Note that we do not need brackets here as the multiplication is done first anyway. If we now copy this formula down the rest of the column we find that a problem occurs, as shown in Figure 10.22.

The 10% reduction has worked correctly on the first price, but none of the other prices have been reduced. If we inspect the formula in E5 we can see why (look in the formula bar in Figure 10.22). Relative addressing has changed the original B4 in the formula to B5, which is correct as this is the price of the next game, but it has also changed B16, where the percentage reduction is held, to B17, which contains nothing. In this situation we do not want that part of the address changed when we copy the formula; we want it fixed on B16. Fixing a cell address so that it does not change is called **absolute addressing**.

To make that part of the formula use absolute addressing we need to return to the formula in E14 and edit it in the formula bar. Click next to the B16 address and then press the F4 key (function key on the top of your keyboard) and $ signs will appear in front of the B and the 16 of the address, as shown in Figure 10.23.

Note that, if you prefer, you can type the $ signs yourself, rather than using the F4 key. Now, if you copy this formula down through the column, the B4 part of the formula will change (due to relative addressing) but the B16 part will not (due to absolute addressing). This modified version of the formula will display reduced prices for all the games, as shown in Figure 10.24.

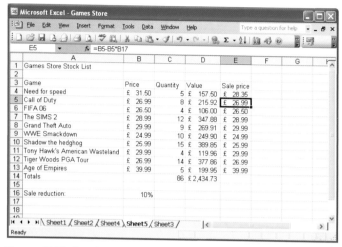

**Figure 10.22** *Copying the formula*

*An **absolute address** is a cell address that does not change when you copy it.*

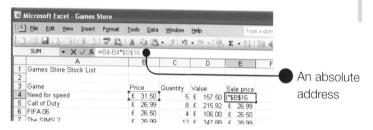

An absolute address

**Figure 10.23** *An absolute address*

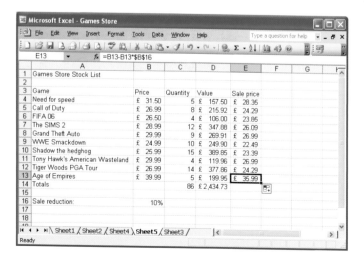

**Figure 10.24** *Reduced prices for all games*

Note that if, for some reason, you wanted to fix only either the row or the column address, rather than both, you could do this by inserting the $ sign in front of the column letter or row number only.

## Further research – using absolute addressing

To complete the spreadsheet, add a formula in column F to calculate the value of the games with their reduced prices (quantity multiplied by sale price). Then use the *AutoSum* button to provide a new total value of the stock in cell F14.

What is the maximum percentage sale reduction that can be given while keeping the total value of the stock above £2000?

## Autofilling cells

Spreadsheet software contains lots of features to make creating large spreadsheets easy, and one of those features is autofill. Many budget spreadsheets have the months across the top of the columns (like the car cost calculator we created earlier). Rather than having to type each month, you can simply type the first month (it does not have to be January, you can start with any month, and you can use the abbreviated version, such as Jan, if you wish). Then use the cell pointer copy box to copy the cell across however many cells you need. Autofill will enter the month names for you, as shown in Figure 10.25.

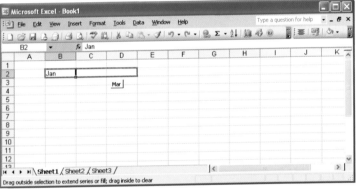

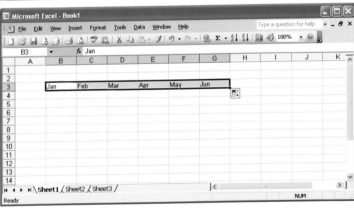

**Figure 10.25** *Using autofill to complete month names*

Autofill will work with days of the week in the same way, either the full names (e.g. Monday) or the abbreviated versions (e.g. Mon). You can also enter a date and autofill will fill in subsequent dates for as many days as you wish.

Autofill will also complete a sequence of numbers or dates if you show it what sequence you want. For example, to number cells sequentially, just type 1 in the first cell you want to number, then 2 in the next one. Then select these two cells by dragging across them with the white-cross mouse shape; then click and drag on the copy box and keep dragging for however many cells you want to number. Autofill will fill in the numbers for you.

Another example would be if you wanted a series of cells to show the dates on each Monday for several weeks. Just enter the first two dates – for example 2nd Jan 2006 is a Monday, and the following Monday is the 9th Jan. With these two dates entered in adjacent cells, select these cells and then use the copy box to list as many Monday dates as you require. This can make creating a timetable or schedule easy, as you do not need to look up each date. Figure 10.26 shows autofill being used to create a weekly schedule of dates.

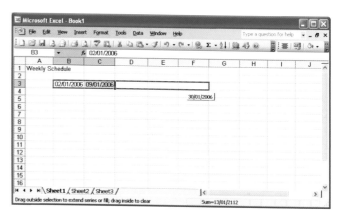

**Figure 10.26** *Using autofill to enter dates*

## Linking worksheets

One of the benefits of having multiple worksheets in one spreadsheet is that you can link information between the worksheets. Once again, the benefit of this is best seen with examples. There are two ways to create links:

- enter links between worksheets as formulas
- use *Paste Link*.

How to –

### *Link spreadsheets using manual links*

Suppose you had two computer games shops – one in Luton and one in Watford – and you kept a record of their sales on two worksheets in the same spreadsheet. The spreadsheet is shown in Figure 10.27, with the Luton shop worksheet currently displayed. Note that the worksheets have been given names, rather than just sheet1, sheet2 etc. You can do this by double-clicking on the sheet name and typing in the name you want.

The worksheet for the Watford shop is exactly the same, except of course that the figures are different. Now we are going to create a third worksheet, called

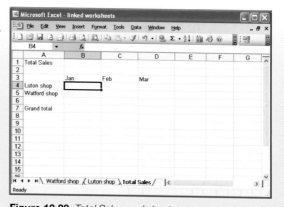

**Figure 10.28** *Total Sales worksheet*

Total Sales, which will show the combined total sales from both the Luton and Watford shops. The basic layout of this worksheet is shown in Figure 10.28.

To copy the values from the other worksheets, the procedure is as follows. First click in cell B4, which is where the January total from the Luton shop should go. Type an equals sign to start a formula, then click on the Luton shop worksheet name to swap to that worksheet. Click in B7 on the Luton shop worksheet (which contains the January total). Notice that, on the formula bar, the address of that cell in that worksheet ('Luton shop'!B7) has been entered. (The worksheet name is in single quotes followed by an exclamation mark and the cell name. This is the format of a cell

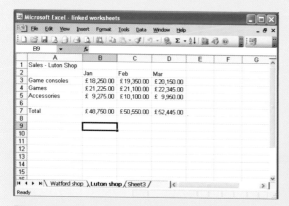

**Figure 10.27** *The Games shops sales spreadsheet*

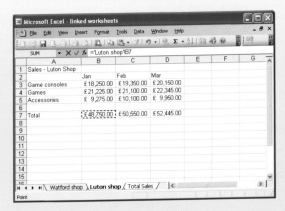

**Figure 10.29** *Linking the worksheets*

relative addressing works in just the same way as it does with cells located on the same worksheet, and the formula adjusts the cell addresses to pick up the correct monthly totals.

The totals for the Watford shop can be inserted in the same way – create a formula that links with the Watford shop worksheet for January then copy the formula across for February and March. The grand totals can be completed using a simple formula (e.g. =B4+B5 for January and so on) and the completed sheet should look like Figure 10.30.

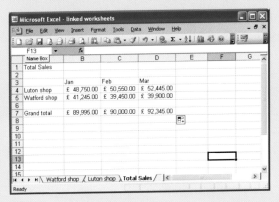

**Figure 10.30** *The completed Total Sales sheet*

address that contains a worksheet name.) See Figure 10.29.

Now press *Enter* to complete the formula. You will be returned to the Total Sales worksheet, with the value from the Luton shop worksheet displayed. Note that this value is linked with the other worksheet and, if a change is made to that value on the Luton shop worksheet, it will change here too.

You can now copy the formula that has been created for the Luton Shop January sales total across to February and March (cells C4 and D4). Note that

How to –

## Link spreadsheets using *Paste Link*

*Paste Link* provides an alternative method for creating links between worksheets. With this method you click on the cell containing the formula you want to copy (e.g. B7 in the Luton worksheet) and choose *Edit / Copy* (or click the copy icon in the toolbar); then go to the cell where you want the formula to be copied into (e.g. B4 in the *Total Sales* worksheet); then choose *Edit / Paste Special*. This will display the *Paste Special*

dialog box. Click the *Paste Link* button and the link formula will be inserted.

However, note that the cell references have been made absolute, so the formulas cannot be copied as described above. Therefore, although *Paste Link* provides an easy way to create links between worksheets, in this example it would be easier to create the linking formulas manually.

## Improving efficiency

Excel provides many shortcut key combinations to make it easy to move around large or multiple worksheets. Some of the more useful ones are listed in Table 10.4.

| Shortcut key | Effect |
|---|---|
| **For moving around a worksheet** | |
| Ctrl + End | Moves cell pointer to the last used cell in a worksheet (bottom right cell) |
| Ctrl + Home | Moves cell pointer to cell A1 |
| Home | Move to the beginning (i.e. column A) of current row |
| Page Down | Move one screen down |
| Page Up | Move one screen up |
| **Selecting cells** | |
| Ctrl + A | Selects the current data region (a data region is an area of cells that contain something and are surrounded by empty cells or the edge of the worksheet) |
| Ctrl | Allows you to select non-adjacent areas (i.e. areas not next to each other) |
| **Moving between worksheets** | |
| Ctrl + Page Up | Move to next worksheet |
| Ctrl + Page Down | Move to previous worksheet |
| **Formatting** | |
| Ctrl + Shift + $ | Apply currency format |
| Ctrl + Shift + % | Apply percentage format |

**Table 10.4** *Commonly used shortcut keys*

There are many more shortcut keys, but it can be difficult to remember them all unless you use them often. You can find out about them all by searching the help menu.

# Combining information

There are some situations, such as when you need to produce a financial report, when you will want to select information created in Excel and insert it into another software package, such as a Word document.

## Simple copy and paste

The simplest way to insert data into a Word document is to just copy the required cells from Excel and paste the data into Word. Once pasted into a Word Document, worksheet cells will become a Word table and can be edited in the normal way. An example is shown in Figure 10.31, although, as you can see, the columns of the table need widening to display the data on one line.

Cells pasted this way are no longer connected with the original spreadsheet.

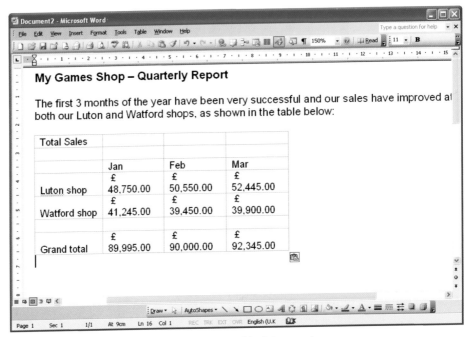

**Figure 10.31** *Excel spreadsheet cells pasted into a Word document*

## Retaining a link to the original data

If you want the pasted cells to remain linked with the original spreadsheet, so that changes made in the spreadsheet will be reflected in the pasted cells in the Word document, this can be done.

How to –

### Retain a link to the original data

Having copied the cells from Excel and switched to the Word document, choose *Paste Special* from the *Edit* menu (you may need to expand the menu to see this option). Then from the menu that appears (see Figure 10.32) choose the *Paste Link* button and select the document type as *Microsoft Office Excel Worksheet Object* from the list box; then click *OK*.

The cells will be inserted in the Word document as before, but not as a Word table. The cells behave as a graphic image. To edit them, double-click on them and the original spreadsheet will open up in Excel but inside Word.

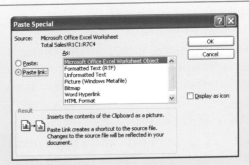

**Figure 10.32** *The Paste Special dialog box*

# File handling

You must, of course, save the spreadsheet file you produce.

## How to –

### *Save a spreadsheet file*

Save a file in Excel by going to the *File* menu and choosing *Save;* to save an existing file with a different name choose *Save As.* Alternatively you can use the *Save* button in the toolbar.

If the spreadsheet has not been previously saved, or you choose *Save As,* you will see the *Save As* dialog box. You will be offered a default file name of *Bookn.xls* where *n* is a number indicating the number of new spreadsheets you have opened on this occasion while using Excel.

It is unwise to use the default name, as it tells you very little about what the spreadsheet contains. It is much better to think up a more descriptive name that gives some clue to the contents of the spreadsheet. For example, you might call a monthly budget spreadsheet 'Budget for Jan 06'.

When you are creating lots of spreadsheets and other files, it is a good idea to create some kind of folder structure to keep related files together.

## Test your knowledge

5   What result would the formula =6^2 give?

6   Explain the term 'relative addressing'.

7   What is the order of mathematical precedence?

8   List the comparison operators and explain what each means.

9   In the formula =B4*$D$9 what do the dollar signs ($) mean?

10   What shortcut key is used to return the cell pointer to cell A1?

11   What is the difference between simply copying and pasting cells from an Excel worksheet into a Word document and using *Paste Special* with the *Paste Link* button?

# Using spreadsheets to present, analyse and interpret data

## Presenting data

So far we have kept our spreadsheets fairly plain, but there are many options to allow us to format the data in a spreadsheet, improving the way it is presented.

### Number formats

We have already used currency and percentage number formats in the spreadsheets we have produced. Both of these formats can be set by using the buttons in the toolbar, by typing the appropriate symbol (a £ sign before the number or a % sign after), or by using the appropriate shortcut keys. The toolbar also has a button for what it calls 'Comma' style. This numeric format will add two digits after the decimal point and a comma after the thousands.

Figure 10.33 shows the same number (1234) formatted in the different ways using the standard toolbar buttons. Note that the percentage format button multiplies a number by 100, so if you want, for example, 50% to be displayed then you must enter 0.5.

Currency button

Percentage button

Comma format button

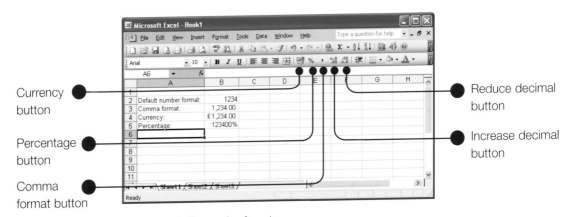

Reduce decimal button

Increase decimal button

**Figure 10.33** *The number formats*

Date format is automatically set in a cell if you enter something that Excel recognises as a date, such as 5/2/06 or 5-Feb-06.

Note that, if you delete the contents of a cell or cells that have been formatted (by selecting the cells with the current cell pointer and pressing *Delete*), although you will delete what is in the cell, you will not remove the formatting. This can result in some confusing results. For example, if you enter a date in a cell, the cell will automatically be formatted as a date. If you then delete the date, but at some time later enter a simple number in the same cell, the number will be displayed as a date. You can, of course, change the formatting by using one of the format buttons in the toolbar. Alternatively, when you delete the date initially, use *Edit*, *Clear*, and *Clear all* from the drop-down menu; this will remove both the contents and the formatting.

Also shown in Figure 10.33 are the *Increase* and *Decrease decimal* buttons, which allow you to control the number of digits displayed after the decimal point.

### Further research – experimenting with number formats

You can set many other number formats, and different versions of the formats already described, using the *Cells* option under the *Format* menu. This brings the *Format cells* dialog box on to the screen. The *Number* tab allows you to choose the different formats for numbers. Have a look at this dialog box and experiment with the different formats. If there are any that you do not understand, or that you want more information about, search under help for 'number formats'.

If you want a real challenge, consider a mythical currency, which we shall call the 'Zap'. This has a rather strange format: the currency symbol is a capital 'Z', and it has 3 digits after the decimal point (there are 1000 pennies in a Zap). The pennies are always preceded by a letter p, so 25 Zap and 75 pennies would be written Z25. p075. Create a custom number format for the Zap currency.

## Display formats

As you would expect, Excel has a full range of facilities to control the way information is displayed, including being able to modify the font, size, attributes (bold, italics, underline) and alignment (within the cell). As with the number formats, many of these can be set using the buttons in the toolbar, but the full range of options can be found in the *Alignment*, *Font*, *Borders* and *Patterns* tabs of the *Format Cells* dialog box in the *Format* menu.

Some of the formats are worth mentioning in more detail:

- **Colours.** You can set both the background colour of the cell and the colour of its contents. The background colour button in the toolbar is a drop-down button called *Fill Color*, which when you click on it displays a swatch of different colours. To add background patterns to a cell, you need to go to the *Format cells* dialog box and choose the *Patterns* tab. The *Font* tab and *Color* button work in a similar way.

- **Borders.** It is often useful to add borders to your spreadsheet, to highlight important information such as totals and to separate data into different sections. The *Borders* button is also a drop-down button; it displays diagrams showing how the borders will be applied to the current selected cell or cells.

  It also offers an option called *Draw borders*, which allows you to use the mouse to apply borders to cells. When you click the button, the mouse pointer changes to a pencil shape and a small *Borders* toolbox appears, which you can use to set the colour and thickness of the borders. You can also use *Draw Border* to create an outline around the edge of the cell region over which you drag the pencil, or *Draw Border Grid*, where all the sides of the cells inside the area have borders added.

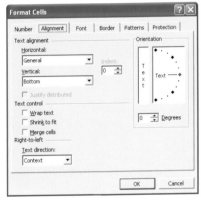

**Figure 10.34** *The Alignment tab of the Format Cells dialog box*

- **Alignment.** By default, numbers are aligned to the right of a cell and text to the left, but you can change this alignment using the buttons in the toolbar. If you select the *Alignment* tab in the *Format cells* menu (see Figure 10.34) you will find some useful additional options you can set.

You can set the vertical alignment in rows for text to be displayed at the top, bottom and centre. You can also set the orientation of text so that you can, for example, have text rotated through 90° (i.e. on its side).

The *Text control* check boxes allow you to set the following options:

- **Wrap text**. Text wraps within the cell (as it does in a text box).
- **Shrink to fit.** The font size is automatically reduced so that text fits in the cell. Without this option, text too large to fit in the cell will overflow across other cells, obscuring their contents.
- **Merge cells.** This allows several cells to be merged so that they are treated as one cell. This option can be useful if you want to enter a lot of text, especially if combined with *Text Wrap*.

There is a wide range of formatting options available. You need to ensure that you use these options to improve the readability and appearance of your spreadsheets. However, make sure you do not overuse them or your spreadsheets will look garish and unprofessional. Also make sure you use formatting in a consistent way, otherwise your spreadsheets will look messy.

## Formatting for printing

Unlike a word-processing program, Excel does not display the spreadsheet while you are editing it as it will look when printed. You therefore need to check how it will look when printed and, if necessary, adjust various settings, such as the position of page breaks and the page orientation. On a spreadsheet larger than a single page of paper, there are several ways of dealing with this:

- Adjust the margins so that the spreadsheet fits on a single sheet of paper. This works only if the spreadsheet is only slightly larger than one page.
- In some cases, adjusting the page orientation will enable a spreadsheet to fit on a single sheet. The page orientation needs to be adjusted in any case to suit the layout of the spreadsheet. For example, if it has more columns than rows, it will print better in landscape.

- Scale the spreadsheet so that it fits on a single sheet of paper. This also only works if the spreadsheet is only slightly larger than one page, otherwise the text can get too small.
- Adjust the position of the page breaks so they occur in convenient places.

To check the way the spreadsheet will look when printed, click the *Print preview* button in the toolbar. You will then see a display similar to Figure 10.35.

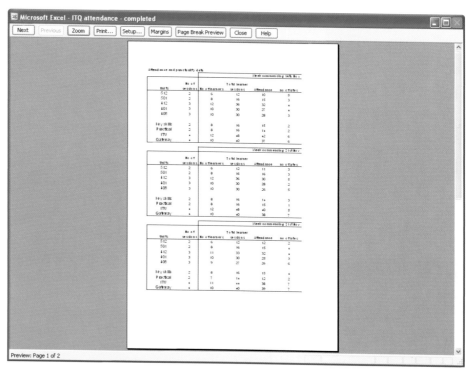

**Figure 10.35** *Print Preview*

On the *Print Preview* screen you can adjust the margins by clicking the *Margins* button. This will display the margins as dotted lines and you can drag them to the desired positions. Clicking the *Setup* button will display the *Page Setup* dialog box, shown in Figure 10.36.

Here, on the *Page* tab, you can set the orientation of the page and also scale the spreadsheet either to a fixed percentage or to fit on a certain number of pages. (Excel works out the percentage scaling for you.) The example spreadsheet shown in Figure 10.35 would, in fact, be better printed in *Landscape* orientation, as the right side of each table would not then go on to another page. The other tabs on this dialog box are as follows:

**Figure 10.36** *The Page Setup dialog box*

- **Margins.** You can set the margins here using numbers, rather than dragging the margin lines as you can on the *Print Preview* screen.
- **Header and Footer.** Here you can choose from a selection of preset header and footer entries using the drop-down boxes. If you prefer, you can click the *Custom header* (and/or *Footer*) button and enter your own information into the header and/or footer. The *Header/Footer* dialog box contains various buttons that allow you to add page numbers, dates etc. and format them. See Figure 10.37 for details.

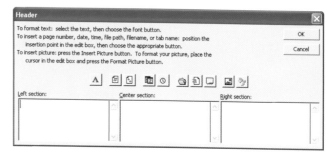

**Figure 10.37** *The Header/Footer dialog box*

■ **Sheet.** This offers several options, which are listed below, though some are greyed out as they are not available when you are in *Print Preview*. (Note: all options are available if you go to *Page Setup* via the main *File* menu.)

The *Sheet* options include:

■ **Gridlines.** Selecting this option means that the lines separating rows and columns, showing on the screen, will appear in print.

■ **Row and Column Headings.** These are the numbers of the rows and letters of the columns on the screen, which would otherwise not appear in print.

■ **Page order.** This offers options on the order in which the pages of data will be printed, as indicated by the picture within the dialog box.

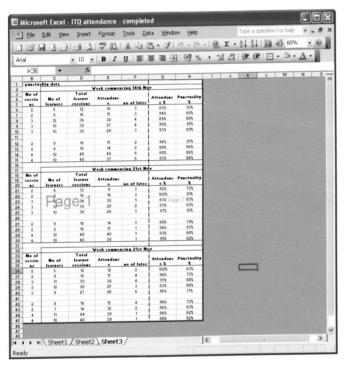

**Figure 10.38** *Page break preview*

Back at the *Print Preview* screen, the *Page Break Preview* button allows you to see and adjust where the page breaks fall in your document. You can drag them to different, more convenient positions with your mouse. However, if you drag the breaks to the right or down, more information needs to fit on a page, the spreadsheet automatically scaling to allow this. See Figure 10.38.

If you do not want to print the whole spreadsheet you can set a print area, using one of the following methods:

■ select the area, then go to the *File* menu and choose *Print Area* and then *Set Print Area*

■ choose *File*, *Page Setup* and select the *Sheet* tab of the *Page Setup* box.

You can also select row or column titles here that will repeat on every page of the printout. This is very useful because, if the titles only appear on the first sheet, it can be difficult to see which titles the columns and rows relate to on subsequent pages.

## Analysing and interpreting data

Excel includes some tools to help you analyse and interpret the data in a spreadsheet. Particularly with large amounts of data, it can be difficult to make sense of it without these tools.

### Charts

One of the best ways to present data in an easy-to-understand format is to display it as a graph or chart. Creating charts in Excel is quite easy, although you need to be careful to ensure the correct data is included.

How to –

# Create a chart using the chart wizard

To create a chart you use the *Chart Wizard* button on the toolbar. The chart wizard works best with blocks of data that have titles along the top and down the left-hand side. Figure 10.39 shows an example of this layout. Before you click the *Chart Wizard* button you should select all the data including the titles.

**Step 1 of 4.** When you click on the *Chart Wizard* button, *Step 1* of the chart wizard appears, asking you to choose the type of chart you want. See Figure 10.40. This, of course, partly depends upon your own preference, but remember the following:

- Line and area charts, where the data points are joined up, should be used for data that represents a continuous change, such as temperature over time.

- With financial data, like the data in Figure 10.39, column or bar charts are better.

- A single pie chart cannot show multiple sets of data, as we have in Figure 10.39 (i.e. we would need separate charts for North, South, East and West regions).

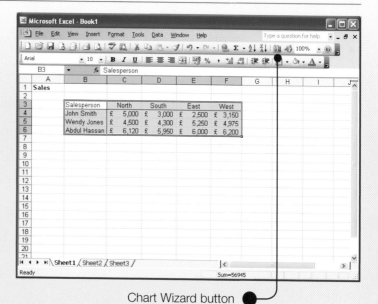

Chart Wizard button

**Figure 10.39** *Selecting the data*

the data is shown. In this example, it will move the sales people to the bottom of the graph (x-axis) and move the regions to the series (the different coloured bars). If we are trying to analyse the sales peoples' performance (rather than comparing regions) then they are best represented as the coloured bars, so leave *Rows* selected.

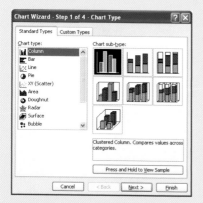

**Figure 10.40** *Step 1 of the chart wizard*

**Step 2 of 4.** When you click *Next*, *Step 2* appears (see Figure 10.41). If you have selected the data correctly, you will see a preview of your chosen chart type. The *Rows* and *Columns* buttons will swap around how

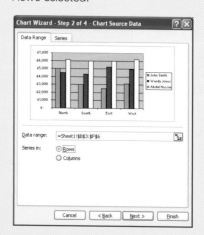

**Figure 10.41** *Step 2 of the chart wizard*

If your data contains empty rows or columns, you may have to delete these rows of columns from the series (sets of data), but we will look at that in a moment.

Click *Next* to move to the next step.

**Step 3 of 4.** *Step 3* of the chart wizard is a tabbed dialog box where you can set various labels for the chart. See Figure 10.42. On the first tab you can give the chart a title, such as 'Sales Performance' and also label the x-axis ('Regions' would be a suitable label) and the y-axis (as this is clearly money it does not really need a title).

Click *Next* again to take you to *Step 4*.

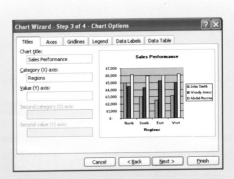

**Figure 10.42** *Step 3 of the chart wizard*

**Step 4 of 4.** This final step asks you if you want to insert the chart as an object in the current worksheet or as a separate sheet. In this example we shall insert it as an object in the current sheet. Click *Finish* to do this.

The chart that is inserted will probably need adjusting in size to produce a reasonable chart. If it is too small then the text appears large while the chart itself is tiny, so use the handles around the chart object to drag the chart box to a reasonable size, as shown in Figure 10.43.

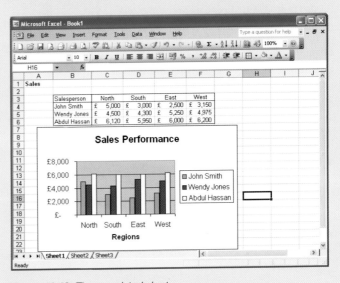

**Figure 10.43** *The completed chart*

The layout of your spreadsheet may make using the chart wizard a little more difficult. For example, consider the spreadsheet shown in Figure 10.44.

The **x-axis** of a chart is the scale or items that run along the bottom of the chart. The **y-axis** is the scale that runs up the side.

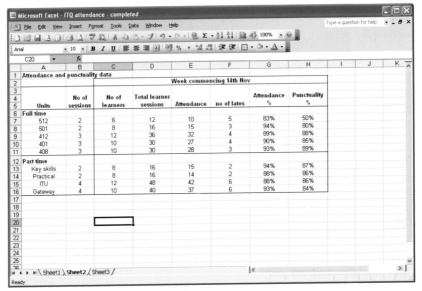

**Figure 10.44** *Attendance and punctuality data*

There are two reasons why this data will prove tricky to create a chart for using the chart wizard:

- We would not want to include all the data in the chart, as we would get a very messy and confusing chart if we did. The important figures are the attendance and punctuality percentages; all the other figures should be left out of the chart.
- Column A contains some subheadings (*Full time* and *Part time*), and there is no data along the rows where these subheadings appear. This will confuse the chart wizard and leave gaps in the chart.

How to –

## Create a chart with complex data

There are a couple of ways we can get around these problems. We could create a copy of the data that we want to use. This would include just the titles and the *Attendance* and *Punctuality* percentages, leaving out the other subheadings. We could then use the chart wizard as before.

Another way is to use the *Ctrl* key while selecting the areas of data we want to chart. This allows us to select non-adjacent areas, as shown in Figure 10.45. Here the rows containing the *Full time* and *Part time* subheading have been left out.

**Figure 10.45** *Selecting non-adjacent areas*

Other unwanted data has still been left in and, if the chart wizard is run again, *Step 2* shows all the columns of data included in the coloured bars (or 'data series' as Excel calls them), including those we do not want. See Figure 10.46.

We can remove them by clicking on the *Series* tab of the *Step 2* dialog box. We then select the series we do not want (everything except *Attendance* and *Punctuality* percentages) and click the *Remove* button to remove them from the chart. The chart will now be redrawn with only the two required data series.

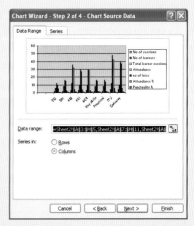

**Figure 10.46** *Chart source data*

In this example we have seen how you can control the data that is included in the chart by using the *Ctrl* key to select only the required areas, and by removing the data series at *Step 2* of the chart wizard. Once your chart has been created, you can then format any part of it.

## Format a chart

Simply double-click on the part of the chart you want to format and a dialog box will appear, showing the formatting options for that part of the chart. For example, if you want to change the format of the text in the chart's title, double-click on the title and a *Format chart title* dialog box will appear as shown in Figure 10.47.

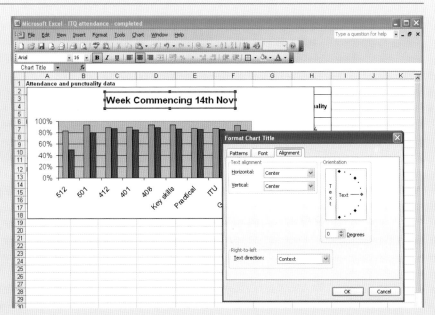

**Figure 10.47** *Format chart title dialog box*

**Figure 10.48** *The Games Store games list*

Excel charts are an excellent way of summarising large volumes of data, so that overall trends can more easily be seen and comparisons made. The chart wizard is quite easy to use, although you may have to use some of the techniques described to make sure that only relevant data is included in your chart.

## Filtering and sorting lists

Dealing with lists and simple databases is one of Excel's many strengths. Many people use Excel to keep track of lists, rather than using a full-blown database product such as Microsoft Access, because it is easier to understand and set up. In fact, all you really need to do to set up a list in Excel is to add field titles at the top.

Figure 10.48 shows a version of the Games Store spreadsheet we used before. We will use it to look at how lists can be filtered and sorted. Every column of data has a title (or 'fieldname' in database terminology); and columns for the types of game and the hardware platform have been added.

## Sort lists

There are various reasons why people want to sorts list – to find the cheapest, the newest, the best-selling and so on. To sort a list, all you need to do is to make sure the current cell pointer is somewhere in the list, then, from the *Data* menu, choose *Sort*. Excel will highlight the whole list and display the *Sort* dialog box, as shown in Figure 10.49.

As long as you have field titles in the first row of your list, they will be displayed in the drop-down boxes. You can sort ascending or descending by up to three criteria. The example in Figure 10.49 shows that the games will be sorted first by hardware platform, then within the different platforms by price. Since ascending order is set for both sort criteria, the platform will be sorted alphabetically (PC first then PS2) and then by price with the cheapest first.

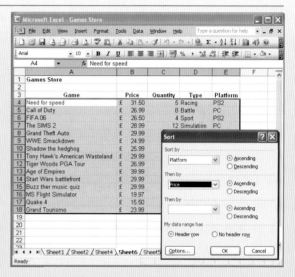

**Figure 10.49** *The Sort dialog box*

## Filter lists

Filtering is rather more sophisticated than sorting, as it lets you pick out a record or records in the list that match certain criteria.

As with sorting you must have the current cell pointer inside the list somewhere; then, from the *Data* menu, choose *Filter*, then *Autofilter*. This will display a little drop-down arrow beside each of the fieldnames in the top row of the list, as shown in Figure 10.50. So, for example, to list only the PS2 games, you would click on the arrow next to the *Platform* title and choose PS2 from the list.

This list will then be filtered with only the PS2 games showing. The arrow next to *Platform* will go blue, showing that this is the field on which the data is filtered.

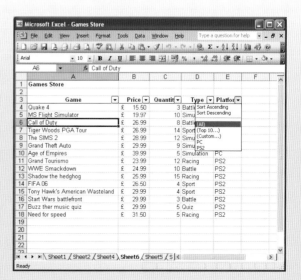

**Figure 10.50** *Filtering a list*

To return to the display of all the data, click the button again and choose *All*.

The *Custom* option under the filter buttons lets you select criteria on which the filtering will be done. For example, suppose you wanted to find all the games costing less than £28. To do this you would click on the button next to *Price*, and choose *Custom*. This would display the dialog box shown in Figure 10.51.

Then you would choose *is less than* from the first drop-down box and type '28' in the second (you can drop this box down to see all the different prices in the list if you want). If you click *OK* now, the list will display only the games under £28. You can also have a second

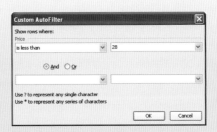

**Figure 10.51** *The Custom Autofilter dialog box*

criterion to make filters such as 'PC games under £28'. The *And* button means both criteria must be true for a record to be displayed, the *Or* button means either criterion may be true for a record to be displayed.

Remember that, when attempting to analyse data from large and complex spreadsheets, you may make more sense of the figures if you restrict your analysis to just their totals or subtotals. Although sorting and drawing charts makes interpreting data easier, if there is a very large amount of data in the first place then the resulting chart, sort or search may not make much sense.

For example, if you draw a bar chart from a very large amount of data then the resulting chart will have so many bars it will be difficult to read. In this situation it may be better to create subtotals based on a date or month range and then graph this data. The resulting chart will be much smaller and, therefore, easier to read and interpret.

## Test your knowledge

12  If a cell contains the number 10, and you use the percentage format button in the toolbar to format the cell, what will be displayed?

13  Your spreadsheet is slightly larger than a single sheet of paper; how can you make it print on just one sheet?

14  How can you select non-adjacent cells (i.e. cells that are not all together in one block)?

15  What must you do before you use the *Autofilter* menu option?

16  Where is the x-axis on a graph, along the bottom or up the side?

# Checking and documenting a spreadsheet solution

## Checking

It is all too easy to assume that, because it is a computer doing the calculations, they must be correct. However, the computer only does what you tell it to do, so you must be careful that the formulas you enter are correct; otherwise the calculations may be done correctly, but they are the wrong calculations! To be sure your formulas are correct, you need to check them manually with a calculator.

You may sometimes find that your formulas produce an error message (error messages displayed within cells all start with a '#') rather than the expected result. The most common errors displayed in cells that contain formulas are as follows:

- **#Value.** This appears when your formula refers to a cell address that contains text when the formula requires a numeric value. To correct the error make sure the formula is referring to the correct cell and that the cell contains a number.

- **#Name.** This error is caused by you misspelling a function name, such as AVERGE rather than AVERAGE. To correct this problem, check the spelling of the function, looking it up in the help menu if you are not sure how to spell it.

- **#DIV/O.** This means you are attempting to divide a value by zero, which is not possible.

Note that Excel will not display an error if a formula contains a cell reference to a cell that is empty. In this case the cell is treated as if it contains zero. You must, therefore, check cell references carefully to ensure they refer to the correct cell.

As well as checking that your spreadsheet works correctly, you also need to check that it meets the requirements of the users you produced it for. This is the 'acid test' for any IT solution – does it do what the user wants? Before you show it to your users you should check it against the design document you produced in the first place. You should, of course, have been regularly checking your progress against this document, as it is a little late now the spreadsheet is complete to find you have forgotten what was originally required. However, this should be a final check to make sure there is nothing you have forgotten.

As students your users will probably not be real, but you should consider asking your teacher or fellow students to review what you have done and compare it to your design. Doing this will help you check that your work meets the requirements of pass grade ('Create a spreadsheet solution to meet a specified user need') and may also provide some evidence for a Distinction ('Evaluate the benefits of a spreadsheet solution').

## Documentation

Documentation is an important part of any solution. Producing a working solution without documentation will lead to problems later. Software often needs to be updated or improved and some problems may only surface after the solution has been in use for a while. It may be that these updates or corrections cannot be done by the person who originally wrote the software, so the documentation is needed to guide those who will do the work.

Of course, you will also need documentation as part of your evidence for this unit. Do not forget to spellcheck and proofread your final version to ensure it is free from errors.

### Test your knowledge

17  You enter a formula in a cell but it displays '#Value'. What is the problem?

18  What error message will be displayed in a cell if you spell a function name incorrectly?

19  Explain why it is important to check the formulas in your spreadsheet.

20  List the things that spreadsheet documentation should include.

## Assessment tasks

The assessment tasks in this unit are based on the following scenario:

*Your school or college has asked you to produce an automated class register using a spreadsheet. It should be formatted in a similar way to a paper-based class register with student names down the side and the date or session numbers of each class across the top. In addition to the things you would normally expect to find on a paper-based register, the spreadsheet version should display percentage attendance rates for each learner as the lessons progress. It should also display a chart showing the attendance across the whole group. As well as the on-screen register, a suitably formatted printed version is required for reports etc.*

> To work towards a Distinction in this unit you will need to achieve **all** the Pass, Merit and Distinction criteria in the unit and have evidence to show that you have achieved each one.

### How do I provide assessment evidence?

You should provide evidence of the spreadsheet that you created. Rather than just being a collection of screen and spreadsheet printouts, your documentation should be made into a proper report with a clear structure and professional presentation.

The documentation to support your spreadsheet should include:

■ details of the original user requirement that your spreadsheet is supposed to meet

# Assessment tasks continued

- the design document you produced at the outset
- annotated screen shots of the spreadsheet showing how it is used and an explanation of how it meets the user's requirements
- printouts of the spreadsheet with the formulas displayed.

All your evidence should be presented in one folder, which should have a front cover and a contents page. You should divide the evidence into three sections corresponding to the three tasks.

## Task 1 (P2, P3, P4)

Create a class register spreadsheet to meet the requirements as described above, including formulas to display the total attendance by learner and by class. Add a chart to the register to allow the learners' attendance to be easily compared.

Use text, date and percentage data types to display data correctly, and formatting to make the appearance of the register clear and professional.

Check that your spreadsheet works correctly, particularly the formulas and functions that have been used. Write up the documentation for the spreadsheet you have created.

## Task 2 (M1)

Create at least one other worksheet, which contains a register for another class that the same group of learners attend. Add a summary sheet, linked to the other two class register sheets, which displays the overall attendance for learners across the two or more classes.

## Task 3 (M2, D1)

Demonstrate how charts, graphs, filtering and sorting can be used to help interpret the data on the spreadsheet. For example you could:

- show how filtering could be used to pick out learners who should go on report because their attendance has fallen below target
- show how sorting could be used to create a 'league table' with the best-attending students at the top.
- create a graph that draws together data from the two different classes, so trends or problem areas (e.g. learners who attend one class but not the other) can be identified.

> To work towards a Distinction you should write a report evaluating the register spreadsheet you have produced. Consider the advantages and disadvantages of your spreadsheet when compared to a paper-based register. Was a spreadsheet the best application to use to create the register, or would another application have been better? Also consider how your spreadsheet register could be refined to make it easier to use and to more closely match the user's requirements. Your teacher or tutor may be able to help you by looking at the spreadsheet you have produced and discussing with you how it could be used for real.

# 16 Mobile Communications Technology

## About this unit

Computing and communications have become increasingly mobile. It is hard to imagine what personal communications were like prior to the mobile telephone, which came into common use only in the 1980s. Laptops and personal digital assistants (PDAs) have also become truly mobile with the use of short-range wireless networks to provide them with access to the Internet. Mobile communications technology is widely used, but it is also quite complex with many different technologies in use, such as Bluetooth, Wi-Fi, 3G and GPRS, each with its own features and applications. There are also several important issues to be considered including security, cost and health.

▶ Continued from previous page

# Learning outcomes

When you have completed this unit you will:

1   understand the characteristics and services of available mobile communications devices

2   understand the implications of mobile communications

3   be able to use mobile communications technologies to meet user needs.

This area of technology is growing and changing very fast. The information in this chapter is up-to-date at the beginning of 2006, but you may need to do your own research on the Internet to get the very latest information.

# How is the unit assessed?

This unit is internally assessed. You will provide a portfolio of evidence to show that you have achieved the learning outcomes. The grading grid in the specification for this unit lists what you must do to obtain Pass, Merit and Distinction grades. The section on Assessment Tasks at the end of this chapter guides you through activities that will help you to be successful in this unit.

# Mobile communications services

## Available technologies

There are a number of different mobile communications technologies currently available. They each have different characteristics, such as the range over which they can operate and the rate at which they can transfer data. These different characteristics make each of the technologies best suited to a particular application. The technologies currently in use can broadly be divided into the following groups:

- wide-range mobile phone networks
- short-range local networks.

We shall look at each of these types of mobile network in detail.

### Wide-range mobile phone networks

The original mobile phone networks were analogue radio communications networks, designed for voice communication. These have now been superseded by digital networks that can carry voice, text, data and, more recently, video. Mobile phone networks are licensed by the government, who sell a limited number of licences to communications service operators such as Vodafone, T-mobile, $0_2$ and Orange. It is illegal to run this type of network unless you have a licence.

Mobile phone networks are sometimes called cell phone networks because of the way they work. Unlike a traditional 'walkie-talkie' (or CB) radio, which transmits over a wide range and only has a limited number of channels, cell phones use a system with a base station transmitter that serves a fairly small area – about 10 square miles. This is called a **cell**, which gives the system its name. Cell phones also use a large number of channels (over 1,000) and can swap between them, and switch from one cell base station to another, without the user being aware of this happening.

There are other systems in use around the world, but the three main international systems are described below and compared in Table 16.1.

### GSM

GSM (Global System for Mobile Communications) is a world-wide standard for mobile telephone networks. It provides for digital voice and text messaging but not data transfer. It is sometimes referred to as a 2G (second generation) network, with the old analogue mobile phone system referred to as 1G.

### GPRS

The problem with 2G networks is that they do not support data transmission. This means you cannot use your mobile phone as a type of modem to provide Internet access on your laptop computer. To get around this problem, a system called GPRS (General Packet Radio

Service) was developed that does allow data transmission over 2G networks; which therefore became known as 2.5G networks.

If you have a mobile phone that supports GPRS then you can plug the phone into a laptop and get on the Internet anywhere there is a mobile phone signal.

### 3G

The third generation mobile phone networks were designed from the start to support both voice and data, and much higher data rates than GPRS. 3G can support data rates of up to 3 Mbits per second, while GPRS can manage only up to 144 Kbits per second. This allows applications such as video to become a reality.

3G networks have been fairly slow to take off, mostly because they require a completely new network so are very expensive to set up.

| Standard | Type | Voice | Text | Data | Video | Transfer rate |
|---|---|---|---|---|---|---|
| 1G | Analogue | Yes | No | No | No | - |
| 2G (GSM) | Digital | Yes | Yes | No | No | - |
| 2.5G (GPRS) | Digital | Yes | Yes | Yes | No | 144 Kbit/s |
| 3G | Digital | Yes | Yes | Yes | Yes | 3 Mbit/s |

**Table 16.1** *Mobile phone standards compared*

## Short-range local networks

There are a number of short range wireless communications technologies that are currently in use, such as Bluetooth and Wi-Fi. These are unlicensed networks, in that the government has allocated a radio frequency band (2.4GHz) in which these networks can operate and anyone who has the equipment can use the network without a licence.

### Bluetooth

Bluetooth was designed for hand-held mobiles devices, such as mobile phones and PDAs, and is low cost and easy to use. Bluetooth is named after a 10th-century Danish king who united Denmark and Norway. The technology originated from the Scandinavian company L.M. Ericsson who thought the name suited something that linked things together.

Bluetooth devices are designed to be easy to use and to connect to each other without user intervention. When they come within range, they converse with each other to see if they should connect and, if they should, they form a personal area network or **piconet**.

Bluetooth is short range, covering only 10 metres. Its low power makes it suitable for battery-operated devices and helps reduce the likelihood of interference between different Bluetooth piconets. Bluetooth devices for laptops and desktop computers can be purchased that run at higher power, stretching the range up to 100m. The data rate of Bluetooth is, however, quite low, which is why it is not very popular for applications

### What does it mean?

*Radio works by creating waves of electromagnetic energy. Radio **frequency** is related to the time taken to complete one wave or cycle and is measured in hertz (Hz); 1 hertz is one cycle per second. Different bands (ranges of frequencies) are allocated to different purposes: for example FM radio uses the 30-300 MHz band (1 MHz = 1 million Hz). Wi-Fi devices and mobile phones user higher frequency bands in the 3–30 GHz range (1 Ghz = 1 million MHz).*

such as providing Internet connections for laptops, where the higher data rates of Wi-Fi are better suited.

With its origin in the mobile phone industry, Bluetooth can handle voice as well as data, and is a popular way to connect hands-free headsets to mobile phones.

## Wi-Fi

Wi-Fi is mainly used to provide laptops and PDAs with a wireless method of connecting to the Internet. The range is much wider than Bluetooth – about 500 metres in an open area, but much shorter where there are walls. The most common arrangement is for a wireless-equipped device to conect to an access point or wireless router which provides a wired connection to the Internet. Figure 16.1 shows a typical home wireless network setup.

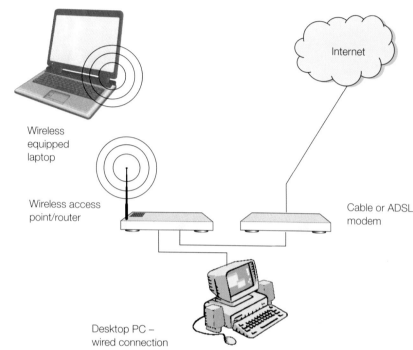

**Figure 16.1** *Typical Wi-Fi home configuration*

The basic standard for Wi-Fi is known as 802.11. This name was given by the Institute of Electrical and Electronic Engineers (IEEE), who developed the standard. However, as Wi-Fi has evolved over several years, there are a number of different standards in use. Table 16.2 compares the different 802.11 standards.

| Standard | Max speed | Approx range | Comments |
|----------|-----------|--------------|----------|
| 802.11a | 54 Mbit/s | Less than 30 m | Although it had higher speed than 802.11b, its higher cost and short range reduced its popularity |
| 802.11b | 11 Mbit/s | Approx 30 m | Low cost made it popular |
| 802.11g | 54 Mbit/s | Approx 30 m | Combined the benefits of the two earlier standards |
| 802.11n | Up to 540 Mbit/s | 30 m or more | Latest version, but the standard has not yet been agreed |

**Table 16.2** *Wi-Fi 802.11 standards*

### Infrared

Infrared wireless communications technology has been around for some time, but has never achieved the popularity of Bluetooth or Wi-Fi. It used to be quite common on laptop computers, PDAs and mobile phones but is now often found only on low-end phones and PDAs or wireless mice.

The main disadvantage of infrared is that devices have to be in line of sight (as little as a 3° angle on some devices) and very close (1 metre or less). Unlike Wi-Fi and Bluetooth, infrared is a point-to-point connection – only two devices can communicate at the same time and the data is not broadcast.

Infrared does, however, have a number of advantages. Due to its physical limitations, it is a secure method of communication; it is very unlikely that someone could hack into an infrared signal without the user being aware, due to the short range of the devices. It is also very low cost.

The standards used by infrared devices are set by an organisation called IrDA (Infrared Data Association). Table 16.3 summarises the features of these different short-range technologies.

| | Max data rate | Max range | Main benefits | Main disadvantages |
|---|---|---|---|---|
| Bluetooth | 1 Mbit/s | 10 m | Low power, ease of use | Low speed, security |
| Wi-Fi | Currently 54 Mbit/s | 30 m | Standard for PC wireless networks | Security |
| IrDA | 16 Mbit/s | 1 m | Secure, low cost | Short range, low speed, devices must be in line of sight |

**Table 16.3** *Short-range wireless communications technologies*

## Wireless networking

### Wireless network adaptors

What do you need to connect a computer to a wireless network or wireless local area network (WLAN)? Most laptops you can buy today come with a wireless network interface card (NIC) already built in. If you have a laptop that does not already have a wireless card, you can purchase an add-on wireless NIC, which will plug into either the USB port or the PCMCIA interface to be found on most laptops. To attach a desktop computer, you can either use a USB wireless NIC or an internal wireless NIC, which plugs into the computer's PCI interface.

To create a wireless network at home, school or in an office, you will also need a wireless access point. This device has an antenna to send and receive the wireless signal, and a standard network connector to connect to a wired LAN. See Figure 16.2.

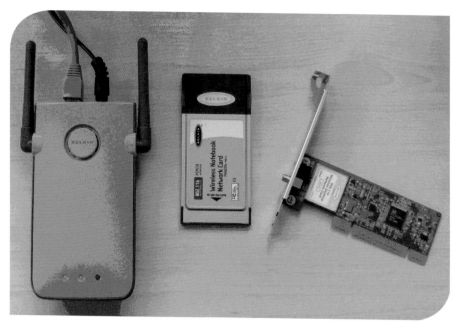

**Figure 16.2** *A wireless access point and PCMCIA and PCI wireless NICs*

## Wireless access points

To use a wireless Internet connection while 'on the road' at a café, hotel, railway station etc. you first need to check that the location has a wireless 'hotspot'. If it does, you will normally need to purchase a voucher that will provide an access key to allow you to use the hotspot for a limited time.

As well as local Wi-Fi hotspots, plans were in place in early 2006 to create much larger Wi-Fi zones, called 'hotzones'. With hotzones, wireless coverage will be provided over a large urban area using multiple access points installed in the street, attached to lampposts or signs.

## Security

Security is a problem for Wi-Fi networks, since anyone in range with a compatible system can gain access to the network. Most access points and NIC have security switched off as a default and many home users do not realise the potential dangers of an insecure WLAN, or do not know how, or cannot be bothered, to turn it on.

There are two ways to improve the security of a WLAN. One is to use WEP (Wired Equivalent Privacy) or WPA (Wi-Fi Protected Access) encryption. This involves encrypting the data sent over the wireless link so that it is less vulnerable to being intercepted.

In order to set up WEP, an encryption key is used, and all the devices on the WLAN must use the same key. The key can be a 64-bit or 128-bit number. Theoretically 128-bit encryption keys are less easily cracked than 64-bit keys. However, WEP has some serious flaws and can be easily cracked.

What does it mean?

**Encryption** *is a way of encoding data so it cannot be read by anyone other than its intended recipients.*

## What does it mean?

*A **MAC address** is a 12-digit hexadecimal number (hexadecimal numbers are base 16-numbers, represented by digits 0 to 9 and letters A to F). A MAC address is used to identify uniquely a computer's network interface card (wireless or wired).*

In response to the problems of WEP, WPA was introduced, although it can be found only on more recent access points and wireless NICs (approximately 2003 onwards). A further improvement in security was made in 2005, called WPA2.

Another option is to use MAC address filtering. Every NIC (wireless or wired) has a unique MAC address, which is a hexadecimal number. MAC address filtering is set up at the access point; a list of valid MAC addresses are entered and these are the only devices the access point will communicate with.

## How to –

### Set up an encryption key

This example shows how to set the encryption key on a Belkin wireless access point. The set-up for other manufacturers or models would be similar. When you are setting up a Wi-Fi network, the wireless access point provides a bridge between the wired and the wireless parts of the network. Having connected the access point to the wired side of the network, you need to install the access point manager software on a PC that is also on the wired side. When you run the manager software, it will find all the access points currently connected, which in this example is only one. See Figure 16.3

**Figure 16.3** *Wireless Access Point Manager software*

To set the encryption key, choose *Command* from the menu bar, then the *Configure AP* option. This opens the dialog box shown in Figure 16.4.

In the dialog box, the encryption level is chosen (64 or 128 bits) and a

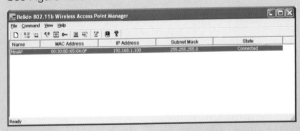

**Figure 16.4** *The Encryption Setting dialog box*

passphrase or key is entered (which is used as a key to generate the encrypted data). The passphrase of 'hellomum' is shown in Figure 16.4. When you click the *Apply* button, encryption is set up and computers equipped with a wireless NIC can access the WLAN only if they know the passphrase.

Figure 16.5 shows the WLAN Monitor software on a wireless-equiped laptop. Note that the *Status* box says 'Enable encryption to join this BSS'. This is because this passphrase has not yet been entered.

To enter the passphrase, the

**Figure 16.5** *WLAN Monitor*

**Figure 16.6** *Entering the passphrase*

*Encryption* tab is selected and the same passphrase used with the access point is entered. See Figure 16.6. The passphrase must be entered in every device that wants to access this WLAN.

The laptop can now join the WLAN and the monitor shows it is connected. See Figure 16.7.

**Figure 16.7** *The WLAN Monitor showing a connection*

How to –

## Set up MAC address filtering

Setting up MAC address filtering requires that you know the MAC address of any device that wants to access the WLAN. The MAC address of the laptop we have been using is shown in Figure 16.7. Unfortunately they are long numbers and not very easy to remember, so many people prefer the passphrase method. However, MAC address filtering is more secure since, while it may be possible to find out or crack the passphrase, MAC addresses are fixed and cannot be altered.

Once you have set up MAC address filtering then only those devices with the listed MAC addresses can access the WLAN. MAC address filtering is set up on the access point, using the manager software. Using the same *Access Point Manager* as before, the *Command* menu is again chosen, this time with the *Set MAC Filter* option. This displays the dialog box shown in Figure 16.8.

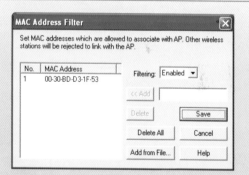

**Figure 16.8** *MAC Address Filter dialog box*

*Enabled* is chosen from the *Filtering* drop-down list and the MAC addresses of all the devices you want to be able to access the WLAN are entered using the *Add* button.

What are the dangers associated with not securing a wireless access point in this way?

## SMS

The Short Message Service (SMS) is available on almost all digital mobile phones and allows text messages up to 160 characters long to be sent. It was originally part of the GSM standard but has also been incorporated in later standards, such as 3G. The first text message was sent in 1992; since then, SMS has grown to be a tremendously popular service throughout the world. In 2004, around 500 billion text messages were sent and this rate is growing rapidly. Text messages generate large revenues for service providers, even though the cost of a single text message is quite low, due to the large number of messages sent.

In addition to sending text messages between mobile phones, the SMS protocol also allows the sending of binary data, such as ring tones, logos and configuration data. Being able to send configuration data via a text message is very useful. For example, you may contact your service provider to configure a special service on your phone, such as picture messaging. In this case, the company will send a text message to your phone to set the correct configuration options automatically.

Most phone companies also now offer an 'SMS to land line service', which allows text messages to be sent to a land line number. This service automatically dials the number and reads the message out using a speech synthesizer.

Sending text messages has also become a popular way for people to take part in radio and TV programs and is used for quizzes, jokes, requests and voting.

## Further research – services using SMS

The SMS text service is used for all sorts of applications: games, notifying people of important events, advertising etc. Do some research into as many different applications as possible and make a list of them. Are there any ways your school or college could (or does) use text messaging to help students?

If you really want a challenge, consider how the popularity of text messaging varies between continents and countries. For example, the most frequent senders of text messages can be found in South-East Asia. Europe comes next, but there are variations between countries, with the Spanish sending the most and the French sending the fewest messages. In the US the sending of text messages is much less popular; why do you think this is?

## Internet access

### WAP

WAP (Wireless Application Protocol) is an international standard for applications, such as Internet access, that use wireless communication devices, e.g. mobile phones. It was designed to provide web page browsing facilities on mobile phones, and takes into consideration the limitations of the very small screens these devices have when compared to a computer screen. It has its own web page creation language, WML, rather than the HTML language that is used for computer-based web pages. WAP pages are, therefore, different from normal web pages and WAP devices cannot view ordinary web pages.

## Case study

### *Instant messaging*

The future of SMS is likely to be **IM** (instant messaging). All the mobile phone companies are keen to set up instant messaging systems, as they have seen how popular these services are on the Internet (such as 'MSN messenger' and 'Yahoo messenger'). IM is more complex than SMS text, since not only are the messages delivered immediately but the chat sessions are often between quite large groups of people rather than one to one, which is normally the case with text messages. 3G mobile phones have the technology and bandwidth to allow IM, but the problem is linking different networks together and agreeing interfaces with the big Internet IM companies such as Yahoo and Microsoft.

In February 2006, 15 mobile operators across the world, including Vodafone, Orange, T-Mobile and China Mobile, agreed to work together to make it easy to link IM across networks; and it is expected that IM services will be launched in 2006. Agreements between networks on how IM will work on mobile phones is important, because it is unlikely to be a success if users on different networks cannot communicate with each other.

IM is a new and developing area for mobile communications and, by the time you read this, the situation is likely to be different from that at the time of writing. By doing some research into the current state of IM on mobile devices you can answer these questions:

**1**   What IM services have been launched by mobile phone operators? Do they link with any of the PC-based IM services?

**2**   Have you or would you use a mobile-phone-based IM service? What advantages and disadvantages do mobile IM services have over PC-based ones?

At the time WAP became available on mobile phones in the late 1990s, users had expectations that it would provide a similar experience to surfing the Internet on a computer. Unfortunately this was not the case; the WAP service was slow and pages were text only. There were also many other technical problems, not least that mobile phones only had black and white screens. WAP was therefore considered a failure at the time.

However, in recent years WAP has recovered some popularity through specific services provided by phone companies, such as Vodafone Live! and T-Mobile T-Zones. Services such as picture messaging (also called MMS – Multimedia Messaging Service) also use WAP combined with SMS.

### i-mode

In Japan, the largest mobile phone operator (NTT) decided not to offer a WAP service. Instead it developed its own system, known as **i-mode**. This was designed to provide web browsing on mobiles phones but also to overcome some of the technical problems associated with WAP. This proved to be very successful in Japan and NTT licensed the technology to service operators in other countries, including $O_2$ in the UK. As with WAP, the key to the success of i-mode has been the provision of suitable content, which users are willing to pay to view.

# Licensing issues

The use of all radio frequencies in the UK is controlled by the government (via Ofcom – Office of Communications. To see the website go to www.heinemann.co.uk/hotlinks, insert the express code 2048P and click on this unit. The complete spectrum of available frequencies is split up into bands, which are allocated to different purposes. This prevents confusion and interference, which could create serious problems. Some bands are used for 'mission critical' applications, such as air traffic control, emergency services or military use, so the regulation of the use of radio frequencies is important. In most bands, you require a licence to operate a transmitter, and the usage of many of the bands is strictly controlled.

Mobile phones operate in several radio frequency bands, including 900 MHz and 1800 MHz. Mobile phone services are controlled by the government and can only be operated by companies that have a licence, such as Orange and Vodafone.

Short-range wireless systems, such as Wi-Fi and Bluetooth, operate in the 2.4 GHz frequency band. This is an unlicensed frequency band in that, as long as the equipment you use complies with the regulations (e.g. transmitter power), you can use it without a licence. Devices such as cordless home phones share this band.

# Mobile wireless network devices

There are many devices that can make use of a mobile wireless network. We have already mentioned some, such as mobile phones and desktop and laptop computers.

## PDAs versus mobile phones

PDAs (Personal Digital Assistants) are popular with professionals who:

- need to combine the functions of a diary and address book
- want a device that can fit in a pocket and yet access network facilities, such as email and the Internet.

PDAs fit between mobile phones and laptops in terms of size and functionality and, indeed, some PDAs include a mobile phone.

Which one is best? It all depends upon the application. For portability and low cost, mobile phones are the best, but their small screen size limits the usefulness of the professional applications they can run. PDAs, with their larger screens, which can be interacted with using a stylus, are better for 'organiser' type applications.

Most PDAs have applications that easily link with established PC software, such as Microsoft Outlook. In addition, many PDAs use Windows-based operating systems. These features make it easy to synchronise a desktop PC and a PDA.

Table 16.4 summarises the differences between these devices.

| Device | Cost | Portability | Functions | Battery life |
|--------|------|-------------|-----------|--------------|
| Mobile phone | Low | Small and light | Phone, camera, video, games, simple organisers, limited Internet access | Good (all day to several days, depending on use) |
| PDA | Medium | Fairly small and light | As mobile, plus 'professional' applications, MS Office compatible | Good (all day) |
| Laptop | High | Large, quite heavy | 'Professional' applications, full Internet access | Limited (several hours) |

**Table 16.4** *Mobile devices*

## Specialised mobile devices

There are many specialised mobile devices in use. You may well have recently had a parcel delivered but, rather than sign a paper form, the delivery person gives you a hand-held terminal on which you sign your name using a stylus.

Organisations with a mobile workforce often equip their vehicles with a mobile computer (sometimes called a **mobile data terminal**) so they can receive information and instructions and report back on progress. Police cars, fire engines and ambulances may have such devices, as do repair and servicing workers, such as breakdown assistance engineers.

Many of these devices communicate using the mobile phone network. They often use the GPRS data communication system – because the data sent and received is mostly text rather than images or video, the higher data rates of 3G are not required. However, the police and other security-sensitive users use such devices over their own secure private wireless communications systems.

## RFID tags

Radio frequency identification (RFID) is a system that uses miniature transponder tags, which can be read by a special radio receiver. The tags can store a wide range of data, which can be used to identify the item they are attached to. The tag contains a silicon chip and a miniature aerial. When the hand-held reader unit emits radio waves in the range of a tag the tag, wakes up and transmits its data, which is then captured by the reader.

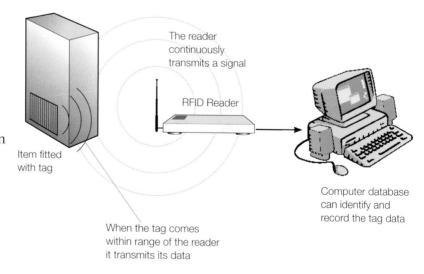

The reader continuously transmits a signal

RFID Reader

Item fitted with tag

When the tag comes within range of the reader it transmits its data

Computer database can identify and record the tag data

**Figure 16.9** *RFID in use*

There are two types of tags: passive and active. Passive tags are small enough to be inserted under the skin and cannot transmit much data as they do not have their own power supply. They are activated by the energy transmitted by the reader, so they have to be very close to it to work (a few centimetres). Active chips are larger and far more versatile. They have their own power supply (which can last for years), a range of tens of metres and they can be used to store more information.

RFID can be used for a wide variety of identification purposes. For example, in Australia, sheep and cattle have been fitted with RFID tags. This allows animals to be automatically identified and, as each animal passes over an electronic weighing scale, its weight can be recorded and compared to ensure the animal is growing as required.

RFID tags are also used to identify pets that travel outside the UK. Before you can take your dog, cat or other pet abroad, you must visit the vet and have the animal tested for rabies (a deadly disease that humans can catch from dogs and other animals, which exists in Europe and elsewhere but not in the UK). The animal is also injected with a tiny RFID tag, about the size of a grain of rice, which remains just under the animal's skin, usually just behind its head. The tag is used to positively identify the animal on its return to the UK, using a hand-held reader. You can read more about the scheme, which is sometimes called the 'pet passport', on the Internet. Go to www.heinemann.co.uk/hotlinks, insert the express code 2048P and click on this unit.

## Case study

### Dart-tag

The Dartford Toll crossing uses a DART-Tag system, which is a type of RFID tag. The Dartford crossing takes the M25 motorway over the River Thames east of London. South-bound drivers use the Queen Elizabeth II bridge, while North-bound drivers use the Dartford tunnel. The crossing is a toll road, which means you must pay to use it. You can pay with cash but it is easier and cheaper for frequent users to purchase a DART-Tag, which is attached to the windscreen of the vehicle.

When a vehicle with a DART-Tag approaches the toll-booth, an RFID reader in the toll booth reads the tag to obtain a customer number and retrieve the customer record. It checks the customer's balance and allows the driver through if the account is in credit. A colour-coded light system is used to inform the driver that the balance on the account is getting low. For more information on DART-Tag on the Internet, go to www.heinemann.co.uk/hotlinks, insert the express code 2048P and click on this unit. A similar system is used on the M6 Toll motorway in the Midlands.

What are the advantages and possible disadvantages of using RFID tags for toll road payment?

Currently, bar-codes are used in many applications where items need to be identified, such as products on a supermarket shelf. In many of these applications, RFID is seen as an ideal successor to the bar-code, because the identification code held in the tag is in digital format, meaning that each tag can have its own unique code, and store much more information than a simple bar-code. So an RFID tag can tell you not only what it is attached to but where the item came from, how much it weighs and its date of production.

## Test your knowledge

1   Explain the difference between GSM, 2.5G and 3G mobile systems.

2   What frequency band does Wi-Fi use?

3   What is the approximate range of Bluetooth devices?

4   What are the advantages of infrared communications over radio systems such as Bluetooth and Wi-Fi?

5   What is a Wi-Fi hotzone?

6   Describe three ways that you can improve the security of a Wi-Fi network

7   What is WAP and what is it used for? What alternatives are there to WAP?

8   What is an RFID tag? Give some examples of applications that RFID tags can be used for.

# Implications of mobile communications

The development of mobile technologies has been rapid, and seems likely to continue. The technologies, especially mobile phones, have had a considerable impact on the way we do things, even creating a modified version of the English language in the abbreviated words used for text messages. These changes have a number of social and ethical implications.

## Social implications

### Changes in social interaction

It is sometimes hard to remember how people used to communicate only 25 years ago! Personal letter-writing is now something most people under the age of 40 never do; it has been replaced by mobile phones, online chat and email.

The availability of mobile communications has not just changed our social lives and methods of personal interaction. Business now no longer has to be conducted in an office; and business people, who have to travel around the country to meet customers and other business contacts, can communicate while on the move.

### Further research – what was it like before mobile phones?

Speak to your parents or grandparents and ask them how they did the things you do now using your mobile phone. Discuss with them the advantages and disadvantages of using mobile technology.

If you would like a real challenge, try estimating what mobile communications will be like in 20 years time. With such a dramatic change in the way we communicate in the last 20–30 years, the changes over the next 20 years are difficult to imagine. Research the subject on the Internet and see what developments in mobile communications are currently in progress.

Internet pioneer Vint Cerf, who is currently employed as the Vice President and 'Chief Internet Evangelist' at Google, often gives lectures and interviews on this subject. Search for his name on the Internet to find out what he thinks will happen to the Internet and mobile communications in the future.

As mobile communications develop to the point were we can be connected to the Internet wherever we are, will we see a change in our lives? Currently most Internet activities (email, chatting, games, online auctions etc.) are carried on at home. Though a Wi-Fi network may give you the freedom to do this from anywhere within your home, in the future you will be able to take all these activities with you when you go out.

This is possible to a certain extent now, but there are two main factors that hold back developments. One is the cost of accessing the Internet outside your home, which is currently quite high compared to the cost of a broadband link at home. The other is the lack of suitable devices that have sufficient battery life to last all day without a recharge. Mobile phones have long battery life but their small screens and keyboards make Internet access difficult, while laptops currently lack the battery life and are not as portable as phones.

## Further research – further developments in mobile technology

What current developments in mobile devices are underway? Fuel cell batteries for laptops promise much longer battery life, but what is currently available?

PDAs provide a compromise between mobile phones and laptops, but so far have not been as popular as mobile phones or laptops. Is this changing? What current developments in PDAs are there?

If you would like a real challenge, attempt to design the specifications for your ideal portable mobile communications device. You need to consider size (in terms of portability, screen and keyboard size), functionality (what networks will it use and what software applications will it run?) battery life and cost. Does it come close to any of the devices currently available?

## Environmental and health issues

There have been concerns for some time that the radiation from wireless equipment may damage health. This largely relates to mobile phones, since these devices are held close to your head while in use. A great deal of research has been done, but little hard evidence of real danger has been found. In 1999, the government commissioned an independent group of experts to look into the potential risks from phones. The result was the Stewart Report, published in April 2000.

This report advises that gaps in our current knowledge mean that we should take a 'precautionary approach' to phone use. For adults, this means using our phones for limited amounts of time. For children, the advice is much stronger; the Stewart Report recommends that under-16s use their phones only for essential calls.

As well as the phones themselves, concerns have been raised that the fixed base-station antennas may cause health problems. According to the Stewart report, there is no evidence of adverse health effects. However, many people up and down the country remain concerned and raise objections when a new base-station is planned.

## Further research – health issues of mobile phone technology

Are there any mobile phone base stations near your home, centre of learning or place of work? Ask around your friends and family and see if they are aware of any local masts and if they are worried about health implications.

Building of new masts often causes a public outcry. Check the BBC News website to see if there have been any recent protests against plans to build masts.

If you would like a real challenge, explore the results of the latest research on the health dangers of mobile phone handsets and masts. Again the BBC News website is a good place to start.

## Moral and ethical implications

Computer systems and mobile communications technology have brought many advantages, but with new technologies come new problems and new opportunities for criminals.

Devices such as mobile phones and laptops are, of course, an easy target for thieves, and many young people have been victims of mobile phone theft. Mobile phone cameras have also been used to victimise and bully vulnerable people in so called 'happy slapping' attacks.

Text messaging has also been used to encourage people to join protests and even riots. In December 2005, Sydney, Australia had a series of violent race riots. Text messages were widely used to encourage people to join them, with large numbers of messages passed round, giving places and times for rioters to assemble. This has led to some calls for incitement to violence by text message to be made a more serious offence.

There is also concern over the security of personal data sent over wireless links. Unlike wired networks, where a physical connection is needed to be able to access information, with a wireless link the data is broadcast, so in theory anyone with suitable equipment can intercept it.

### Security of personal data

#### RFID tags

RFID tags, as discussed earlier, have been the subject of fears over privacy. With bar-codes on supermarket products, the shopper is well aware when the bar-code is being scanned, as it must be placed in very close proximity to the bar-code reader, and at a certain angle to be read. However, RFID tags can be read without the shopper being aware and could, in theory, be used as a tracking device, even after the shopper has left the shop.

Considerable controversy arose in 2003 when Tesco ran a trial of RFID tags at a shop in Cambridge. The system was used in an attempt to prevent shoplifting of razor blades (a popular item with shoplifters).

Packets of Gillette razor blades were fitted with RFID tags. Anyone picking up a packet was automatically registered by the system and then monitored by CCTV. Following complaints, the system was withdrawn.

notags.co.uk is an independent consumer organisation that campaigns against the use of RFID tags. You can read more about RFID tags, and their potential impact on privacy on their website. Go to www.heinemann.co.uk/hotlinks, insert the express code 2048P and click on this unit.

## Case study

### *Privacy issues with identity cards and RFID chips*

The debate about whether we should introduce ID cards in the UK has raged for a number of years and we could start being issued with them from 2008 when applying for a passport. The cards will include a microchip that will hold 'biometric' data such as a fingerprint and iris scan. This data will also be included in a type of RFID chip in new-style passports to be issued from 2006. (In these types of applications they are often called 'contactless proximity chips' and can only be read when in very close proximity to the reader, about 0–2 cm.)

You can read about biometric passports on the Internet. You can also read about ID cards by going to the UK Home Office ID card website. For these websites go to www.heinemann.co.uk/hotlinks, insert the express code 2048P and click on this unit. The possible use of RFID chips in these ways causes many concerns about privacy and the possibility that the devices could be used to track an individual's movements.

Why are identity cards considered necessary?

What are the benefits of including chips on the cards?

Why are people concerned about the possible use of RFID chips on passports and ID cards?

### Security and Bluetooth

Since Bluetooth devices actively seek out other devices in range (only about 10 metres), there are a number of ways this feature can be misused (although users can switch off the feature by setting their device into non-discoverable mode). These various vulnerabilities have different names:

- **Bluejacking** is where users send 'business cards' anonymously to other users. It does not involve removal of any personal data or any other negative effects, so is really just done for fun. The cards normally have a clever or flirtatious message and the aim of the 'game' is to listen for the other phone to 'ping' and observe the user's reaction to the card.

- **Bluebugging** exploits a security hole in some versions of some devices. This allows hackers with specialist skills to access another person's device and run commands without the other person's knowledge. This could allow them to eavesdrop on phone calls and access user data.

- **Bluesnarfing** is similar to Bluebugging but exploits a different vulnerability and affects different devices. Bluesnarfing allows the hacker to access personal data including the phone's IMEI (International Mobile Equipment Identity) number.

It should be remembered that, unlike computer hacker and virus attacks, these vulnerabilities can only be exploited by the hacker when they are within range of a vulnerable Bluetooth device. Device manufacturers have produced updates that prevent these attacks and new devices are not vulnerable to them.

The Cabir worm is a virus which is passed from one phone to another using Bluetooth. It affects phones that run only the Symbian Series 60 User Interface (type of operating system for portable devices). Users have to accept the software manually and install it for the phone to be infected.

## Hacking activities on Wi-Fi networks

The need to set up security options on Wi-Fi networks, such as WEP encryption and MAC address filtering, has already been explained. In this section we shall look at some of the means hackers can use to attempt to gain access to a Wi-Fi network.

### Wardriving

The term 'wardriving' has been used to describe the activity that involves driving around in a car with a wireless-equipped laptop, looking for insecure Wi-Fi networks to gain access to. It is named after war dialing, which was a method used in the 1980s and 90s to gain access to computers via their dial-up modems. The term war dialing originates from the 1983 sci-fi film War Games, in which a hacker inadvertently sets in motion a nuclear missile attack. Wardriving is also know as 'LAN jacking' or 'WiLDing' (Wireless Lan Driving).

Wardriving is a well known method of gaining access to Wi-Fi networks. The software needed (called Netstumbler) is freely available on the Internet, and can be used for legitimate purposes, such as testing a WLAN. The only hardware needed is a wireless-equipped device such as a laptop or PDA, although some people buy or make special directional antennas to improve the likelihood of detecting WLANs.

Wardriving is not strictly illegal, and simply detecting a WLAN is harmless. However, unauthorised use of someone else's Internet connection, or extracting personal information, is illegal.

### Packet sniffing

In order to be able to steal personal information from a WLAN, a hacker needs to be able to inspect the traffic on the WLAN and extract the desired information. Inspecting traffic on a wired or wireless LAN is known as packet sniffing. This is done using a piece of software sometimes called a LAN monitor. As with the Netstumbler program, LAN monitors are freely available on the Internet (e.g. Ethereal) and have legitimate uses in network testing and troubleshooting.

### What does it mean?

*A **hacker** is a person who attempts to gain unauthorised access to computer systems through a variety of methods, including exploiting security loopholes in operating systems. The intentions of hackers vary; some have criminal intentions, such as stealing personal information like credit card or bank details, and are sometime called **crackers**. Others do it for amusement, to demonstrate their skills or to help identify where systems may be vulnerable to attack.*

These programs require a detailed knowledge of the technical workings of networks, so they are not particularly easy to use, but with that knowledge it is possible to steal personal information from unprotected WLANs. However, if the data is encrypted (using the WEP or WPA encryption methods) it cannot be directly read, even with a packet sniffer. The hacker would first need to crack the encryption code.

## Defend a WLAN from 'wardriving'

There are a number of things you should do to enhance the security of a WLAN.

Every WLAN has an SSID (Service Set Identifier), which is basically the name of your WLAN. Access points and wireless NICs will come with these set to a default value. They may also be set to allow any device to join the WLAN without knowing the SSID. Figure 16.10 shows the *AP setting* dialog box from the Belkin Access Point Manager software we have seen before.

The SSID is shown set to the default name of 'WLAN'. This would be very easy for a hacker to guess, especially if they already know the default setting for Belkin access points. Also the check box marked *Accept 'ANY' SSID* is checked, which means that a device can join the WLAN with its SSID set to 'ANY'.

These settings leave the WLAN wide open to hackers, so the SSID should be set to something personal that

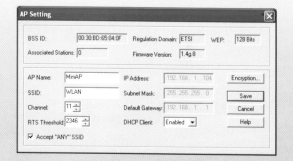

**Figure 16.10** *The AP setting dialog box*

would be difficult to guess (such as Arsenal4ever – although, if the hacker knew you were an Arsenal fan, this might be easy to guess!) and the *Accept 'ANY' SSID* box should be unchecked.

You should of course also set up WEP, or preferably WPA encryption (if your access point supports it), as described earlier.

## Legal issues

The law that covers hacking in the UK is the Computer Misuse Act. This law was passed in 1990, and activities such as hacking and spreading viruses are offences under the act. The act lists three specific offences:

- **Unauthorised access to computer material** (for example, a program or data). An example would be accessing a company's computer system and viewing their database of customers, or unauthorised access to your next door neighbour's Wi-Fi LAN. Note that it is illegal to access programs or data, even if you do not actually do anything with them.
- **Unauthorised access to a computer system with intent to commit a serious crime**. An example would be accessing a bank's computer system and transferring money into your own account.

■ **Unauthorised modification of computer data or programs**. This covers what many viruses do, even if they do not do any damage to the computer data.

If found guilty, offenders can be jailed for up to five years. Hacking into a wireless network is also covered by the Communications Act, which makes it illegal to dishonestly obtain an electronic communications service.

## Further research – vulnerability of wireless systems

Virus writers and hackers who get caught often end up in the news, but have there been any recent cases of wireless hackers being caught? The first case of its type in the UK came to court in July 2005, when a man from London was fined £500 for illegally accessing a wireless network while using his laptop sat in his car outside a house. Find out if there have been any more recent cases. The BBC News web site is a good place to start.

If you would like a real challenge, conduct a survey amongst your friends and family. How many of them have, or would like, wireless networks at home? Are they aware of the potential security hazards? Produce a simple leaflet for non-expert users that explains about the dangers and how to protect against them.

## Advantages

It is not difficult to see the advantages of mobile communications. The tremendous popularity of the technology clearly shows that, for most people, these outweigh any disadvantages. Let us just remind ourselves what some of the advantages are:

■ **Cable free convenience.** For the home and personal user, mobile data communications technology provides convenience. Internet access can be provided anywhere in the home and there is no need to install wires. Away from home it is possible to catch up with the latest information via the Internet, and communicate with friends and family via text, video or email.

■ **Increased efficiency.** For business people, who must travel around the country to do their job, wireless networking means they can carry on working and keep in touch even when they are out of the office. For example, imagine a situation where a sales person has a meeting with a customer who wants a quotation for some products they wish to purchase. After the meeting is over, the sales person does not need to return to their office, which may be hundreds of miles away; they can visit a local café with a wireless hotspot and set up their laptop to prepare the quotation. They can use their mobile phone to check with their boss on some pricing, then finish off the quotation and email it to the customer. Not only does the customer get the quotation more quickly, but the sales person can fit in another meeting in the afternoon, rather than having to drive back to the office to prepare the quote.

- **Greater flexibility.** Wireless communications allows people to be more flexible in how they spend both work and leisure time. As shown in the previous example, business people are no longer tied to the office phone and computer. They can work more flexibly, at home, on the road, and at times and places convenient to them. At home, people no longer have to use their computer in a fixed location; they can surf the Internet, check their emails, chat to friends etc. anywhere in the house or, if the weather is nice, in the garden! They do not even have to stay at home to use the Internet; they can do so wherever there is a wireless hotspot.

## Case study

### BT Open Zone

You can access the Internet from a wireless-equipped laptop or PDA in more and more places. Public access wireless networks are sometimes called 'Internet hotspots' and can be found in cafés, railway stations, hotels and many other places. BT Openzones are an example of a type of hotspot. To access a BT openzone hotspot you need a wireless (IEEE 802.11b) equipped laptop or PDA. You can then visit the Openzone website where you can find a directory of all the different hotspots around the country. To visit the site, go to www.heinemann.co.uk/hotlinks, insert the express code 2048P and click on this unit. You can also download the access manager software from the site, which automatically configures the network settings on your laptop to work with the hotspot. The final step is to purchase credit, which is currently priced at 20p per minute.

People who run cafés, hotels or other businesses that the public use, and where they might want to access the Internet, can purchase their own 'Hotspot in a box' kit from the BT Openzone website. This includes the hardware required (a wireless access point), promotional materials (posters, stickers etc.) and access vouchers that can be sold to customers.

Visit the BT Openzone website and find out where the nearest BT Openzone hotspot to you is.

What benefits do you think using Wi-Fi hotspots, such as BT Openzone, might have to both recreational and business users of the Internet?

What benefits might a café owner have from including a wireless hotspot in his or her café?

## Disadvantages

There are clearly many advantages to the mobile communications systems, but there are a number of disadvantages too:

- **Security.** All networked computer systems are vulnerable to security breaches, but mobile systems, due to their broadcast rather than wired method of transmission, are even more susceptible. Users need to be aware of the dangers and take the necessary actions to make sure their wireless communications are secure.
- **Effective range.** All mobile communications systems have limits on their range and this can be frustrating for users. We all know how

annoying it is to have an important call to make, but to find that your mobile phone has no service. Wi-Fi networks have very limited range and many users find that the actual range of the devices inside a building is much shorter than the maximum range quoted by the manufacturer. Interference from other devices can also be a problem.

■ **Perceived health hazards.** As explained earlier, although there is currently no clear evidence of any health hazards associated with mobile radio equipment, many people remain sceptical and this can, for example, make it difficult for mobile phone companies to erect transmission masts in areas where coverage is poor.

## Test your knowledge

9   Explain what wardriving is.

10   List the three specific offences covered by the Computer Misuse Act.

11   Briefly explain the recommendations of the Stewart Report.

12   Name the three security vulnerabilities that currently affect Bluetooth devices.

13   Describe two ways in which mobile phones can encourage criminal activities.

# Uses of mobile communication

In this section we shall look at how to set up two different mobile communications connections:

- a Bluetooth connection between a PC and a mobile phone
- a Wi-Fi connection for a laptop computer.

The examples shown here use equipment from certain manufacturers. Since the equipment at your centre of learning or place of work may be different, the details of the installation may differ, but the overall steps should be the same.

## Making a Bluetooth connection

In order to allow a mobile phone and a PC to communicate using Bluetooth, the following are required:

- a Bluetooth-enabled mobile phone
- a Bluetooth device with software drivers for the PC
- PC connection software for the phone.

The Bluetooth device we shall use for the PC connects via the USB port, as shown in Figure 16.11.

**Figure 16.11** *Bluetooth USB device and driver software*

How to –

### Make a Bluetooth connection

Step one is to install the Bluetooth USB device in the PC. To do this, the software is first installed from the CD that came with the device, following the on-screen instructions. Then the device itself is installed, by inserting it in a free USB port.

Once the installation is complete you should have a Bluetooth icon in the system tray, and a *My Bluetooth Places* icon in the *My Computer* window, as shown in Figure 16.12.

Step two is to pair the mobile phone and the Bluetooth USB device. How this is done will depend on the mobile phone in use but normally involves setting a 'passkey' (a numeric password) on both the computer and the phone.

**Figure 16.12** *My Bluetooth Places icon*

Step three is to install the connection software for the mobile phone. This provides an easy-to-use interface to allow you to access files on the phone, such as photos you have taken and videos you have recorded. The example shown here uses the Nokia phone software, which is called 'Nokia PC Suite'. It can be downloaded free of charge from the Nokia website. To visit the site go to www.heinemann.co.uk/hotlinks, insert the express code 2048P and click on this unit. Once in the website choose the *Support* link, then *Download software*. Once downloaded, the software can be installed following the on-screen instructions.

The PC Suite software can now be run and will display a menu of options, as shown in Figure 16.13.

Choosing the *File manager* option will display a window similar to the normal Windows Explorer, showing the phone and various folders inside the phone's memory. This is known as the Nokia phone browser and is shown in Figure 16.14.

Photos, videos and other media can now be copied in the normal way from the phone to a folder on your computer via the Bluetooth link.

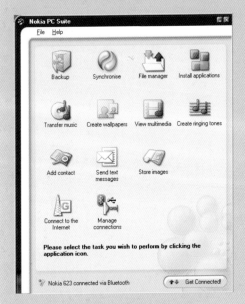

**Figure 16.13** *Nokia PC Suite menu*

**Figure 16.14** *Nokia phone browser*

### Making a Wi-Fi connection with a laptop

This example describes how to install a Belkin PCMCIA Wi-Fi wireless network card. This type of card slides into the PCMCIA expansion slot found on the side of most laptops. The card could be used to allow a laptop to access a Wi-Fi network at home or at work, or to access a Wi-Fi hotspot in a public place.

How to –

## Make a Wi-Fi connection with a laptop

Step one is is to install the software drivers, which come on a CD when the card is purchased and must be installed before the card is placed in the laptop.

Once the software is installed, following the on-screen instructions, the card can be inserted in the PCMCIA slot in the laptop. Unlike some expansion cards, PCMCIA cards are 'hot-swappable', which means they can be safely inserted and removed while the computer is running.

Once the card is inserted, the installation process should be complete and the card will try to connect to any Wi-Fi network in range. For example, if you have a wireless access point in your centre of learning or place of work, the card will attempt to connect to the network.

While the card is inserted in the laptop, the monitor software will run and display various pieces of important information. Figure 16.15 shows the monitor software running. If you have set an SSID for the network (as described earlier) you will need to set the same SSID in the card. The SSID for the card can be seen in Figure 16.15.

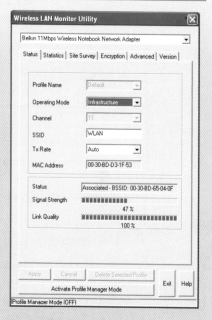

**Figure 16.15** *Wireless LAN monitor software*

If any of the security options described earlier are set up on the Wi-Fi network, such as encryption or MAC address filtering, you will need to configure the card and the router to work with these settings. For example, if you are using encryption, then you will need to enter the same passphrase as used on the access point. If you use MAC address filtering, you will need to add the MAC address of the card to the list of addresses that the access point will accept. The MAC address of the card can also be seen in Figure 16.15.

Once the card is successfully connected to the WiFi network you can access any of the facilities available on the network, such as an Internet connection, shared folders or printers, as if the computer were connected to the LAN via a wired connection.

## Test your knowledge

**14** List the steps required to make a Bluetooth connection between a mobile phone and a laptop computer.

**15** What hardware is required to connect a computer to a Wi-Fi network?

**16** Give an example of a business application of a Wi-Fi hotspot.

# Assessment tasks

The assessment tasks in this unit are based on the following scenario:

*You work as an IT consultant for an insurance company. They have office-based staff, and also sales people and insurance assessors who travel around the country. Insurance assessors visit people and companies who are making insurance claims (e.g. following an accident or robbery) to assess how much money the company should pay out to them and to ensure their claim is genuine. You have been asked to carry out research into mobile communications for the company management, as they are considering how they can use these technologies in the company.*

> To work towards a Distinction in this unit you will need to achieve **all** the Pass, Merit and Distinction criteria in the unit and have evidence to show that you have achieved each one.

## How do I provide assessment evidence?

You can present your written findings as a report. Alternatively, you could discuss the topics with your tutor, who can provide observation records.

All of your evidence should be presented in one folder, which should have a front cover and a contents page. You should divide the evidence into two sections corresponding to the two tasks.

## Task 1 (P1, P2, P3, M1, M2)

Describe the current mobile technologies, including devices, standards and licensing. Explain the important issues relevant to mobile communications, such as security. Also describe the social, moral and ethical implications of the use of mobile communications equipment. Describe the advantages and disadvantages of two different methods of mobile communication.

Compare the ways that different mobile communications technologies could be used to meet the needs of the sales people and assessors in the company. Explain how the social, moral and ethical implications of using mobile communications equipment can be dealt with.

## Task 2 (P4, D1)

You have been asked to test out ways that the insurance assessors could make use of mobile communications technologies to make them more efficient. The assessors often take photographs of the damage to claimants property and these, along with a written report, need to be sent back to their head office as soon as possible so the insurance claim can be processed.

Set up and configure two different mobile communications technology devices to demonstrate how the insurance assessors could connect their mobile phones and laptops to achieve the required functionality.

> To work towards a Distinction you should evaluate three different, currently available mobile communications devices, explaining the advantages and disadvantages of each in terms of security, range, transfer speed, ease of use and suitable applications.

# Glossary

**Absolute address** A cell address that does not change when you copy it.

**Access code** A password that allows limited access to a system.

**ADSL** Stands for asynchronous DSL, which just means higher rates in one direction, i.e. for downloading data. q

**Analogue signals** A continuously varying set of electromagnetic waves, e.g. the voice data sent along a telephone landline.

**Audit trail** Can be set up using an audit trail program. This is used not just for keeping track of individual users, but also, for example, to trace transactions as they go through a system. The audit trail can tell the network administrator where a transaction is in the system at any time, or where a user is logged on and what he or she is accessing, downloading or printing.

**Backup** A copy of software and data that is kept in case the original becomes damaged.

**Bandwidth** The capacity that an information channel has, i.e. how much data can be carried at one time.

**Bar code scanner** An input device that reads a series of lines of different thickness and shading. The scanner is passed over the bar code on a product and a light on the scanner is read. The bar code is then processed automatically and converted to a code. It is this code that identifies the product. If you look at a bar code on a product, you will see that because scanner systems are not 100% reliable, the code that the bars represent is also printed underneath the pattern of lines to enable manual data entry.

**Binary (or bit) pattern** Any combination of bits in a sequence.

**Biometric data** Data that measures something to do with the biology of the user, such as a fingerprint or a voice pattern.

**Boundaries** The points at which a system interacts with the end user or with another system. For example, the user interface will be a boundary, as will any components that need to perform networking or printing.

**Broadband** The name now given to any communication method that has a faster transmission rate than that of the fastest telephone line.

**Brownout** The opposite of a spike; it is a period of under-voltage that might be caused by excessive demand on the electrical supply grid.

**Bug** An error in software that causes it to work in an unintended way. The process of trying to find errors in computer programs and to correct them is called **debugging**.

**Bulletin board** Like an electronic notice board.

**Capacity** The amount of data that can be stored. Capacity is measured in bytes, Kilobytes (KB), Megabytes (MB) or Gigabytes (GB). 1 KB is approximately one thousand bytes, 1 MB is approximately one million bytes, and 1 GB is approximately one thousand million bytes.

**CCTV** Stands for closed circuit television.

**Character** Any letter or symbol that can be stored in a computer system. The standard characters include all the letters of the alphabet (both upper and lower case), the digits from 0 to 9, and all the punctuation marks and symbols shown on a normal keyboard (including the space). Additional characters can be stored as well, such as letters and symbols used in other languages, like é, ß and ¥.

**Client** Any workstation connected to a server. It may also be the software that is designed specifically to work with a server application. For example, web browser software is client software; it is designed to work with webservers.

**Closed source software** Software that is distributed in only binary (compiled) form. Companies using this business model usually make most of their money from selling the software.

**Coaxial** The parts of the cable share the same axis. Thus, when you cut through the cable, they appear as a series of rings around the central core.

**Concept keyboard** Has different keys from that of a QWERTY keyboard. For example, a concept keyboard may be attached to the weighing scales in the green grocery section of a supermarket. The customer places produce on the scales and presses a button to say what type of food is being weighed, e.g. carrots, potatoes, mushrooms. The food is weighed and the cost calculated, based on the weight and the price per kilo of the produce. A ticket is then printed, and this is stuck on the bag ready for the checkout assistant. Some systems are designed to do the weighing at the checkout.

**Consumables** The products that a user uses and then needs to replace from time to time. Consumables include paper, toner and ink cartridges for printers, removable data storage media such as floppy disks and writable CDs and DVDs, and batteries for some peripherals.

**Contingency plan** Identifies what to do if something goes wrong.

**Cookie** A small file that records information about your visit to a particular website. It stores personal information such as your password, so you do not have to re-key this data every time you visit the same site.

**Criterion** A rule that is used to select data. Note that the plural of criterion is criteria.

**CSMA/CD** Stands for carrier sense multiple access with collision detection.

**D**

**Data encryption** The coding – or scrambling – of data prior to transmission and the unscrambling of it on arrival, to prevent those without the code understanding the data.

**Data integrity** Means ensuring that the data correctly matches the facts.

**Data transfer rate** Calculated on the basis of it's the amount of data transmitted through a channel, per second. Analogue transmissions are measured in cycles per second. Digital transmissions are measured in bits per second.

**Database** A collection of data. It is organised so that different kinds of information can be retrieved from it by the users.

**Dedicated lines** A permanent connection to a WAN is set up.

**Defaults** The settings that are selected by the program maker, and the ones used unless the program user changes them.

**Digital data** Any data which is stored or transmitted using binary patterns.

**Digital signals** Discrete voltage pulses, measured in bits per second, e.g. the data sent into a television via a digital cable.

**Disaster recovery** The process of following a contingency plan, adapted or otherwise, when a disaster happens.

**Distribution list** A collection of email addresses, relating to the members of a group. Rather than having to complete the *To:* field for every member of the group, the sender can just refer to the group name. All those on the distribution list then appear in the *To:* field. The distribution list can be kept up to date by adding new members and deleting members, or amending their email addresses if these change.

**Dongle** A hardware device that has to be in place before a user can gain full access to some software.

**Downtime** Any time when an ICT system is not working.

**DSL** Stands for digital subscriber line.

## E

**e-commerce** The use of the Internet for selling goods and services to customers.

**EDI** Stands for electronic data interchange.

**Electronic whiteboard** A shared work area in a window on the monitor of a networked computer. It is designed to be used while video or voice contact is taking place. More than one person at a time, in different locations, can see the window and can change drawings or documents that are on view.

**Email address** A string of characters that identify a user. It will enable the user to receive email. For example, _hp123@example.com_ could be the email address of user hp123 who works for a company with the domain _example.com_.

**Email** An abbreviation for 'electronic mail'.

**Email virus** or **worm** Can send on emails – and the virus – to all your contacts using data from your address book

**Encryption** A way of encoding data so it cannot be read by anyone other than its intended recipients.

**Escalation** Means passing on a problem to someone who knows more than you – or has higher authority than you to act – and should be able to solve the problem for you.

**ESD** Stands for electrostatic discharge.

**External communication** Any communication that involves someone inside the organisation being in contact with anyone from outside the organisation.

## F

**Fault diagnosis system** A piece of software that helps someone to solve a problem.

**Field** A category used for data in a database. The name of the field is called the fieldname.

**Firewall** A type of security system, used primarily to protect networks from external threats.

**Footer** Text which prints at the bottom of every page, often used for things like page numbers.

**Form** An on-screen user interface designed to view the data in a database.

**FTP** Stands for file transfer protocol.

**Functional area** The overall name given to each of the different departments within an organisation. For example, the Sales department would be the functional area for most jobs to do with sales within that organisation.

## G

**Graphical user interface** Incorporates graphics into the visual display. The graphics are not simply used as decoration, but are used to replace text and to convey meaning to the user.

## H

**Hacker** A person who attempts to gain unauthorised access to computer systems through a variety of methods, including exploiting security loopholes in operating systems. The intentions of hackers vary; some have criminal intentions, such as stealing personal information like credit card or bank details, and are sometime called 'crackers'. Others do it for amusement, to demonstrate their skills or to help identify where systems may be vulnerable to attack.

**Header** Text that prints at the top of every page.

**Hotline** A phone number that end users can call when they need ICT support.

**HTML** Stands for hypertext mark-up language.

**Hub** A type of electronic switching box; its purpose is to control the traffic flow around the network.

**Hungarian notation** Originally developed by Charles Simonyi. Because he was originally from Hungary, and code written in this style is not plain English, Simonyi's co-workers at Microsoft christened this style Hungarian notation.

**Hyperlink** The common term for a link. Hyperlinks can link to pages that are in different files or directories, and that can be anywhere on the Web.

**Hypermedia** A multimedia system that includes hyperlinks to other pages.

## I

**IDE** Stands for integrated development environment. A program that includes an editor where you can type the programming code, a compiler for converting the code into binary codes understood by the computer, and a tool called a debugger, which can help you to find errors in the program.

**Identifier** The string of characters used to identify a particular variable, constant or function. For example, in the code `widgets = 3`, the identifier is `widgets`.

**Identity theft** Involves using another person's personal details, such as credit card information, to purchase goods and services fraudulently.

**Infra-red communication** Uses infra-red waves to transmit and receive data. Infra-red waves are longer than light waves but shorter than radio waves.

**Integration** The process of bringing together software components, perhaps written by different development teams, into a single piece of software.

**Internal communication** Any communication within an organisation.

**Internet enabled system** A computer or network of computers with a link to the Internet. This allows the exchange of email communication and access to the World Wide Web.

**Intranet** A closed system that has many of the features of the Internet but which is accessible only within an organisation.

**Invoice** A request for payment for a sale of goods or services that has been made.

**ISDN** Stands for integrated services digital network.

**ISP** Stands for Internet service provider.

## K

**Keyboard shortcut** A key combination that runs a certain command. For example, the built in shortcut Ctrl+S will save a document in most office applications.

## L

**LAN** Consists of computers connected across a small geographical area.

**Leased line** A permanent or switched connection that links a user's computer to a service-provider WAN.

**Link** A text or graphic on a page. When it is clicked another page in the same file or directory is loaded. For example, a page in the Help file for an applications package will contain links to other pages in the same file.

## M

**MAC address** A 12-digit hexadecimal number (hexadecimal numbers are base 16-numbers, represented by digits 0 to 9 followed by letters A to F). It is used to identify uniquely a computer's network interface card (wireless or wired).

**Macro** A method of automating a series of functions within an office application.

**Macro virus** Hides within a macro – so care must be taken when enabling macros.

**Mailshot** A leaflet, letter or brochure – or maybe an email – that is sent from an organisation to a wide range of customers. The listing of customers that are to be sent the mailshot will be collated by the organisation. All those on the listing will receive exactly the same message, although it may be personalised, for example, starting Dear Mr X, or Dear Mrs Y. Sometimes organisations will target certain customers only. For

example, if the new product has certain advanced functions, the organisation might send the promotional material only to those customers whose mobile phones do not yet have this additional functionality. To target customers so carefully, a database of information about individual customers and the products they currently own has to be maintained.

**Maintenance** Consists of all the routine tasks that have to be done to keep hardware and software running properly.

**Manual** A document traditionally provided as a printed book. But it may also be available in electronic form, often on CD-ROM, or downloadable from a website.

**Margins** The gaps between the edge of a piece of paper and where the text starts.

**Media** The traditional ways of providing news to the general public, such as newspapers, radio and television, became known as communication media (or simply, 'the media'). The word 'media' is the plural for 'medium', i.e. the means whereby information is transmitted. Websites, email, interactive television and mobile phones are referred to as the new media.

**Modem** The word 'modem' is made up from the names of two processes involved in the conversion of digital to analogue signals and back again – **mo**dulate and **dem**odulate.

**Multimedia** Refers to systems which handle data in a variety of formats, such as sound, graphics and animation.

**Multi-tasking** The ability to hold several programs and files in memory simultaneously, so that the user can switch between one task and another.

## N

**Navigation** Refers to the way visitors finds their way around a website, using links provided on the pages. Text or images can act as navigation links, and image links are often called buttons. Some of the most important links may be positioned together in a navigation bar.

**Network** A system that allows people to share information with each other.

**Network access methods** Ways in which users can gain access to the network without interfering with other users on the network.

**Networked computer** A computer connected to others so that software and hardware resources can be shared, and communication is possible between them.

**Newsgroup** An interactive area on a network, where users can communicate in real time. Each user is accessing and using information simultaneously, and can respond immediately to something that someone else is typing.

**NIC** Stands for network interface card.

## O

**Open source software** Freely available for anyone to look at and modify. Companies using this business model make their money from paid support instead of from charging for the software.

## P

**Page orientation** How print will be displayed on the paper: with the long side along to top it is known as landscape orientation; with the short side on the top (the normal setting for letters etc.) it is known as portrait.

**Password** A series of characters that a user has to enter to gain any access at all to a system or to a particular file.

**Password cracker** A piece of software that tries all possible passwords – as listed in cracker dictionaries – in an attempt to guess a password.

**Patch** A change to a larger program to fix a problem. In Windows, patches are usually executable files that modify or replace software components that have already been installed on the computer. A good example of this is 'Patch Tuesday': on the second Tuesday of each month, Microsoft makes security patches available, which can then be downloaded and installed by the Microsoft Update software.

**Performance** A way of describing how well a device in a computer system does its job. This often relates to the speed at which it works.

**Peripheral** A hardware component that is connected to a computer, e.g. a printer.

**Personal data** Data that relates to a living person, is private to that person and so could be used to identify that person.

**Platform** The underlying operating system, for example, Mac OS or Windows.

**Primary key field** The field in a table in which the data uniquely identifies each record. The data in a primary key field in one record is known as the primary key (or record key) for that record.

**Programming language** Instructions that are written in English-like statements, which are easier for people to understand than binary codes. These English-like statements are converted into the binary codes that the computer understands using a piece of software called a **compiler**.

**Property** Controls aspects of the appearance and behaviour of objects, such as text boxes and buttons, contained in Visual Basic forms. When you click on an object in the Visual Basic Environment, its properties are displayed in the *Properties* window in the bottom-right of the screen. You can change properties by modifying them in the *Properties* window or by setting them in the program's code.

**Protocol** A set of rules that determines how data is transmitted between computers.

**Public relations** The overall name given to how an organisation is seen by its customers and how the organisation deals with customers.

**Q**

**Query** A method for searching and displaying a selection of data in a database.

**R**

**Record** The data, held in a database, about a single item in the real world.

**Relative address** A cell address that changes when it is copied to a different cell.

**Rescue disk** Contains enough software to restart your PC, plus anti-virus software so that you can clean your infected PC.

**Router** Used to connect networks. It decides what route the file or message will take towards its destination.

**S**

**Scope** The set of features that will need to be inside the system itself. Other features may be recorded in the requirements document, but noted as **out of scope** if they are not in the direct control of the software system. For example, a requirement may be that the system's log files do not exceed a certain size; if it is the system administrator's responsibility to archive the log file before it reaches that size then this requirement will be **out of scope** (although there may be an **in scope** requirement to alert the administrator when the log file reaches a certain size).

**Search engine** A software tool that can be used to find pages on the Internet. Search engines track millions of web pages and create an index based on the text appearing on the pages, or on the keywords provided by the web designer. The user enters search terms (one or more words) and the search engine then finds and lists relevant websites. Well-known search engines include Google and Yahoo.

**Security audit** Reviews the ICT system and lists weaknesses that may result in a security breach.

**Server** A networked computer, used to manage software and/or hardware resources for all users (clients).

**Shortcut keys** (also known as **hot keys**) Combinations of key presses that achieve the same effect as making certain selections from a menu.

**Single-table database** A database in which all the data can be written down as a single list or table.

**Sort key field** The field that is used to sort the data into alphabetical or numerical order (including date order).

**Source code** The HTML program that makes up a web page file. A browser interprets the source code and presents it on screen as a web page.

**Spike** (or **power surge**) A sudden and short lived large voltage that can be caused by an anomaly such as a lightning strike.

**Spyware** Any application that tracks your behaviour in accessing websites without your knowledge or consent.

**Standalone computer** A computer that is not linked permanently to others in a network.

**Storage media** The actual disks or tapes that are used to store digital data. Storage media are placed in a disk or tape drive, which then reads the data or writes new data to the medium. Storage media include hard disks, floppy disks, CDs, DVDs and digital tapes. Note that 'media' is the plural for 'medium'.

**Surveillance** Involves watching at a given moment in time.

**Syntax** Defines the rules which govern how programs are constructed in a programming language.

**System slowdown** The noticeable effect of too many background tasks being run while the user is trying to work in the foreground, e.g. to write a letter.

### T

**Tab key** Situated above the Caps Lock on the left-hand side of your keyboard. The character it produces, known as a **tab**, is used to create columns of text. A tab character is not a fixed width; instead it expands to fill up to the next **tab stop**, defined in terms of a number of characters.

So, for example

| Name[tab]Age | might appear as | |
|---|---|---|
| | Name | Age |
| Bill[tab]50 | Bill | 50 |
| Jennifer[tab]35 | Jennifer | 35 |

**Table** A two-dimensional arrangement of data, usually written in rows and columns.

**TCP/IP** Stands for transmission control protocol / Internet protocol. This protocol dictates the way in which networked computers are named and addressed, how different networks can be connected together and how messages are sent across a wide variety of networks that are linked together to make up the Internet.

**Technical specification** A list of a device's properties. It usually refers to the capacity and performance of the device.

**Template** A document, written in a software package, that can be used over and over again for a variety of purposes. Typical examples are headed letter stationery or memo formats.

**Throughput** The amount of work done by a system.

**Toolbars** Groups of icons used by all office software to control the functions of the program. The default setting for toolbars places them at the top of the program window under the menu bar. However, toolbars are 'floating' and can be dragged into any position in the program window. Different toolbars can be displayed if required, using the *Toolbars* option under the *View* menu.

**Topology** The way in which the **nodes** – the workstations and servers and other peripherals – are connected, and how information travels around the network.

**Touch typing** Using the keyboard with all your fingers without looking at it (you look at the screen not the keyboard). Professional typists touch type and achieve very high typing speeds.

**Transaction** A single action such as placing an order, making a phone call, making a booking or withdrawing cash.

**Trojan virus** Hides in a file that has a name you would expect to find on your PC.

**Troubleshooting** Solving a problem as it arises.

## U

**UPS** Stands for uninterruptible power supply.

**User ID** An access code that identifies the user, so that activity by that user can be tracked. For example, which applications are used and when, which files are accessed and when.

**User interface** The point of contact between a user and the software. It consists of a visual display on the screen, which may be controlled using both the keyboard and a mouse or other device. Some user interfaces incorporate sound as well.

**User support staff** The technical staff in an organisation who help the rest of the employees with any ICT problems that they have.

**UTP** Stands for unshielded twisted pair.

## V

**Validation** A process carried out automatically by a database. It checks that data entered into a field matches rules laid down for that field.

**Variable** An area of memory that a program uses to store a value while it is running. Variables have names, so that they can be referred to in the program, and a data type, which sets the type of data that the variable can hold, such as text or numbers.

**Version control** (or **revision control**). The management of multiple versions of software components. Software tools, such as Microsoft Source Safe, allow programmers to inspect old versions of their programs, e.g. to see when a particular bug was fixed (or introduced). Every professional software development team should also use version control software.

**Video conferencing** A meeting between two or more people where they can see and talk to each other through a computerised video link. The computer screen is the visual link and speakers are used for the sound link. A video camera attached to each computer sends the images through telephone lines, while a microphone captures the sound.

**Virus** A small computer program that can cause damage to a computer system. Viruses are usually spread by being attached to programs or documents, which are then distributed on disk or by email.

**Virus protection software** Attempts to trap viruses and, therefore, prevent them from damaging data and software.

## W

**WAN** Consists of computers connected across a large geographical area.

**Workstation** A computer that is linked to a network.

## X

**x-axis** The scale or items on a chart that run along the bottom.

## Y

**y-axis** The scale or items on a chart that run up the side.

# Index

Notes: Page numbers in **bold** indicate definitions of key terms. Microsoft applications are to be found under the generic name eg, for Microsoft Excel look under Excel.